# Object-Oriented Programming with C++ and OSF/Motif

Douglas A. Young

*Silicon Graphics, Inc.*
*Mountain View, California*

PRENTICE HALL, Englewood Cliffs, New Jersey 07632

Cover design: LUNDGREN GRAPHICS, L.T.D
Pre-press buyer: MARY ELIZABETH MCCARTNEY
Manufacturing buyer: SUSAN BRUNKE
Acquisition editor: GREGORY G. DOENCH

The publisher offers discounts on this book when ordered
in bulk quantities. For more information, write:

Special Sales/Professional Marketing
Prentice-Hall, Inc.
Professional and Technical Reference Division
Englewood Cliffs, New Jersey 07632

Printed in the United States of America

10   9   8   7   6   5   4   3   2   1

ISBN   0-13-630252-1

Prentice-Hall International (UK) Limited, *London*
Prentice-Hall of Australia Pty. Limited, *Sydney*
Prentice-Hall Canada Inc., *Toronto*
Prentice-Hall Hispanoamericana, S.A., *Mexico*
Prentice-Hall of India Private Limited, *New Delhi*
Prentice-Hall of Japan, Inc., *Tokyo*
Simon & Schuster Asia Pte. Ltd., *Singapore*
Editora Prentice-Hall do Brasil, Ltda., *Rio de Janeiro*

*To Teresa, my wife and best friend*

# Contents

# Preface

This book grew out of a simple question: "How do I use the Motif user interface toolkit when programming in C++?" The most direct answer to this question, one that provides only the mechanics of the solution, is fairly simple. But fully addressing all the surrounding issues is a more complex task. In particular, a complete answer must discuss how to coordinate the programming model supported by X and Motif with the C++ object-oriented programming model. This is the central topic of this book.

This book has another underlying theme that is at least as important. In the past few years there has been a fundamental shift in the type of software programmers develop. The textbooks we study in school often focus on algorithms and basic data structures. Wirth said in the title of his popular text that *Algorithms + Data Structures = Programs* [Wirth76]. While no one would dispute that data structures and algorithms are the heart of any application, most modern programs cannot be considered complete without additional elements. For most applications written today, choosing appropriate data structures and determining the right algorithms are only the beginning.

Much of the emphasis in contemporary applications is on interactive user interfaces based on window systems such as X, the Macintosh Toolbox, Microsoft Windows, NeXTStep, and others. Estimates of the effort required to develop the user interface portion of a window-based application range from 50 to 90% of the total effort, which leaves only a small remainder to the task of developing the computational portion of the program. This does not diminish the importance of algorithms, it simply provides one measure of the additional complexity introduced by the interface component of contemporary interactive software.

Programmers sometimes find it difficult to develop these new types of programs, partly because developing a good interactive interface is inherently difficult, but also because interactive programs require a different type of architecture. Programmers who have never encountered this type of application before may be unsure where to begin. The type of algorithm usually studied in school generally involves a single function that takes some data as input and returns other data as output. Interactive programs are different. First, modern interactive programs are real-time applications. In addition, modern applications are often expected to coordinate the presentation of data in multiple areas of the screen, recover from errors in a user-friendly way, provide an appropriate interface for both expert and novice users, and much more.

One of the goals of this book is to help the reader understand how to structure applications to address some of these issues. Simply understanding how to display and manipulate user interface components such as Motif widgets is only the beginning. It is also necessary to understand the subtle constraints X and Motif impose on the architecture of an application.

Object-oriented programming matches the needs of modern interactive systems very well. However, object-oriented programming also requires programmers to alter the way they think about developing software. In object-oriented programming, much of the emphasis is on structure. Programmers who use object-oriented techniques are generally more concerned with defining interfaces and relationships between objects than developing algorithms. Programmers usually find that they need to approach such programs with a completely different mindset. One of the goals of this book is to demonstrate an object-oriented approach within the context of interactive Motif applications.

Someone is sure to ask, "Why should I use an Xt-based toolkit like Motif with C++ in the first place? Shouldn't I use a 'true' object-oriented toolkit?" There are many X-based object-oriented user interface toolkits available to those who feel that object-oriented software must use nothing but pure object-oriented libraries. For example, the Interviews toolkit developed at Stanford University, the ET++ toolkit developed at the University of Zurich, and the OI toolkit developed by Solbourne are all written in C++. Each of these toolkits has strong points and may be useful to C++ programmers. Some may have promising futures. But for now, none of these have Xt's and Motif's momentum, support, and wide acceptance by both programmers and users. There are some who will maintain that it is sacrilege to use a C-based toolkit like Motif with C++. If you fall into that camp, I can only say that this book is not written for you.

There are literally hundreds of user interface toolkits available today, supporting a variety of languages and programming styles. You must decide which toolkit you want to use, based on your needs and the merits of each. There is much more to consider than the implementation language used internally by a toolkit. Issues such as present and future availability, acceptance by users and programmers, support, reliability, and so on, must be considered. You must also consider the environment in which your application will be used, and whether the user interface style supported by any given toolkit will be compatible with other applications in that environment. In many cases, or perhaps even most cases, these issues will be the most critical factors in your decision. This book is written for those who decide to use Motif, and would also like to take advantage of the object-oriented facilities offered by C++. For those who choose C++ and Motif, I hope this book is useful.

All software in this book was tested on a Silicon Graphics Iris Indigo running IRIX 4.0. The examples were compiled using cfront, AT&T's C++ translator, and linked with the X11R4 Xt Intrinsics and Motif 1.1.3. The examples are designed to be self-sufficient, and depend on nothing but standard UNIX and C++ libraries, X, and Motif. Notice that self-sufficiency places some limitations on the design of any software. For example, many of the classes described in this book could be improved or simplified by using a good library of general purpose data structures. The most obvious need is for a generic List class, although others could be useful as well. For those examples that could use such generic data structures, my available choices were to diverge from the central topic of the book to implement the necessary classes, to use a library that might not be available to the reader, or to implement the examples without the benefit of such classes. Since the topic of reusable classes that implement common data structures could be a book in itself, I chose the last approach. For the purposes of this book, the internal implementation of any individual class is of less interest than the external behavior of each class and the collective behavior of all classes in a system.

Writing a book is very much like developing a large piece of software. In both cases, the idea that one can ever find the "last bug" is an illusion. I have tried to make this book as error-free as possible, and I am grateful for the assistance of many people, mentioned below, who helped in that effort. However, I have no doubt that errors and deficiencies remain, in spite of my best efforts. Readers, of course, have an uncanny knack for immediately spotting errors that the author has overlooked repeatedly! My primary goal has been to produce a book that conveys useful information. I hope this book achieves that goal in spite of any errors you encounter.

## Acknowledgments

I would like to thank the many people who helped me with this book. Jolly Chen, Jean-Daniel Fekete, Ken Fischer, Steve Friedl, Oliver Jones, Rick Kelly, David Lewis, Howard Look, Anil Pal, Kim Rachmeler, and Rebecca Wirfs-Brock helped by reviewing early drafts. Their suggestions were invaluable in defining the final form of this book. My wife, Teresa, helped by copy-editing at all stages. I owe a special thanks to Shiz Kobara, who provided the visual design of the TicTacToe game described in Chapter 4. I approached Shiz with the idea of trying to capture a small part of the interaction between a software developer and a user interface designer. The portions of Chapters 4 and 5 that address the interface design of TicTacToe are based on his work and our discussions. Finally, I would like to thank my son, Douglas, for creating the artwork that brightens the cover of this book. He calls this piece "Puzzle", which serves as an appropriate metaphor for a software development technique that assembles complete systems by connecting objects of all shapes and sizes.

*Douglas A. Young*

# Introduction to C++ and Motif

This book presents an object-oriented approach to developing interactive applications using C++ and the OSF/Motif user interface toolkit. Motif is based on the Xt Intrinsics, a library that supports an object-oriented architecture implemented in C. C++ is a language derived from C, but which provides direct support for object-oriented programming. The objects supported by Xt and Motif are completely different from C++ objects, which may give some programmers the false impression that they can only write Motif applications in C, or that they must use some type of C++ wrapper around the Motif widgets. However, the fact that Motif uses an object-oriented architecture internally is of no consequence to applications that use Motif. Motif provides a function-oriented interface and the internal implementation details of Motif and Xt are seldom of interest to applications that call these functions. Outwardly, Motif is no different than any other C language library. Fortunately, C++ was designed to allow programmers to continue to use C libraries like Motif with minimal effort. In fact, C++ provides an excellent way for programmers to take advantage of Motif, while simultaneously using object-oriented programming techniques.

When using Motif and C++, the programmer must first overcome the feeling that *everything* in a program, including Motif widgets, must be C++ objects. Objects and classes are, of course, a central feature in any object-oriented program, but C++ programs usually involve other data structures and functions as well. For example, most UNIX programs make system calls, use various UNIX library functions, and so on, even when they are written in C++. Although one could create an object-oriented interface to the file system or the operating system, it is usually sufficient to call the functions provided by various C-based UNIX libraries.

In many cases, the key benefit of object-oriented programming lies in the impact this technique has on an application's architecture. Whether or not each individual element of a program is implemented as an object is seldom of critical importance. However, to fully realize the benefits of object-oriented programming, it is important that the programmer, designer, or architect understand and apply object-oriented principles when identifying and implementing a system's major components.

Languages like C++ allow programmers to use object-oriented techniques when creating the larger architectural components of an application while still taking advantage of system calls, libraries and other non-object-oriented elements of underlying software platforms, including the X Window System. By making it easy to mix object-oriented and more traditional approaches to writing software, C++ allows programmers to benefit from object-oriented techniques without losing the efficiency of C and without having to re-implement standard C libraries such as X and Motif.

## How to Use this Book

To get the most out of this book, the reader needs some basic knowledge of both Motif and C++. Chapter 1 provides a very brief and high-level introduction to X and Motif. The material in this book assumes the reader has already been introduced to, and can at least read, C++. Many useful books have been written about X, Motif, and C++, and programmers who need more information about these topics have a large selection from which to choose. In particular, the books listed below represent the definitive documentation for Xt, Motif, Xlib, and C++, respectively, as this book goes to press.

Asente, Paul, and Ralph Swick, *The X Window System Toolkit*, Digital Press, 1990.

Open Software Foundation, *OSF/Motif Programmer's Reference*, Version 1.1, Prentice Hall, 1990.

Scheifler, Robert W., and James Gettys, X *Window System*, Second Edition, Digital Press, 1990.

Stroustrup, Bjarne, *The C++ Programming Language*, Second Edition, Addison-Wesley, 1991.

These books provide comprehensive and authoritative coverage of topics that are outside the scope of this book, and are highly recommended as reference material to augment the discussions in the following chapters. The Bibliography on page 424 lists additional sources of information. This book focuses primarily on ways the programmer can structure an application to take advantage of C++ and Motif. Except when crucial to the main point of the discussion, this book does not provide extensive explanations of how individual X or Motif functions work, because that information is readily available elsewhere (for example, in the books listed above).

This book is divided into two sections. Part I introduces the mechanics of using C++ and Motif with an emphasis on object-oriented techniques. Part II explores additional ideas for using Motif and C++, while developing a small library of useful classes that support applications based on Motif.

Many of the examples in this book place a strong emphasis on the thought process behind the development of each program. In many cases, the discussion includes reasons for various decisions, and proposes alternate approaches. The intent is not to present a single "right" way to develop Motif applications with C++, but to explore and discuss various approaches and possibilities.

This book is written with the assumption that it will be read from beginning to end. However, because readers' backgrounds and interests vary widely, it is likely that many readers will not do that. The following chapter summaries serve as a guide for those who want to get to the essential material quickly, or who do not need the background information discussed in the opening chapters.

Part I, Introduction to C++ and Motif

*Chapter 1, A Motif Tutorial using C++*, introduces the X Window System, the Xt Intrinsics and the Motif widget set from the perspective of a C++ programmer. Those already familiar with Motif or another Xt-based toolkit may be tempted to skip this chapter. However, everyone should at least skim the examples and read those parts that discuss the impact of the C++ language's strong typing on Motif programs. This discussion begins on page 13.

*Chapter 2, C++ Classes and Widgets, introduces the approach used in this book to take advantage of both C++ classes and Motif widgets. This chapter provides essential information that serves as a basis for the remainder of this book.*

*Chapter 3, Designing with Objects*, discusses some techniques for designing object-oriented applications. The design techniques and notation described in this chapter are used in examples throughout the rest of this book.

*Chapter 4, TicTacToe: Design*, applies the techniques discussed in Chapter 3 to design a simple Motif program.

*Chapter 5, TicTacToe: Implementation*, presents an implementation of the design developed in Chapter 4, using the techniques introduced in Chapter 2.


Part II, Application Frameworks

*Chapter 6, The MotifApp Application Framework,* introduces the architecture of a simple *application framework*, a reusable class library implemented with C++ and Motif. This chapter describes an Application class and a MainWindow class that serve as the foundation of a framework named *MotifApp*. Following chapters discuss other classes in the framework.

*Chapter 7, Dialogs*, discusses ways dialogs can be used in Motif applications and presents some classes that make it easier for applications based on MotifApp to use dialogs.

*Chapter 8, Command Classes*, discusses a collection of abstract classes used to model commands in the MotifApp framework.

*Chapter 9, A Simple Menu Package*, presents the MotifApp menu system, which is based on the classes introduced in Chapter 8.

Chapter 10, Lengthy Tasks, discusses the difficulties programmers face when an interactive application must support an operation that requires an extended period of time to perform. This chapter describes some facilities a framework like MotifApp can provide to help programmers handle this common problem.

Chapter 11, A Color Chooser, provides an example of a fairly complex, self-contained user interface component written in C++. This reusable component, which allows users to choose colors interactively, is based on an object-oriented architecture known as Model-View-Controller (MVC).

*Chapter 12, An Example Application*, presents an extended example that uses many of the features of the MotifApp framework developed in earlier chapters.

## Conventions Used in this Book

This book follows several naming and coding conventions common in C++ and object-oriented programming. All variable and class names use a mixed case convention in which words are capitalized and concatenated. Names of classes begin with a capital letter, while names of instances begin with a lower-case letter. For example:

```
MainWindow *myWindow;
```

Data members and member functions also use mixed case, and start with a lower-case letter. For example:

```
myWindow->className();
```

Occasionally, it is only possible or reasonable for one instance of a particular class to exist in a program. When this situation occurs in this book, the name of that instance begins with the word "the". For example:

```
Application *theApplication;
```

All classes in this book use encapsulation as much as possible. Therefore, classes contain no public data members. Following a common convention used by C programmers to indicate private symbols, data members are preceded by a "_" character as a further reminder that the member is private. When other classes need access to a data member, the class provides an inline access function. Using an underscore for the private data member allows the access function to have the same name as the data member, but without the underscore. So, a sample class that contains some data needed outside the class can be written as:

```
class SampleClass {

  private:

    int   _someData;   // An internally-used int member
    char *_aString;   // An internally-used string member

  public:

    SampleClass();   // Constructor

    // Access functions
```

```
    int someData() { return ( _someData ); }
    const char *const aString() { return ( _aString ); }
};
```

If a class needs to allow an outside entity to set the value of a data member, the class can provide a function that assigns a new value to the protected data. In the above example, if we wish to extend the previous example to allow the _someData member to be changed, we can provide a setSomeData() member function like this:

```
class SampleClass {

  private:

    int    _someData; // An internally-used int member
    char * _aString;  // An internally-used string member

  public:

    SampleClass();    // Constructor

    // Access functions

    int    someData() const { return ( _someData ); }
    const char *const aString() const { return ( _aString ); }

    // Function sets private data

    void   setSomeData ( int newValue ) { _someData = newValue; }
};
```

This book presents many C++ classes. It is usually most convenient to maintain each C++ class separately, in two files. The class is declared in a header file, while the member functions are implemented in a separate source file. The name of the header file is usually the name of the class, with a .h suffix (i.e., Stack.h), while the name of the source file is the name of the class with a .C suffix (i.e., Stack.C). Unfortunately, there is no standard source file suffix for C++, and your environment may use .C, .c, .cc, .cxx, or some other convention. Some programmers also use a .H suffix for the header file. This book uses .h and .C.

This book displays line numbers to the left of most code listings. Code may be discussed in small segments, usually consisting of individual functions. However, the line numbering is continuous within any given file, and restarts at 1 for each new file. Occasionally, there may be small examples that are incomplete or are otherwise not associated with a file. These code segments do not have line numbers to distinguish them from the others.

To prevent problems with multiple declarations, which can easily occur when header files are nested, all class header files have the form:

```
#ifndef CLASSNAME_H
#define CLASSNAME_H

// class declaration goes here

#endif
```

In each file, CLASSNAME is replaced by the name of the class. For example, a header file for a class named Stack would look like this:

```
1    /////////////////////////////////////////////////////
2    // Stack.h: Header file for the Stack class
3    /////////////////////////////////////////////////////
4    #ifndef STACK_H
5    #define STACK_H
6
7    class Stack {
8
9      public:
10
11       Stack();  // Constructor
12       // Miscellaneous members
13   };
14   #endif
```

The file Stack.C contains the implementation of all Stack member functions, as follows:

```
1    /////////////////////////////////////////////////////
2    // Stack.C: Implementation file for the Stack class
3    /////////////////////////////////////////////////////
4    #include "Stack.h"
5
6    Stack::Stack()
7    {
8      // Various initialization statements
9    }
```

Notice that Stack.C includes Stack.h, which contains the class declaration. Any other class that references an object belonging to the Stack class needs to include the file Stack.h as well. Because class headers may be included in many different source files in a program, it is important that the header contain only declarations, and not define functions (except for inline functions) or variables.

The terminology used by C++ differs slightly from that used by many other object-oriented languages. C++ defines *member functions* instead of *methods*, calls a member function for an object instead of sending a *message*, creates *base classes* and *derived classes* instead of *subclasses* and *superclasses*, and so on. This book primarily uses the C++ terminology, but occasionally slips into the more traditional object-oriented mode when these terms make more sense in the context of a discussion.

# Chapter 1
# An X/Motif Tutorial using C++

This chapter introduces the X Window System and the Motif widget set. The X Window System, also known simply as "X", is an industry-standard window system that provides a portable base for applications with graphical user interfaces. Motif is a higher-level toolkit that provides common user interface components needed by X-based applications. This chapter uses C++ for all examples, but does not address object-oriented programming techniques. Chapter 2 presents an object-oriented approach to using Motif and C++.

Section 1.1 introduces the architecture of X and the Motif widget set. Next, Section 1.2 discusses function prototypes and shows how to link C libraries like X and Motif with C++ applications. Section 1.3 introduces the basic programming model used by all Motif applications. Section 1.4 provides an overview of the user interface components in the Motif widget set. Finally, Section 1.5 introduces the X resource manager, a facility for customizing applications and widgets.

## 1.1   The X/Motif Architecture

Motif applications are built on three distinct layers. Xlib provides a low-level interface to the basic services of the underlying window system, the Xt Intrinsics library provides a higher-level toolkit architecture, and Motif provides a collection of components for creating user interfaces. This section discusses the basic features of the X Window System and shows the relationships between X, the Xt Intrinsics, and Motif.

## Clients and Servers

The architecture of the X Window System is based on a *client-server* model. A single process, known as the *server,* is responsible for all physical input and output devices. The server creates and manipulates windows on the screen, displays text and graphics, and receives all input. Applications based on X never draw anything directly to the screen, but instead request the X server to perform the drawing. Similarly, X applications never receive input directly from the keyboard or mouse. Instead, applications rely on the X server to inform them when input is available from these devices. By handling all input and output, the server provides a portable layer between applications and the display hardware. When written correctly, X-based applications can display windows, text, or graphics on any hardware that supports the X protocol.

A *client* is an application that uses the facilities provided by the X server. A client communicates with the X server via a network connection. Multiple clients can connect to a single server concurrently, and an individual client can also connect to one or more servers. It is important to understand that the X server is a *process*, as are the clients. The X server and clients can execute on different machines on a network, or run on the same machine.

## Requests and Events

When a client wishes to use a service provided by X, it sends a *request* to the X server. For example, a client might request the server to create a window or to draw a line on the screen. A request is simply a packet of information. The X server processes requests from any given client in the order in which the client makes the requests. However, the server queues all requests and may not process them immediately. Also, it is not possible to guarantee the order in which the server will process requests from multiple clients, because the server and all clients run asynchronously with respect to each other.

The server notifies each client when input is available by sending the client an *event*. X presents each event to clients as a union of C structures. Each event structure indicates the specific type of event, and also supplies additional information about the event. For example, when the user presses a key on the keyboard, the X server generates a `KeyPress` event. Besides the type of the event, the `KeyPress` event structure reports what key the user pressed, the location of the mouse cursor when the event occurred, and other relevant information.

The X server places events in a per-process FIFO event queue, where the application can read the event. The server reports each event only to those clients that have specifically requested events of that type for the window in which the event occurred. Although the server reports all events in the order in which they occurred, clients do not necessarily process the events immediately. Applications can read their event queues at any time, and they may be busy when the event occurs.

In general, all X applications must be designed to poll the event queue continuously and respond to incoming events as quickly as possible, for several reasons. One reason is that X windows are not persistent; that is, they can lose their contents if they are moved, resized, or covered and then uncovered. X maintains the background pattern of each window and an optional border around the window. Anything a client chooses to display inside a window is transient and can be lost. X notifies applications whenever this happens by sending an `Expose` event to clients that have asked to be notified when a particular window's contents are lost. Well-designed clients should be prepared to receive such events and redraw the contents of their windows at any time.

# Windows

The X server's primary responsibility is to display and manipulate windows. In X, a *window* is a rectangular region on the screen. The server creates, destroys, and manipulates windows at the request of a client. Each window has a unique identifier, which clients must provide in all requests to manipulate that window.

Windows in X form a hierarchical structure. When the X server starts, it creates one special window, called the *root window*, that covers the entire screen. All other windows are either direct children of the root window or *descendents* of the root window. Every window may have children, and every window except the root window has a parent.

X supports an overlapping window model in which windows can be stacked much like papers on a desk. Each set of sibling windows (windows that share the same parent) has a *stacking order*. The stacking order determines which window or windows appear to be "on top" and which appear to be partially or completely covered by the others.

Windows do not necessarily appear on a display device (a CRT or screen). When the server first creates a window, it is not visible. Clients can request the server to display a window on the screen by issuing a *map* request. Windows can be removed from the screen by requesting the server to unmap the window. Windows can be manipulated (moved, resized, destroyed) whether they are mapped or not.

Clients may request the server to manipulate windows on their behalf. This includes raising or lowering windows within their stacking order, moving their positions relative to their parents, mapping and unmapping them, and so on. Windows are always created at the request of an individual client, and generally go away when that client exits or disconnects from the server. However, while a window exists, any client that knows that window's ID can request the X server to manipulate the window.

# X Graphics Facilities

X provides some basic drawing capabilities. Clients can request the server to draw lines, circles, rectangles, or polygons in any window. X allows lines to be drawn in various widths, in any color supported by the display device, and using various patterns. Figures can also be filled with a pattern or solid color. The basic X protocol supports only an integer coordinate system.

All graphics requests must be made relative to a *drawable*, which can be either a window or a *pixmap*. A pixmap is just a chunk of off-screen memory that can be the target of graphics requests. Pixmaps can be used to store or compose an image off-screen before copying it to a window. Pixmaps are maintained in the X server and have unique identifiers, the same as windows.

# Window Managers

In X, the term *window manager* refers to an X client that allows the user to manipulate each application's top-most window. A window manager allows the user to move windows, raise or lower windows relative to the others on the screen, iconify windows, and so on. An X window manager is simply a client that uses the server to manipulate other clients' windows. All window managers are expected to obey a specific protocol for interacting with clients. This protocol is documented in the *InterClient Communications Conventions Manual* (ICCCM). The images in this book show the

Motif Window Manager (mwm), but any ICCCM-compliant window manager can be used with X and Motif applications.

## The Layering of X-based Libraries

Applications based on Motif use at least three distinct libraries. The highest-level library is the Motif widget library, which contains common user interface components such as buttons, scrollbars, and menus. The second library is the Xt Intrinsics, which this book usually refers to simply as "Xt". This library provides some common facilities needed to construct the components defined by Motif, and defines the architecture used by all widgets. The lowest-level library is the Xlib C language interface to X, which provides primitive operations that allow applications to create windows, draw text and simple graphics, and so on.

Figure 1.1 shows how these libraries relate to one another. The X server is a process that normally runs on a local machine and communicates with clients across a network protocol. The Xlib (libX11.a) layer handles the network traffic on the client side and presents a low-level C language interface to the facilities of the X server. The Xt Intrinsics library, libXt.a, is built on top of Xlib and hides many of Xlib's lower-level details. Motif is built primarily on the Xt Intrinsics layer, but occasionally calls Xlib functions directly. Motif applications typically use functions from all three libraries.

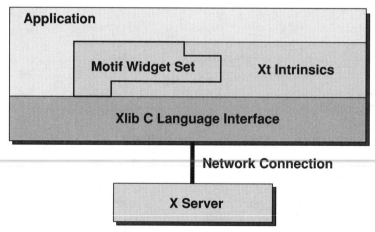

**Figure 1.1**  The architecture of the X Window System.

### Xlib

Xlib provides the principal C language interface to the services supplied by the X server. This library encapsulates the mechanisms for connecting to the X server, sending requests to the server, and receiving events back from the server. Xlib contains approximately 290 functions that allow applications to create windows, move and resize windows, draw text and graphics to windows, communicate with other clients, and much more. A detailed discussion of Xlib is beyond the scope of this book. For more information, the definitive book on Xlib is *X Window System, C Library and*

*Protocol Reference*, by the creators of X, Robert Scheifler and J. Gettys [Scheifler90]. For a more tutorial introduction to Xlib programming, see *Introduction to the X Window System*, by Oliver Jones [Jones88].

At the Xlib level, one notable attribute of X is its "mechanism, not policy" philosophy. X does not dictate the look or feel of any application. Windows are simply rectangular regions on the screen, with no identifying decorations. Xlib also does not impose any strict programming style on applications that use it. But there are preferred ways to accomplish various tasks, and X programmers have developed many stylistic conventions. Some of these are specified in the InterClient Communications Conventions Manual (ICCCM). However, many other techniques and conventions exist only as common practice among X programmers.

This book assumes X, Version 11 Release 4, which includes header files that are compatible with C++. Later releases should be adequate as well. The X11 library is normally installed as /usr/lib/libX11.a, while the header files are normally located in /usr/include/X11.[1] Following C++ conventions, these header files may also be found under the directory /usr/include/CC/X11 on some systems. However, the versions found in this directory should be identical to the header files found in /usr/include/X11.

## The Xt Intrinsics

Xlib defines a programmatic layer that is lower than many programmers prefer to deal with. In relation to the other libraries discussed in this section, one could compare Xlib to the assembly code level. Even a program that simply displays a short string on the screen can consist of hundreds of lines of code. The Xt Intrinsics library was designed to make it easier to write X applications by providing more support for the kinds of things programmers want to do with a window system, while hiding many of the details of Xlib.

Xt defines an object-oriented architecture for constructing user interface components. Like Xlib, the Xt Intrinsics are written in C, and Xt-based objects are not compatible with objects implemented in C++. Xt defines only a few user interface components itself, and like Xlib, strives to be independent of any particular look and feel. To use object-oriented terminology, Xt defines the abstract base classes on which user interface components can be built. It also defines the external protocol used by applications to interact with all components based on Xt.

The user interface components supported by Xt are called *widgets*. Typical widgets include buttons, scrollbars, and menus. A widget consists of a structure that contains data and supports procedures that operate on those data. Each widget has an X window associated with it, in which the widget displays itself.

There are many Xt-based widget sets; the OSF/Motif widget set and the Open Look widget set (known as OLIT, for *Open Look Intrinsic Toolkit*) are both widely-used commercial widget sets based on Xt. The Athena widget set, which is is freely available as part of the standard X Window

---

[1]   The location of the X and Motif header files and libraries is subject to wide variations between systems. The locations discussed here are only likely places to look, and it is important to check local conventions. For example, some installations may support older versions of headers and libraries. For example, X11R4 headers may be kept under an R4 directory, while another directory contains headers for other releases. Similarly, some installations use different library naming conventions. Environments that support shared libraries may also have sharable versions of the X libraries. A local expert should be able to locate the correct libraries and header files.

System distribution, is another popular widget set. This book uses the Motif widget set, although most of the techniques described in the following chapters apply equally to any Xt-based widget set.

The Xt library is usually installed as /usr/lib/libXt.a[2], and its associated header files are usually kept in /usr/include/X11. Following C++ conventions, these header files are sometimes installed in /usr/include/CC/X11.

## The Motif Widget Set

Motif is a standard user interface toolkit developed and supported by the Open Software Foundation (OSF) and its member companies. Motif consists of several parts:

- The Motif widget set is based on the Xt Intrinsics. The standard Motif widgets include components that support user interaction, such as buttons, popup and pulldown menus, and so on. The Motif widget set also includes components that handle assorted screen layouts, dialogs that can be used to display error and warning messages, and so on.

- The Motif style guide contains rules and recommendations for achieving visual and behavioral consistency with other Motif applications.

- The Motif window manager, mwm, is an ICCCM-compliant window manager whose appearance and behavior complements the Motif widget set.

- UIL (User Interface Language) offers an alternative to the C-language programmatic interface for Motif-based applications. UIL is a language that can be used to describe an application's window layout in a separate file from the rest of the program.

This book uses the Motif widget set, and does not discuss the Motif window manager, the Motif Style Guide, or UIL.

The Motif widget set contains many components, including scrollbars, menus, buttons, and so on, that can be combined to create user interfaces. Unlike Xlib and Xt (which provide only the underlying mechanisms), the Motif widget set supports a very specific appearance and behavior. Motif has a distinctive three-dimensional appearance and provides strong support for the interface style described in the Motif Style Guide. Section 1.4 introduces some specific Motif widgets and shows how they can be used to build a simple program.

Unlike Xlib and Xt, Motif is not freely available, but many companies include Motif as part of their system software, at little or no additional cost. Versions are also available from the OSF and many other sources for a fee. The Motif library is normally found in /usr/lib/libXm.a and the header files are commonly installed in /usr/include/Xm. C++ installations may put these headers in /usr/include/CC/Xm as well. Examples in this book are based on Motif Version 1.1.3, which is based on the X11R4 Xt Intrinsics and includes headers that are compatible with C++. Later versions of Motif should be compatible with C++ as described here, but specific features of individual widgets are subject to change.

These three libraries, Xlib, Xt, and the Motif widget library, provide a powerful and flexible base upon which to create user interfaces. The following sections discuss the programming model used by applications based on Xt and Motif from the perspective of the C++ programmer.

---

[2] Some installations of Motif include a special version of the Xt Intrinsics specifically intended for use with Motif. The Intrinsics library may have some other name, perhaps libXt_m.a or libXtm.a. If your system has such a library, it most likely contains a version of Xt that has minor bug fixes appropriate for the version of Motif on your system.

## 1.2    Mixing C and C++

Before looking at an example that uses Motif with C++, it is important to understand a few simple things about mixing C and C++ code in the same program. An important feature of the C++ language is that it is simple to call existing C functions from C++. When programming in C++, all the familiar C libraries, like Xlib and Motif, are still available.

However, there are a few simple things to watch out for. The first thing to be aware of is *function prototypes*. Function prototypes are used to declare the types of all arguments to C++ functions.

X and Motif are written in pre-ANSI C. Functions are defined in pre-ANSI C like this:

```
void aFunction ( x, y, z )
    int x, y, z;
{
    /* Empty Body */
}
```

This code segment defines a function that takes three integer arguments and has no return value.

C programs sometimes declare functions before they are used, like this:

```
void aFunction();
```

In pre-ANSI C, this declares aFunction() to be a function with no return value. In C, it is only necessary to declare a function before it is used when the function returns a type other than int, or when a pointer to the function is needed. C assumes that all undeclared functions return an int.

In C++, all functions must be declared before they are referenced in any way. In addition, the type of each argument must also be declared. In C++, the above function would be declared like this:

```
void aFunction ( int, int, int );
```

This states that aFunction() is a function with no return value that takes three integers as arguments. This declaration is referred to as a function prototype. Notice that the declaration

```
void aFunction();
```

is still valid, but in C++ this declaration means that aFunction() is a function with no return value that takes no arguments.

C++ function definitions also include type declarations immediately preceding each argument. For example:

```
void aFunction ( int x, int y, int z )
{
    // Empty Body
}
```

Like the C version of aFunction(), this is a function that takes three integer arguments and has no return value.

Before a C function can be called from C++, the function must have a prototype. As of Motif Version 1.1, all public Motif header files include function prototypes for all public functions. The prototypes are ifdef'd with the flag _NO_PROTO. The default is to use function prototypes. For example, an excerpt from the file Xm.h might look something like this:

```
#ifndef _NO_PROTO
Widget XmCreateForm ( Widget, String, ArgList, Cardinal );
#else
Widget XmCreateForm();
#endif
```

Function prototypes are also necessary for any Xt Intrinsics and Xlib functions called from C++. Fortunately, as of X11R4, all standard X and Xt header files also supply function prototypes. To enable these function prototypes, the symbol FUNCPROTO must be defined when compiling. Note that Motif or Xt header files whose names end in a "P" (LabelP.h, for example) are private. These files do not generally define prototypes and are not meant to be included by applications.

X programs, particularly those based on the Xt Intrinsics, often pass pointers to functions as parameters to other functions. C programmers tend to be fairly sloppy about properly declaring type information for functions because pre-ANSI C offers only weak type-checking. Programmers moving from C programming with Motif to C++ often encounter some initial difficulty with C++'s strong type-checking, particularly when passing pointers to functions.

## Specifying C Linkage

In addition to providing prototypes for all functions, all X and Motif functions must be declared to be external C-language functions because the C++ preprocessor *mangles* the names of nearly all C++ functions. If the C++ preprocessor or compiler is allowed to mangle the names of X or Motif functions called from a C++ program, the linker will not be able to find these functions in the X and Motif libraries. This problem can be solved by surrounding all C function prototypes, or the header files for any C libraries with an extern "C" declaration. For example,

```
extern "C" {
#include "aCheader.h"
extern void aCfunction ( int, int, char * );
}
```

Notice that simply bracketing a function declaration with an extern "C" declaration does not eliminate the need for function prototypes.

As of Release 1.1, all Motif header files include extern "C" declarations. Normally, this declaration does not need to be made explicitly in an application's code. If a Motif or X header file does not include this statement, the extern "C" statement can be placed around the problem header file in the application code. The same technique can also be used to call functions from other C libraries within C++.

# 1.3    Programming with Motif and the Xt Intrinsics

The Xt Intrinsics and all toolkits based on the Xt Intrinsics define a strong programming model that must be followed when writing applications. Because Motif is based on the Xt Intrinsics, Motif applications follow the same model. Most Motif applications perform the following basic steps:

- **Initialize Xt**. This step initializes some internal data structures defined by the Xt Intrinsics. Every application must also open a connection to the X server and load a resource database containing customization information. Applications must also create a data structure known as an *application context*.

- **Create a Shell**. All applications must create one or more shell widgets to serve as containers for all other widgets in the program. A shell widget acts as an intermediary between the application and the window manager. Every application that displays windows has one shell widget for each top-level application window. When using the Xt functions described in the following section, this step is performed by the same function that initializes the Intrinsics.

- **Create widgets**. Widgets are the user interface components with which the user interacts. Most widgets can be customized by passing various parameters as arguments at creation time, or after the widget has been created.

- **Register callback functions**. Callbacks are functions that perform some application-specific action in response to some user input. For example, a program might register a function to be called when the user presses a button, or selects an item from a menu.

- **Manage all widgets**. Widgets form a hierarchy similar to the X window tree. Widgets that have children act as containers that group other widgets together into some logical collection. Each container is responsible for determining the size and position of its children. This process is known as *managing* widgets. All widgets must be managed before they can appear on the screen. Programmers often use a convenience function that creates and manages a widget in a single step.

- **Realize all widgets**. Realizing a widget creates an X window on the screen in which the widget can display itself. Widgets can be created, manipulated, managed, and so on without being visible on the screen. Once everything is ready, realizing all widgets makes the application's windows appear on the screen.

- **Handle events**. All Xt applications must enter an event loop to receive events from the X server. The event loop never returns and just continuously checks the event queue for new events. When an event occurs, the event loop removes the first pending event and dispatches the event to the appropriate widget for further handling.

## A Simple Example

The previous sections discussed the X architecture and Xt programming model somewhat abstractly. Of course real applications must deal with many concrete details. Let's get started by looking at a C++ example that uses Motif. This first example displays the string "Hello World" in a window.

```
1     /////////////////////////////////////////////////////
2     // hello.C, Hello World using C++ and Motif
3     /////////////////////////////////////////////////////
4     #include <Xm/Xm.h>
5     #include <Xm/Label.h>
6
7     main ( unsigned int argc, char **argv )
8     {
9         Widget        label, toplevel;
10        XtAppContext app;
11        XmString      xmstr;
12        Arg           args[10];
13        int           n;
14
15        // Initialize the Intrinsics
16
17        toplevel = XtAppInitialize ( &app, "Hello", NULL, 0,
18                                     &argc, argv, NULL, NULL, 0 );
19
20        // Create a compound string to display the Hello message
21
22        xmstr = XmStringCreateSimple ( "Hello World" );
23
24        // Create a label widget to display the string
25
26        n = 0;
27        XtSetArg ( args[n], XmNlabelString, xmstr ); n++;
28        label = XtCreateManagedWidget ( "label", xmLabelWidgetClass,
29                                        toplevel, args, n );
30
31        // Free the compound string when it is no longer needed
32
33        XmStringFree ( xmstr );
34
35        // Realize all widgets and enter the main event loop
36
37        XtRealizeWidget ( toplevel );
38        XtAppMainLoop ( app );
39    }
```

Now let's look at this program, step by step. We can break the program down into the steps normally performed by all Xt-based applications, approximately as outlined in the previous section.

## Initialization

Every C or C++ program includes a certain amount of code that is nearly the same from program to program. This includes header files, declarations, and other statements that are required by all programs. The hello.C program begins by including Xm.h, the primary Motif header file. Xm.h must be included before any other Motif header file in all files that reference Motif functions or widgets. Xm.h includes the required Xt header files, such as Intrinsic.h, and also includes all required Xlib header files, such as Xlib.h. Programs that use Motif do not need to include these files directly. Following Xm.h, each file must include the header file for any widget referenced in the file. Each widget has its own header file. This example uses only the Motif XmLabel widget, so it includes only the file Label.h.

The main body of the program declares several variables needed by the example, and then, on line 17, calls the function

```
Widget XtAppInitialize ( XtAppContext      *appContext,
                         const String       className,
                         XrmOptionDescList options,
                         Cardinal           numOptions,
                         Cardinal          *argc,
                         char             **argv,
                         const String      *fallbackResources,
                         ArgList            args,
                         Cardinal           numArgs );
```

XtAppInitialize() is normally called first, before any other Xt function. This function is a convenience function that performs many steps with a single call. XtAppInitialize() initializes various Xt data structures, opens a connection to the X server, and creates and returns a shell widget. Applications that require more control over the initialization process can call the functions XtToolkitInitialize(), XtCreateApplicationContext(), XtOpen-Display(), and XtAppCreateShell() to perform these steps individually. For most applications, XtAppInitialize() is a simpler choice.

The first argument to XtAppInitialize() returns an application context, a data structure that is required by many other Xt functions. The application must define an application context by declaring a variable of type XtAppContext and passing its address to XtAppInitialize(). Every application must create one application context, and it is often necessary to declare the application context as a global variable so that it can be accessed throughout the program.

The second argument, className, is a string that specifies the *class* of the application. By convention, the application's class name should be the intended name of the program, with the first letter changed to be upper-case. Note that this does not mean the programmer should change argv[0] to uppercase. It means that if the program's nominal name is "emacs", the class name should be "Emacs." The className argument identifies the program even if the user renames the application.

The second and third arguments are used to supply a description of command-line arguments that should be recognized by the application. All Xt applications recognize a number of common command-line options. The options argument allows applications to add application-specific arguments to those already recognized by Xt. If no additional options are required, as in this example, the options argument can be given as NULL.

The fifth argument must be a *pointer* to argc, followed by the array argv, as passed to the application from the command line. Xt searches the argv array for command-line options it recognizes. If any are found, Xt removes them and places them in the application's resource database.

Notice that the function `main()` in this program declares `argc` as an `unsigned int`. This is unusual for a C or C++ program, and `argc` is usually expected to be declared as an `int`. Unfortunately, the X11R4 Intrinsics expects `argc` to be passed to other functions as a `Cardinal`, which is typically an `unsigned int`. Therefore, programs must either define `argc` to be an `unsigned int` in the prototype for `main()`, or use type-casting when passing `argc` to other functions.[3] In this book, all examples declare `argc` as an unsigned int, although this is non-standard.

Most Xt applications have an associated application resource file that specifies the values of various customizable parameters used by the widgets in the application. Typically, the application resource file is found in /usr/lib/X11/app-defaults/<class>, where <class> is the class name of the application. Some applications need to be sure certain parameters are set to function properly. In this case, the required resource specifications can be passed as an array of strings to `XtApp-Initialize()` as *fallback resources*. If the application resource file does not exist, the resources specified in the `fallbackResources` argument are used. If no fallback resources are required, this argument can be given as `NULL`. (See Section 1.5 for more information about resources and resource files.)

The last two arguments to `XtAppInitialize()` allow the program to specify additional arguments, in the form of an `ArgList`, to be passed to the shell widget created by `XtApp-Initialize()`. We will discuss how to use an `ArgList` to customize widgets later in this chapter.

## Creating Shell Widgets

All widgets in an application must be contained by a special widget that acts as an interface between the program and the window manager. This widget is called a "shell" widget because it forms a shell around the other widgets created by the program. There are several types of shell widgets, each serving a slightly different purpose. The convenience function `XtAppInitialize()` creates and returns an ApplicationShell widget, which can be used as an application's main shell.

There are two ways to create shells for multi-window applications. The first is to use the shell returned by `XtAppInitialize()` for the first window, and to create additional windows using `XtCreatePopupShell()`. This approach works best when the application has one window that clearly serves as the primary window, with all other windows playing a secondary role. When an application has multiple top-level windows that act as equals, it is best to create all windows as popup children of the initial shell returned by `XtAppInitialize()`. When using this approach, the parent shell returned by `XtAppInitialize()` is not realized and does not appear on the screen.

The function `XtCreatePopupShell()` is declared as follows:

```
Widget XtCreatePopupShell ( String        name,
                            WidgetClass   widgetClass,
                            Widget        parent,
                            ArgList       *args,
                            Cardinal      numArgs );
```

---

[3]  This problem has been fixed in the R5 Intrinsics by changing the Xt functions that use `argc` to expect an `int`.

The first argument to `XtCreatePopupShell()` specifies the name of the popup shell, and the second argument indicates the widget class of the shell to be created. The third argument specifies a parent for the shell. Popup shells must be children of some other widget. The final two arguments allow additional parameters to be passed to the shell widget in an `ArgList`.

## Creating Widgets

The next major step is to create the widgets that form the application's user interface. The hello.C example creates only one widget in addition to the shell, a Motif XmLabel widget that displays the "Hello World" string. The function `XtCreateWidget()` provides the simplest way to create a widget:

```
Widget XtCreateWidget ( const String    name,
                        WidgetClass     widgetClass,
                        Widget          parent,
                        ArgList         args,
                        Cardinal        numArgs );
```

The first argument to `XtCreateWidget()` specifies the name of the widget to be created. The name can be an arbitrary character string, but should ideally be unique within any set of widgets that share the same parent. The widget class is a pointer to the widget class structure declared in the public header file of the widget to be created. In this example, the class pointer for the XmLabel widget class is `xmLabelWidgetClass`. In general, the class pointer for a particular widget class can be determined by looking in the widget's header file, or consulting a Motif reference manual. However, Motif uses a straightforward naming convention. All class pointers start with the letters xm, followed by the basic class name of the widget (i.e., Label, RowColumn, PushButton), followed by the word WidgetClass.

The third argument to `XtCreateWidget()` specifies the parent of the new widget. Except for Shell widgets, every widget must have a parent. In this example, the shell widget, `toplevel`, serves as a parent for the XmLabel widget. The last two arguments specify additional arguments that modify the widget's behavior. We will discuss this in a moment.

Motif also provides a convenience function for each widget class, which can be used instead of `XtCreateWidget()`. These functions have the form

```
Widget XmCreate<widget> ( Widget     parent,
                          String     name,
                          ArgList    args,
                          Cardinal   numArgs )
```

where *<widget>* is replaced by the class of the widget to be created. For example, the function `XmCreateLabel()` creates a new XmLabel widget, and the function `XmCreateRow-Column()` creates an XmRowColumn widget. Notice that the argument order of these convenience functions differs from the argument order of `XtCreateWidget()`. In `XtCreateWidget()`, the name of the widget precedes the parent, while the convenience functions reverse this order.

All widgets except shell widgets must be *managed* by a parent widget. A widget's parent manages the widget's size and location, determines whether or not the widget is visible, and may also control input to the widget. Widgets may be managed by calling a separate function after the widget has been created, or they can be created and managed in a single step using the function `XtCreateManagedWidget()`. This convenience function has the same arguments as `XtCreateWidget()`.

The "Hello World" example uses `XtCreateManagedWidget()` to create an XmLabel widget on line 28, as shown below. The name of this widget is "label" and the widget class to be created is `xmLabelWidgetClass`. The parent is the `toplevel` shell widget. There is one additional argument specified in the `args` array.

```
label = XtCreateManagedWidget ( "label",
                                xmLabelWidgetClass,
                                toplevel,
                                args, n );
```

## Customizing Widgets

Programmers can alter the default behavior of most widgets by providing additional parameters when the widget is created. These additional arguments can be passed to `XtCreateWidget()` or `XtCreateManagedWidget()` using an `ArgList`. An `ArgList` is an array of type `Arg`, which is declared as:

```
typedef struct {
    String    name;
    XtArgVal value;
} Arg, *ArgList;
```

The `name` member of the `Arg` structure is a string that specifies a customizable parameter supported by the widget, while the `value` member indicates a value for this parameter. These customizable widget parameters are called *resources*. If the size of the value stored in the `value` member is less than or equal to the size of `XtArgVal`, the value is stored directly in the `Arg` structure. Otherwise the `value` member of a structure represents a pointer to the value. The definition of `XtArgVal` is system-dependent, but is generally the size of an address.

`XtCreateWidget()` allows a list of values to be passed to a widget at creation time. The widget compares the resource names in the list against those it recognizes, and copies the corresponding values into its own space.

It is often convenient to use the following macro to initialize an `ArgList`:

```
XtSetArg ( Arg arg, String name, XtArgVal value )
```

This macro is often used with a counter, as shown in the code segment below. Because `XtSetArg()` is a macro that evaluates its first parameter twice, the counter must not be incremented inside the macro.

```
int n;
Arg args[10];
// ...
n = 0;
XtSetArg ( args[n], XmNwidth, 200 ); n++;
XtSetArg ( args[n], XmNheight, 300 );n++;
XtCreateWidget ( name, xmRowColumnWidgetClass, parent, args, n );
```

This code segment specifies values for two resources in an `Arg` array. The second argument to each `XtSetArg()` macro is a macro that represents a character string. These are defined in Xm.h. For example, the macros used above are defined as:

```
#define XmNwidth    "width"
#define XmNheight  "height"
```

Using these macros allows the compiler to catch spelling errors that might go unnoticed if character strings were used directly.

As of X11R4, the Xt Intrinsics also supports *vararg* versions of many functions. These functions accept a variable number of name/value pairs in place of an `ArgList`. The names of all vararg functions begin with the prefix `XtVa`. One such function is `XtVaCreateWidget()`, which can be used in place of `XtCreateWidget()`. Using the vararg version, the XmRowColumn example above could be written as:

```
XtVaCreateWidget ( name, xmRowColumnWidgetClass, parent,
                XmNwidth,  200,
                XmNheight, 300,  NULL );
```

Any number of resources can be specified in name/value pairs as arguments to `XtVaCreate-Widget()`. The final argument *must* be a `NULL` to terminate the argument list. There are currently no vararg versions of the `XmCreate<widget>` convenience functions. There are vararg versions of most Xt calls, however, including `XtVaCreateManagedWidget()`, `XtVaCreatePopupShell()`, and even `XtVaAppInitialize()`.

These vararg functions may be particularly attractive to C++ programmers, because eliminating the calls to `XtSetArg()` generally makes the code look a little cleaner and less C-like. Using vararg routines can also be less error-prone by eliminating the possibility of overflowing a fixed length `Arg` array, or passing an incorrect argument count to the non-vararg routines. However, the argument list to all vararg functions *must* be `NULL` terminated, which is a different source of hard-to-detect errors. The vararg routines are also slightly more expensive, because the functions do additional work to process the variable length arguments. This is seldom a significant factor in the performance of most applications.

Many widget resources can be altered after the widget has been created by constructing an `ArgList` and calling the function

```
void XtSetValues ( Widget    w,
                ArgList   args,
                Cardinal  numArgs )
```

For example, we can specify the size of an XmRowColumn widget by creating the widget first, and then setting the size, as follows:

```
int     n;
Arg     args[10];
Widget rc;
// ...
rc = XtCreateWidget ( name, xmRowColumnWidgetClass, parent, args, n );
n = 0;
XtSetArg ( args[n], XmNwidth,  200 ); n++;
XtSetArg ( args[n], XmNheight, 300 );n++;
XtSetValues ( rc, args, n );
```

There is also a vararg version of XtSetValues():

```
void XtVaSetValues( Widget, ... )
```

Using XtVaSetValues(), the above code segment can be written as:

```
Widget rc;// ...
rc = XtCreateWidget ( name, xmRowColumnWidgetClass, parent, args, n );
XtVaSetValues ( rc,
                XmNwidth,  200,
                XmNheight, 300,
                NULL );
```

## Compound Strings

In the "Hello World" example, an ArgList is passed to the function XtCreateManaged-Widget() to specify the label displayed by the widget. The value expected by the XmLabel widget for the XmNlabelString resource must be a *compound string*. Compound strings are an abstraction used by Motif to represent text. The primary purpose of compound strings is to support international character sets and to eliminate dependencies on ASCII character strings. The function

```
XmString XmStringCreateSimple ( char  *string );
```

creates a compound string from an array of ASCII characters. The "Hello World" example creates a compound string on line 22, as follows

```
xmstr = XmStringCreateSimple ( "Hello World" );
```

The "Hello World" program uses the macro XtSetArg(), on line 27, to construct an ArgList that specifies a compound string as an XmNlabelString resource. The XmLabel widget uses this resource as the string to display in its window. Finally, because the XmLabel widget makes its own copy of the compound string, the program frees the compound string on line 33.

Compound strings can also be created using the function:

```
XmString XmStringCreateLtoR ( char  *string, char *charset );
```

This function creates a compound string whose direction is left-to-right using a character set specified by the `charset` argument. Normally, this argument is specified as the symbol `XmSTRING_DEFAULT_CHARSET`.

### Registering Callbacks

The next step in most Motif applications is to register any callback functions or other similar functions defined by the application to handle input or events. The hello.C example does not define any callbacks. The XmLabel and Shell widgets created by the "Hello World" program handle events, but they do so without requiring any action by the programmer. The Label widget automatically redraws the contents of its window when `Expose` events occur, repositions the displayed text when the window is resized, and so on. Callback functions are useful when the application needs to take some action in response to user input. The hello.C program is so simple that there are no actions to be taken.

### Managing Widgets

All widgets except shell widgets must be *managed* by a parent widget. A widget's parent manages the widget's size and location, determines whether or not the widget is visible, and may also control input to the widget. For example, some widgets arrange their children to form rows and columns, while others group their children into resizable panes. Still others allow the user or the programmer to specify the location of each child widget.

To add a widget to its parent's managed set, applications must call the function:

```
void XtManageChild ( Widget child )
```

The "Hello World" example creates and manages the XmLabel widget in a single step using the function:

```
Widget XtCreateManagedWidget ( const String   name,
                               WidgetClass    widgetClass,
                               Widget         parent,
                               ArgList        args,
                               Cardinal       numArgs );
```

### Realizing Widgets

Before a widget can be seen on the screen, it must create an X window in which to display itself. The process of creating an X window is called *realizing* the widget. A widget can be realized by passing it as an argument to the function:

```
void XtRealizeWidget ( Widget w );
```

Normally, applications only realize the top-level shell widget directly, because `XtRealize-Widget()` recursively realizes all children of the specified widget. Notice that a widget cannot be realized before its parent, because every X window must have a parent that already exists. The "Hello World" example realizes the top-level shell widget on line 37.

## Entering the Event Loop

Once the "Hello World" program has created the widgets it uses, it enters an event loop on line 38. The event loop is encapsulated by the Xt function:

```
XtAppMainLoop ( XtAppContext app )
```

This function never returns. Xt implements `XtAppMainLoop()` like this:

```
XtAppMainLoop ( XtAppContext app )
{
    for ( ;; )
    {
        XEvent event;
        XtAppNextEvent ( app, &event );
        XtDispatchEvent( &event );
    }
}
```

`XtAppNextEvent()` waits until an event is available in the application's event queue. When one or more events are available, it removes the first event from the head of the queue and returns. Then, `XtDispatchEvent()` looks up the widget associated with the window in which the event occurred and forwards the event to that widget for further processing.

## Compiling the Example

Compiling a C++ Motif program is much the same as building a comparable C program. The shell command CC usually invokes the C++ compiler or translator. The program described in the previous section can be built using the following shell command:

```
CC -DFUNCPROTO -o hello hello.C -lXm -lXt -lX11
```

This is, of course, nearly the same way an equivalent C program would be built, except that this command uses the C++ compiler. Notice also that the source file in this example uses a capital C as the file suffix. Normally the C++ compiler does not care what file extension is used, although auxiliary tools such as make, and editors such as emacs, may not recognize arbitrary suffixes.

Some systems may require other libraries, in addition to those shown here. For example, the X extension library (libXext.a) may need to be linked before the Xlib library. On some systems, Motif applications that use the FileSelectionBox widget may also require libPW.a to be linked. Some systems may also require additional libraries for network support.

### Running the Example

To test the program, go to a terminal emulator window (xterm, or similar) and type:

```
% hello
```

If all goes well, a window that looks like Figure 1.2 should appear on the screen.

**Figure 1.2**  The "Hello World" window.

The hello.C program creates only the middle portion of this window, the "Hello World" label, and the flat area around the label. The Motif window manager adds the surrounding decoration. Using a different window manager may produce a different appearance.

## Callback Functions

Most widgets provide hooks that allow applications to define functions to be called when some widget-specific condition (usually related to user input) occurs. These hooks are called *callback lists*. The application's functions are known as *callback functions*, or simply *callbacks*, because the widget uses them to make a "call back" to the application.

Callbacks provide a way to associate an action with some user input. For example, the Motif XmPushButton widget allows the programmer to register a function to be called when the user "pushes" the button. Programmers can register functions with the Motif XmScrollBar widget to be called when the user scrolls up or down a page, up or down a line, and so on. Most Motif widgets support many types of callbacks.

Each widget maintains a callback list for each type of callback it supports. The types of callbacks a particular type of widget supports can be found in the UNIX man page for that widget, or in a Motif reference guide. Callback lists are identified by strings, although programmers usually use macros defined in the file Xm.h instead. For example, every widget supports an XmNdestroyCallback callback list. If a widget's XmNdestroyCallback list is not empty, each callback function on the list is invoked before the widget is destroyed. The symbol XmNdestroyCallback is defined in Xm.h as:

```
#define XmNdestroyCallback "destroyCallback"
```

Applications can use the following function to add a callback to a widget's callback list:

```
void XtAddCallback ( Widget        widget,
                     const String  callbackName,
```

```
                    XtCallbackProc  proc,
                    XtPointer       clientData )
```

The first argument specifies the widget to whose callback list the function is to be added. The second argument, `callbackName`, identifies the callback list to which the third argument, the callback function `proc`, is to be added. The application can use the final argument, `clientData`, to specify some application-defined data to be passed to the registered callback function when it is called.

Because of the strong typing provided by C++, extra care must be taken when declaring callback functions. Both the type of each argument passed to the callback and the function's return type are important. The Xt Intrinsics defines the prototype for a callback function as:

```
    typedef void ( *XtCallbackProc ) ( Widget, XtPointer, XtPointer )
```

This declares that the type `XtCallbackProc` indicates a pointer to a function that has no return value and that expects three arguments whose types are `Widget`, `XtPointer`, and `XtPointer`. A typical callback function would be written as follows:

```
    void quitCallback ( Widget, XtPointer clientData, XtPointer callData )
    {
        exit ( 0 );
    }
```

This is a typical callback function that could be used to exit an application. It might be registered to be called when the user clicks on a quit button, or when the user selects "Quit" from a menu.

The C++ compiler or translator will probably give warning messages about the `callData` and `clientData` parameters being unused in the `quitCallback()` function. These warnings are harmless, but they can be eliminated by removing the unused parameters, leaving only the type declarations. Making this change, the above callback could be written as:

```
    void quitCallback ( Widget w, XtPointer, XtPointer )
    {
        exit ( 0 );
    }
```

The first argument passed to every callback function is the widget for which the callback is called. (There is nothing to prevent the programmer from registering any given function as a callback for multiple widgets.) The second parameter is the `clientData` specified by the application in the call to `XtAddCallback()`.

The last argument contains data provided by the widget. The type and purpose of this argument can be determined by checking the documentation for the specific widget class. In Motif, the `callData` argument is always a pointer to a structure. At a minimum, the `callData` structure contains a widget-specific code that indicates the reason the function was called and a pointer to the X event that indirectly triggered the callback. Some callbacks cannot be easily related to a specific event, in which case the `event` member is NULL. The structure that contains this basic information is defined as:

```
typedef struct {
    int       reason;
    XEvent   *event;
} XmAnyCallbackStruct;
```

Some Motif widgets define more complex structures to report additional information to callback functions, but these structures always include the `reason` and `event` fields as the first two members of the structure.

We must resort to type-casting to retrieve the data represented by the `clientData` and `callData` parameters. For example, we can retrieve the `reason` member of the `callData` structure passed to a callback like this:

```
void quitCallback ( Widget w, XtPointer, XtPointer callData )
{
    XmAnyCallbackStruct *cb = ( XmAnyCallbackStruct * ) callData;

    if ( cb->reason == XmCR_ACTIVATE )
    {
        exit ( 0 );
    }
}
```

Let's see how callbacks work with a brief example. The following program, pushme.C, is very similar to the "Hello World" program discussed earlier. However, this program creates a Motif XmPushButton widget instead of an XmLabel widget, and registers a function to exit the program when the user clicks on the button. The XmPushButton widget class supports three callback lists:

```
XmNactivateCallback        XmNarmCallback        XmNdisarmCallback
```

When the user presses a mouse button while the mouse cursor is inside an XmPushButton widget, the widget invokes the functions on the `XmNarmCallback` list. If the user releases the mouse button while the mouse cursor is within the bounds of the XmPushButton widget, the functions on the `XmNactivateCallback` list are called, followed by the functions on the `XmNdisarm-Callback` list. If the user moves the mouse cursor out of the XmPushButton widget's window before releasing the mouse button, only the functions on the `XmNdisarmCallback` list are invoked.

Let's look at the code before discussing the example.

```
1  //////////////////////////////////////////////////////
2  // pushme.C, Using callback functions in C++
3  //////////////////////////////////////////////////////
4  #include <stdlib.h>  // Needed for exit prototype
5  #include <Xm/Xm.h>
6  #include <Xm/PushB.h>
7
8  static void quitCallback ( Widget, XtPointer, XtPointer );
9
```

```
10  main ( unsigned int argc, char **argv )
11  {
12      Widget        button, toplevel;
13      XtAppContext app;
14      XmString      xmstr;
15
16      // Initialize the Intrinsics
17
18      toplevel = XtAppInitialize ( &app, "Pushme", NULL, 0,
19                                   &argc, argv, NULL, NULL, 0 );
20
21      // Create a compound string
22
23      xmstr = XmStringCreateSimple ( "Push Me" );
24
25      // Create an XmPushButton widget to display the string
26
27      button = XtVaCreateManagedWidget ( "button",
28                                         xmPushButtonWidgetClass,
29                                         toplevel,
30                                         XmNlabelString, xmstr,
31                                         NULL );
32
33      // Free the compound string after the XmPushButton has copied it
34
35      XmStringFree ( xmstr );
36
37      // Register the quitCallback callback function
38      // to be called when the button is pushed
39
40      XtAddCallback ( button,
41                      XmNactivateCallback,
42                      quitCallback,
43                      NULL ); // No client data needed
44
45      // Realize all widgets and enter the main event loop
46
47      XtRealizeWidget ( toplevel );
48      XtAppMainLoop ( app );
49  }
50
51
52  // Callback invoked when button is activated
53
54  void quitCallback ( Widget, XtPointer, XtPointer )
55  {
56      exit ( 0 );
57  }
```

There is very little difference between this example and the previous one, and there are only a few new items to discuss in pushme.C. First, instead of creating an XmLabel widget, the pushme program creates an XmPushButton widget on line 27. This example uses the vararg function `XtVaCreateManagedWidget()` to create the XmPushButton widget, which eliminates the need for an `ArgList`.

Notice that this program uses the `XmNlabelString` resource to specify the label displayed by the XmPushButton widget. The XmLabel widget in the previous example accepted the same resource. Motif uses an object-oriented architecture, implemented in ordinary C, that supports a type of inheritance. The XmPushButton widget is a subclass (an Xt-style subclass, not a C++ derived class) of XmLabel. Therefore, the XmPushButton widget inherits most of the behavior and resources supported by the XmLabel widget, and also adds some additional behavior of its own.

Another difference between pushme and the earlier example is the call to `XtAddCallback()` to register the `quitCallback()` function. The `quitCallback()` function is registered with the XmPushButton widget's `XmNactivateCallback` list, and invoked when the user presses and releases the left mouse button while the mouse cursor is over the widget.

Notice that the structure of this program is unchanged from the "Hello World" example on page 16. Both programs call XtAppInitialize() to open a connection to the X server and create a shell widget. Then, they create widgets that serve as each application's primary interface and register functions to be called when use input occurs. Finally, all widgets are managed, the shell is realized, and each program enters an event loop. Even more complex programs follow this same model.

We can compile the pushme.C example the same way as the previous program:

```
CC -DFUNCPROTO -o pushme pushme.C -lXm -lXt -lX11
```

Figure 1.3 shows the window created by running the pushme program.

**Figure 1.3**  The pushme program.

## The Architectural Impact of Event-driven Programming

The architecture of X and Xlib imposes several subtle but powerful constraints on an application's structure. Applications must be aware of the client-server model, especially the fact that applications run asynchronously with respect to each other and with respect to the server. Programmers must also be aware that the server is a shared resource and that clients must cooperate by not burdening the server unnecessarily. Most of all, it is important to understand the ramifications of the event-driven model used by X and Xt. All X and Motif applications must be designed to process events continuously. This has several implications:

- Programs cannot block while waiting for input, as older-style programs might do when calling a function like `scanf()`. If a program blocks while waiting for a response to a question asked of the user, it cannot receive other events. If an application does not process the event queue in a timely manner, the application's windows will not be redrawn when a window is exposed. The application's buttons and menus will not respond to user input, and so on. Applications can usually be structured to avoid the need for blocking input. It is possible to simulate blocking behavior in such a way that the user believes the program is blocked while waiting for input. Chapter 7 discusses this topic in more detail.

- If a program is busy performing some task and does not read the event queue, there is no user-friendly way to interrupt the application. Users in a UNIX environment take for granted the ability to type a Control-C at any time to interrupt a process. To an X application, a Control-C key sequence typed into an application's window is just another sequence of events for the server to send to the application. If the application never reads its event queue, it has no way to detect an interrupt key. Chapter 10 treats this topic in more detail.

- The program should avoid performing any task that will take longer than the user's perception of a reasonable response time. If the program must perform a task that requires longer than this amount of time, it is best to break the task up into smaller tasks. Depending on the situation, the task could be done as a concurrent background task, or some other means could be used to do the job.

The last point requires some elaboration. As many user interface researchers have pointed out, the amount of time a user thinks is "reasonable" varies with the task. If the user simply wants to delete a character in some text, anything other than instantaneous response will be perceived as slow. But if the user requests all names that match a certain pattern from a database containing the equivalent of a large phone book, the user may be willing to wait a very long time.

However, the requirements of an X application change this scenario considerably. Imagine an X-based database program. The user may still be willing to wait a long time (even several minutes) for a complex operation to be completed. But the user will probably be dismayed if he or she moves or uncovers the application's window while waiting for the result, only to find that the window is not redrawn correctly. This can easily happen if the program is busy and does not handle `Expose` events that accumulate in the event queue. When a program is too busy to handle events, the user may think the program is dead, instead of understanding that the program is busily working on a complex operation.

The issue of response time can show up in more subtle ways as well. If a program does not perform a task quickly and return to the event loop, the user may start to wonder what is happening, and try to press other buttons. Discovering that the button does not respond, he or she tries others. These events are queued by the X server for the application to handle when it can. When the program finally returns, it processes all the mouse events generated by the user while it was busy. Obviously, this could lead to unexpected, and even disastrous, consequences.

One way to handle such situations is to always provide continuous feedback whenever a program is busy. It is also possible to disable device events until an application is ready to handle them. Xt allows applications to disable user input by making widgets *insensitive* to device events. Chapter 10 also discusses additional techniques for handling user input while an application is busy.

# 1.4    The Motif Widget Set

The Motif widget set contains many components, including scroll bars, menus, buttons, and so on that can be combined to create user interfaces. The most noticeable characteristic of the Motif widget set is its three-dimensional, bevelled appearance. Most Motif widgets contain a border whose top and left sides can be set to a different color than the bottom and right sides. By setting these areas to the appropriate colors, a three-dimensional shading effect can be achieved, as shown in Figure 1.4.

**Figure 1.4**  The Motif 3D shadow effect.

If a widget's top shadow is lighter than the background and the bottom shadow is darker, the widget appears to protrude from the screen, as seen in the widget on the left in Figure 1.4. Reversing these colors makes the widget appear to be recessed into the screen, as demonstrated by the widget on the right side of Figure 1.4. The colors that create this three-dimensional effect can be set by the user or the programmer. By default, Motif automatically generates the appropriate top and bottom shadow colors, based on each widget's background color.

The Motif widget set is designed to encourage the programmer to follow the Motif Style Guide, which is based on the behavior of Microsoft's Presentation Manager. However, Motif widgets can be customized in the same way as other widget sets. So, while Motif encourages the Presentation Manager style, the style is not strictly enforced by the widget set. Programmers who want their applications to fit smoothly with other Motif-based applications should try to adhere to the conventions described in the *Motif Style Guide* [OSF90] as closely as possible.

We can divide the widget classes provided by Motif into several categories based on the general functionality they offer. For example, some widgets display information, while others allow the user to select from a set of choices. Still others allow other widgets to be grouped together in various combinations. The following sections describe the Motif widgets, divided into the following categories:

1. **Display widgets**. These are simple buttons, labels, text editors, and so on.

2. **Manager or Container widgets**. These are used to contain, or group, other widgets.

3. **Dialog widgets**. These are temporary windows, used to communicate some information to the user or ask questions.

4. **Menus**. Motif supports popup, pulldown and option menus that allow the user to select

from a set of choices.

5. **Gadgets**. Gadgets are more efficient versions of the Motif display widgets. Using gadgets can greatly improve a program's performance, although they have some restrictions that can limit their use.

## Display Widgets

Motif provides many widgets whose primary purpose is to display information or to interact with the user. These widgets include:

| | | |
|---|---|---|
| XmArrowButton | XmDrawnButton | XmLabel |
| XmList | XmPushButton | XmScrollBar |
| XmSeparator | XmText | XmToggleButton |
| XmScale | XmCascadeButton | XmTextField |

The following sections discuss several of these widget classes.

### The XmLabel Widget

One of the simplest Motif display widgets is the XmLabel widget used in the "Hello World" example. The XmLabel widget simply displays a string or a graphical image (in the form of a *pixmap*) in a window. As in nearly all Motif widgets, the string displayed by the XmLabel widget must be a compound string. The XmLabel widget does not support any callbacks (other than the XmNdestroyCallback supported by all Xt widgets and the XmNhelpCallback list supported by all Motif widgets). Figure 1.5 shows a simple XmLabel widget displaying some text.

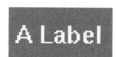

**Figure 1.5** A Motif XmLabel widget.

### Motif Button Widgets

Several subclasses of XmLabel, such as XmPushButton, XmArrowButton, XmToggleButton, XmCascadeButton, and XmDrawnButton, act as buttons that allow the user to issue commands. When a button is "pushed," its three-dimensional appearance changes, providing the illusion that the button has been pressed into the screen. When the user releases the mouse button, the button's appearance returns to normal.

The XmArrowButton is similar to the XmPushButton widget, except that it displays a triangular arrow that can point up, down, left, or right. The XmDrawnButton widget is also similar, but allows each program to draw its own text or images in the button. The XmCascadeButton is used primarily in menus as a button that supports a pulldown or cascading menu pane. The XmToggleButton is somewhat different and alternates between two states. If the toggle is "set," a small indicator beside the label changes its appearance. Figure 1.6 shows the Motif button widgets.

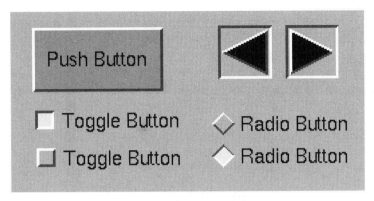

**Figure 1.6** Motif button widgets.

All Motif button widgets provide callbacks to allow a program to perform an action when the button's state changes. The XmPushButton, XmArrowButton, XmCascadeButton, and XmDrawn-Button widget classes support similar callback lists, which include the `XmNarmCallback`, `XmNdisarmCallback`, and `XmNactivateCallback` callback lists. Functions registered as these types of callbacks are called when the button is pressed (armed), released (disarmed), or activated. A button is normally activated when it is armed and then disarmed while the mouse cursor is within the button widget. Motif buttons can usually be activated by the <Return> key as well.

The XmToggleButton widget supports a different set of callbacks than the other button widgets. Functions registered with the `XmNvalueChangedCallback` list are invoked when the toggle button changes state. The call data structure supplied with this callback reports the current state of the toggle.

## The XmText and XmTextField Widgets

The XmText widget allows the user to edit single or multiple lines of text. In single-line mode, the XmText widget allows the user to enter a short string. In multi-line mode, it functions as a complete text editor. The XmText widget supplies many convenience functions that allow the programmer to scroll the text, toggle the widget between edit and read-only mode, retrieve text from the widget, programmatically add text to the widget, and so on. In Motif version 1.1, the XmText widget is the only Motif widget that uses ASCII character strings instead of compound strings. This is expected to change in the near future.

Motif provides two versions of the text widget: the XmText widget and the XmTextField widget. The XmTextField widget can display only a single line of text, and is intended to be more efficient than the XmText widget when only a single line text entry area is needed.

Figure 1.7 shows a Motif XmText widget with a pair of vertical and horizontal scrollbars. The XmText widget does not include scrollbars itself, but programmers can use the XmScrollBar widget to scroll the contents of an XmText widget, or use the XmScrolledWindow widget, as shown here. There is also a convenience function, `XmCreateScrolledText()` that creates an XmText widget as a child of an XmScrolledWindow widget and handles all the scrolling automatically.

```
main ( unsigned int argc, char **
{
        Widget          toplevel, rc, fc
                        sw, runButton,
                        quitButton, can\
        XtAppContext app;
        Display      *dpy;
        Arg          wargs[10];
        int          n;

        // Initialize the Intrinsics

        XtToolkitInitialize();
```

**Figure 1.7**  A Motif scrolled text widget.

## The XmScrollBar Widget

The XmScrollBar widget displays a slider that moves in a trough. The user can move the slider, using the mouse, to scroll other windows. The XmScrollBar widget also provides arrows at either end of the trough, which can be used to move the slider in the direction of the arrow. Applications can register callback functions to be called when the user moves the slider. The callback lists supported by the XmScrollBar widget include `XmNvalueChangedCallback`, called whenever the slider moves, and `XmNdragCallback`, called when the user continuously drags the slider. In addition, the XmScrollBar widget supports many special-purpose callbacks, such as `XmNto-TopCallback` and `XmNtoBottomCallback`, called when the user moves to the top or bottom of the scrollbar's range, and `XmNpageIncrementCallback` and `XmNpageDecrement-Callback`, called when the user scrolls one page.

Figure 1.8 shows a Motif XmScrollBar widget.

**Figure 1.8**  The Motif XmScrollBar widget.

## The XmSeparator Widget

The XmSeparator widget displays a straight line, which can be drawn vertically or horizontally. The XmSeparator widget is primarily a decorative widget, used to visually separate different sections of a window. Figure 1.9 demonstrates the visual styles supported by the XmSeparator widget, which are controlled by the `XmNseparatorType` resource. In addition to the styles shown, the XmSeparator widget allows programmers to specify an arbitrary pixmap pattern to be used as the background pattern of the line.

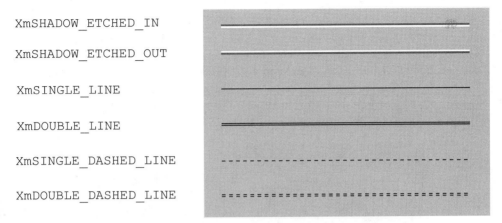

XmSHADOW_ETCHED_IN

XmSHADOW_ETCHED_OUT

XmSINGLE_LINE

XmDOUBLE_LINE

XmSINGLE_DASHED_LINE

XmDOUBLE_DASHED_LINE

**Figure 1.9**  Styles supported by the Motif XmSeparator widget.

## The XmList Widget

The XmList widget displays a list of text items and allows the user to select entries on the list. The items displayed by the XmList widget are specified as an array of compound strings. The XmList widget supports several selection styles and selection callback lists. For example, the XmList widget can be configured to allow the user to select single or multiple lines. Multiple selections can be either contiguous or non-contiguous. The programmer can register callback functions to be called when the user selects items from the list, when the user double-clicks on an item in the list, and so on. The XmList widget can also be used in conjunction with the XmScrolledWindow widget to create scrollable lists. Motif provides a convenience function `XmCreateScrolledList()` that can be used to create and automatically configure an XmScrolledWindow and an XmList widget.

Figure 1.10 shows two XmList widgets with scrollbars.

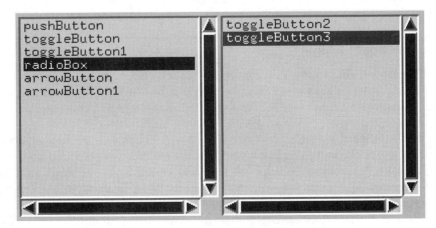

**Figure 1.10**  A scrolled List widget.

## The XmScale Widget

Figure 1.11 shows the XmScale widget, a scrollbar-like widget. Like the XmScrollBar widget, it has a movable slider that slides in a trough area. The user can move the slider to choose a value within a pre-specified range. The scale also supports a label area, and displays the current value represented by the widget above the slider. The slider supports several callbacks that notify applications when the user moves the slider. The XmScale widget is a subclass of XmManager, and is therefore more correctly categorized as a container widget. However, it usually functions as a display widget and allows the user to control a numerical value.

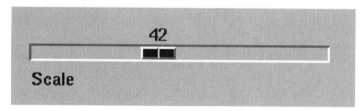

**Figure 1.11**   The Motif XmScale widget.

# Container Widgets

The Motif widget set provides many widgets that can be used to combine other widgets into composite panels. Composite widgets allow endless combinations of buttons, scrollbars, text panes, and so on, to be grouped together in an application. Complex interfaces are constructed by combining display widgets or collections of display widgets in different arrangements. The layout of each collection of widgets is determined by the container widget that manages that collection.

The Motif container widgets include:

| | | |
|---|---|---|
| XmDrawingArea | XmFrame | XmMainWindow |
| XmRowColumn | XmForm | XmScrolledWindow |
| XmPanedWindow | XmBulletinBoard | |

The following sections discuss several typical Motif container widget classes.

## The XmBulletinBoard Widget

The XmBulletinBoard widget class is a container widget with a very simple layout policy. The XmBulletinBoard widget allows children to be placed at absolute $(x, y)$ coordinates within the widget. If no coordinates are provided for the XmBulletinBoard widget's children, the children are placed at $(0, 0)$.

The XmBulletinBoard widget is often used when the programmer wants to maintain complete control over the layout of a collection of widgets. Because children can be placed anywhere within the parent, complex layouts can be achieved relatively easily. However, the XmBulletinBoard widget provides no automatic way to dynamically adjust the layout when the user resizes a window. In addition, widget layouts based on the XmBulletinBoard and hard-coded positions often exhibit problems if the user changes the font sizes used by the children. Most widgets resize in response to changes in font size, which means that a layout based on one font size may not work for another.

## The XmRowColumn Widget

The XmRowColumn widget is a subclass of the XmManager widget class that organizes its children as a grid of rows and columns. A large set of resources control the XmRowColumn widget's behavior. For example, the `XmNorientation` resource determines whether children are displayed in row-major or column-major order. The `XmNnumColumns` resource controls the number of columns when the orientation is vertical or the number of rows when the orientation is horizontal. The `XmNpacking` resource can be set to `XmPACK_TIGHT` to pack all children as tightly as possible, or to `XmPACK_COLUMN` to force all children to be aligned in evenly-spaced rows and columns.

Figure 1.12 shows an XmRowColumn widget with six XmPushButton widgets as children. The six children would ordinarily have different sizes, based on the length of their labels. The layout in Figure 1.12 is achieved by setting the `XmNnumColumns` resource to 3 and the `XmNpacking` resource to `XmPACK_COLUMN`. In this mode, the XmRowColumn widget forces all children to have the same width, and to line up in evenly-spaced columns.

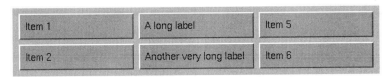

**Figure 1.12**  The Motif XmRowColumn widget, configured to display three columns.

The XmRowColumn widget's children do not normally change size when the XmRowColumn widget is resized. However, the last widget in each row stretches and shrinks with its parent if the `XmNadjustLast` resource is set to `TRUE`.

If the `XmNnumColumns` resource is set to 1, the XmRowColumn widget's layout changes to that shown in Figure 1.13. Here, the XmRowColumn widget still forces all children to be the same size, but the children are placed in a single column.

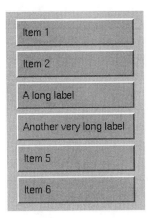

**Figure 1.13**  The Motif XmRowColumn widget, configured to display a single column.

Changing the XmNpacking resource to XmPACK_TIGHT produces the layout shown in Figure 1.14. In this mode, the XmRowColumn widget positions each child next to the previous child as long as there is sufficient space left in the row. When a child doesn't fit on the current row, a new row is begun. When XmNpacking is set to XmPACK_TIGHT, the layout of the XmRowColumn widget's children changes dynamically when the XmRowColumn widget changes size.

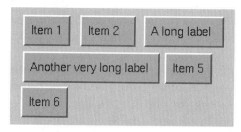

**Figure 1.14**  The Motif XmRowColumn widget, with XmNpacking set to "pack_tight".

The XmRowColumn widget can be used to provide general layout, but more often serves other, more specialized, purposes. For example, the XmRowColumn widget can be used as a RadioBox widget that allows only one child out of a set of children to be selected at one time. In this mode, the children are generally some type of button widget. The XmRowColumn widget is most often used as a menu pane or menubar. The XmRowColumn widget is less useful as a general container widget because it imposes several restrictions on its children. For example, the XmRowColumn widget always forces all children to have the same height.

## The XmForm Widget

The XmForm widget is one of the most flexible of the Motif manager widgets, and is often used as the topmost container in an application (excluding the shell widget). The primary advantage offered by the XmForm widget is that it is possible to create a collection of widgets that dynamically resize themselves according to a layout description that describes relationships between widgets. The XmForm widget offers more flexibility than the XmRowColumn widget and more support for dynamically resizable layouts than the XmBulletinBoard widget.

The XmForm widget manages its children based on constraints that specify the position of each widget relative to another widget, known as a *reference widget*. Each child can have a top, bottom, left, and right reference widget. Each child of an XmForm widget can also support an "attachment" for each of its top, bottom, left, and right sides. The attachment specifies how the child's position relates to the reference widget's position. Programmers can also specify that any side of a child of an XmForm should be attached to a particular position, relative to its parent XmForm widget.

By carefully setting the attachments and reference widgets, it is possible to specify how the children of a XmForm widget should be positioned, and how those positions should be affected when the XmForm widget's size changes. For example, the function below creates an XmForm widget with four children:

```
void createForm ( Widget parent )
{
    // Create a form and four children

    Widget form, widgetA, widgetB, widgetC, widgetD;

    form = XtCreateManagedWidget ( "form",
                                   xmFormWidgetClass,
                                   parent,  NULL, 0);
    widgetA = XtCreateManagedWidget ( "widgetA",
                                      xmPushButtonWidgetClass,
                                      form, NULL, 0 );
    widgetB = XtCreateManagedWidget ( "widgetB",
                                      xmPushButtonWidgetClass,
                                      form, NULL, 0 );
    widgetC = XtCreateManagedWidget ( "widgetC",
                                      xmPushButtonWidgetClass,
                                      form, NULL, 0 );
    widgetD = XtCreateManagedWidget ( "widgetD",
                                      xmPushButtonWidgetClass,
                                      form, NULL, 0 );

    // Attach widgetA to the left, top, and bottom of the form

    XtVaSetValues ( widgetA, XmNtopAttachment,    XmATTACH_FORM,
                             XmNbottomAttachment, XmATTACH_FORM,
                             XmNleftAttachment,   XmATTACH_FORM,
                             XmNrightAttachment,  XmATTACH_NONE,
                             NULL );

    // Attach widgetB to the top of the form, the right side of
    // widgetA, the top of widgetC, and the the left side of widgetD

    XtVaSetValues ( widgetB, XmNtopAttachment,    XmATTACH_FORM,
                             XmNbottomAttachment, XmATTACH_WIDGET,
                             XmNbottomWidget,     widgetC,
                             XmNleftAttachment,   XmATTACH_WIDGET,
                             XmNleftWidget,       widgetA,
                             XmNrightAttachment,  XmATTACH_WIDGET,
                             XmNrightWidget,      widgetD,
                             NULL );

    // Attach widgetC to the bottom of the form, the
    // right side of widgetA, and the left side of widgetD

    XtVaSetValues ( widgetC, XmNtopAttachment,    XmATTACH_NONE,
                             XmNbottomAttachment, XmATTACH_FORM,
                             XmNleftAttachment,   XmATTACH_WIDGET,
                             XmNleftWidget,       widgetA,
```

```
                              XmNrightAttachment,  XmATTACH_WIDGET,
                              XmNrightWidget,       widgetD,
                              NULL );

    // Attach widgetD to the top, bottom, and right of the form

    XtVaSetValues ( widgetD, XmNtopAttachment,    XmATTACH_FORM,
                             XmNbottomAttachment, XmATTACH_FORM,
                             XmNrightAttachment,  XmATTACH_FORM,
                             XmNleftAttachment,   XmATTACH_NONE,
                             NULL );

}
```

Figure 1.15 illustrates the attachments and approximate initial positions of the XmForm widget's children, as specified by the function above. The arrows in the figure indicate an attachment to a reference widget.

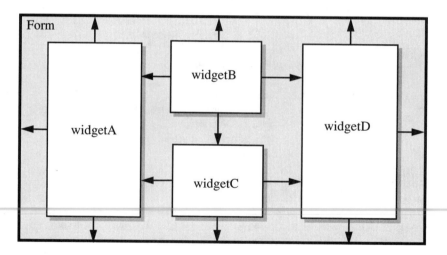

**Figure 1.15** Attachments between children of an XmForm widget.

The primary reason to use an XmForm widget is to allow the layout of the form's children to change dynamically when the form widget changes size. Therefore, the attachments shown above should be viewed as a behavior specification, not just a static layout description.

For example, let's see what happens to the layout described above when the parent XmForm widget changes size. Figure 1.16 shows the initial layout when the widgets created by the createForm() function are first managed. Notice that the layout is almost exactly as drawn in Figure 1.15. Each widget's width is determined primarily by the width of its label. The two widgets on each end are twice as tall as the middle widgets, because they are attached to the top and bottom of the XmForm.

**Figure 1.16**  The Motif XmForm widget, initial layout.

Figure 1.17 shows the same window, after it has been resized to be much taller. Notice that widgetC maintains the same height, but widgetB has grown significantly. This is because widgetC has no top attachment, and therefore is not stretched vertically. However, widgetB is attached to the top of widgetC and the top of the form, and must grow to maintain this relationship. If we detached the bottom of widgetB and attached the top of widgetC to the bottom of widgetB, widgetC would grow instead. Both widgetA and widgetD have stretched to match the height of the form, because these widgets are attached to both the top and bottom of the form.

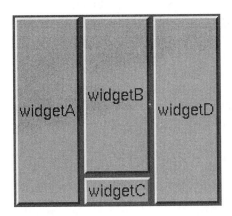

**Figure 1.17**  The Motif XmForm widget, after resizing vertically.

Figure 1.18 shows what happens if the form widget is resized to be wider. Here, widgetA and widgetD still maintain the same width because they each have only a single horizontal attachment. However, widgetB and widgetC are both attached to the right side of widgetA and the left side of widgetD and must grow horizontally to maintain that relationship.

It is often rather difficult to determine the correct attachments to achieve a particular layout or a particular dynamic behavior. One common problem programmers encounter when using an XmForm widget is that it is easy to specify circular constraints, which the XmForm widget cannot resolve. For example, we could easily specify(incorrectly) that widgetB is to be attached to the top of widgetC, and that widgetC is to be attached to the bottom of widgetB. Drawing figures similar to Figure 1.15 can help visualize the correct attachments. In general, it is best to specify the smallest number of attachments necessary to describe the layout.

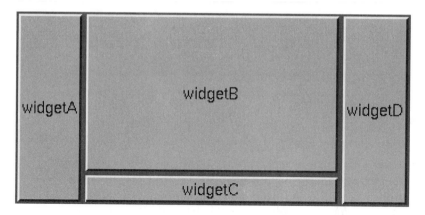

**Figure 1.18**   A wide layout.

The XmForm widget also supports the ability to attach a widget to a particular position. For example, in the above example, we could attach `widgetA` to the left side of the form and to a position equal to 33% of the form's width. Then, `widgetB` and `widgetC` could be attached on the left to the 33% position, and on the right to the 66% position. The top and bottom positions of `widgetB` and `widgetC` could be set such that each widget occupies 50% of the height. Finally, `widgetD` could occupy the remaining 33% of the width. This type of layout would initially look the same as Figure 1.16. However, the window's behavior when resized would be quite different from that shown in Figure 1.17 and Figure 1.18. When position attachments are used, each widget maintains the same relative size and position regardless of the size of the XmForm.

Each of these behaviors can be useful in different situations, depending on the desired layout. It is also possible to mix the two approaches, so that some widgets are attached to positions and others are attached to widgets. The XmForm widget requires a great deal of patience and practice to use successfully, but it is usually possible to achieve almost any layout desired by specifying the right set of attachments.

### The XmDrawingArea Widget

Motif provides an XmDrawingArea widget for those applications that simply want to display their own text or graphics in a window. The XmDrawingArea widget is a container widget and can support children, but it is generally used as a simple drawing canvas. The XmDrawingArea widget supports callbacks that notify the application when the window is resized or exposed. The widget also supports an input callback for handling keyboard or mouse input within the drawing area.

### The XmPanedWindow Widget

The XmPanedWindow widget places all children in a vertical stack. The user can dynamically alter the size of each pane by using the mouse to move a small "sash" associated with each pane. Figure 1.19 shows an XmPanedWindow widget with three XmScrolledWindow widgets as children.

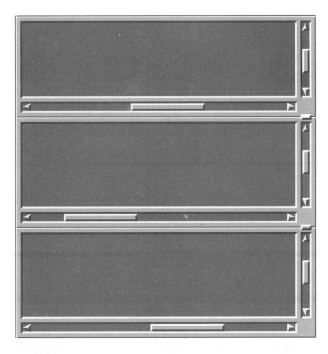

**Figure 1.19**   The Motif XmPanedWindow widget.

## The XmScrolledWindow Widget

The XmScrolledWindow widget provides vertical and horizontal scrollbars and a scrollable work area. The XmScrolledWindow widget can be configured to automatically scroll any child widget, or the programmer can register callbacks with the scrollbars to handle the scrolling.

Motif provides many convenience functions that combine the XmScrolledWindow widget with other widgets. The convenience functions configure the XmScrolledWindow widget to best match the needs of the child widget. For example, `XmCreateScrolledList()` creates an XmList widget managed by an XmScrolledWindow widget, while `XmCreateScrolledText()` creates an XmText widget as a child of an XmScrolledWindow widget. Figure 1.7 shows an XmScrolled-Window used with an XmText widget, while Figure 1.19 shows several XmScrolledWindow widgets managed by an XmPanedWindow widget.

## Using Containers

Let's look at a simple program that demonstrates how to use several Motif container widgets to build a more complex interface than the hello and pushme examples discussed earlier. The following program creates a window layout that has two command buttons in a single row along the top of the application. A scrolled work space area occupies most of the application's window below the command buttons. Figure 1.20 illustrates this window arrangement.

**Figure 1.20**  A typical Motif window layout.

To create the window layout in Figure 1.20, we must combine several container widgets, a Shell widget, an XmForm widget, an XmRowColumn widget, and an XmScrolledWindow widget, with the simpler XmPushButton and XmDrawingArea widgets. The widgets form a hierarchical structure, known as the application's widget tree. Figure 1.21 shows the hierarchy corresponding to the window layout in Figure 1.20. Each node of the tree shows the name of a widget, with the widget's class name shown below in italics. The hierarchy does not include the scrollbars, which are considered to be part of the XmScrolledWindow widget.

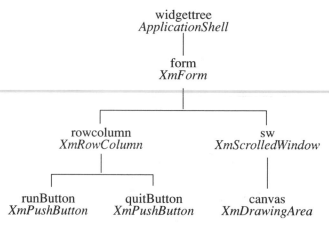

**Figure 1.21**  The widget tree for the window in Figure 1.20.

The following program creates the widget tree shown in Figure 1.21, and configures the various widgets to achieve the layout shown in Figure 1.20. As written, the program doesn't do anything, but some actions or behavior could be added simply by assigning callbacks to the XmPushButton and XmDrawingArea widgets. Look at the code below, and then we will discuss it.

```
1    ////////////////////////////////////////////////////
2    // Widgettree.C, Demonstrate a typical widget hierarchy
3    ////////////////////////////////////////////////////
4    #include <Xm/Xm.h>
5    #include <Xm/RowColumn.h>
6    #include <Xm/Form.h>
7    #include <Xm/ScrolledW.h>
8    #include <Xm/DrawingA.h>
9    #include <Xm/PushB.h>
10
11   main ( unsigned int argc, char **argv )
12   {
13       Widget      toplevel, rc, form,
14                   sw, runButton,
15                   quitButton, canvas;
16       XtAppContext app;
17
18       toplevel = XtAppInitialize ( &app, "Widgettree", NULL, 0,
19                                    &argc, argv, NULL, NULL, 0 );
20
21       // All other widgets are contained in a Form widget
22
23       form = XtCreateManagedWidget ( "form",
24                                      xmFormWidgetClass,
25                                      toplevel,
26                                      NULL, 0 );
27
28       // Attach a RowColumn widget top along the top edge of the Form
29
30       rc = XtVaCreateManagedWidget ( "rowcolumn",
31                                      xmRowColumnWidgetClass,
32                                      form,
33                                      XmNleftAttachment,   XmATTACH_FORM,
34                                      XmNrightAttachment,  XmATTACH_FORM,
35                                      XmNtopAttachment,    XmATTACH_FORM,
36                                      XmNbottomAttachment, XmATTACH_NONE,
37                                      NULL );
38
39       // A ScrolledWindow widget occupies the bottom portion
40       // of the window, and spans the entire width
41
42       sw = XtVaCreateManagedWidget ( "sw",
43                                      xmScrolledWindowWidgetClass,
44                                      form,
45                                      XmNleftAttachment,   XmATTACH_FORM,
46                                      XmNrightAttachment,  XmATTACH_FORM,
47                                      XmNbottomAttachment, XmATTACH_FORM,
48                                      XmNtopWidget,        rc,
49                                      XmNtopAttachment,    XmATTACH_WIDGET,
```

```
50                                          NULL );
51
52        // A DrawingArea widget provides a scrollable work area
53
54        canvas =  XtCreateManagedWidget ( "canvas",
55                                          xmDrawingAreaWidgetClass,
56                                          sw,
57                                          NULL, 0 );
58
59        // Create various buttons as children of the RowColumn widget
60
61        runButton = XtCreateManagedWidget ( "runButton",
62                                            xmPushButtonWidgetClass,
63                                            rc,
64                                            NULL, 0 );
65
66        quitButton = XtCreateManagedWidget ( "quitButton",
67                                             xmPushButtonWidgetClass,
68                                             rc,
69                                             NULL, 0 );
70
71        //
72        // Assign callbacks, etc. here
73        //
74
75        // Realize all widgets and enter the main event loop
76
77        XtRealizeWidget( toplevel );
78        XtAppMainLoop( app );
79    }
```

This program uses a Motif XmForm widget to set up the basic layout of the scrolled work area and the row of buttons. The layout shown in Figure 1.20 is achieved by attaching the XmRow-Column container widget to the top, left, and right sides of the XmForm widget. The XmScrolledWindow widget must be attached to the left, right, and bottom of the XmForm, and to the bottom of the XmRowColumn widget. These attachments are specified by sets of resources passed to `XtVaCreateManagedWidget()` when each widget is created. The XmScrolled-Window widget manages an XmDrawingArea widget, while the XmRowColumn widget manages two XmPushButton widgets that allow the user to issue commands.

This example provides just one simple example of how different types of widgets can be used to form an application's interface. The various Motif container widgets can be combined in nearly endless ways to achieve many complex layouts. Learning how to combine the available widgets to create different panels can require some investment of time. It is very helpful to develop a feel for the basic behavior of each type of widget, as well as a general understanding of the many options supported by each widget class.

# Menu Widgets

The Motif widget set provides a versatile collection of widgets that allow applications to create popup, pulldown and option menus. A menu pane consists of a popup Shell widget that manages an XmRowColumn widget containing buttons, labels, and occasionally other types of widgets. The buttons are the selectable entries in the menu. Actions can be associated with each menu entry by registering a callback function with each button in the menu. By combining different types of widgets, the programmer can create many different types of menus: pulldowns, popups, cascading pulldowns, cascading popups, option menus, and so on.

The following widgets can be used to construct menus:

- The **XmRowColumn** widget class functions as a menubar as well as both popup and pulldown menu panes. When used as a menu pane, the XmRowColumn widget must be created as a child of an XmMenuShell widget. Motif provides convenience functions to create both the XmMenuShell and the XmRowColumn widget at once. These functions are:

```
XmCreatePopupMenu ( Widget   parent,
                    String   name,
                    ArgList  args,
                    Cardinal nargs )

XmCreatePulldownMenu ( Widget   parent,
                       String   name,
                       ArgList  args,
                       Cardinal nargs )

XmCreateOptionnMenu ( Widget   parent,
                      String   name,
                      ArgList  args,
                      Cardinal nargs )
```

- **XmPushButton** widgets are used as selectable items in a menu pane. XmPushButton widgets are used exactly as demonstrated earlier in this chapter. Callback functions registered for the `XmNactivateCallback`, `XmNarmCallback`, or `XmNdisarmCallback` lists are called when the user activates, arms, or disarms a menu button.

- The **XmToggleButton** widget can be used in a menu to toggle between two states.

- The **XmCascadeButton** widget supports submenus. The XmCascadeButton widget looks much like an XmPushButton widget. However, the XmCascadeButton widget can have a pulldown menu associated with it, which appears when the user arms the XmCascadeButton widget. XmCascadeButton widgets can be used in a menu bar to create pulldown menu panes, or in a menu pane to create menu panes that cascade to the right of a menu entry.

- The **XmLabel** widget class is often used to add titles or subtitles to a menu.

- The **XmSeparator** widget can be used to delineate different sections of a menu. For example, an XmSeparator widget can be used to set a title or subtitle off from other menu items.

Figure 1.22 shows an example of a Motif menu bar, with a pulldown menu pane. The menu pane also has a second menu pane that cascades from the main menu pane to the right.

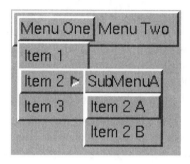

**Figure 1.22**  A Motif menubar, with a cascading pulldown menu.

## Motif Dialog Widgets

The Motif widget set builds on the underlying popup facilities provided by the Xt Intrinsics to provide a versatile set of dialog widgets. Motif uses a subclass of the Shell widget class, the XmDialogShell widget class, as the basis of most dialogs. However, the programmer seldom needs to deal with the XmDialogShell widget class directly because Motif provides convenience functions that create different types of dialogs and popups. Most Motif widgets know when they are children of the XmDialogShell widget class and automatically pop up and pop down their parent shell when managed and unmanaged.

The following are the Motif widget classes designed to be used as dialog widgets.

- **XmBulletinBoard**. This widget is the base for many dialogs. It does not impose any ordering or geometry constraints on its children. The XmBulletinBoard widget provides special support for automatically popping up or down dialogs when an "OK" or "Cancel" button is activated.

- **XmCommand**. The XmCommand widget provides a command input region and a command history region that lists previously entered commands.

- **XmFileSelectionBox**. This widget class allows the user to select from a list of files and navigate through the file system.

- **XmForm**: The XmForm widget uses constraints attached to each managed child to determine the position of each child.

- **XmMessageBox**. The XmMessageBox widget class displays a message to the user. The XmMessageBox widget provides a message area, a symbol area, and three buttons labeled "OK", "Cancel", and "Help".

- **XmSelectionBox**. This widget class allows the user to select from a list of choices displayed in a scrolled list. The XmSelectionBox widget class also provides "OK", "Cancel", and "Help" buttons.

By setting appropriate resources, many types of dialogs can be created from these basic widget classes. Motif provides a large set of convenience routines to make dialogs easier to create and use. These convenience functions create the following types of dialogs:

| | | | |
|---|---|---|---|
| BulletinBoardDialog | ErrorDialog | FileSelectionDialog | FormDialog |
| InformationDialog | MessageDialog | PromptDialog | QuestionDialog |
| SelectionDialog | WarningDialog | WorkingDialog | |

The corresponding convenience functions add "XmCreate" before these names. These dialogs are not really new widget classes, but are combinations of an XmDialogShell widget and one of the manager widgets described earlier in this chapter. These convenience functions each return the corresponding manager widget, not the XmDialogShell widget created as the parent of the manager widget. Motif tries to hide the XmDialogShell widget as much as possible.

Figure 1.23 shows some example Motif dialog widgets.

**Figure 1.23**  Typical Motif dialog widgets.

## Gadgets

In addition to widgets, Motif provides user interface components known as *gadgets*. Gadgets are nearly the same as widgets, except that they have no windows of their own. A gadget must display text or graphics in the window provided by its parent, and must also rely on its parent for input. Because reducing the number of windows in an application reduces the number of server requests, using gadgets can result in a much more efficient application.

For the most part, gadgets can be used just like other display widgets, although there are a few restrictions, primarily because the gadgets do not have associated windows. In Motif, a gadget can only have the same foreground and background colors as its parent widget.

Gadgets can support callback functions and have the same appearance as their corresponding widgets. Motif provides both widget and gadget versions of several interface components. The Motif gadget classes include:

| | | |
|---|---|---|
| XmArrowButtonGadget | XmLabelGadget | XmPushButtonGadget |
| XmSeparatorGadget | XmToggleButtonGadget | XmCascadeButtonGadget |

Gadgets can be created using `XtCreateWidget()` by specifying a gadget class pointer as the class argument. For example:

```
XtCreateWidget ( "label", xmLabelGadgetClass, toplevel, NULL, 0 );
```

Motif also provides convenience functions that can be used to create gadgets. For example, an XmLabelGadget can also be created using the function:

```
XmCreateLabelGadget ( Widget   parent,
                      String   name,
                      ArgList  args,
                      Cardinal numArgs )
```

Gadgets can provide a significant performance improvement and are useful whenever the restrictions mentioned above are not a problem. Gadgets are particularly useful in menus. Menus often have many entries, and it is usually possible to greatly improve performance and start-up time by using gadgets for all menu entries.

# 1.5   Customization and Resources

Nearly all widgets can be customized by the user or the programmer. Widgets are customized by specifying values for various resources supported by the widget. These resources affect how widgets behave as well as how they their appear. For example, the XmRowColumn widget supports a resource that determines how many rows and columns it has. All widgets support a resource that controls their background colors.

We saw how programmers can set resources programmatically on page 20, in the "Hello World" example. There, the program controlled the label displayed by the XmLabel widget by specifying a value for the widget's `XmNlabelString` resource. Often it is useful to specify the values of various resources in a file, instead of the program. Motif (and all Xt-based widgets) use a facility known as the *resource manager* to load resources from various customization files. The resource manager is just a collection of related functions in Xlib and Xt.

## Resource Files

The resource manager creates an internal resource database and loads resources from several files when a program starts. Resource files are simply text files that contain specifications of the form:

```
resourceName: value
```

If multiple values are specified for the same resource, the last specification overrides earlier ones.
The resource manager loads four distinct resource files. These are:

- The *application defaults file*. This file is most often found in /usr/lib/X11/app-defaults/ *classname*, where *classname* indicates the class of the application as specified by an argument to `XtAppInitialize()` or `XtOpenDisplay()`. (See page 17.) The exact location of this file is site-dependent and depends on the language being used and a search path determined by the value of an `XFILESEARCHPATH` environment variable. The application defaults file usually contains resources provided by the programmer(s) who wrote the application. These resources may be required to enable the application to run properly.

- The *per-user application defaults file*. This file is loaded using a complex path-resolution scheme that involves several environment variables and search paths. A file with the same name as the application's class is loaded from a directory found by searching a path designated by the `XUSERFILESEARCHPATH` environment variable. The per-user application defaults file allows the user to add to, or selectively override, some of the resources in the application's defaults file. By default, if the `XUSERFILESEARCHPATH` variable is not set, the per-user application defaults file is loaded from a directory specified by the environment variable `XAPPLRESDIR`. If that environment variable is not defined, Xt searches for a file whose name is the same as the application's class name in the user's home directory, as specified by the value of `$HOME`.

- The *user's defaults*. These resources are loaded from a file named .Xdefaults in the user's home directory or from the `RESOURCE_MANAGER` *property* on the root window. (See [Scheifler90] for an explanation of window properties.) Users can use the program `xrdb` to store resources in the `RESOURCE_MANAGER` property. Many systems are set up to invoke `xrdb` automatically when the user logs in, to initialize this property. The user's defaults generally contain user-preferences such as color and font specifications.

- The *user's per-host defaults file*. This file is determined by the value of the `XENVIRONMENT` environment variable. If the environment variable does not exist, the file $HOME/.Xdefaults-*host* is loaded, where *host* is the name of the system on which the application is executing.

In addition to these four files, the Xt Intrinsics recognizes and loads various command-line arguments into the resource database. These are loaded after the resource files, and therefore take precedence over similar resources specified in the files discussed above.

The exact algorithm used to find and load these files is very complex. See [Asente90] for details on the loading sequence and the format of the various search paths and environment variables.

## Resource Specifications

In Xt, all widgets, applications, and resources must have both a name and a class. A resource name can be specified relative to a program and a specific widget by combining the name and class of a resource with the widget names and classes in the program. A complete resource name consists of the name of a program, the name of each widget in a path through the widget tree, and the name of the desired resource. Let's look at the widgets created by the widgettree.C program on page 45.

Suppose we want to change the label on the quit button in this example. If we name the program `widgettree`, we can identify the resource name of this label as:

```
widgettree.form.rowcolumn.quitButton.labelString
```

We can specify a label for the quit button with the following resource specification:

```
widgettree.form.rowcolumn.quitButton.labelString:   Quit
```

We can also use class names, like this:

```
Widgettree.XmForm.XmRowColumn.XmPushButton.LabelString: Quit
```

Names and classes can also be mixed:

```
Widgettree.form.XmRowColumn.quitButton.labelString:   Quit
```

The "*" character serves as a wild card and can be used in place of one or more names in a resource specification. So, we can also specify the label of the quit button like this:

```
Widgettree*quitButton.labelString:   Quit
```

or even

```
*labelString:    Quit
```

When more than one pattern applies to a given resource, the resource manager uses a complex matching algorithm to determine which specification to apply. See [Scheifler90] for a complete discussion of the resource manager's matching algorithm.

Most X applications are accompanied by an application resource file, which is normally installed in the application resource (app-defaults) directory. For example, the window layout shown in Figure 1.20 can be specified by the following application resource file:

```
!!!!!!!!!!!!!!!!!!!!!!!!!!!!!!!!!!!!!!!!!
!!  Widgettree Application Resources
!!!!!!!!!!!!!!!!!!!!!!!!!!!!!!!!!!!!!!!!!

! Provide labels for buttons

Widgettree*runButton*labelString:    Run
Widgettree*quitButton*labelString:   Quit

! Rowcolumn has 2, evenly sized columns

Widgettree*XmRowColumn*packing:      pack_column
Widgettree*XmRowColumn*numColumns:   2
```

```
Widgettree*XmRowColumn*adjustLast:   FALSE

! Make sure scroll bars are always displayed

Widgettree*XmScrolledWindow*scrollingPolicy:          automatic
Widgettree*XmScrolledWindow*scrollBarDisplayPolicy: static
```

Any resource file can contain any resource specifications. However, some resources, such as color choices, are usually left up to the user, and should not be specified in an application resource file. Different users may have different color preferences, and may also use different displays with varying color capabilities and characteristics.

It is also important to note that any resources set in the program itself (such as the XmLabel string resource in the "Hello World" program) cannot be changed in a resource file. Programmers must use good judgement when setting resources programmatically. Resources that are clearly the domain of user preference should not be overridden in the program. On the other hand, programmers should not allow resources that are essential to the operation of the program to be accidently overridden by the user.

# 1.6  Summary

This chapter discussed the basic elements of the X Window System and introduced programming with Motif using C++. We saw how to initialize the Xt Intrinsics, create and manage widgets, and register callbacks to deal with user input. One of the first things programmers must learn when using Motif is how to assemble the various widgets to form the more complex panels needed for an application. Programmers can choose from an assortment of container widgets that support many different layout policies. Learning to assemble these components to achieve the desired result takes practice and experimentation.

This chapter used C++ for all examples, although the programs are not much different than if we had written them in C. The primary difference is in the introduction of function prototypes and stronger type checking. Chapter 2 introduces some techniques for using Motif and C++ with an object-oriented style.

# Chapter 2

# C++ Classes and Widgets

There are two principal issues that must be resolved to use Motif effectively with C++. The first is a simple question of how to call functions in C libraries, such as Motif, from programs written in C++. This is straightforward and is discussed in the Motif tutorial in Chapter 1. The second issue is a matter of style, particularly when using the object-oriented features of C++. This chapter begins to address the style issue by discussing ways to use Motif with C++ classes.

After mastering the mechanics of mixing C++ and C, the next difficulty C++ programmers usually encounter is that, like C++, Motif supports an object-oriented architecture. In spite of some surface similarities, the two object systems are different and incompatible. C++ programmers often work with object-oriented libraries by creating new subclasses of various classes in the library, specializing them to suit the needs of their applications. Programmers who have used this approach may wonder how they can create a C++ class that is a subclass of a Motif widget. The obvious answer is that you cannot. While the inability to subclass from existing widgets may appear to be a major obstacle at first, it is not really a problem, as we will see.

Chapter 1 discussed one way to mix Motif and C++. That approach is simply not to use the object-oriented features of C++ and to write applications in a style similar to that used for C programs, with the addition of strong type-checking. While this approach may be acceptable in some cases, and is certainly no worse than programming in C, it does not take full advantage of the C++ language, nor of the many benefits of object-oriented programming techniques.

A second approach involves wrapping each Motif widget class in a C++ class. This method offers the advantage that all Motif widgets appear to be C++ classes to the application. Wrappers allow the programmer to maintain the appearance of an object-oriented flavor throughout an application by hiding the normal programmatic interface to Motif. This approach often appeals to programmers who prefer C++ syntax and find the C syntax used by Motif to be un-aesthetic within a C++ application.[1] Wrapping widgets in C++ classes provides no additional functionality, and can even cause some problems. The programmer must always remember that the classes are wrappers around a widget class, and not the widget class itself. For example, deriving a new class from a widget wrapper class allows programmers to extend the wrapper, not the widget itself.

A third approach is to use C++ to create higher-level user interface components that combine one or more widgets into a logical grouping. The goal here is not to wrap individual widgets in separate classes. Instead, the intent is to implement the key components of an application and its interface as C++ classes, using Motif widgets as primitives. Notice that from this perspective, it doesn't matter whether Motif is object-oriented or not. C++ programmers can call Xt and Motif functions to create primitive Motif widgets, just as C++ programmers can call C functions to make UNIX system calls.

We can summarize these three approaches by observing that the first approach addresses programming with Motif in C++, but ignores the object-oriented capabilities of C++. The second approach addresses programming with C++ and Motif using an object-oriented style, but assumes that widgets are interesting objects within the application, or that Motif widgets should be made to look like C++ objects for some reason. The third approach, which is used throughout this book, addresses object-oriented programming with C++ and assumes that the classes in a program represent the interesting architectural elements of the application. Classes that have a user interface component use Motif widgets as primitive elements from which to construct that interface.

The remainder of this chapter focuses on techniques for creating user interface components by encapsulating collections of widgets in C++ classes. Section 2.1 begins by exploring the basic concept of a user interface component and introduces a base class that implements some basic features used by all user interface classes in this book. Section 2.2 discusses some more advanced techniques for using Motif and C++, which include handling widget destruction and using the resource manager to initialize C++ classes. This section also describes an abstract base class that provides support for these features. Section 2.3 summarizes the protocol defined by the two classes described in Sections 2.1 and 2.2 and discusses the responsibilities of derived classes. Finally, Section 2.4 discusses the trade-offs between encapsulating existing widgets in a C++ class and writing a new widget in C.

# 2.1    User Interface Components

Nearly all Motif applications create collections of widgets that are related in some way. For example, many applications support a system of menus. The user sees a menubar as a single logical

---

[1]  A complete set of C++ wrappers has been developed by the University of Lowell, Lowell, Massachusetts. A second set of C++ widget wrappers is available as part of the Widget Wrapper Library (WWL) developed at the Laboratoire de Recherche en Informatique in France. Both implementations use macros that expand into C++ class definitions that shadow each widget class. These packages attempt to be as lightweight as possible, and simply provide a C++ syntax for Motif widgets, relying heavily on macros and inline functions.

component of the user interface. However, the Motif programmer must construct menus from many individual widgets. Usually, the programmer uses functions to build up higher abstractions that let applications deal with a "menu" rather than the individual pieces of the menu.

Similarly, interfaces often contain various panels, which may be composed of buttons, input areas, and so on. Like menus, these may appear to the user to be one logical user interface component, but they actually consist of many individual widgets. Using this approach, the body of a typical Motif program written in C might look like the following:

```
1   /***********************************************************
2    * dummy.c: skeleton of a typical Motif C application
3    ***********************************************************/
4   #include <Xm/Xm.h>
5   extern Widget createMainWindow();
6   extern Widget createMenus();
7   extern Widget createCommandPanel();
8
9   main ( argc, argv )
10      unsigned int argc;
11      char          *argv[];
12  {
13      Widget toplevel, mainWindow, menuBar, cmdPanel1, cmdPanel2;
14      XtAppContext app;
15
16      /* Initialize Xt */
17
18      toplevel = XtAppInitialize ( &app, "Dummy", NULL, 0,
19                                   &argc, argv, NULL, NULL, 0 );
20
21      /* Set up the major pieces of the interface */
22
23      mainWindow = createMainWindow ( toplevel );
24      menuBar    = createMenus ( mainWindow );
25      cmdPanel1  = createCommandPanel ( mainWindow );
26      cmdPanel2  = createCommandPanel ( mainWindow );
27
28      /* Realize everything and go */
29
30      XtRealizeWidget ( toplevel );
31      XtMainLoop ( app );
32  }
```

The above example uses individual functions to separate the task of creating menus from the task of creating a command panel. Each function creates a portion of the application's complete widget tree. With some care, these functions can even be used to create multiple, similar collections of widgets. For example, the above program calls the function `createCommandPanel()` twice, presumably instantiating a new collection of widgets each time. (Notice that this example is over-simplified. In a realistic implementation, it would be necessary to supply names, callbacks, and so on.) The function `createCommandPanel()` returns the root of the widget subtree it creates for further manipulation by the program. This approach allows the programmer to deal with large numbers of widgets by viewing them as a collection of widgets, within a single subtree.

C offers the programmer only limited facilities for organizing and managing such collections of widgets. In C++, we can do much better by encapsulating a collection of widgets within an object. The mechanics of creating widgets, specifying widget locations and other resources, assigning callbacks, and so on can all be captured in a C++ class.

This simple idea is the basis of all examples in the remainder of this book. We will refer to such classes as user interface *components*. A component not only encapsulates a collection of widgets, but defines the behavior of the overall component as well. Widget sets like Motif provide simple, low-level building blocks, like buttons, scrollbars, and text fields. Components are C++ classes that use these simple building blocks to create higher-level objects like file browsers, command panels, menus, and so on.

For example, consider the following simple C++ class, which combines an XmLabel widget and an XmText widget to create a labeled text area:

```
1  ///////////////////////////////////////////////////////
2  // LabeledText.h: A simple C++ component class
3  ///////////////////////////////////////////////////////
4  #ifndef LABELEDTEXT_H
5  #define LABELEDTEXT_H
6  #include <Xm/Xm.h>
7
8  class LabeledText {
9
10    private:
11
12      Widget _rowColumn;    // A container for the text and label
13      Widget _text;         // Input area
14      Widget _label;        // The label
15
16    public:
17
18      LabeledText ( Widget, char * ); // Requires a parent and a name
19  };
20  #endif
```

The LabeledText class encapsulates three widgets, represented by the _rowColumn, _text, and _label data members. The constructor creates these widgets, which form a widget subtree below the parent widget specified as an argument to the constructor.

```
1  ///////////////////////////////////////////////////////
2  // LabeledText.C: A simple C++ component class
3  ///////////////////////////////////////////////////////
4  #include "LabeledText.h"
5  #include <Xm/Xm.h>
6  #include <Xm/RowColumn.h>
```

```
7   #include <Xm/Label.h>
8   #include <Xm/TextF.h>
9
10  LabeledText::LabeledText ( Widget parent, char * name )
11  {
12      // Use an XmRowColumn widget to contain a label
13      // and a single line text field
14
15      _rowColumn = XtCreateManagedWidget ( name,
16                                           xmRowColumnWidgetClass,
17                                           parent, NULL, 0 );
18      _label    = XtCreateManagedWidget ( "label",
19                                           xmLabelWidgetClass,
20                                           _rowColumn,  NULL, 0 );
21      _text     = XtCreateManagedWidget ( "text",
22                                           xmTextFieldWidgetClass,
23                                           _rowColumn,  NULL, 0 );
24  }
```

This example uses a class to combine several widgets in a very simple and limited way. The class has several obvious shortcomings. For example, how can the rest of the program interact with any of these widgets? Widgets are seldom displayed on the screen for no reason. The application must be able to access and manipulate these widgets, to change the information displayed by labels or text, or to receive and act on user input.

C++ classes provide a natural way to associate such actions and behaviors with logical collections of widgets. To show how this is done, we must first discuss how to use callbacks and other similar functions within C++.

## Callbacks and Member Functions

The previous section introduced a simple technique for using a C++ class to combine groups of widgets to create more complex user interface components. Such a class not only creates a collection of widgets, but also defines the overall behavior of the user interface component. The intent is not just to wrap up a collection of widgets in a C++ class. Instead, the goal is to create the primary classes needed by an application, some of which use widgets to implement a user interface component.

For example, we might wish to write a class similar to the LabeledText class shown above, but which can be used to request a password from the user, and to perform some action, depending on the validity of the password. To handle such a situation, we must be able to handle user input, which is normally done by registering a callback function with one or more widgets. Ideally, we could combine the functions that perform such tasks with the widgets by encapsulating both as members of a class.

However, callbacks pose a minor problem for C++ classes. C++ member functions have a hidden first argument, which is used to pass the this pointer to the member function. This hidden argument makes ordinary member functions unusable as callbacks for Xt-based widgets. If a member function were to be called from C (as a callback), the this pointer would not be supplied, and the remaining arguments would be incorrect. If we want to use member functions to define the behavior of a C++/Motif user interface component, we have to arrange another way for a member function to be called as a result of a widget callback.

Fortunately, there is a simple way to handle this problem, although it requires the overhead of one additional function call. The approach is simply to declare a member function to perform the desired task, and then arrange for a function that does not have the hidden this argument to call that member function. There are two basic ways to do this. The first is to use a normal function, just as we did in Chapter 1, which can invoke the appropriate member function. The only catch is that the callback function needs a way to access the appropriate instance whose member function is to be called. This can be provided by specifying a pointer to the object as client data when registering the callback.[2]

For example, let's create a Password class that is similar to the LabeledText class previously discussed, but which calls a checkPassword() member function when the user types <RETURN> in the text area. The header file for the Password class can be written like this:

```
1   ///////////////////////////////////////////////////////
2   // Password.h: Retrieve and check a password
3   ///////////////////////////////////////////////////////
4   #ifndef PASSWORD_H
5   #define PASSWORD_H
6   #include <Xm/Xm.h>
7
8   class Password {
9
10    private:
11
12      Widget _rowColumn;    // Manages the text and label widgets
13      Widget _text;
14      Widget _label;
15
16    public:
17
18      Password ( Widget, char * );
19      void checkPassword();  // Check the validity of password entered
20                             // in the _text area
21  };
22
23  #endif
```

The implementation file, Password.C, declares an external function, checkPassword-Callback(), which is registered as an XmNactivateCallback function in the class constructor on line 32, in the next code segment. Notice that the this pointer, passed as client data on line 35, must be cast to type XtPointer to match the type expected by XtAddCallback().

---

[2] Some programmers may be concerned that they cannot use the callback's client data parameter for other purposes when using this approach. This is seldom a problem. The approach presented in this chapter encourages the use of classes to encapsulate widgets and all related functions and data. The information normally passed as client data in C programs is not needed, because all data that any callback function needs to access can be contained with the classes themselves.

```
1   //////////////////////////////////////////////////////
2   // Password.C: A simple C++ component class
3   //////////////////////////////////////////////////////
4   #include "Password.h"
5   #include <Xm/Xm.h>
6   #include <Xm/RowColumn.h>
7   #include <Xm/Label.h>
8   #include <Xm/TextF.h>
9
10  // A callback function used by the Password class
11
12  void checkPasswordCallback ( Widget, XtPointer, XtPointer );
13
14  Password::Password ( Widget parent , char * name )
15  {
16      // Use an XmRowColumn widget to manage a label
17      // and a single line text field
18
19      _rowColumn = XtCreateManagedWidget ( name,
20                                           xmRowColumnWidgetClass,
21                                           parent, NULL, 0 );
22      _label    = XtCreateManagedWidget ( "label",
23                                           xmLabelWidgetClass,
24                                           _rowColumn,  NULL, 0 );
25      _text     = XtCreateManagedWidget ( "text",
26                                           xmTextFieldWidgetClass,
27                                           _rowColumn,  NULL, 0 );
28
29      // Register a callback function with the text widget's
30      // XmNactivateCallback list. Pass "this" as clientData
31
32      XtAddCallback ( _text,
33                      XmNactivateCallback,
34                      checkPasswordCallback,
35                      ( XtPointer ) this );
36  }
```

The function checkPasswordCallback() is called when the user types a <RETURN> in the text widget encapsulated by the Password class. The callback function must retrieve the object pointer from the client data and call that object's checkPassword() member function, like this:

```
37  void checkPasswordCallback ( Widget, XtPointer clientData, XtPointer )
38  {
39      // Cast the clientData to the expected object type
40
41      Password *obj = ( Password * ) clientData;
42      obj->checkPassword(); // Call the corresponding member function
43  }
```

The checkPassword() member function has full access to the other members of the Password class and uses XmTextGetString() to retrieve the contents of the _text widget. The function shown here is incomplete. A complete implementation would need to check the retrieved password and take appropriate action if the password was right or wrong.

```
44   void Password::checkPassword()
45   {
46       // Retrieve password from text widget
47
48       char *passwd = XmTextFieldGetString ( _text );
49
50       // Validate password here
51   }
```

The only problem with the approach demonstrated here is that it requires an outside function to have access to all member functions that could be involved in actions related to callbacks and user input. Sometimes this might be satisfactory, but it would often require classes to expose details that are more correctly kept private.

One solution is to declare callback functions such as the checkPasswordCallback() function shown above as a friend of the corresponding class. The function would then be able to call private and protected member functions, and the class would not be forced to expose more than necessary.

Another solution is to use *static member functions*. A static member function is similar to a friend function in that it is a regular function that does not expect a this pointer when it is called. However, a static member function is a member of a class, and as such has the same access privileges as any other member function. It can also be encapsulated so it is not visible outside the class.

Let's rewrite the above example using the static member function approach:

```
1    /////////////////////////////////////////////////////
2    // Password.h: Retrieve and check a password
3    /////////////////////////////////////////////////////
4    #ifndef PASSWORD_H
5    #define PASSWORD_H
6    #include <Xm/Xm.h>
7
8    class Password {
9
10     private:
11
12       Widget _rowColumn;  // Manager widget that contains others
13       Widget _text;
14       Widget _label;
15
16       void checkPassword(); // Called when user hits the <RETURN> key
17
18       // Static member function serves as an interface between
19       // widget callback and member function
```

```
20
21      static void checkPasswordCallback ( Widget, XtPointer, XtPointer );
22
23    public:
24
25      Password ( Widget, char * );
26   };
27   #endif
```

Notice that both the checkPassword() member function and the checkPassword-Callback() static member function are now declared in the private portion of the class. These members could be declared in any part of the class. However, if a member function is not part of the class's external protocol, there is no reason for the function to be made visible. The static member function is only called by the widget with which it is registered, so there is seldom any reason for such callback functions to be declared publicly.

The Password constructor registers the checkPasswordCallback() function as an XmNactivateCallback function in the class constructor, just as before. The this pointer is cast to type XtPointer and passed as client data. Notice that the address of a static member function must be taken explicitly (using the & operator) and that the function must be qualified by the class to which it belongs.

```
1    /////////////////////////////////////////////////////
2    // Password.C: A simple C++ component class
3    /////////////////////////////////////////////////////
4    #include "Password.h"
5    #include <Xm/Xm.h>
6    #include <Xm/RowColumn.h>
7    #include <Xm/Label.h>
8    #include <Xm/TextF.h>
9
10   void checkPasswordCallback ( Widget, XtPointer, XtPointer );
11
12   Password::Password ( Widget parent, char * name )
13   {
14       // Create the widgets
15
16       _rowColumn = XtCreateManagedWidget ( name,
17                                            xmRowColumnWidgetClass,
18                                            parent, NULL, 0 );
19       _label     = XtCreateManagedWidget ( "label",
20                                            xmLabelWidgetClass,
21                                            _rowColumn,  NULL, 0 );
22       _text      = XtCreateManagedWidget ( "text",
23                                            xmTextFieldWidgetClass,
24                                            _rowColumn,  NULL, 0 );
25
26       // Register a callback function with the text widget's
27       // XmNactivateCallback list. Pass "this" as clientData
```

```
28
29      XtAddCallback ( _text,
30                         XmNactivateCallback,
31                         &Password::checkPasswordCallback,
32                         ( XtPointer ) this );
33  }
```

This version of `checkPasswordCallback()` is nearly identical to the earlier version, except that this member function is encapsulated by the Password class. The `checkPassword()` member function itself is unchanged, except that it is now declared as a member of the Password class.

```
34  void Password::checkPasswordCallback ( Widget,
35                                          XtPointer clientData,
36                                          XtPointer )
37  {
38      // Cast the clientData to the expected object type
39
40      Password *obj = ( Password * ) clientData;
41      obj->checkPassword(); // Call the corresponding member function
42  }
```

The static member function and the friend function approaches are very similar. However, the static member offers better encapsulation, and is the approach favored in the remainder of this book.

## Callbacks and Virtual Member Functions

One interesting variation of the technique discussed in the previous section involves the use of virtual member functions. In the Password example in the previous section, the static member function `checkPasswordCallback()` calls an ordinary member function, `check-Password()`, to perform the actual task supported by the class. If the `checkPassword()` function is declared as a virtual member function, derived classes can override the function. The static member function can then call the member function belonging to the derived class whenever the callback is invoked.

For example, assume Password is declared as follows:

```
1   ////////////////////////////////////////////////////
2   // Password.h: Retrieve and check a password
3   ////////////////////////////////////////////////////
4   #ifndef PASSWORD_H
5   #define PASSWORD_H
6   #include <Xm/Xm.h>
7
8   class Password {
9
10     private:
11
```

```
12          Widget _rowColumn;   // Main container
13          Widget _text;        // Input area
14          Widget _label;       // The label
15
16          // Callback called when password is entered
17
18          static void checkPasswordCallback ( Widget, XtPointer, XtPointer );
19
20      protected:
21
22          virtual void checkPassword();   // Called from callback
23
24      public:
25
26          Password ( Widget, char * );
27  };
28  #endif
```

As before, the callback function is declared as private to the Password class, which means it is not accessible from derived classes. However, the checkPassword() function is declared as a protected member, which allows derived classes to call it or override it. We can now derive a new class that inherits the widgets and callbacks set up by Password, but which defines its own behavior by overriding the checkPassword() member function. For example:

```
1  ///////////////////////////////////////////////////////////////
2  // StrictPassword.h: Check a password more closely than usual
3  ///////////////////////////////////////////////////////////////
4  #ifndef STRICTPASSWORD_H
5  #define STRICTPASSWORD_H
6  #include <Xm/Xm.h>
7
8  class StrictPassword : public Password {
9
10     protected:
11
12        void checkPassword();   // Overrides Password::checkPassword
13
14     public:
15
16        StrictPassword ( Widget w, char * name ) : Password ( w, name ) {}
17  };
18
19  #endif
```

Combining virtual functions with callbacks (implemented as static member functions) provides an interesting way to create abstract user interface components. The base class can determine the widgets supported by the component, and the overall layout, while deferring the precise behavior of the component to derived classes. Later chapters explore this technique in more detail.

# The BasicComponent Class

The classes discussed in the previous sections used an ad hoc approach. Each class merely supported the widgets, callbacks, and members it required. While this simple approach suffices for many situations, it is often more useful to define some guidelines or common features that should be provided by all component classes.

   For example, because each component creates a widget subtree, each component must have a parent widget. It would be a good idea for all components to deal with their parents in the same way. Also it would be convenient if each component supported simple operations such as managing and unmanaging the root of the widget tree it represents. To work well with the resource manager, widgets should have unique names. Therefore, all C++ user interface classes should allow a unique name to be specified when a class is instantiated.

   In short, it would be useful to define a simple protocol that all user interface components can follow to ensure consistency between different components, and to enable different components to work together easily. For example, the following are a few features supported by nearly all user interface components described in this book:

- Components create one or more widgets in the class constructor. Normally, callbacks and other setup are handled here as well. Each component creates a single widget that forms the root of a widget tree represented by the class. All other widgets are children or descendents of this widget, which we will call the "base widget."

- Components take a widget as an argument in the constructor. This widget serves as the parent of the component's base widget.

- Components assign the root of the widget subtree created by the component to a protected instance variable. Using the same variable name in each class helps programmers understand the implementation of a class.

- Components accept a string as an argument in the class constructor. This string is used as the name of the root of the component's widget tree. Each instance of a component class should be given a unique name to allow each widget in an application to correspond to a unique path through the application's widget tree. If each widget can be uniquely identified, the X resource manager can be used to customize the behavior of each widget by setting appropriate values in a resource file. Widgets within a component can have hard-coded names, because they can be qualified by the name of the root of the component subtree.

- Each component class provides an access method that can be used to retrieve the root widget of the component's subtree. While the goal of a component class is to encapsulate the behavior of a single logical collection of widgets, classes occasionally need to expose at least the root widget of the widget tree. For example, if an application needs to position the entire component in a Motif XmForm widget, it needs to be able to set the base widget's constraint resources. Normally, other widgets inside a component should not need to be exposed.

- Component classes allow the widget subtree encapsulated by the class to be managed and unmanaged. Examples in the previous sections managed all widgets as soon as the widgets were created. This is sometimes undesirable. Programmers may want to create a collection of widgets to be displayed at a later time, or may need to remove a collection of widgets from the screen while a program is running. Most of the time, components should be treated as a logical group, and only the root of the widget subtree should need to be managed or unmanaged. Other widgets should be managed in the constructor when they are created, but the root widget should be left unmanaged.

- Components handle the destruction of widgets within the component's widget tree. The widgets encapsulated by an object should be destroyed when the object is destroyed.

Some of these features must be implemented by each individual user interface class. However, some can be captured in an abstract class, from which other classes can be derived. Let's look at a very simple class that supports some of these features. We will call this class the BasicComponent class.

The BasicComponent class is declared as follows:

```
1    ///////////////////////////////////////////////////////////////
2    // BasicComponent.h: First version of a class to define
3    //                   a protocol for all components
4    ///////////////////////////////////////////////////////////////
5    #ifndef BASICCOMPONENT_H
6    #define BASICCOMPONENT_H
7
8    #include <Xm/Xm.h>
9
10   class BasicComponent {
11
12   protected:
13
14       char    * _name;
15       Widget   _w;
16
17       // Protected constructor to prevent instantiation
18
19       BasicComponent ( const char * );
20
21   public:
22
23       virtual ~BasicComponent();
24       virtual void manage();    // Manage and unmanage widget tree
25       virtual void unmanage();
26       const Widget baseWidget() { return ( _w ); }
27   };
28
29   #endif
```

The BasicComponent class supports a _w data member that, by convention, represents the base widget that serves as the root of every component's widget tree. The class also provides a baseWidget() member function that provides public access to this widget. BasicComponent also supports a _name member that stores the name of the object. Normally, this character string serves as the name of the _w widget. Occasionally, classes may be able to use this string for other purposes as well.

The BasicComponent constructor is declared in the protected portion of the class to prevent the class from being instantiated directly. The class does not contain any pure virtual members, but is intended to be an abstract class. Declaring the constructor to be protected is one way to prevent direct instantiation. Derived classes can still call the BasicComponent constructor from their own constructors, but applications cannot instantiate the BasicComponent class directly.

The BasicComponent class also defines two member functions, manage() and unmanage(), which manage and unmanage the component's base widget. These functions are part of the class's public protocol, and allow other classes or parts of the application to display or hide the widget collection represented by any component class. These member functions are declared as virtual to allow derived classes to alter this behavior, if needed. Some classes might need to perform other actions when a component is added or removed from the screen in addition to managing or unmanaging the base widget. Therefore, the manage() and unmanage() functions should not be viewed as just a C++ wrapper around the corresponding Xt calls. Instead, they should be thought of as a way to make an entire component visible or to remove it from the display.

Unlike other classes described so far in this book, the BasicComponent class is intended specifically to serve as a base class for other classes. As such, it is important to pay particular attention to the interface provided for derived classes, and also to the class's role in defining the protocol to be followed by all derived classes. In addition, base classes, or potential base classes, need to help programmers detect errors that could be introduced by derived classes that do not use the base class correctly.

Toward that end, BasicComponent uses the assert() macro defined in the system header file assert.h, found on most UNIX systems. The assert() macro prints an error message and aborts, producing a core dump, if a specified condition is not true. The core file allows a programmer to use a debugger to trace the sequence of steps that led to the problem, and correct it. The assertion can be completely removed from code, once the code has been tested, by compiling with the symbol NODEBUG defined. Therefore, this macro provides a way to add checks that are useful to a developer when deriving new classes from a class like BasicComponent, without forcing finished applications that use the class to incur unnecessary overhead at run-time.

The BasicComponent constructor initializes _w to NULL and also makes a copy of the name parameter. The strdup() function allocates enough space for a copy of the given string, and then copies its argument into the new string. The BasicComponent constructor uses the assert() macro to check for the existence of the name parameter. This serves two purposes. First, the strdup() function may fail if given a NULL string. Second, using assert() provides a way to enforce the rule that all components must have a name. The BasicComponent class cannot determine if the name is really unique, but at least it can ensure that it is non-NULL.

```
1   ////////////////////////////////////////////////////////
2   // BasicComponent.C: Initial version of a class to define
3   //                   a protocol for all components
4   ////////////////////////////////////////////////////////
5   #include "BasicComponent.h"
6   #include <assert.h>
7   #include <stdio.h>
8
9   BasicComponent::BasicComponent ( const char *name )
10  {
```

```
11        _w = NULL;
12        assert ( name != NULL );    // Make sure programmers provide name
13        _name = strdup ( name );
14    }
```

Constructors for classes derived from BasicComponent are expected to accept a name as an argument and pass this argument on to BasicComponent. References to an instance's name within the derived class should use the _name member. The BasicComponent constructor simply initializes the _w member to NULL. The BasicComponent constructor cannot determine what type of base widget to create; that task is left for derived classes.

The destructor calls XtDestroyWidget() to destroy the root of the component's widget tree. Because destroying a widget also destroys the widget's children, the BasicComponent destructor effectively destroys the entire widget tree encapsulated by the object being destroyed. The destructor checks that the _w member is non-NULL before calling XtDestroyWidget().

```
15    BasicComponent::~BasicComponent()
16    {
17        if ( _w )
18            XtDestroyWidget ( _w );
19        delete _name;
20    }
```

The manage() member function calls XtManageChild() to manage the root of the widget tree. The manage() function also uses the assert() macro to make sure the widget actually exists before calling XtManageChild(). This serves two purposes. First, it prevents manage() from calling XtManageChild() with a NULL widget, which would cause a core dump that might be hard to trace. Second, it attempts to enforce the BasicComponent subclass protocol which expects derived classes to create a base widget. It would be better if the BasicComponent class could detect errors immediately after all constructors are called, but C++ does not provide any way for base classes to know when all derived class constructors have been called. As implemented here, the BasicComponent class at least catches any derived class that does not create a base widget before the manage() method is called.

```
21    void BasicComponent::manage()
22    {
23        assert ( _w != NULL );
24        XtManageChild ( _w );
25    }
```

The unmanage() member function is similar. It also uses the assert() statement to guarantee that a widget exists before calling XtUnmanageChild(). This serves the same purpose as the assert() statement in the manage() function.

```
26    void BasicComponent::unmanage()
27    {
28        assert ( _w != NULL );
```

```
29      XtUnmanageChild ( _w );
30   }
```

The BasicComponent class supports only a minimal feature set, and does not address every issue listed at the beginning of this section. There are several topics that must be introduced before a more complete class can be presented. However, the following section uses the BasicComponent class as the basis of several components, to demonstrate how C++ user interface components based on such a class can be used in an application.

## An Example

This section demonstrates a simple "stopwatch" application. The program displays two buttons and a labeled text area that reports elapsed time. One button initializes the elapsed time to zero and starts the stopwatch, while the other stops the clock, leaving the final time displayed in the text area.

This is a simple application, and the interface could be constructed in many different ways. As implemented here, the buttons are Motif XmPushButton widgets, which are managed by an XmRowColumn widget. The labeled text area consists of two XmLabel widgets, grouped within an XmRowColumn widget. One XmLabel widget is used as a label, while the other serves as an output area whose contents can be changed. The second XmLabel widget is a child of an XmFrame widget, which displays a Motif-style shadow around the widget to offset it from the label. These two logical collections of widgets (the buttons and the output area) are managed by yet another XmRowColumn widget. Figure 2.1 shows the widget tree created by the stopwatch program.

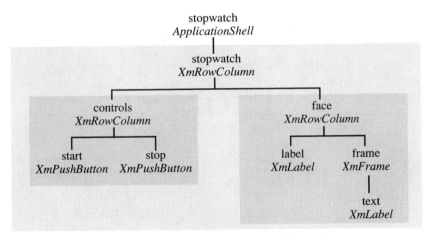

**Figure 2.1**  The stopwatch widget hierarchy.

The gray boxes in Figure 2.1 indicate logical groupings, or components, within this application. These collections of widgets are related, not only by their positions on the screen, but also because they serve a cohesive function within the application.

The boxed region on the left represents a control panel that supports start and stop operations. These widgets can be created by a Control class that registers appropriate callbacks with each button, and directs the user's commands to the rest of the application.

The box on the right represents the "face" of the stopwatch, and displays the current elapsed time. This subtree can be implemented as a Face class that handles the widget creation and layout and also provides an interface for changing the contents of the display.

The Timer class handles the task of updating the elapsed time displayed by the Face component. The Timer class is not a user interface component, but interacts with the other classes to display elapsed time.

Finally, the entire stopwatch can be viewed as a logical component, as indicated by the larger box around the larger subtree whose root is "stopwatch." This component is implemented as a Stopwatch class that collects the Face, Control, and Timer classes and binds them together into a distinct, self-contained component.

The following section examines each of these classes.

## The Control Class

The Control class, which is derived from BasicComponent, creates the start and stop buttons used by the stopwatch program. The Control class supports `start()` and `stop()` member functions, which forward corresponding messages to a Timer object. The Timer object associated with this object is specified in the Control constructor, and maintained in the private portion of the class.

Figure 2.2 shows an instance of the Control class as it might appear on the screen. The user interface portion of the Control class is trivial, and just displays two buttons.

**Figure 2.2**  The Control user interface component.

The class header file, Control.h, is written like this:

```
1    ////////////////////////////////////////////////////////////////////////////
2    // Control.h: A start/stop pair of buttons for the stopwatch program
3    ////////////////////////////////////////////////////////////////////////////
4    #ifndef CONTROL_H
5    #define CONTROL_H
6    #include "BasicComponent.h"
7
8    class Timer;
9    class Stopwatch;
10
11   class Control : public BasicComponent {
12
13     private:
14
```

```
15      void start();  // Called when the user hits the start button
16      void stop();   // Called when the user hits the stop button
17
18      // Static member functions that interface the above member
19      // functions with Motif widget callbacks
20
21      static void startCallback ( Widget, XtPointer, XtPointer );
22      static void stopCallback ( Widget, XtPointer, XtPointer );
23
24    protected:
25
26      Timer       *_timer;      // The timer controlled by this class
27      Stopwatch  *_stopwatch;   // The stopwatch containing this control
28      Widget      _startWidget; // The start button
29      Widget      _stopWidget;  // Stop button
30
31    public:
32
33      Control ( Widget, char *, Stopwatch *, Timer * );
34    };
35    #endif
```

The Control class declares only the constructor in the public portion of the class. The protected portion contains pointers to several widgets used within the component, as well as some pointers to associated objects. These might be useful to any class derived from Control. All other members are declared to be private to the Control class.

The Control constructor takes four arguments, a parent widget, a name for the top widget in the class's widget tree, and pointers to Stopwatch and Timer objects. The constructor stores pointers to the Timer and Stopwatch objects for later use and then creates the widgets needed by this component.

```
1   /////////////////////////////////////////////////////////////////////
2   // Control.C: A start/stop pair of buttons for the stopwatch program
3   /////////////////////////////////////////////////////////////////////
4   #include "Control.h"
5   #include <Xm/Xm.h>
6   #include <Xm/RowColumn.h>
7   #include <Xm/PushB.h>
8   #include "Timer.h"
9   #include "Stopwatch.h"
10
11  Control::Control ( Widget      parent,
12                     char       *name,
13                     Stopwatch  *stopwatch,
14                     Timer      *timer ) : BasicComponent ( name )
15  {
16
17      _timer     = timer;     // Keep a pointer to the timer
```

```
18        _stopwatch = stopwatch; // Remember stopwatch
19
20        // Create the component's widget tree
21
22        _w = XmCreateRowColumn ( parent, _name, NULL, 0 );
23
24        _startWidget = XtCreateManagedWidget ( "start",
25                                                xmPushButtonWidgetClass,
26                                                _w,  NULL, 0 );
27        _stopWidget = XtCreateManagedWidget ( "stop",
28                                                xmPushButtonWidgetClass,
29                                                _w, NULL, 0 );
30
31        // Register callbacks, specifying the object's instance
32        // pointer as client data
33
34        XtAddCallback ( _startWidget,
35                        XmNactivateCallback,
36                        &Control::startCallback,
37                        ( XtPointer ) this );
38
39        XtAddCallback ( _stopWidget,
40                        XmNactivateCallback,
41                        &Control::stopCallback,
42                        ( XtPointer ) this );
43    }
```

The top of the Control widget hierarchy is an **XmRowColumn** widget, which is assigned to the _w member inherited from the BasicComponent class. The _name member, also inherited from the BasicComponent class, specifies the name of the widget. The start and stop buttons are created next, as children of the XmRowColumn widget. Finally, the constructor registers the two static member functions, startCallback() and stopCallback(), as XmNactivateCallback callback functions for the two buttons. Notice that the XmRowColumn widget is not managed within the constructor; this is left under the control of the code that instantiates the Control class.

The startCallback() static member function retrieves the instance pointer from the client data and calls the object's start() member function. The Control::start() function, in turn, calls the start() member function supported by the Timer object with which this object is associated. Control::start() also calls the Stopwatch object's timerStarted() member function, which will be discussed shortly.

```
44  void Control::startCallback ( Widget, XtPointer clientData, XtPointer )
45  {
46      Control *obj = ( Control * ) clientData;
47
48      obj->start();
49  }
50
51  void Control::start()
```

```
52  {
53      _timer->start();
54      _stopwatch->timerStarted();
55  }
```

The Control class's `stop()` member function is handled in the same way as the `start()` member function. The static member function, `stopCallback()` retrieves the instance pointer from the client data, and calls the `Control::stop()` member function, which calls the `_timer` object's `stop()` function and the `Stopwatch::timerStopped()` member function as well.

```
56  void Control::stopCallback ( Widget, XtPointer clientData, XtPointer )
57  {
58      Control *obj = ( Control * ) clientData;
59
60      obj->stop();
61  }
62
63  void Control::stop()
64  {
65      _timer->stop();
66      _stopwatch->timerStopped();
67  }
```

## The Face Class

The Face class is also derived from BasicComponent. The Face class encapsulates an output area and a label, along with an interface for displaying a floating point number in the text area. This component supports no callbacks, but simply displays the data it is given. Figure 2.3 shows how an instance of the Face class might appear on the screen.

**Figure 2.3** The Face user interface component.

The Face class is declared in the file Face.h as follows:

```
1  /////////////////////////////////////////////////////////
2  // Face.h: A simple digital clock face for a stop watch
3  /////////////////////////////////////////////////////////
4  #ifndef FACE_H
5  #define FACE_H
6  #include "BasicComponent.h"
7
8  class Face : public BasicComponent {
9
```

```
10    private:
11
12      Widget _frame;   // Frame around the output area
13      Widget _label;   // Label for the elapsed time area
14      Widget _time;    // Widget that displays elapsed time
15
16    public:
17
18      Face ( Widget, char * );
19      void setTime ( float );   // Change the displayed time
20  };
21  #endif
```

The Face constructor requires a widget to be used as the parent of the object's base widget, plus a name. The constructor creates the label and output areas, managed by an XmRowColumn widget. The second XmLabel widget, which serves as the text output area, is managed by an XmFrame widget to provide some visual separation between the elapsed time and the label. Notice that the text displayed by the label is not specified here; the label can be set in a resource file.

```
1   /////////////////////////////////////////////////////
2   // Face.C: A simple digital clock face for a stopwatch
3   /////////////////////////////////////////////////////
4   #include "Face.h"
5   #include <Xm/Xm.h>
6   #include <Xm/RowColumn.h>
7   #include <Xm/Label.h>
8   #include <Xm/Frame.h>
9   #include <stdio.h>
10
11  Face::Face ( Widget parent, char *name ) : BasicComponent ( name )
12  {
13      // Create all widgets
14
15      _w = XmCreateRowColumn ( parent, _name, NULL, 0 );
16
17      _label = XtCreateManagedWidget ( "label",
18                                       xmLabelWidgetClass,
19                                       _w, NULL, 0 );
20      _frame = XtCreateManagedWidget ( "frame",
21                                       xmFrameWidgetClass,
22                                       _w, NULL, 0 );
23      _time  = XtCreateManagedWidget ( "time",
24                                       xmLabelWidgetClass,
25                                       _frame, NULL, 0 );
26  }
```

The only other member function supported by the Face class is setTime(). This function accepts a floating point number as its only argument. The value of this argument is displayed in the _text widget as a six-digit number, with three decimal point precision. The floating point number is displayed in the XmLabel widget by first using sprintf() to convert the float to a character string. Once the string is formatted, the Motif function XmStringCreateSimple() converts the character string to the compound string form expected by the XmLabel widget.

Note that the decision to use two XmLabel widgets in the Face class is completely arbitrary. There are several other ways to achieve similar results. For example, we could replace both the output text label and the XmFrame widget that surrounds it with an XmTextField widget. The XmTextField widget expects ASCII text instead of compound strings, which could be an advantage or disadvantage, depending how the widget is being used. If we switched to an XmTextField widget, it would be best to configure the widget to be read-only and to hide the text insertion cursor, to make it clear that the Face object is an output-only region. Alternately, the Face class could be redesigned to present an analog display. In any case, such decisions do not alter the external interface to the Face class. By providing an external interface based on the semantics of the class and not the widgets used to implement it, such changes can be made easily, without affecting the rest of the program.

```
27   void Face::setTime ( float value )
28   {
29       char     buf[50];
30       XmString xmstr;
31
32       // Format value as a string
33
34       sprintf ( buf, "%6.3f", value );
35
36       // Convert to compound string
37
38       xmstr = XmStringCreateSimple ( buf );
39
40       // Display the string in the XmLabel widget
41
42       XtVaSetValues ( _time, XmNlabelString, xmstr, NULL );
43
44       // The compound string can be freed once passed to the widget
45
46       XmStringFree ( xmstr );
47
48   }
```

## The Timer Class

The Timer class is the only class in the stopwatch program not derived from BasicComponent. The Timer class uses the Xt function XtAppAddTimeOut() to supply a clock. The Timer class supports a start() member function and a stop() member function. When the clock is started, the Timer calls the setTime() member for the associated Face object at regular intervals. The interval between calls is determined by a parameter passed to the Timer constructor, and maintained by the class.

The file Timer.h contains the following class declaration:

```
1   /////////////////////////////////////////////////
2   // Timer.h: Provide clock for the stopwatch
3   /////////////////////////////////////////////////
4   #ifndef TIMER_H
5   #define TIMER_H
6   #include <Xm/Xm.h>
7
8   class Face;  // Timer objects send messages a Face object
9
10  class Timer {
11
12    private:
13
14      // Static member function used for TimeOut callback
15
16      static void tickCallback ( XtPointer, XtIntervalId* );
17
18      void tick();  // Called every _interval milliseconds
19
20      Face *_face;        // The Face object updated with each tick
21      int   _counter;     // Current number of ticks
22      int   _interval;    // Time in milliseconds between updates
23      XtIntervalId _id;   // Identifier of current TimeOut
24      XtAppContext _app;  // Required by Xt functions
25
26    public:
27
28      Timer ( XtAppContext, Face *, int );
29
30      void start();       // Resets, and starts the clock ticking
31      void stop();        // Stops the clock
32      float elapsedTime(); // Returns time since timer started
33  };
34  #endif
```

Timer.C contains the member function implementations for the Timer class. The constructor requires three arguments. The first is an XtAppContext, which is required for the XtAppAddTimeOut() function used to implement the clock. The second is a pointer to the Face object to be updated by the Timer. The third argument indicates the length of time, in milliseconds, between updates. Because the Timer class is not a user interface component, the constructor simply initializes all data members.

```
1   /////////////////////////////////////////////////
2   // Timer.C: A clock class for the stopwatch
3   /////////////////////////////////////////////////
4   #include "Timer.h"
5   #include "Face.h"
6   #include <Xm/Xm.h>
```

```
7
8  Timer::Timer ( XtAppContext app, Face *face, int interval )
9  {
10     _face     = face;
11     _id       = NULL;
12     _app      = app;
13     _counter  = 0;
14     _interval = interval;
15 }
```

The Timer class uses the Xt timeout callback mechanism to implement a simple clock. The function

```
XtIntervalId XtAppAddTimeOut ( XtAppContext       app,
                               unsigned long      interval,
                               XtTimerCallbackProc callback,
                               XtPointer          clientData )
```

registers a function of type XtTimerCallbackProc to be called at a later time. The second argument specifies the number of milliseconds until the function is to be called. XtAppAddTimeout() returns a unique identifier associated with this timeout.

The XtTimerCallbackProc is a callback, much like other callbacks discussed earlier. The form of all XtTimerCallbackProc functions is

```
void timerCallback ( XtPointer clientData, XtIntervalId *id )
```

Here, the clientData parameter is the clientData passed to XtAppAddTimeout() when the callback was registered. The second argument is a pointer to the identifier returned by XtAppAddTimeout().

The same techniques used for the widget callbacks discussed earlier can be used to handle timeout callbacks from C++. The actual callback function can be a static member function that calls a member function in turn. Normally, the object's instance pointer is passed as client data to XtAppAddTimeout(), just as in previous widget callbacks.

The start() member function uses XtAppAddTimeOut() to register the static member function tickCallback() to be called in _interval milliseconds.

```
16 void Timer::start()
17 {
18     // Reset the elapsed time
19
20     _counter = 0;
21
22     if ( _id ) // If a previous callback is still in effect, remove it
23     {
24         XtRemoveTimeOut ( _id );
25         _id = NULL;
```

```
26      }
27
28      // Register a function to be called in _interval milliseconds
29
30      _id = XtAppAddTimeOut ( _app,
31                              _interval,
32                              &Timer::tickCallback,
33                              ( XtPointer ) this );
34
35  }
```

Before registering a timeout callback, the start() function resets the _counter member to zero and calls XtRemoveTimeOut() to remove the previous timeout, if any. This allows the start button to be pressed at any time. Even if the stopwatch is already running, starting the stopwatch a second time resets the elapsed time to zero.

The stop() member function simply removes any installed timeout function and sets the _id member to NULL. This effectively stops the clock.

```
36  void Timer::stop()
37  {
38      // Remove the current timeout function, if any
39
40      if ( _id )
41          XtRemoveTimeOut ( _id );
42
43      _id = NULL;
44  }
```

The tickCallback() function is a static member function that provides an interface between the Xt timeout mechanism and the Timer class. Like other callbacks, the tickCallback() function retrieves the instance pointer from the function's client data, and calls the corresponding member function for that object.

```
45  void Timer::tickCallback ( XtPointer clientData, XtIntervalId * )
46  {
47      // Get the object pointer and call the corresponding tick function
48
49      Timer *obj = ( Timer * ) clientData;
50
51      obj->tick();
52  }
```

The tick() member function updates the _counter member each time it is called. It then calls the elapsedTime() member function, which uses the value of _counter to compute the approximate elapsed time in seconds. The resulting value is sent to the Face object as a floating point number. The time calculated by elapsedTime() is approximate because the timeout callback mechanism may not be accurate. The function is not necessarily called exactly when the specified time elapses. If greater accuracy is required, the `elapsedTime()` function can be changed to make a system call to determine the time more accurately.

Finally, `tick()` calls `XtAppAddTimeOut()` to re-register `tickCallback()`. Once Xt calls a timeout function, it removes the callback automatically. Because the Timer needs to have a repeated, regular clock, the callback must be re-installed each time.

```
53  void Timer::tick()
54  {
55      // Increment a counter for each tick
56
57      _counter++;
58
59      // Display the current time in the Face object
60
61      _face->setTime (  elapsedTime() );
62
63      // Reinstall the timeout callback
64
65      _id = XtAppAddTimeOut ( _app,
66                              _interval,
67                              &Timer::tickCallback,
68                              ( XtPointer ) this );
69
70  }
```

The `elapsedTime()` member function computes the elapsed time based on the number of times the `_counter` member has been incremented and the Timer's clock rate.

```
71  float Timer::elapsedTime()
72  {
73      return ( ( float ) _counter * _interval / 1000.0 );
74  }
```

## The Stopwatch Class

It is often useful to create component classes that contain not only widgets, but also other components. Because other components are just classes that encapsulate a widget tree, this is easy to do. The Stopwatch class is one example of a class that encapsulates other components. The primary purpose of the Stopwatch class is to connect the Face, Control, and Timer classes discussed in previous sections into one entity.

The Stopwatch class creates an XmRowColumn widget, seen as a root of part of the widget tree in Figure 2.1. The XmRowColumn widget manages the Face and Control components' base widgets.

The file Stopwatch.h contains the declaration of the Stopwatch class. The class supports three protected data members, one for each of the objects that compose the stopwatch component. The Stopwatch also allows the Control class to access its private and protected members by declaring Control to be a friend. This allows the Control class to call the Stopwatch class's `timer-`

Stopped() and timerStarted() member functions, without making these functions part of
the Stopwatch's public interface.

```
1    ////////////////////////////////////////////////////////////
2    // Stopwatch.h: Group subcomponents into one stopwatch component
3    ////////////////////////////////////////////////////////////
4    #ifndef STOPWATCH_H
5    #define STOPWATCH_H
6    #include "BasicComponent.h"
7    #include "Timer.h"
8
9    // Header file doesn't need the full declaration of these classes
10
11   class Face;
12   class Control;
13
14   class Stopwatch : public BasicComponent {
15
16       friend Control; // Let Control call protected Stopwatch functions
17
18     private:
19
20       Face    * _face;    // The display of the stopwatch
21       Timer   * _timer;   // The object that keeps the time
22       Control * _control; // Control panel that starts and stops timing
23
24     protected:
25
26       virtual void timerStarted();    // Subclass hooks called when
27       virtual void timerStopped();    // timer starts and stops
28       float elapsedTime() { return ( _timer->elapsedTime() ); }
29
30     public:
31
32       Stopwatch ( Widget, char * );
33       virtual ~Stopwatch();
34   };
35
36   #endif
```

Only the Stopwatch constructor and destructor are declared in the public portion of the
Stopwatch class. The elapsedTime(), timerStarted(), and timerStopped() functions
are specifically provided to allow derived classes to perform additional actions when the timer is
started and stopped. Therefore, these functions are defined in the protected portion of the class. All
other members are kept private to the Stopwatch class.

The Stopwatch constructor creates a single XmRowColumn widget that serves as a parent for
the widgets created by the Face and Control classes. The constructor instantiates each of these
classes, as well as an instance of the Timer class, and sets up the connections between them. The

`XtAppContext` required by the Timer object is retrieved from the parent widget passed as an argument to the Stopwatch constructor, using the Xt function `XtWidgetToApplication-Context()`.

```
1   //////////////////////////////////////////////////////////////
2   // Stopwatch.C: Group subcomponents into one stopwatch component
3   //////////////////////////////////////////////////////////////
4   #include "Stopwatch.h"
5   #include <Xm/Xm.h>
6   #include <Xm/RowColumn.h>
7   #include "Timer.h"
8   #include "Face.h"
9   #include "Control.h"
10
11  Stopwatch::Stopwatch ( Widget parent, char *name ) :
12                                              BasicComponent ( name )
13  {
14      // Create a manager widget to hold all components
15
16      _w = XmCreateRowColumn ( parent, _name, NULL, 0 );
17
18      // Instantiate the three sub-components of the stopwatch
19
20      _face  = new Face ( _w, "face" );
21      _timer = new Timer ( XtWidgetToApplicationContext ( parent ),
22                           _face,
23                           1000 );
24      _control = new Control ( _w, "control", this, _timer );
25
26      // Manage the two user interface sub-components
27
28      _face->manage();
29      _control->manage();
30  }
```

The Stopwatch destructor deletes the objects instantiated by the Stopwatch constructor whenever a Stopwatch object is destroyed. The BasicComponent destructor, which is called *after* the Stopwatch destructor, destroys the component's base widget.

```
31  Stopwatch::~Stopwatch ( )
32  {
33      delete _face;
34      delete _timer;
35      delete _control;
36  }
```

The Stopwatch class defines two virtual functions that serve as hooks for derived classes. The Control object encapsulated by a Stopwatch object calls these functions when the user starts or stops the time. These hooks, along with the `elapsedTime()` function, allow programmers to derive classes that perform some additional task when the user starts and stops the stopwatch. Without these functions, the Stopwatch class may be useful to the user in a stand-alone program, but it cannot be connected to, or used to control, other objects in a system.

```
37  void Stopwatch::timerStarted()
38  {
39      // Empty
40  }

41  void Stopwatch::timerStopped()
42  {
43      // Empty
44  }
```

Figure 2.4 shows the inheritance relationships between the classes used in the stopwatch program. Face, Stopwatch, and Control are derived from the BasicComponent class, while Timer has no base class.

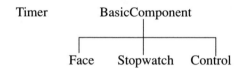

**Figure 2.4**  Inheritance hierarchy of the stopwatch classes.

### The stopwatch Program

The driver for the stopwatch program is quite simple. The program initializes the Xt Intrinsics and then creates an instance of the Stopwatch class, specifying the top-level shell widget as the component's parent. The program then manages the Stopwatch component, realizes the top-level shell, and enters the Xt main event loop.

```
1   /////////////////////////////////////////////////
2   // stopwatch.C: main driver for stopwatch
3   /////////////////////////////////////////////////
4   #include <Xm/Xm.h>
5   #include "Stopwatch.h"
6
7   main ( unsigned int argc, char **argv )
8   {
9       XtAppContext   app;
10      Widget         toplevel;
11
12      // Initialize the Intrinsics
13
```

```
14      toplevel = XtAppInitialize ( &app, "Stopwatch", NULL, 0,
15                                   &argc, argv, NULL, NULL, 0 );
16
17      // Instantiate a Stopwatch object and manage its base widget
18
19      Stopwatch *stopwatch = new Stopwatch ( toplevel, "stopwatch");
20      stopwatch->manage();
21
22      XtRealizeWidget ( toplevel );
23
24      XtAppMainLoop ( app );
25  }
```

The program can be built by compiling the files Face.C, Timer.C, Control.C, Stopwatch.C, and stopwatch.C, and then linking the resulting object files with the Motif, Xt, and X libraries. Figure 2.5 shows the initial appearance of the final program.

**Figure 2.5**  Initial layout of the stopwatch program.

The aesthetics of the stopwatch interface can be improved somewhat by choosing appropriate resources and placing them in the stopwatch program's application resource file. For example, the following resources produce the window layout shown in Figure 2.6.

```
!!!!!!!!!!!!!!!!!!!!!!!!!!!!!!!!!!!!!!!!!!!!
!! Appdefaults for stopwatch program
!!!!!!!!!!!!!!!!!!!!!!!!!!!!!!!!!!!!!!!!!!!!
Stopwatch*face.orientation:             horizontal
Stopwatch*face*label*labelString:       Elapsed Time:
Stopwatch*face*time*labelString:        000.000
Stopwatch*face*frame*shadowType:        shadow_in
Stopwatch*control.orientation:          horizontal
Stopwatch*control.start.labelString:    Start
Stopwatch*control.stop.labelString:     Stop
```

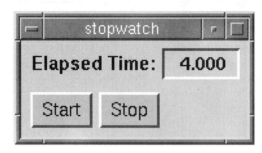

**Figure 2.6** Layout specified by the Stopwatch application resource file.

The Stopwatch component is a completely self-contained user interface component, much like a widget. This component can be instantiated within other components, or even instantiate multiple times within an application. Creating several instances in a single program provides one test of how independent and self-contained a class really is. For example, it is easy to modify the file stopwatch.C to instantiate two (or more) Stopwatch objects, as shown in Figure 2.7. Here, two instances of the Stopwatch class are displayed in the same window, separated by an XmSeparator widget. Both Stopwatch objects function independently.

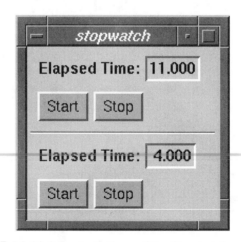

**Figure 2.7** Multiple instantiations of the Stopwatch component.

Notice that, from the perspective of a program that uses the Stopwatch class, the Stopwatch component appears to be a single, self-contained entity. The stopwatch program deals only with the Stopwatch class, and does not interact with the Clock, Timer, or Face objects directly. In fact, it might seem as if splitting the Stopwatch component into four separate classes is unnecessary. The entire functionality could simply be implemented as a single class.

The choice of how to split a system into objects is a design decision, of course, and no two programmers are likely to make the same decisions. For an extremely simple example like the stopwatch program, it would be reasonable to implement the functionality as a single class. However, in real applications, the type of division demonstrated here becomes more useful. Object-oriented programs often trade the quickest, easiest way to implement a given piece of functionality for a more robust, modular, potentially general solution that may save time and effort later on.

The ability to change, improve, or even redesign one portion of a program without affecting the others is one of the main reasons for using object-oriented techniques. If, in addition, some of the smaller pieces of a particular program could be implemented as self-contained objects, the chances that these objects may be useful in some other context becomes an important factor. For example, classes similar to the Timer class and the Face class may be useful in other applications that are quite different from the Stopwatch component.

## 2.2   The UIComponent Class

The previous section demonstrated how the BasicComponent class could be used as a basis for other component classes. The BasicComponent class implements some basic features useful to all component classes. However, there are several additional facilities that may be useful to many user interface classes as well. Some of these can be handled in a base class so that all classes are not forced to duplicate code.

The following sections examine issues related to widget destruction and the X resource manager and show how these issues can be addressed by an enhanced base class, UIComponent. The UIComponent class is derived from the BasicComponent class discussed earlier in this chapter, but adds support for handling widget destruction and uses the resource manager to customize and initialize classes.

The UIComponent class is declared as follows:

```
1    /////////////////////////////////////////////////////////////////
2    // UIComponent.h: Base class for all C++/Motif UI components
3    /////////////////////////////////////////////////////////////////
4    #ifndef UICOMPONENT_H
5    #define UICOMPONENT_H
6
7    #include <Xm/Xm.h>
8    #include "BasicComponent.h"
9
10   class UIComponent : public BasicComponent {
11
12     private:
13
14       // Interface between XmNdestroyCallback and this class
15
16       static void widgetDestroyedCallback ( Widget,
17                                             XtPointer,
18                                             XtPointer );
```

```
19
20     protected:
21
22       // Protect constructor to prevent direct instantiation
23
24       UIComponent ( const char * );
25
26       void installDestroyHandler(); // Easy hook for derived classes
27
28       // Called by widgetDestroyedCallback() if base widget is destroyed
29
30       virtual void widgetDestroyed();
31
32       // Loads component's default resources into database
33
34       void setDefaultResources ( const Widget , const String *);
35
36       // Retrieve resources for this clsss from the resource manager
37
38       void getResources ( const XtResourceList, const int );
39
40     public:
41
42       virtual ~UIComponent();   // Destructor
43
44       // Manage the entire widget subtree represented
45       // by this component (Overrides BasicComponent method)
46
47       virtual void manage();
48
49       // Public access functions
50
51       virtual const char *const className() { return ( "UIComponent" ); }
52   };
53
54   #endif
```

The UIComponent class defines several new member functions that implement new features that may be useful to derived classes. Each of these new features is described individually in the following sections.

Like the BasicComponent class, the UIComponent class is intended to define a basic protocol for all derived classes and also to support programmers who create new derived classes. Therefore, the UIComponent class pays particular attention to error handling, and uses the assert() macro frequently. The UIComponent class also makes frequent use of const declarations for the same reason.

The UIComponent constructor is located in the file UIComponent.C, along with the other UIComponent member functions. It is written as:

```
1    //////////////////////////////////////////////////////////
2    // UIComponent.C: Base class for all C++/Motif UI components
3    //////////////////////////////////////////////////////////
4
5    #include "UIComponent.h"
6    #include <assert.h>
7    #include <stdio.h>
8
9    UIComponent::UIComponent ( const char *name ) : BasicComponent ( name )
10   {
11        // Empty
12   }
```

All remaining member functions are discussed in the following sections.

## Widget Destruction

Some simple programs create all widgets at start-up, and never destroy widgets while the program is running. However, more complex programs often create and destroy various parts of the interface dynamically. When widgets are destroyed, it is easy to leave dangling references – pointers to memory that once represented a widget, but which are no longer valid. Dangling references are a problem in any program, but can be particularly troublesome in Xt-based applications for two reasons. First, when a widget is destroyed, its children are also destroyed. It is often very difficult to keep track of the references to these children. Second, Xt uses a two-phase destroy mechanism. The first pass simply marks the widget to be destroyed, while the second does the actual destruction. The second pass may not occur immediately, depending on how and when the widget is destroyed.

The Intrinsics' destruction sequence for widgets is particularly troublesome, although necessary. For example, consider the stopwatch example described earlier in this chapter. If an instance of the Stopwatch class is deleted, the BasicComponent destructor is called. The BasicComponent destructor then calls `XtDestroyWidget()` to destroy the base widget of the component. When the widget is destroyed, Xt automatically destroys all the widget's children. So, destroying a Stopwatch object ultimately destroys the widgets created by the Face and Control objects contained by the Stopwatch, even though the Face and Control objects have not been freed. Therefore, the Stopwatch destructor indirectly frees memory (a widget) that is supposedly accessible only within the Face and Control classes. This represents a fairly serious breach in the encapsulation of the component.

The situation described above can lead to several problems, depending on how objects are deleted and how widgets are destroyed. The least serious problem is that an application may have a "memory leak." The widgets that form the interface of a component may be destroyed, but the object that formerly contained these widgets may still exist. The interface is no longer visible on the screen and as long as no other part of the program interacts with the object, no problems will occur. However, the object still occupies space within the program, even though its user interface portion does not appear on the screen.

The second problem is more serious. It is fairly easy to write a program that accidently references the widgets in a class after the widgets have already been destroyed through a "back door." In some cases, applications may try to delete a widget twice, which usually causes the program to crash.

Calling XtSetValues() or other Xt functions with a widget that has been destroyed is also an error that can occur easily in this situation.

The UIComponent class provides some support for handling these problems. The widgetDe-stroyedCallback() function is a static member function that can be installed as an XmNdestroyCallback function by all subclasses of UIComponent. The widgetDe-stroyedCallback() function retrieves a pointer to the UIComponent object from the client data passed to the callback. Then, instead of taking any specific action itself, the callback calls the virtual member function widgetDestroyed(). No other class needs to access this static member function, so it is declared as private to the UIComponent class.

The following function implementation continues where we left off in the previous section, on line 13 of the file UIComponent.C:

```
13  void UIComponent::widgetDestroyedCallback ( Widget,
14                                               XtPointer clientData,
15                                               XtPointer )
16  {
17      UIComponent * obj = ( UIComponent * ) clientData;
18
19      obj->widgetDestroyed();
20  }
```

The default widgetDestroyed() function just sets the _w member to NULL, so that the UIComponent class, as well as derived classes, can catch any references to a component's base widget after it has been destroyed. However, subclasses can override the widgetDestroyed() method if needed. Derived classes might need to perform additional cleanup when the widget tree is destroyed.

```
21  void UIComponent::widgetDestroyed()
22  {
23      _w = NULL;
24  }
```

The UIComponent class cannot register the widgetDestroyedCallback() function in the UIComponent constructor, because derived classes have not yet created a widget at this point. Rather than force every derived class to install the widgetDestroyedCallback() function directly, the UIComponent class provides a protected installDestroyHandler() member function that performs this task. Classes derived from UIComponent are expected to call installDestroyHandler() immediately after the base widget has been created.

The function installDestroyHandler() is written as:

```
25  void UIComponent::installDestroyHandler()
26  {
27      assert ( _w != NULL );
28      XtAddCallback ( _w,
29                      XmNdestroyCallback,
30                      &UIComponent::widgetDestroyedCallback,
```

```
31                          ( XtPointer ) this );
32  }
```

Ideally, the UIComponent base class could force derived classes to install the `widgetDe-stroyedCallback()` function, or install it automatically. However, this is difficult to do, because of the way C++ constructors work. As a partial solution, the UIComponent `manage()` member function checks to see if an `XmNdestroyCallback` has been installed and attempts to enforce this mechanism. Checking for a registered `XmNdestroyCallback` function is not a fool-proof test, but catches most cases. The test is not fool-proof because Xt does not provide a way to determine if a particular function has been registered as a callback, only whether or not some function has been registered. This approach also does not provide any warning for objects whose widgets are destroyed before they are managed.

An alternate approach to providing the `installDestroyHandler()` function would be to simply install the `widgetDestroyedCallback()` in the `UIComponent::manage()` member function. However, this also fails to handle widgets that are destroyed before the component is managed. Also, a derived class may override the `manage()` member function. Because the callback cannot be installed reliably in the UIComponent class, it seems best to document it as a responsibility that should be handled by derived classes.

The `manage()` method can be written as follows:

```
33  void UIComponent::manage()
34  {
35      assert ( _w != NULL );
36      assert ( XtHasCallbacks ( _w, XmNdestroyCallback ) ==
37                                              XtCallbackHasSome );
38      XtManageChild ( _w );
39  }
```

Notice that the `manage()` member function uses the `assert()` macro to test for the presence of an `XmNdestroyCallback`. This test is intended to help programmers make proper use of the UIComponent class, but the test should not be necessary once a program has been tested. The `assert()` macro allows programmers to remove this test from production-quality code, or even to turn such tests off during development, if desired.

The UIComponent destructor is called before the BasicComponent destructor when an object is deleted. As discussed earlier, it is possible for a component's base widget to be destroyed before a component's destructor is called. In this case, the UIComponent class's `widgetDestroyed()` member function should have already been called, which sets the _w member to NULL. If the _w member is non-NULL, the UIComponent destructor removes the `XmNdestroyCallback` regis-tered by the `installDestroyHandler()` function. Removing this callback prevents Xt from trying to call the `widgetDestroyedCallback()` function again with an invalid `this` pointer.

```
40  UIComponent::~UIComponent()
41  {
42      // Make sure the widget hasn't already been destroyed
43
44      if ( _w )
```

```
45      {
46              // Remove destroy callback so Xt can't call the callback
47              // with a pointer to an object that has already been freed
48
49              XtRemoveCallback ( _w,
50                                 XmNdestroyCallback,
51                                 &UIComponent::widgetDestroyedCallback,
52                                 ( XtPointer ) this );
53      }
54  }
```

It may appear that handling widget destruction correctly is a major obstacle to using Motif with C++. However, it is important to understand that the problems discussed in this section have little to do with C++. C programmers face the same difficulties with any program that dynamically destroys widgets. Programmers have to deal with dangling pointers, as well as the consequences of the two-phase widget destruction process, regardless of the implementation language. By allowing programmers to encapsulate all references to a collection of widgets in a class, C++ provides an effective way to manage these difficulties that is not easily available to C programmers.

## Customizing Components

It is often useful to allow users or programmers to customize the behavior of a class, particularly a user interface component. X and Motif provide a mechanism that allows individual widgets to be customized by specifying resources for each widget. This section presents a way to use the X resource manager with C++ classes. The mechanism allows users to customize the behavior of an entire user interface component, instead of just individual widgets.

The X resource manager is a very powerful facility for customizing both applications and individual widgets. The resource manager allows the user or programmer to modify the behavior of a widget by changing an appropriate value or values in a resource file. Typical customizations range from simple color choices to more complex behavioral modifications. Ideally, programmers should be able to use the same mechanism to customize not only the widgets within a C++ component, but also the component itself.

For example, it might be useful to allow end users to specify the precision displayed by the stopwatch program described earlier in this chapter, or control the rate at which the component updates the elapsed time. These parameters cannot be set using existing widget resources because this type of information is application-specific.

The usual way to allow the user to select options like these is to support command line arguments, or to use the Xt function XtGetApplicationResources() to retrieve application-specific resources specified by the user. These resources are retrieved relative to the name and class of the application, and are generally maintained within an application as global variables or members of a global structure. This approach works fine in many situations, but in an object-oriented system, forcing a class to rely on global application-level parameters compromises the encapsulation of the class.

Furthermore, if there were a way to associate additional resources with a class instead of an application, then a class could support the same customizations in any application that uses it. Associating resources with each class would free applications from the responsibility of retrieving and setting various global parameters for each class. One of the assumptions behind the idea of "components" is that many of these classes can be used in a variety of situations. Any component that is meant to be reusable must be as self-contained as possible, including any support for user-customization facilities.

Fortunately, Xt provides a way to use the resource manager that works nicely with C++ classes used as user interface "components." Because each C++ component can be viewed as a subtree within an application's widget hierarchy, we can use the Xt function XtGetSubresources() to initialize member data in a class from the resource database. Before showing how to use this technique with a C++ class, the following section briefly discusses what the XtGetSubresources() function does.

## The XtGetSubresources() Function

The Xt Intrinsics function XtGetSubresources() retrieve values from an application's resource database based on resource names and classes, a widget hierarchy, and the name and class of a "subpart" of the widget (more on this later). The retrieved values can be stored in a structure by giving the base address of the structure and an offset within the structure. XtGetSubresources() is declared as:

```
void XtGetSubresources ( Widget        w,
                         XtPointer     base,
                         String        subpartName,
                         String        subpartClass,
                         XtResourceList resources,
                         Cardinal      numResources,
                         ArgList       args,
                         Cardinal      numArgs );
```

Resources to be retrieved are described in an array of type XtResource, which is declared as:

```
typedef struct {
    String     resource_name;
    String     resource_class;
    String     resource_type;
    Cardinal   resource_size;
    Cardinal   resource_offset;
    String     default_type;
    XtPointer  default_addr;
} XtResource, *XtResourceList;
```

This may look complex, but XtGetSubresources() is simple to use. Let's assume that we have an XmLabel widget named "text" that, with its parents, corresponds to the following class and name resource lists:

```
Stopwatch.XmRowColumn.XmRowColumn.XmFrame.XmLabel
stopwatch.stopwatch.face.frame.text
```

The first list represents the class resource list for the widget, and the second is the assumed name resource list. These lists correspond to a path through the widget tree of the stopwatch program described earlier in this chapter. (See the widget hierarchy in Figure 2.1.)

Now, suppose we want to retrieve a resource named "precision", whose class is "Precision", and store the retrieved value in a member of the following structure:

```
typedef struct {
      int decimalPlaces;
} aStructure;
```

In addition, assume that we want to retrieve the value of the "precision" resource as if the resource belonged to the label widget supported by the Face class. In other words, we would like to allow the user to specify values like

```
*text*precision: 5
```

in a resource file.

This can be done as follows:

1.   Define an `XtResourceList` that describes the resource. The following `XtResource` array defines one resource, whose name is "precision", and whose class is "Precision". The value is to be retrieved as an integer, and stored in the `decimalPlaces` member of a structure of type `aStructure`. The specification also provides a default value of 2, given as a string, to be used if no value is found in the resource database. The Xt type converter mechanism automatically handles converting between the string and integer data types used here. (See [Asente90] for detailed information about type-converters.) The macro `XtOffset()` computes the relative address of a field in structure.

```
XtResource resources[] {
  {
    "precision",          // Name of resource
    "Precision",          // Class of resource
    XmRInt,               // Required type
    sizeof ( int ),       // Size of expected type
    XtOffset ( aStructure *, decimalPlaces ), // destination addr
    XmRString,            // Type of default value
    ( XtPointer ) "2"     // Default value
  },
};
```

2.   Create the various widgets and define a variable of type `aStructure` in which to store the resource.

```
aStructure myData;
//...
// Create widget tree

text = XmCreateLabel( /* ... arguments */ );
```

3.  Now, we can simply call `XtGetSubresources()` to retrieve the value of "precision" relative to the XmLabel widget from the resource database and store it in the `myData` structure:

```
XtGetSubresources ( text,
                     ( XtPointer ) &myData,
                     "subpartname",
                     "SubpartClass",
                     resources,
                     XtNumber ( resources ),
                     NULL,
                     0 );
```

Notice the "subpartname" and "SubpartClass" arguments in this function call. These are strings that `XtGetSubresources()` considers to be "subparts" of the specified widget. This function attempts to retrieve a resource whose full specification (assuming the widget tree listed on the previous page) is given as:

```
Stopwatch.XmRowColumn.XmRowColumn.XmFrameXm.Label.SubpartClass.Precision
stopwatch.stopwatch.face.frame.text.subpartname.precision
```

`XtGetSubresources()` is intended for internal use by widgets that contain multiple "subparts." There is no subpart in this case, but we can use this feature to our advantage, as we will see shortly.

After the `XtGetSubresources()` function is called, `myData.decimalPlaces` is set to the value found in the resource database, or to 2, if no value is found. The user can now set values in a resource file, such as:

```
stopwatch*precision: 5
```

or

```
stopwatch*text*precision:   3
```

or

```
stopwatch*SubpartClass*precision: 4
```

## Using XtGetSubresources() with C++ Classes

Because C++ classes are simply structures, `XtGetSubresources()` can be used to initialize data members with values in the resource database. With components, we can also use a simple trick to get the complete resource name to match the widget tree to which the component belongs, plus the name and class of the component. The UIComponent class provides a `getResources()` member function, which can be called by derived classes after the component's base widget has been created to initialize other class data members from the resource database.

The UIComponent class defines a virtual member function, `className()`, that returns the name of the class. Each class derived from UIComponent is expected to override this method, which provides a rudimentary way to identify the class to which an object belongs. The `getResources()` member function uses this information to load resources relative to the class name of the class to which an object belongs.

The member function `getResources()` takes an `XtResourceList` that describes the set of resources to be retrieved, and an argument that specifies the size of the resource list. After checking for error conditions, `getResources()` calls `XtGetSubresources()` to retrieve values for all resources in the specified list.

```
55   void UIComponent::getResources ( const XtResourceList resources,
56                                     const int numResources )
57   {
58       // Check for errors
59
60       assert ( _w != NULL );
61       assert ( resources != NULL );
62
63       // Retrieve the requested resources relative to the
64       // parent of this object's base widget
65
66       XtGetSubresources ( XtParent( _w ),
67                           ( XtPointer ) this,
68                           _name,
69                           className(),
70                           resources,
71                           numResources,
72                           NULL,
73                           0 );
74   }
```

Look carefully at the arguments to `XtGetSubresources()`. The first argument specifies the *parent* of this component's base widget. The second argument specifies the object's instance pointer as the base address of the structure in which the resources are to be stored. The contents of the `XtResourceList` are expected to specify offsets that indicate data members within this class.

The third parameter, which is supposed to identify a "subpart," is set to the name of the object. The fourth argument specifies the class name of the C++ class to which this object belongs. These arguments effectively identify this object as a subpart of the parent widget specified when the component is instantiated. The final two arguments can be used to provide a list of resources and values to override values found in the resource database.

Let's look at a new version of the Stopwatch class that uses this mechanism. The new version of Stopwatch is derived from UIComponent and allows the user to specify the rate at which the stopwatch updates its displayed time. The new Stopwatch class is declared as follows:

```
/////////////////////////////////////////////////////////////////
// Stopwatch.h: Group subcomponents into one stopwatch component
/////////////////////////////////////////////////////////////////
#ifndef STOPWATCH_H
#define STOPWATCH_H
#include "UIComponent.h"
#include "Timer.h"

 // Header file doesn't need the full declaration of these classes

class Face;
class Control;

class Stopwatch : public UIComponent {

    friend Control; // Let Control call protected Stopwatch functions

  private:

    // Encapsulate a resource specification used to init this class

    static XtResource _resources[];

    Face    * _face;    // The display of the stopwatch
    Timer   * _timer;   // The object that keeps the time
    Control * _control; // Control panel that starts and stops timing

  protected:

    virtual void timerStarted();    // Subclass hooks called when
    virtual void timerStopped();    // timer starts and stops
    float elapsedTime() { return ( _timer->elapsedTime() ); }
    int _interval;

  public:

    Stopwatch ( Widget, char * );
    virtual ~Stopwatch();
    virtual const char *const className() { return ( "Stopwatch" ); }
};
#endif
```

This version of Stopwatch has two new members. The _resources member is an XtResourceList that specifies how resources should be retrieved and loaded into the Stopwatch class. It is declared as a static member to encapsulate the resource list within the class. The array is declared in the private section of the class because it is only used at initialization time to load resources, and does not need to be accessed from any other class.

The second new member is the `_interval` data member. The new version of the Stopwatch class uses this value to indicate how often the value displayed by the stopwatch component should be updated. The original stopwatch program passed a hard-coded value of 1000 milliseconds to the Timer class. The new version of Stopwatch passes the `_interval` value instead. Furthermore, the value of this data member can be specified by the end user using the X resource manager.

The new version of the file Stopwatch.C begins by initializing the `_resources` member. The first member of this array specifies a resource whose name is "interval" and whose class is "Interval". The value is to be retrieved as an integer and stored in the `_interval` member of a structure (an object) belonging to the Stopwatch class. Finally, the last two parameters specify a default value for the resource. If no corresponding value is found in the resource data base, the default value is used. Xt handles the conversion between the specified character string and the expected integer type.

```
/////////////////////////////////////////////////////////////////
// Stopwatch.C: Group subcomponents into one stopwatch component
//              Customizable, UIComponent version
/////////////////////////////////////////////////////////////////
#include "Stopwatch.h"
#include <Xm/Xm.h>
#include <Xm/RowColumn.h>
#include "Timer.h"
#include "Face.h"
#include "Control.h"

XtResource Stopwatch::_resources [] = {
{
    "interval",
    "Interval",
    XmRInt,
    sizeof ( int ),
    XtOffset ( Stopwatch *, _interval ),
    XmRString,
    ( XtPointer ) "1000",
  },
};
```

The new Stopwatch constructor is similar to the earlier version, but with several additions. After the component's base widget is created, the constructor calls both the `installDestroy-Handler()` function discussed in the previous section and the `getResources()` function. The `_resources` array is specified as the first argument to this function, while the second argument uses the Xt macro `XtNumber()` to determine the size of the `_resources` array. Once the `getResources()` function is called, the `_interval` member will be set to the value found in the resource database, or to 1000 if no value is found. This value is then passed to the Timer constructor and used to determine the clock rate at which the Face component is updated.

```
Stopwatch::Stopwatch ( Widget  parent,
                       char   *name ) : UIComponent ( name )
{
    // Create a manager widget to hold all components

    _w = XmCreateRowColumn ( parent, _name, NULL, 0 );

    // Call UIComponent hook to set up destruction handler

     installDestroyHandler();

    // Retrieve customizable parameters for this class

    getResources ( _resources, XtNumber ( _resources ) );

    // Instantiate the three sub-components of the stopwatch

    _face = new  Face ( _w, "face" );
    _timer = new Timer ( XtWidgetToApplicationContext ( parent ),
                         _face,
                         _interval );
    _control = new Control ( _w, "control", this, _timer );

    // Manage the two user interface components

    _face->manage();
    _control->manage();
}
```

The new version of the Stopwatch class allows users to specify the update rate in resource files with statements such as:

```
*interval:    500
```

or

```
*Stopwatch*interval:   100
```

Notice that the "Stopwatch" name used in these resource specifications refers to the Stopwatch class, not the stopwatch demo program described earlier in this chapter. These resources apply to any instance of the Stopwatch class, regardless of the program in which the component is used.

## Specifying Component Default Resources

Resource files provide a way for end users to customize applications to fit their personal tastes and preferences; but, that is not the only purpose of resource files. It is customary for X applications to specify as much as possible in a resource file to allow applications to be integrated into new environments without modifying source code. Resources that properly belong in a resource file include geometries, labels, and perhaps some layout specifications. Some applications even define bindings between application functions and keys or mouse buttons in resource files so that these can be changed easily.

It is important to draw a distinction between application defaults and user-preference items. User preferences are usually relatively unimportant to the operation of the application, and include such things as color, top-level window position, and so on. These are usually specified in a per-user resource file, like the .Xdefaults file in the user's home directory. Application default resources may be necessary for the proper operation or appearance of a program, and are normally found in a system app-defaults directory.

For example, the stopwatch program provides a set of application defaults, listed on page 83, that could be regarded as important for the proper layout of the component. These resources were originally specified as application defaults for the stopwatch program. However, that description is not entirely accurate. This file really specifies resources needed by the Stopwatch *component*. Ideally, any application that needs a component like the Stopwatch component should be able to instantiate one or more instances of the Stopwatch class. Because the component is self-contained, it has the potential to be used as a reusable component in many applications.

The fact that this component relies on a set of externally-defined resources reduces the degree to which the component is really self-contained. There are several ways to address this problem. One is to use `XtSetValues()`, or an equivalent function, to hard-code all resources needed by the component within the class. However, when a program sets a widget resource programmatically, it overrides user specifications for that resource. In some situations, this might be an adequate solution. However, in other cases, taking such a drastic step would make the component unusable to some programs. If the defaults cannot be changed, some programmers who could potentially reuse the class may have to write a nearly duplicate class, just to change an unsuitable resource setting.

Notice that many widget resources can be changed programmatically after the widget has been created. Therefore, derived classes can sometimes change the behavior of widgets created by base classes by setting new resource values in the derived class constructor. However, this does not allow the user to customize a component, nor does it allow applications to alter a component's behavior without deriving a new class. Also, some widget resources cannot be changed after the widget has been created.

Another approach is to set most resources in resource files rather than in the code, and to make the resource settings needed by a class available to any application that might use the component. For example, imagine a library that contains a collection of component classes. In addition to the binary library file and the various class header files, the library could also have an associated set of resource files required by various components. Programmers who use this library would then be expected to copy the resources for any components used in their programs into the application defaults file used by their program. This is a difficult approach to manage, because once a programmer copies the resources into another file there is no way to manage changes to the original, or even track the origin of the resources.

Fortunately, there is another alternative. We can use some functions provided by Xlib to merge a set of resource specifications with those normally loaded by the program. These resources can be encapsulated within any component that needs to supply resources. Although the resources are specified programmatically, they can be overridden by applications that use the class, or by end users in resource files. However, the default values are specified by the component class and cannot be separated from the class accidently. If a programmer changes a class's implementation, he or she can also change the resource defaults when necessary, knowing that applications that use the class will receive both changes simultaneously.

The UIComponent member function `setDefaultResources()` supports derived classes that need to specify default resources. This function should normally be called by the derived class's constructor before any widgets are created, in case any resources apply to the component's base widget.

The `setDefaultResources()` function expects a NULL-terminated array of strings that specify resources and values. For example, a default resource specification for the Stopwatch component would look like this:

```
String Stopwatch::_defaults[] = {
    "*face.orientation:          horizontal",
    "*face*label*labelString:    Elapsed Time:",
    "*face*time*labelString:     000.000",
    "*face*frame*shadowType:     shadow_in",
    "*control.orientation:       horizontal",
    "*control.start.labelString: Start",
    "*control.stop.labelString:  Stop",
     NULL,
};
```

This is the same set of default resources listed on page 83, but in the form of a NULL-terminated array of character strings. Notice that if we want to encapsulate this set of resources in the class, as shown here, we must also add a line to the class declaration, declaring the array as a static member of the Stopwatch class. This is similar to the way the `XtResource` array was handled in the previous section.

The UIComponent `setDefaultResources()` member function is written as follows:

```
75  void UIComponent::setDefaultResources ( const Widget w,
76                                           const String *resourceSpec )
77  {
78      int         i;
79      Display     *dpy = XtDisplay ( w );  // Retrieve the display pointer
80      XrmDatabase rdb = NULL;               // A resource database
81
82      // Create an empty resource database
83
84      rdb = XrmGetStringDatabase ( "" );
85
86      // Add the Component resources, prepending the name of the component
87
88      i = 0;
89      while ( resourceSpec[i] != NULL )
90      {
91          char buf[1000];
92
```

```
93              sprintf(buf, "*%s%s", _name, resourceSpec[i++]);
94              XrmPutLineResource( &rdb, buf );
95          }
96
97          // Merge them into the Xt database, with lowest precedence
98
99          if ( rdb )
100             {
101                 XrmMergeDatabases ( dpy->db, &rdb );
102                 dpy->db = rdb;
103             }
104     }
```

The setDefaultResources() function begins by using the function XrmGetString-Database() to create an empty database. Then it loops through the list of resources adding each line to the newly created database. The Xlib function XrmPutLineResource() takes a single resource string and adds it to a resource database.

Notice that before adding each resource, the name of the specific instance is prepended to the resource. Prepending the object's name partially solves one potential problem with this technique. We need to define these resources on a per-component basis. Because many components may be mixed within a single application, there is a reasonable chance for collisions to occur between the resource settings of different components, unless the resources are qualified on a per-component basis. Failing to qualify the resources in any way would mean that an object might load resource specifications like

```
*orientation: vertical
```

which would almost certainly coincide with some other part of the program and cause difficulties.

It would be best if we could use a technique similar to that described in the previous section, and qualify all resources by a component's class name (i.e., "Stopwatch"). However, the resources in this resource list apply to the widgets within a component, which know nothing of the "Stopwatch" class name.

Although the class of the component is not useful in this situation, the resources can be qualified by the name of the instance, which is also used by convention as the name of the component's base widget. However, an object's name is not known until runtime. So, setDefaultResources() constructs a new resource specification, qualifying each entry by the instance name of the component, before loading the resources into the resource database. For this approach to work, resources must be specified relative to the root of the component's base widget, but must not include the name of the base widget. Resources that apply to the base widget itself can be specified using the name of the resource, preceded by a "*".

Notice that this scheme does not guarantee that collisions will be prevented; however, collisions are common in the X resource scheme. The probability of a collision is, at worst, no more likely than any other collisions that occur between resources specified in the various resource files. This approach may also seem somewhat inefficient. However, it should be no less efficient than reading resources from various files. In most cases, it should be much faster.

Once all entries are loaded into the new resource database, the function `XrmMergeDatabases()` merges the new database with the existing application database. The application database is created and loaded when the application opens the display. It would be ideal if we could pre-load this database before the application and user defaults are loaded, but there is no reasonable way to do that. We can, however, merge the existing application database into the new database, and then assign the new database to be the one used by the entire application. This effectively places the resources specified by the component at the beginning of the resource database, which allows resources listed later to override the defaults.

Using this mechanism appropriately requires some judgment on the part of the programmer. The component defaults should be specific enough that they cannot be overridden accidently, but not so specific that the user, or application, cannot override them intentionally. The precedence order used in arbitrating resource specifications is complex. See [Scheifler90] for more information on the precedence rules used to arbitrate collisions in resource files.

To see how this mechanism works, we can rewrite the Stopwatch constructor one last time, as follows:

```
Stopwatch::Stopwatch ( Widget  parent,
                       char    *name ) :  UIComponent ( name )
{
    // Load the Stopwatch default resources into the database

    setDefaultResources ( parent, _defaults );

    // Create a manager widget to hold all components

    _w = XmCreateRowColumn ( parent, _name, NULL, 0 );

    // Call UIComponent hook to set up the destruction handler

     installDestroyHandler();

    // Retrieve customizable parameters for this class

    getResources ( _resources, XtNumber ( _resources ) );

    // Create the sub-components of the stopwatch

    _face = new  Face ( _w, "face" );
    _timer = new Timer ( XtWidgetToApplicationContext ( parent ),
                         _face,
                         _interval );
    _control = new Control ( _w, "control", this, _timer );
    _face->manage();
    _control->manage();
}
```

This version of the Stopwatch constructor calls `setDefaultResources()` before creating the component's base widget. Applications that use this version of the Stopwatch class do not need to set any resources in the program's application defaults resource file to support the Stopwatch component. The UIComponent default resource mechanism allows user interface classes to better stand on their own. Programmers can specify the correct defaults for a component without resorting to hard-coding the resources in the program.

# 2.3    User Interface Component Guidelines

The approach used in this book encapsulates fairly large-grained user interface components within C++ classes. These classes construct collections of widgets that provide some cohesive function within an application. This function may be strictly related to the user interface (for example, the LabeledText class described earlier in the chapter), or may embody some higher-level operation in addition to supporting a user interface (for example, the Password class described in this chapter).

In this book, all such classes are derived from the UIComponent class. It is not strictly necessary to use the UIComponent class. However, the UIComponent class defines a common protocol and provides some features that can be shared by all derived classes. Classes derived from UIComponent will be referred to as *components* in the remainder of this book.

Earlier in this chapter, on page 65, we discussed some basic guidelines for using C++ classes that serves as user interface components. The following list expands those original guidelines to apply specifically to components based on the UIComponent class:

- All components support one or more widgets.

- Widgets encapsulated by a component should form a single-rooted subtree below a single base widget.

- The root of the widget subtree created by a component is referred to as the *base widget* of the object. The base widget must be created by the derived class, and assigned to the `_w` member inherited from the UIComponent class.

- Components should usually create the base widget and all other widgets in the class constructor. The constructor should manage all widgets except the base widget, which should be left unmanaged. The entire subtree represented by a component can be managed or unmanaged using the member functions supported by UIComponent.

- All constructors should take at least two arguments, a widget to be used as the parent of the component's base widget, and a string to be used as the name of the base widget. The name argument should be passed on to the UIComponent constructor, which makes a copy of the string. All references to a component's name should use the `_name` member inherited from UIComponent.

- All component classes should override the virtual `className()` member function, which is expected to return a string that identifies the name of the class.

- Components should define any callbacks required by the class as static member functions. These functions are normally declared in the private section of the class, because they are seldom useful to derived classes. All callback functions should be passed the `this` pointer as client data. Callback functions are expected to retrieve this pointer, cast it to the expected object type and call a corresponding member function. By convention, static member functions used as callbacks have the same name as the member function they call, with the word "Callback" appended. For example, the static member function `startCallback()` calls the member function `start()`. This convention is simply meant to make the code easier to read and understand.

- Member functions called by static member functions are often private, but may also be part of the public or subclass protocol of the class. Occasionally it is useful to declare one of these functions to be virtual, allowing derived classes to change the function ultimately called as a result of a callback.

- Derived classes should call `installDestroyHandler()` immediately after creating a component's base widget.

- Derived classes that need to specify default resources to function correctly should call the function `setDefaultResources()` with an appropriate resource list before creating the component's base widget.

- Derived classes that wish to initialize data members from values in the resource database should define an appropriate resource specification and call the function `getResources()` immediately after the `installDestroyHandler()` function.

## 2.4   Writing C++ Classes vs. Writing Widgets

One decision that must be made once the need for a new user interface component has been identified is whether to implement the type of C++ component described in this chapter, or to write a new widget. There is no clear-cut answer to this question. The best course depends on the programmer's experience, the amount of time available, and what the component is supposed to do.

There are several advantages to writing a user interface component as a C-based widget, using the architecture defined by the Xt Intrinsics. Widgets have access to the internal data structures of all widgets and can also legitimately use many private utility functions. Because of various private facilities supported by Xt and Motif, there are many things that can be done inside a widget that are difficult to do from the outside.

For example, all manager widgets can control the sizes and positions of their children. Xt notifies each manager widget when its set of managed children changes, making it easy to implement interesting and dynamically changing layouts. This is not possible to do reliably from outside the widget architecture. Therefore, if a component must move or manipulate other widgets, it may be better to write the component as a real widget using the C-based Xt architecture.

In some situations, it may be possible to use an XmBulletinBoard widget as a base of such a component, and move children of the XmBulletinBoard. However, it is usually easier and more efficient to manipulate widgets using their private, internal protocol, rather than going through the `XtSetValues()` interface.

It also may be a good idea to write a C-based widget if a component could be generally useful to many other programmers. The more generally useful a component is, the more it makes sense to design it to obey the same protocol as the rest of Motif. Components that are useful to a single project, but are unlikely to be used by many programmers, are likely candidates for a C++ class. Although the number of C++ programmers is growing rapidly, there are currently more C programmers than C++. So if a particular component might be widely used, it would be best to implement it as a C-based widget.

On the other hand, widgets are relatively hard to write because they require the programmer to follow a complex set of conventions, which are not enforced by a compiler. The conventions required by Xt are thoroughly documented, but Motif adds additional conventions, which are not currently documented. For programmers who have never written a widget before, creating a new widget may prove to be a daunting task. In general, C++ classes such as those described in this book are easier to write, mostly because C++ provides language support for object-oriented techniques.

Widgets are usually designed to be highly customizable, and must be very flexible so that they interact correctly with other widgets. Most Motif widgets provide many customizable resources that alter the widget's behavior. All Motif widgets use the Xt translation manager to handle input, support resolution-independent size specifications, and provide a variety of convenience functions. This large set of features is expected of a generally useful widget. If this is more than a particular user interface component requires, using a C++ class may be a more suitable approach.

Let's consider a couple of examples. Suppose we need a popup dialog component that prompts a user for a name and a password and processes the input. Should this be a widget or a C++ component? It could be implemented as either. However, this component can be built easily from existing widgets and has no special layout needs that would make it hard to write as a C++ class.

This class would simply create a manager widget, a couple of label widgets, and two XmText widgets. The task of retrieving the name and password, as well as preventing the password from being echoed to the screen can be handled by registering the appropriate callbacks. In addition, the process of looking up and verifying the password goes beyond the role of a simple user interface component like a widget. This makes it a prime candidate for the type of C++ class described in this book.

On the other hand, this seems like a component that could find wide use, if it is well implemented. Code that could potentially be distributed to a wide audience might be best implemented as a widget, simply to address a greater range of potential users within the X community.[3]

Now, let's imagine we wish to display a set of rectangular objects in a "deck of cards" arrangement, as shown in Figure 2.8. The component should allow the user to shuffle the cards, raise any card to the top of the deck, and so on. The component should allow any type of widget to be used as a card. Should this component be implemented as a widget or as a C++ class?

---

[3] There is an opposing argument that is deliberately neglected in this book. Suppose we want to write a component that can be widely used, and which is not constrained to the Motif or even the X programming community. A C++ class could define the external interface to such a component and handle the details of running on multiple platforms. The class could detect the environment in which it is instantiated and create the user interface components appropriate for that platform. Such components are beyond the scope of this book.

This user interface component could be implemented as either a C++ class or a widget, but in this case, there are definite advantages to implementing it as a widget. If we assume that each card in the deck can be an arbitrary widget or gadget, the component could be implemented as a manager widget. The architecture of the Xt Intrinsics provides facilities for notifying parents when children are added or deleted. Also, the parent of a widget has the power to dictate a child's position and size. A C++ class would have to do all of this from outside the widget architecture, which would be much more difficult and more clumsy.

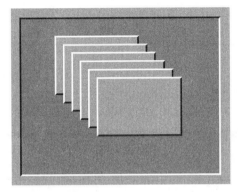

**Figure 2.8**  A hypothetical "deck of cards" manager.

## 2.5   Summary

This chapter introduces several techniques for using Motif widgets with the object-oriented features of C++. The basic mechanism for using callback functions and other indirect C function-calling techniques with C++ classes is straightforward. Techniques for handling widget destruction, default resources, and so on, are more complex. However, supporting mechanisms can be provided by a base class for all derived classes to use.

This chapter also suggests a few style conventions for using widgets with C++ classes. These style conventions are not required to use Motif with C++, but can help collections of user interface components to behave more consistently. The UIComponent class also defines a simple protocol for all C++ classes that create widget-based user interfaces. The UIComponent class provides support for interfacing C++ classes to Motif widgets and the Xt Intrinsics. The remainder of this book derives all user interface classes from the UIComponent class.

The next chapter discusses some techniques for designing object-oriented applications based on classes like those discussed in this chapter, and develops an approach used in the rest of the book for describing and documenting C++ classes such as the UIComponent class.

Chapter 3
# Designing with Objects

Chapter 2 introduces a technique for building Motif-based applications using C++ classes. One natural question to ask when using this approach is "how does one decide what classes to create?" In fact, the first step in developing any object-oriented system must be to determine the set of classes that can be used to implement the application. The nature of the classes that make up a system, and also the interaction between these classes, defines the architecture of an object-oriented application. The process of identifying the classes in a system and determining how each class interacts with others is one of the most important activities when developing any application using an object-oriented approach.

The discussion in Chapter 2 does not offer any rationale for the classes used in the stopwatch example. For such a simple example, programmers can often use their intuition to choose appropriate classes, particularly once they have some experience with object-oriented programming. However, complex applications may involve a large number of classes. In such systems, it is much more important to identify the key classes and determine how they fit together before implementing the entire system. Before preceding further, it would be useful to examine some techniques for choosing the classes and objects that can be useful in an application.

There are many well-known design approaches for applications based on more traditional programming styles. However, object-oriented programming is relatively new, and techniques for designing object-oriented systems are not as well-defined. Many design strategies have been proposed, but few are widely accepted or practiced. Some proposed approaches emphasize comprehensive, theoretical techniques for developing object-oriented systems, while others are based on rapid-prototyping in interpretive environments. In spite of their differences, the goal of each of these techniques is to allow the programmer or designer to start from a problem and develop a set of classes that can be used to implement a solution.

This chapter discusses one technique that helps programmers develop and maintain an object-oriented point of view when designing applications and discusses some issues related to object-oriented design. Section 3.1 discusses some basic steps found in most object-oriented development processes. Section 3.2 presents a technique known as CRC, which can help developers identify and characterize the classes in a system. Section 3.3 describes a notation based on CRC, which is used to document and present object-oriented designs throughout the rest of the book. Section 3.4 discusses some practical issues related to designing classes to be reused in more general situations.

# 3.1    Object-oriented Design and Development

In spite of many differences between various approaches to object-oriented design, many people agree that the process of developing an object-oriented application can be broken down into a few basic steps, at least at a very high level. The process of object-oriented development is often described as consisting of some variation of the following four stages:

- Identify the objects and classes of objects in the system
- Characterize what each object does
- Specify the relationships between the objects in the system
- Implement the classes.

These are not necessarily sequential steps. The designer of an object-oriented system (really, the designer of any system) must constantly weigh all kinds of information at each stage of design. If a designer is aware of certain implementation constraints (such as the language to be used) from the beginning, this information will affect the more abstract design decisions made early in the process. Likewise, even when a programmer is coding the various classes, better abstractions, better ways to define the external interfaces between classes, or better ways to decompose the problem, may be discovered. The development process usually requires several iterations; each cycle contributes to and clarifies the final design.

The existence of libraries of reusable classes, as well as the ability to produce a reusable class, has a major impact on the object-oriented development process, even though reuse is not explicitly mentioned in the four stages listed above. Reusability is one of the most important advantages of object-oriented programming and should not be ignored when designing a system.

A reusable class is generally one of two types. The first type of reusable class can be instantiated directly, while the second is used indirectly, by deriving new classes from an abstract base class. If at all possible, programmers should recognize the existence of such classes at the earliest possible stages of design. Part of the design process involves making trade-offs between implementing new classes from scratch and molding the system to take advantage of existing classes.

Another characteristic of the object-oriented development process is the iterative development of reusable classes. Programmers often start from simple existing classes, and derive new classes that add additional features or alter the behavior of the original base class. These new classes can often serve as a foundation for further expansion and reuse.

Derived classes may be either specializations or generalizations of the original base class. Specializations start from a general-purpose base class and move toward a specific purpose. For example, Chapter 2 discussed the idea of a general PromptForInput class that from which a more specific Password class could be derived. Sometimes the derived class adds additional features and is intended to be used in a wider range of situations than the base class. For example, the UIComponent class extends the protocol defined by the BasicComponent class to provide a more generally useful class.

Reusable classes often evolve in the opposite direction as well. Often, features originally developed as part of a derived class are propagated upwards to base classes to allow other classes to take advantage of these features as well.

The process described in this section is necessarily an over-simplification. The software development process involves a seemingly endless stream of small details, which cannot be completely captured in the simple steps described here. However, these steps provide a useful framework for understanding the object-oriented approach.The following sections discuss each of the steps in the object-oriented development process briefly.

## Identifying Classes and Objects

A common question asked by newcomers to object-oriented programming is, "How do I find the objects?" Identifying the precise objects or classes of objects needed to construct a program is a basic design decision that can only be made in the context of a specific problem. What objects are ultimately chosen (or "found") is a function of the designer's experience, preferences, and creativity. There is seldom a single right answer.

The process of identifying a collection of objects that can be used to implement a program is analogous to the process of decomposing a program into modules and functions in a functional decomposition approach. When using object-oriented programming, the goal is to decompose a program, or each module of a program, into objects and classes of objects. In early stages, it is often easier to think about individual objects and their role in a system, than to try to identify classes. Once individual objects have been identified, classes are usually fairly obvious.

One often-recommended technique for "finding the objects" is to start from a written description of the system to be built and underline all nouns and verbs. The nouns tend to become the objects in the program, while the verbs indicate what the objects do. The description can be a complete requirements specification or a simple description written just for this purpose. This approach may seem too simple to work, but it is often useful as a starting point. For example, if we were to describe the stopwatch program in Chapter 2, it is likely that we would use nouns like "stopwatch," "clock" or "timer," "face," "control." We might also use verbs like "stop" and "start." These words might eventually lead us to identify the classes and methods used in the Stopwatch component. Chapter 4 explores this technique in more detail.

## Characterizing What Each Object Does

A second activity when developing an object-oriented application involves deciding exactly what each object in the system does. This process is closely related to the process of identifying the objects themselves. When using the nouns and verbs approach mentioned above, the verbs usually provide some indication of what various objects do. For example, we know that there is a control (noun) object that starts (verb) and stops (verb) the stopwatch, which could lead us to identify a Control class that supports start and stop methods.

Sometimes it is clear that a task needs to be performed, but it is less clear which object should do it. It is useful to consider all the activities in a system and be sure some object is responsible for each action. Sometimes, the responsibility for a particular task can be assigned to an object that has already been identified. At other times, the action may suggest that a new type of object should be added to the system. For example, when discussing the Password class in Chapter 2, it became apparent that there was a need to maintain a list of valid passwords somewhere. After deciding that this responsibility did not really belong in the user interface component that accepted the password from the user, we created a second class, a PasswordDatabase class, to perform that function.

## Identifying Relationships Between Objects

Objects seldom exist in isolation. In fact it is difficult to design a single class without considering how objects belonging to that class interact with other objects in the system. The exact behavior supported by any given class is closely associated with its relationships with other parts of the system. Defining relationships between different objects can help clarify the responsibilities of each class. As various relationships between classes are established, the overall structure of the system starts to emerge as well.

There are many possible types of relationships that can exist between objects (or classes). *Dependency* relationships occur when one object depends on another to perform a task. Objects may be mutually dependent, and cooperate closely to fill a particular function, or may have unilateral dependencies. For example, the Password class discussed in Chapter 2 has a unilateral dependency on the PasswordDatabase class. Other classes may exhibit *container* relationships. The Stopwatch class in Chapter 2 serves mainly as a container for the other objects. And of course, *inheritance* relationships are common in object-oriented programming. Here, the relationship includes not only elements that a derived class inherits from a base class, but also any protocol between the two classes (in C++, the protected part of the base class).

## Implementing the Classes

The final development stage is the implementation stage. Here, the programmer/designer has to consider more pragmatic issues, often related to the programming language being used. Issues such as how to write the code efficiently, how to reuse other classes or libraries that may be available, and so on, may play a significant role in the final design. In the case of C++ user interface classes, such as those used in this book, the programmer has to decide what widgets to use to create the visible portion of the component and how to map the programmatic interface to these widgets to the other parts of the class. And of course, the code must actually be written, debugged, and tested.

This brief discussion is not meant to minimize the amount of effort required to actually implement the classes in a system. Most of this book is devoted to the implementation details of using C++ classes and Motif widgets. However, at the early stages of design, it is often more appropriate to emphasize the more abstract qualities of various objects, as well as the structure of the overall program. A good understanding of the environment in which an object will exist can make the task of implementing an appropriate class somewhat less difficult.

## 3.2   CRC: Classes/Responsibilities/Collaborators

Ward Cunningham and Kent Beck have developed a method for designing object-oriented systems that helps programmers follow the steps outlined in the previous section. This method is known as Classes/Responsibilities/Collaborators, or CRC [Beck89]. The approach uses abstract principles that apply to any object-oriented system, regardless of the implementation language. CRC helps the designers identify objects and relationships between objects, while building a common under-standing of a system. Beck and Cunningham have referred to CRC as "a laboratory for teaching object-oriented thinking," because the approach helps designers think about problems in object-oriented terms.

CRC is most useful at the earliest stages of design. The primary goal of CRC is to help the programmer identify classes that can be used to construct a system. The method concentrates on identifying the key *responsibilities* of each class, and also identifying relationships between classes. Other classes that are involved in fulfilling a responsibility are known as *collaborators*. Classes may depend on collaborators to provide information, or to perform operations.

Although CRC can be used by an individual, it seems most effective when used by a team. Typically, a group of designers gather around a table, equipped with a package of 3x5 note cards. A line is drawn down the middle of each card. Starting from some initial statement of the problem, the members of the design team suggest names of objects and classes that might be in the system.

As each new class is identified, its name is written across the top of a note card. Each card will eventually contain a list of the class's responsibilities and a list of other classes that collaborate with the class.   Figure 3.1 shows the format of a typical CRC card.

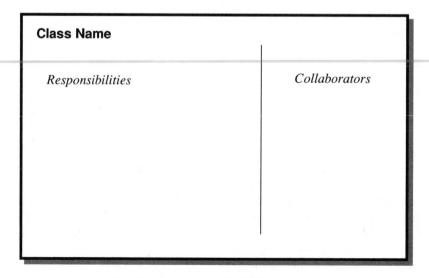

**Figure 3.1**  Format of a CRC class card.

As the design proceeds, the group continues to discuss the architecture of the system, seeking to understand how the system might be divided into objects and classes, and the role each part plays. Often this process takes the form of asking "what if?" As various scenarios are examined, new classes may be identified and assorted tasks that must be performed begin to emerge. In an object-oriented system, all tasks must be the *responsibility* of some class.

Each newly-identified responsibility is recorded along the left side of the card that represents a class that assumes that responsibility. A responsibility is typically a short verb phrase that identifies a particular problem solved by an object. In keeping with the object-oriented paradigm, the responsibility should indicate *what* the object does, but not *how* the task is accomplished. For example, the Password class discussed in Chapter 2 might have the phrase "*validate user's password*," as a responsibility.

Often, identifying one responsibility leads to other questions. For example, if the Password class is to validate a password when it is entered, the question naturally arises "Where are valid passwords kept?" The answer to this question is a design decision, which may lead to added responsibilities for some existing object, or may introduce other objects. One possibility in this example is to define an additional responsibility for the Password class, which could be stated as "*maintains valid passwords.*" Another obvious question is, "How does the system get a password from the user?" In response to this question we could add the responsibility, "*requests password from user*," to the Password class.

It often becomes apparent that an object must interact, or *collaborate*, with another object in some way to accomplish its responsibilities. When a designer identifies such a collaboration, the collaborating class is listed on the right-hand side of the card. For example, instead of maintaining the list of valid passwords itself, perhaps each Password object could rely on a PasswordDatabase object. The PasswordDatabase class would be listed on the Password class card as a collaborator. The resulting Password class card could be written as shown in Figure 3.2. Continuing this process, a list of classes, responsibilities, and relationships (collaborations) can built, until the structure of the entire system emerges.

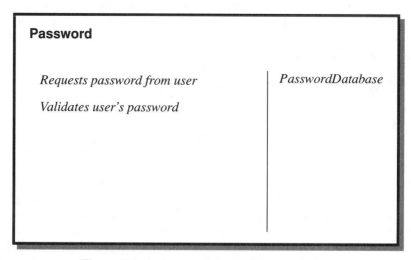

**Figure 3.2** A class card for the Password class.

One interesting characteristic of the CRC approach is that the distinction between objects and classes is deliberately blurred. At early stages of design, it is not always necessary to distinguish between instances of a class and the class itself. Generally, the concentration is on objects that exist in the system, although the information of a card generally indicates a class. In general, it should be clear that the entities that interact in a program are objects, but the behavior of these objects is defined by classes.

The CRC approach seems to draw much of its strength from the group dynamics of the design team. The team may start with little or no common understanding of the problem. The cards, and the exercise of identifying objects, helps focus the group's attention on the behavior and characteristics of the system. The design team develops a common understanding of the problem as new classes are discovered.

One key benefit of CRC is that it keeps the attention of the design team focused on the architectural issues at the early stages of design. Instead of getting bogged down in extraneous detail, the team is encouraged to think about major components in a system and determining what they do and how they interact.

The fact that cards can easily be thrown away, erased, or modified contributes to an overall feeling of free-wheeling brain-storming. CRC encourages designers to think out loud and breaks down inhibitions that might arise if a design team begins to focus on more detailed decisions too early in the process. For example, suppose we were to decide that the Password class should maintain the list of valid passwords itself. It would be quick and easy to cross out the PasswordDatabase collaborator, and add the new responsibility to the Password class card.

Beck and Cunningham have used CRC to teach object-oriented concepts as well as to design systems. Class cards can also be useful for explaining or documenting the design of an overall system. They often provide an appropriate level of detail for a first introduction to a class. For example, the Password class card in Figure 3.2 contains enough information to convey the primary function of the class. Ideally, someone who did not participate in the design should be able to look at the Password card and deduce that a Password object accepts a password from a user and checks the password against a list of valid passwords maintained by another object. In practice however, Beck and Cunningham report that the cards are often meaningless to those who do not participate in the initial design. It seems that much of the information about the behavior of the system remains in the heads of the design team. The cards act as a catalyst for the design process, and record an important part of design, but do not capture the entirety.

## Responsibility-driven Design

The book *Designing Object-Oriented Software* [Wirfs-Brock90] describes a design approach which expands the simple ideas found in CRC into a more comprehensive and detailed process. This method, which the authors refer to as a *responsibility-driven approach*, involves 26 distinct steps, divided into two separate phases.

The responsibility-driven approach varies in many subtle ways from the simple CRC technique described in the previous section. CRC cards simply list all collaborators along the right side of the class card. Wirfs-Brock, et al., introduce the idea that collaborators should be closely associated with a specific responsibility. For example, Figure 3.3 shows a slightly revised class card for the Password class. This class card lists the collaborator, PasswordDatabase, directly to the right of the responsibility it fulfills. The Password class card also contains numbered responsibilities, which will become useful shortly. The responsibility-driven approach uses class cards whose format differs slightly from the CRC-style class cards. The diagrams shown in this section are loosely inspired by both approaches, but have been slightly modified. (This is one advantage of CRC cards. They are simple enough that developers can easily customize them to suit their needs.)

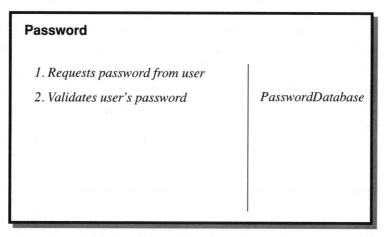

**Figure 3.3**  Revised Password class card.

Collaborations can be mutual relationships between two classes, or they can be uni-directional. For example, Figure 3.4 shows a class card for the PasswordDatabase class. Notice that the PasswordDatabase card does not list Password as a collaborator. The Password class uses the services of the PasswordDatabase class, but the PasswordDatabase doesn't know or care what class requests a name/password pair to be validated. The Password class lists PasswordDatabase as a collaborator because it depends on PasswordDatabase. The Password class must interact with the PasswordDatabase class to fulfill its responsibilities.

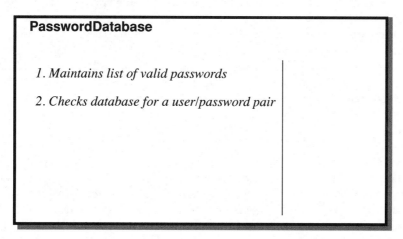

**Figure 3.4**  PasswordDatabase class card.

The responsibility-driven approach introduces another technique, along with a supporting notation, which is very useful for developing and describing designs. This notation is known as a *collaboration graph*. A collaboration graph shows the various relationships between the collaborators identified on the class cards. Collaboration graphs can help programmers visualize the overall architecture of an object-oriented system.

Figure 3.5 shows a very simple collaboration graph containing the Password and PasswordDatabase classes. The rectangular boxes represent individual objects (or classes). The semi-circle along the side of the box on the right represents a responsibility handled by the class. A vector connecting two classes represents a collaboration between those classes. The arrow points to a relevant responsibility handled by the collaborating class. For example, the arrow in Figure 3.5 indicates a collaboration, or dependency, between the Password and PasswordDatabase classes that involves the PasswordDatabase class's first responsibility, as listed on its class card.

In the complete responsibility-driven approach, collaboration graphs tend to be more sophisticated, and involve the concept of a *contract* between two classes. A complete discussion of this idea is beyond the scope of this book, and contracts are not used here.

**Figure 3.5**  A simple collaboration graph.

# 3.3    A Design Notation

This book uses a simple notation to describe the design of various examples throughout the remainder of the book. The notation is based largely on the CRC and responsibility-driven approaches described in the previous section, although with some custom features that differ from those approaches. This book uses four types of diagrams as aids when discussing classes and applications built using C++ classes. These are: class cards, collaboration graphs, message diagrams, and inheritance graphs. The following sections introduce the diagrams used in the remainder of this book, and demonstrates them using the stopwatch example from Chapter 2.

## Class Cards

This book uses CRC cards similar to those described in the previous sections to record the responsibilities and interdependencies between classes during the early design stages. The class cards used here are primarily inspired by the original Cunningham-style CRC cards, but borrow a few ideas from [Wirfs-Brock90]. For example, collaborators are listed beside the responsibility with which they are associated. Responsibilities do not necessarily need to be associated with a collaborator, but when a collaborator exists, the card indicates this relationship.

The upper left corner of the class card lists the name of the class the card represents. If a class is known to be derived from some other class, this fact can be indicated on the class card by listing the base class after the class name, separated by a colon, in a style similar to C++. The upper right corner of a class card contains a word that indicates whether a class is an abstract class or a *concrete* (non-abstract) class. This region of the card can also identify a class as a *subsystem*. A subsystem is an object that serves as a *module* that loosely binds a set of related objects. Subsystems can be either concrete or abstract.

Finally, all responsibilities are numbered, beginning with 1. Each card starts its own numbering sequence, which allows a responsibility to be referenced without having to repeat the entire phrase. This feature is particularly useful in conjunction with collaboration graphs.

Figure 3.6 shows a class card for the UIComponent class developed in Chapter 2. The UIComponent class has no collaborators, but lists five responsibilities. Notice that the responsibilities specify what the class does, but not how. The card does not contain sufficient information to allow a programmer to use the class. It provides enough information however, to explain why the class exists, and to remind the designer of what the class does.

Also notice that the class card does not list every operation supported by the UIComponent class. For example, the UIComponent class implemented in Chapter 2 supports a `baseWidget()` member function that returns the root of a component's widget tree. This information could be included, but this seems like a relatively inconsequential feature (or perhaps an implementation detail) of the class. A good class card conveys the basic flavor of a class, not every detail.

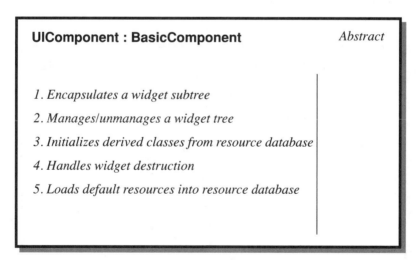

**Figure 3.6** UIComponent class card.

Figure 3.7 demonstrates a class card that includes a collaborator. This card describes the Timer class implemented in the previous chapter. The class has three responsibilities, all of which involve maintaining and reporting the elapsed time. The Timer class collaborates with the Face class, which actually displays the time.

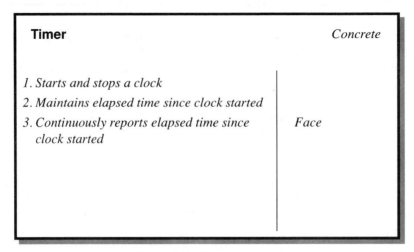

**Figure 3.7**  Timer class card.

Figure 3.8 shows a class card for the Face class. The Face class is responsible for displaying a floating point number, used here to represent elapsed time in a digital format. The Face class has no collaborators, because it simply displays a value in response to messages, which can come from any part of a program.

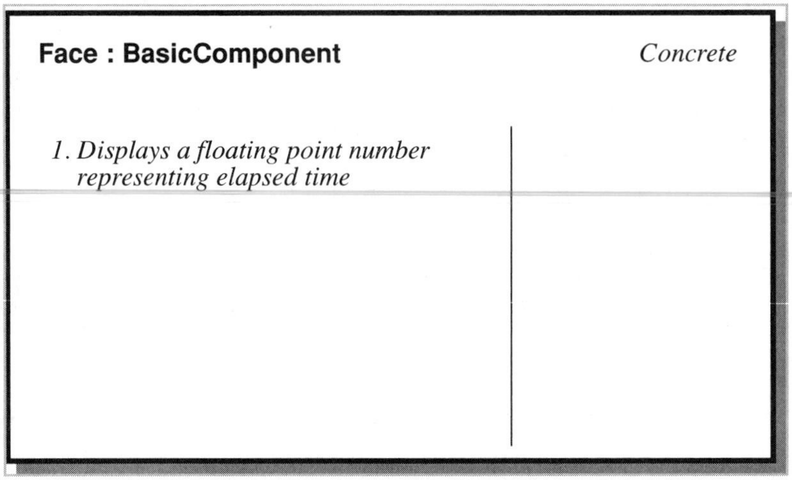

**Face : BasicComponent**                                          *Concrete*

*1. Displays a floating point number*
   *representing elapsed time*

**Figure 3.8**  Face class card.

Figure 3.9 shows the Control class card. The Control class is a user interface component that allows the user to issue a stop or start command. The Control class passes stop and start commands on to a Timer object, which is listed as a collaborator on the Control class card.

| Control : BasicComponent | *Concrete* |
|---|---|
| *1. Starts and stops counting elapsed time* | *Timer* |

**Figure 3.9**  Control class card.

Figure 3.10 shows the Stopwatch class card. As implemented in Chapter 2, the Stopwatch class does very little. Its primary purpose is to instantiate and connect a Control object, a Face object, and a Timer object. However, this is an implementation-oriented point of view. When deciding what should go on the Stopwatch class card, we must consider the external view of the class. The Stopwatch class completely wraps, and effectively hides, the other classes. To a programmer who needs the functionality of a class like Stopwatch, the fact that the class ties three other objects together is not particularly important.

| Stopwatch : BasicComponent | *Concrete Subsystem* |
|---|---|
| *1. Measures elapsed time* | *Timer* |
| *2. Displays counter showing elapsed time* | *Face* |
| *3. Allows user to start and stop timing* | *Control* |

**Figure 3.10**  Stopwatch class card.

It would be useful however, to know that the Stopwatch class measures and displays continuous elapsed time, and that the class provides an interface that allows the user to start or stop the time. From an external viewpoint, these are the responsibilities of a Stopwatch object, as noted on the Stopwatch class card. Notice that the card identifies Stopwatch as a subsystem, which indicates that it encapsulates other objects. The Stopwatch class has three collaborators, upon which the Stopwatch class depends to fulfill its responsibilities.

## Collaboration Graphs

As classes begin to be identified and class cards are being developed, it is often useful to visualize how various objects and classes in a system are related. The collaborations listed on the class card provide some indication, but it is often helpful to view this information more graphically. [Beck89] mentions that designers often find it helpful to position the class cards to indicate various relationships. For example, all classes that collaborate may be placed together to indicate a close relationship.

Figure 3.11 shows the Stopwatch class card and its various collaborators in a single group. In addition to showing that the classes collaborate by overlapping the cards, the position of the cards may imply other relationships. For example, the Stopwatch class card is on top, which might indicate a supervisory role. Note that such meanings are not well-defined, and teams may develop different conventions as new needs arise.

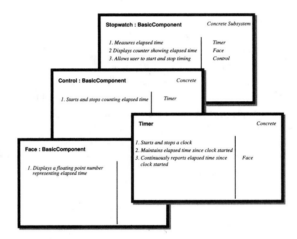

**Figure 3.11**  Showing relationships by positioning class cards.

As mentioned earlier, [Wirfs-Brock90] goes further and constructs a diagram, known as a *collaboration graph*, that shows the relationships between collaborators. A collaboration graph shows the connections between various classes based on numbered contracts supported by various classes. Although this book does not use the idea of contracts, showing collaborations graphically can be very useful. When designing with actual note cards, a simple collaboration graph can be created by positioning cards near those with which they collaborate, as shown in Figure 3.11. Alternatively, a simple graph can be drawn that shows the collaborations between the various classes.

Figure 3.12 shows a simple diagram that represents each collaboration as a vector leaving a class and pointing to a collaborator. Like collaborations, this connecting line can be uni-directional or bi-directional. For example, Control collaborates with Timer, but not vice versa. Classes that collaborate with each other are shown with an arrow at both ends of the line. The rectangular boxes in Figure 3.12 represent concrete classes, and the box with rounded corners indicates that Stopwatch is a subsystem, which contains the other classes.

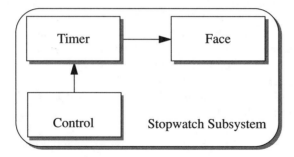

**Figure 3.12** Simple Stopwatch collaboration graph.

The collaboration diagram in Figure 3.12 simply shows that some relationships exist between various classes, without providing additional information. This diagram can be thought of as an entity-relationship diagram in which the only relationship is "collaborates," where "collaborates" can be loosely interpreted as a dependency. In most cases, a collaboration indicates that one or more messages are exchanged between the objects. It may be useful to start with simple diagrams such as this, and add more detailed information later.

We can convey slightly more information in a collaboration graph by referring to the responsibilities on each class card. Borrowing from [Wirfs-Brock90], classes and subsystems can be annotated with numbered semi-circles. Each semi-circle indicates a responsibility as listed on the corresponding class card. With this addition, all arrows between classes point to a specific responsibility of that class.

Figure 3.13 shows a revised collaboration graph for the Stopwatch subsystem.

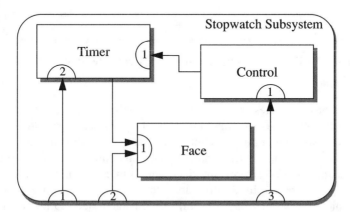

**Figure 3.13** Revised Stopwatch collaboration graph.

In this figure, the nature of each collaboration is shown by the numbered semi-circles to which each arrow points. For example, the Timer class is listed as a collaborator on the Control class card. The collaboration involves the Timer's first responsibility, which is to start and stop the clock.

Similarly, the Timer class depends on the Face class to display the time. The Face class is listed as a collaborator on the Timer class card, and the collaboration graph shows that the Timer class depends on the Face class's first responsibility, as listed on its class card

The collaboration graph handles subsystems a little differently than other classes, because the subsystem's primary purpose is to encapsulate the other objects and provide a single external interface. For example, the first responsibility of the Stopwatch subsystem is to measure elapsed time. This responsibility is delegated to the Timer class, as shown by the arrow pointing to the second Timer responsibility, which, from the Timer class card in Figure 3.7, is to maintain elapsed time.

Sometimes it is easier to show the connections in a subsystem by showing the subsystem object twice. For example, Figure 3.14 shows both the Stopwatch subsystem and the Stopwatch class, as if they were two separate objects.

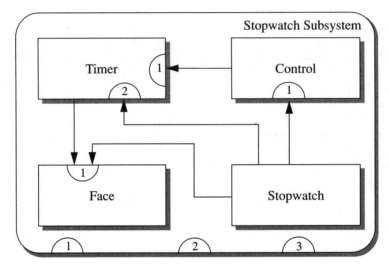

**Figure 3.14** A collaboration graph with a separate Stopwatch object.

The subsystem box indicates the external responsibilities and shows that the Stopwatch subsystem contains the other classes, while the internal Stopwatch class shows the collaborations with the other classes. Notice that this does not mean that there are two distinct Stopwatch objects. The diagram in Figure 3.14 simply differentiates between the Stopwatch class's role as an encapsulating subsystem that provides an external interface, and its internal relationships with other objects.

Collaboration graphs contain little information that is not already present on the class cards. However, the graphical format provides a useful view of the system. Often, attempting to draw a collaboration graph reveals structural flaws in the system that would not otherwise be seen. Drawing a collaboration graph may uncover missing responsibilities or unusual collaborations. The class cards may be revised many times while drawing the collaboration graphs. Therefore, it is useful to create collaboration graphs as class cards are being developed. Correctly identifying classes and assigning appropriate responsibilities often requires many passes. Collaboration graphs are just one more tool that helps support the designer's thought process.

## Message Diagrams

Notice that the connections in a collaboration graph do not necessarily indicate messages between objects. The arrows indicate a collaboration related to the responsibilities of the classes. These may or may not map directly to messages (calls to member functions in C++) when the classes are implemented. As a design develops further, it may be useful to graph the messages that could be sent between objects belonging to various classes. Graphing the messages between the classes in the stopwatch example results in the diagram shown in Figure 3.15. This diagram ignores the constructors and object creation, but otherwise shows an arrow from the caller to the class that supports each member function.

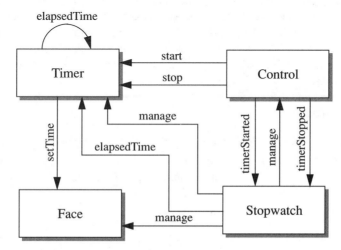

**Figure 3.15**  A message flow diagram of the Stopwatch subsystem.

Message diagrams are similar to collaboration graphs, but there are significant differences as well. Complete message diagrams of real systems are often too complex to be useful for large systems. However, message diagrams of restricted subsets of a system may be useful for documenting or visualizing the structure of that part of the system. In systems that exhibit some hierarchy it may be feasible to diagram the messages between subsystems at various levels of abstraction. For example, programs that use the Stopwatch component can show messages to and from the Stopwatch class, but need not include the Timer, Face, and Control classes in an application-level message diagram.

Note that, unlike the other notations discussed in this chapter, message diagrams are more suitable for documenting and examining completed systems than as vehicles for discussing early designs. By the time a programmer can specify the precise messages sent between each object in a system, the initial design is most likely complete, and the system is close to the implementation phase.

Message diagrams provide a useful tool for presenting various examples throughout the remainder of this book, although they do have some limitations. For example, message diagrams can only provide a static view of a system. This is often a serious limitation, because object-oriented systems tend to be very dynamic. For example, notice that Figure 3.15 shows messages between classes, not messages between instances. The stopwatch example contains a single instance of each class, but many object-oriented systems create and destroy many objects dynamically. Such dynamic behavior cannot be shown on a static diagram of a system. Similarly, message diagrams cannot show what messages are actually sent between objects in the system. They only show what messages could *potentially* be sent between instances of various classes.

It is also difficult to show the effects of inheritance. Normally, we should not care whether the member function that eventually handles a particular message is defined in a base class or a derived class. However, it may sometimes be useful to indicate in a message diagram that a message is actually handled by a base class, particularly in the case of non-virtual functions. Also, messages that involve the subclass protocol between a base class and derived classes, may need to be shown. In these situations, programmers should do whatever makes sense for each specific case. Message diagrams do not capture enough information to replace a programming language, and do not have to be complete in every detail. They are useful for describing the structure of a system, and should include whatever information is most useful to help document or understand interactions within each particular set of classes.

## Inheritance Graphs

In addition to considering relationships between objects and classes in a system, it is also useful to visualize the inheritance relationships between various classes. This can be done easily using an inheritance graph. Figure 3.16 shows the inheritance graph of the classes in the Stopwatch example.

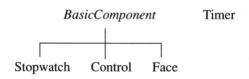

**Figure 3.16**  Stopwatch inheritance graph.

In this diagram, as well as the collaboration graphs and message diagrams used in this book, abstract classes are shown in italics. When working with pencil and paper, some other technique can be used to differentiate between abstract and concrete classes. The classes could be underlined, or some symbol could be drawn beside the class. For example, [Wirfs-Brock90] displays each class in a box, and fills a triangular area in the upper right corner of all abstract classes.

# 3.4    Designing for Reusability

*Reusability* is a word that is almost certain to turn up in any discussion of object-oriented programming. Nearly everyone agrees that reusing existing code is a key element in the search for greater software productivity. It is often said that the primary value of using object-oriented programming techniques is that the approach gives programmers the ability to package code into reusable pieces.

However, simply packaging code into a class does not automatically make the code reusable. Writing a truly reusable component can be a surprisingly difficult task. Object-oriented programming languages and techniques can provide a mechanism to support the construction of reusable components, but that is only the beginning. In general, programmers must plan for reuse from the beginning; it seldom happens by accident. This section discusses a few of the design issues that must be addressed to produce reusable classes.

It is important to realize that not all classes must be, or even can be, reusable. There is nothing wrong with writing a class that serves only one specific purpose. A trade-off must always be made between the time required to write the class required in a given application and the additional time required to implement a more general solution that might be useful at some later time. Sometimes, the additional effort is not worthwhile. Often however, a small initial effort is repaid many times.

The first, perhaps somewhat obvious, requirement of any reusable component is that it must solve a general problem. Good candidates for reusability are usually applicable to many situations. This is one reason most books that discuss reusable classes present examples such as arrays, hash tables, linked lists, and other common data structures. Such objects are so general that they are usually needed over and over again, by nearly everyone. The requirement that a class be generally useful is a relative statement. While lists, stacks, and hash tables may be applicable to most programs, many applications may have domain-specific or application-specific needs that can take advantage of a reusable class.

The task of creating reusable classes begins at the earliest stages of design, when objects and classes are being identified. There is almost always more than one way to decompose a problem into objects. In particular, there is at least one set of objects that solves only the specific problem under consideration and perhaps another set of objects that solves the problem in a more general way. The most direct, and least reusable, solution is usually the easiest to identify and to implement. The more general solution requires more care and more effort, but may produce a class or classes that can be reused on other situations, providing greater productivity later.

Programmers who have learned to think in terms of reusable classes are always looking for a more general solution to any problem. For example, consider the Password and PasswordDataBase classes discussed in Chapter 2. If fully and carefully implemented, these would both be good examples of reusable classes. They perform a single, isolated task that is needed by many different programs.

However, we should ask whether these classes could be made even more useful. For example, the Password class displays a prompt and allows the user to type into a text field, performing some action when the user types the <RETURN> key. This functionality is needed in many situations. Perhaps we should implement a general PromptForInput class that captured as much general functionality as possible. Then, we could have created the Password class as a subclass. In this way, the Password class could be useful to other programs, and the basic functionality could also be used in an even wider set of circumstances.

Similarly, the PasswordDatabase class is just one example of a class that looks up a string in some type of table. The fact that it is a table of passwords may impose some security constraints, but otherwise this class provides a general facility. It would be unfortunate if it were restricted to just handling passwords instead of handling a more general case.

It is interesting to note that many reusable classes begin as specific, non-reusable classes, which are then generalized to fit a broader set of requirements. This progressive move toward more generality often happens iteratively, beginning with the first recognition that some portion of a class's functionality could be moved into a more general base class. We might even speculate that this is a preferred way to create reusable, general-purpose classes. It is difficult to write a good general solution from scratch. Often, classes written without a specific need to drive the design are not useful to anyone. However, when designs move from a specific need to a general solution, the results are sure to meet the needs of at least one situation, and may be applicable to others as well. To make this approach work, a programmer has to watch for opportunities to create reusable classes and constantly think about ways to make classes more general.

Good reusable classes often require several rounds of redesign specifically aimed at improving reusability before they evolve into truly reusable classes. Reusable classes must be designed to minimize dependencies on other classes and provide a consistent, well-thought-out protocol. The implementation must be robust as well. Not all classes are worth this additional effort.

Another requirement for a reusable component is that it must be easier to reuse the component than to write one from scratch. This may seem like an obvious statement, but it is easier said than done. For example, for a class to be easy to reuse, programmers must be able to find it easily. They must know of its existence at the appropriate time. More code has probably been rewritten because the programmer didn't know that a routine already existed than for any other reason.

Assuming the programmer can find a promising piece of code to reuse, the component must be easy for the programmer to understand. At a minimum, the component should be well-documented. Unfortunately, documentation is usually the weakest part of any software library.

Sometimes classes are not reused because they provide more functionality than is needed for a particular application. A programmer might decide not to reuse a class because it has features that will not be used in the targeted application, but which are costly in terms of space or efficiency. Inheritance provides a useful way to address this issue. It is often useful to begin with a simple class that implements the absolute minimum functionality required for a given situation. Then, additional functionality can be added in derived classes, creating a hierarchy of classes with continually increasing functionality. Programmers who wish to reuse such classes can choose the point in the inheritance hierarchy that best fits their needs and do not need to pay for features they don't need. Programmers who need a simple class can create new subclasses from a class near the top of the hierarchy, while those who need more features can choose from derived classes.

Suppose a programmer needs a simple timer module that displays elapsed time. After spending some time looking for such a class, he or she discovers the Stopwatch class described in Chapter 2. However, suppose that the programmer only needs a programmatic interface for starting and stopping time. In that case, the Stopwatch provides user interface components that incur some additional cost, and may make the class unusable. The programmer may be able to use some of the other classes in the Stopwatch subsystem. More likely, because he or she will have to spend the time to figure out how the Stopwatch works before even attempting to use the other classes, the Stopwatch will just be thrown away and a new class will be written.

A critical requirement for a truly reusable class is that it must be self-contained. For best results, the class must not rely on any outside references, or require any supporting environment. This obviously means a component should not use any global variables, but the requirement can be more subtle. For example, a class may assume a particular initialization order, or may assume the existence of some other class or classes. Such assumptions can reduce a class's reusability.

Unfortunately, most C++ classes must have outside references. Few objects can exist, or be useful, in complete isolation. Any object that calls a member function belonging to another object must have a pointer to that object. Furthermore, because of the strong type-checking provided by C++, the exact type declaration of such objects must be known at compile time.

Objects can receive input (messages) without being aware of the class of the sending object. Classes that only receive messages, such as the Face class discussed in Chapter 2, are often the easiest to reuse. The Face class, for example, contains no references to other classes. It could be used in many situations in addition to the Stopwatch class for which it was built. (Notice that the Face class has other limitations that may limit its potential reusability. It only displays floating point numbers, assumes a certain precision, and so on.)

The Timer class, on the other hand, produces output by sending messages to a Face object. In fact, the way the Timer class is written, it can only send messages to a Face object (or an object instantiated from a class derived from Face). This is unfortunate because it seriously limits the reusability of the Timer class. There should be many applications for a class that produces a clock tick at any specified interval and which can be started and stopped programmatically. However, the fact that the Timer class has a hard-coded dependency on the Face class prevents it from being useful in many situations.

There are several solutions to this problem. One solution is to make the Timer class a parameterized type, or *template* as described in [Stroustrup91]. Parameterized types allow classes to be treated as type-independent templates that separate the algorithms implemented by the class from the data types, including classes, upon which the algorithms operate. For example, if the Timer class were implemented as a parameterized type, the type of the object to which the tick message is to be sent could be specified when the class is instantiated. This allows a programmer to create a StopwatchTimer class for the Stopwatch example, and to use the Timer to interact with completely different classes in other applications.

Parameterized types are not widely available in the 2.0 versions of C++, but are supported in later implementations of the language, where they are called *templates*. Programmers often simulate templates using macros that expand into different classes, depending on the type required. This technique is outside the scope of this book, and somewhat difficult to use for all but very simple cases. (See [Shapiro90] for an example of this technique.)

Although templates are not currently available, there are some other solutions available for programmers who wish to make classes as reusable as possible. The issue is how to connect the "output" of one class to another, without tying the two classes together. Basically, there are three ways to implement a class that needs to send messages to another class.

The first way is to call the other object's member function directly. This requires that the declaration of the other class be known at compile time, and binds the class tightly to the other class. The Timer class in Chapter 2 uses this approach. Calling member functions directly is the most expedient way to connect different objects, but results in the least reusable code, unless parameterization is used.

The second approach is to defer the connections to derived classes. This can be done by designing classes to call virtual member functions, which can or must be implemented by derived classes, instead of referring to outside classes directly. For example, let's rewrite the Timer class to support a protected pure virtual member function, `reportTime()`, which is called from the `tick()` member function. The class declaration for the new Timer class looks like this:

```
1    /////////////////////////////////////////////////////
2    // Timer.h: A generic clock class, abstract
3    //          version with pure virtual reportTime
4    /////////////////////////////////////////////////////
5    #ifndef TIMER_H
6    #define TIMER_H
7    #include <Xm/Xm.h>
8
9    class Timer {
10
11     private:
12
13       // Static member function used for TimeOut callback
14
15       static void tickCallback ( XtPointer, XtIntervalId* );
16       void tick();  // Called every _interval milliseconds
17
18       int   _counter;    // Current number of ticks
19       int   _interval;   // Time in milliseconds between updates
20       XtIntervalId _id;  // Identifier of current TimeOut
21       XtAppContext _app; // Required by Xt functions
22
23     protected:
24
25       // Called at each clock tick (Derived classes must override)
26
27       virtual void reportTime ( float ) = 0;
28
29     public:
30
31       Timer ( XtAppContext, int );
32       void start();          // Resets, and starts the clock ticking
33       void stop();           // Stops the clock
34       float elapsedTime (); // Returns time since timer started
35    };
36    #endif
```

All member functions are the same as previous versions, except for the constructor and the tick() member function The new constructor requires only an application context and the update interval and no longer expects a Face object.

```
Timer::Timer ( XtAppContext app, int interval )
{
    _id       = NULL;
    _app      = app;
    _counter  = 0;
    _interval = interval;
}
```

The new version of `tick()` calls the `reportTime()` virtual function instead of updating the Face directly. The `tick()` member function can be written as follows:

```
void Timer::tick()
{
      _counter++;  // Increment a counter for each tick

      // Call derived class function to report time

      reportTime ( elapsedTime() );

      // Reinstall the timeout callback

      _id = XtAppAddTimeOut ( _app,
                              _interval,
                              &Timer::tickCallback,
                              ( XtPointer ) this );
}
```

This approach eliminates the dependency on any outside class, and produces a more reusable Timer class. However, to use the class, the programmer must create a new derived class that overrides the `reportTime()` member function. To use the new Timer class in the stopwatch example, we must create a derived class that provides an interface to the Face class. We can write such a derived class as follows:

```
1   //////////////////////////////////////////////////////
2   // StopwatchTimer.h: A clock class for the stopwatch
3   //////////////////////////////////////////////////////
4   #ifndef STOPWATCHTIMER_H
5   #define STOPWATCHTIMER_H
6   #include "Timer.h"
7   class Face;
8
9   class StopwatchTimer : public Timer {
10
11    private:
12
13      Face *_face;
14
15    protected:
16
17      void reportTime ( float );
18
19    public:
20
21      StopwatchTimer ( XtAppContext, Face *, int interval );
22  };
23  #endif
```

The implementation file contains only a constructor and the `reportTime()` member function, both of which are very simple. The constructor simply calls the Timer constructor and saves the pointer to the Face object. The `reportTime()` member function simply calls the Face object's `setTime()` member function.

```
1   /////////////////////////////////////////////////////
2   // StopwatchTimer.C: A clock class for the stopwatch
3   /////////////////////////////////////////////////////
4   #include "StopwatchTimer.h"
5   #include "Face.h"
6
7   StopwatchTimer::StopwatchTimer ( XtAppContext   app,
8                                    Face          *face,
9                                    int            interval ) :
10                      Timer ( app, interval )
11  {
12      _face = face;
13  }
14
15  void StopwatchTimer::reportTime ( float time )
16  {
17      _face->setTime ( time );
18  }
```

This approach allows the Timer class to be used in more situations by eliminating the dependency on the Face class. However, it requires some additional programming to create the derived class. For a simple class like the Timer class, it may be almost as easy to reimplement the class each time it is needed. However, for more significant classes, this approach can be very effective.

The third way to allow a class to communicate with another is to use a callback technique similar to that used by Xt and Motif. With this approach, the Timer class must be given a function to be called with each clock tick. Applications that use the Timer class can define the function to make the actual connection to another class.

For example, consider the following version of the Timer class:

```
1   /////////////////////////////////////////////////////
2   // Timer.h: A generic clock class, "callback" version
3   /////////////////////////////////////////////////////
4   #ifndef TIMER_H
5   #define TIMER_H
6   #include <Xm/Xm.h>
7
8   typedef void ( *TimerCallback )( float, void * );
9
10  class Timer {
11
12    private:
13
```

```
14        // Static member function used for TimeOut callback
15
16        static void tickCallback ( XtPointer, XtIntervalId* );
17
18        void tick();   // Called every _interval milliseconds
19
20        TimerCallback _func;
21        void        *_data;
22        int    _counter;    // Current number of ticks
23        int    _interval;   // Time in miliseconds between updates
24        XtIntervalId _id;   // Identifier of current TimeOut
25        XtAppContext _app;  // Required by Xt functions
26
27   public:
28
29        Timer ( XtAppContext, TimerCallback, int interval, void *data );
30
31        void start();       // Resets, and starts the clock ticking
32        void stop();        // Stops the clock
33        float elapsedTime(); // Returns time since timer started
34   };
35
36   #endif
```

This version of Timer is similar to the original, except that instead of requiring a pointer to a Face object as an argument to the constructor, the Timer class requires a pointer to a function of type TimerCallback and some optional client data. The TimerCallback function is defined as a void function that expects two arguments, a float and an untyped pointer (void *).

The Timer constructor maintains a pointer to the specified function, to allow it to be called later.

```
1    /////////////////////////////////////////////////
2    // Timer.C: A clock class for the stopwatch
3    /////////////////////////////////////////////////
4    #include "Timer.h"
5    #include <Xm/Xm.h>
6
7    Timer::Timer ( XtAppContext  app,
8                   TimerCallback callback,
9                   int           interval,
10                  void          *data )
11   {
12       _func     = callback;
13       _data     = data;
14       _id       = NULL;
15       _app      = app;
16       _counter  = 0;
17       _interval = interval;
18   }
```

The only other member function that differs from the original version of the Timer class is the tick() member function. This version uses the _func member to invoke the function passed to the class when it was instantiated. Notice that the latest version of Timer requires no knowledge of any other class.

```
19  void Timer::tick()
20  {
21      _counter++;   // Increment a counter for each tick
22
23      // Compute the time in seconds and update the Face object
24
25      if ( _func )
26          ( *_func )( elapsedTime(), _data);
27
28      // Reinstall the timeout callback
29
30      _id = XtAppAddTimeOut ( _app,
31                              _interval,
32                              &Timer::tickCallback,
33                              (XtPointer) this );
34
35  }
```

All remaining functions are the same as the original Timer class in Chapter 2. Now, let's see how the Stopwatch class can use this new Timer class to display the elapsed time in a Face object. First, the file Stopwatch.C implements a function, updateFace(), that expects a floating point number and an untyped pointer. In this case, the pointer is expected to be a Face object. Once the pointer is cast to the proper type, updateFace() calls the Face class's setTime() function for the object.

```
1   /////////////////////////////////////////////////////////////////
2   // Stopwatch.C: Group subcomponents into one stopwatch component
3   /////////////////////////////////////////////////////////////////
4   #include "Stopwatch.h"
5   #include <Xm/Xm.h>
6   #include <Xm/RowColumn.h>
7   #include "Timer.h"
8   #include "Face.h"
9   #include "Control.h"
10
11  // Callback function used to communicate between
12  // the Timer and Face objects
13
14  void updateFace ( float time, void *data )
15  {
16          Face *face = ( Face * ) data;      // Coerce to expected type
17          face->setTime ( time );            // Display time in Face object
18  }
```

The Stopwatch constructor must specify the `updateFace()` callback function when the Timer is instantiated. It must also pass a pointer to the appropriate Face object as the client data argument to the Timer constructor. The client data will be passed back to the `updateFace()` function when it is called.

```
19   Stopwatch::Stopwatch ( Widget parent,
20                            char  *name ) :  BasicComponent ( name )
21   {
22         // Create a manager widget to hold all components
23
24         _w = XmCreateRowColumn ( parent, _name, NULL, 0 );
25
26         // Instantiate the three sub-components of the stopwatch
27
28         _face = new  Face ( _w, "face" );
29         _timer = new Timer ( XtWidgetToApplicationContext ( parent ),
30                              updateFace,
31                              1000,
32                              ( void * ) _face);
33
34         _control = new Control ( _w, "control", this, _timer );
35
36         // Manage the two user interface components
37
38         _face->manage();
39         _control->manage();
40   }
```

All other Stopwatch member functions are the same as in the previous version. This approach allows the Timer object to be reused in a variety of situations and is the simplest way to make the Timer class reusable because it requires the programmer to write the least amount of additional code. Anyone who wants to use the Timer class simply has to write a single function that performs the appropriate action at each tick of the clock.

Notice, however, that the approach presented here is *not* type-safe. It is completely up to the programmer to ensure that the object passed into the constructor is in fact a Face object, as expected by the `updateFace()` function.

For very simple classes, such as those described here and in Chapter 2, the techniques described can help reduce dependencies on external objects and produce more reusable classes. Unfortunately, the solutions presented here cannot always be applied to all situations. Most classes are much more complex than those discussed so far. Not all classes are simple combinations of uni-directional input and output. For example, if two objects must interact closely, the techniques just described may not be adequate. Some classes are simply not able to stand alone, and are not likely candidates for future reuse.

However, the technique of grouping collections of collaborating classes into a single, self-contained subsystem can also be useful. For example, even if the original Timer class is not reusable by itself, the Stopwatch class, combined with the other classes in the Stopwatch subsystem, forms a reusable module.

## 3.5   Summary

The process of designing an object-oriented program differs significantly from the more traditional approaches to designing software. Although many people have tried to find a mechanical, step-by-step approach for moving from a problem to a software solution, the process of designing a program remains more an art than a science. The CRC approach, as well as the responsibility-driven approach described in this chapter, are particularly attractive because they provide a framework in which to explore object-oriented design ideas without being overly constraining.

Object-oriented programming offers the ability to package code in such a way that it can be reused many times. Reusability is a worthwhile goal, because it can improve programmer productivity, reduce maintenance costs, and improve software quality. However, truly reusable classes are surprisingly hard to write. This chapter examined a few pragmatic issues related to reuse by trying to redesign the Timer class from Chapter 2 to be more reusable. Classes can be designed to be reusable, but it takes extra care and attention at all stages of development.

One of the goals of the UIComponent class and its corresponding model was to provide a base for general-purpose user interface components based on C++ and Motif. C++ user interface components are meant to be higher-level than Motif widgets, and may be developed for a specific application. However, with some care, it is feasible to create more general-purpose components based on the UIComponent class.

This chapter represents a very simple, brief, and incomplete overview of a complex topic. The main intent is to provide some basic tools that can be used to explore and explain the design of the examples in following chapters. Readers can turn to many sources for more comprehensive information on object-oriented design, as well as alternative approaches and viewpoints. The Bibliography on page 424 lists several sources of additional information. *Designing Object-Oriented Software*, by Rebecca Wirfs-Brock, Brian Wilkerson, and Lauren Wiener [Wirfs-Brock90] describes a simple approach to object-oriented design that inspired much of the material in the first part of this chapter. Their technique, which focuses on identifying objects and interactions between objects, can help programmers develop a clean object-oriented architecture for a system before embarking on an implementation. For those looking for more pragmatic tips and techniques for designing with C++ classes, *The C++ Programming Language*, by Bjarne Stroustrup [Stroustrup91] devotes several chapters to object-oriented design.

The next two chapters apply the basic design techniques discussed in this chapter to a more realistic example. Chapter 4 develops a high-level design for a simple program, based on the CRC approach described in this chapter. Chapter 5 uses the component approach for mixing Motif and C++ to implement the design described in Chapter 4.

# Chapter 4
# TicTacToe: Design

This chapter begins an extended case study that exercises some of the techniques discussed in Chapter 3, and also provides further examples that use Motif with C++. The case study discusses the design and implementation of a simple computer version of the well-known tic-tac-toe game. We will call the computer version "TicTacToe." The emphasis in this chapter is on developing the early design of the program. The exercise starts with a simple statement of the problem, and then begins to identify a set of classes with which to model the system. The design proceeds until a complete set of class cards is developed, along with a collaboration graph that details the architecture of the program. Chapter 5 presents an implementation based on the design developed in this chapter.

The simple design process described in the previous chapter addresses only the internal architecture of a system. In interactive programs, designing an adequate user interface is equally important. After discussing the internal design, Section 4.5 turns to the issue of designing the user interface portion of an application like TicTacToe.

This chapter and the next also present the first realistic use of the complete UIComponent class, along with the notion of user interface components based on C++ classes, as introduced in Chapter 3. The discussion attempts to begin the design process with as few assumptions as possible. However, there is an underlying assumption that the program will be implemented in C++ using Motif as the user interface platform.

The exercise in this chapter tries to trace a realistic design process, complete with occasional false turns, missteps, and second guessing. Good designs are seldom achieved in a single pass, and the design discussion that follows does not always take a straight path to the eventual solution. The goal is to demonstrate and evaluate a design process based on the CRC approach in the context of a typical application based on C++ and Motif, not to simply spell out the final solution.

## 4.1    Defining the Problem

The first step when developing any application is to identify or clarify the goals of the project. A good place to start is with a written description of the program to be developed. This description can be used as the first step in finding the objects and classes in the program. If the project has not already been defined by someone else, the programmer or project team can always write a description. The following is a brief description of the tic-tac-toe game to be developed in this chapter and the one that follows.[1]

> TicTacToe is an interactive computerized version of the familiar game, tic-tac-toe. The game displays a 3 by 3 grid of squares. Each square in the grid can display an "X" or an "O." The user can mark an X in any unmarked square by selecting the square with the mouse. Each time the user selects an X square, the program responds by displaying an "O" in a different square. The first player (the user or the program) to get three Xs or Os in a straight line wins the game. The program should prompt the user to make a move when it is his or her turn, and also report the winner when either player gets three marks in a row. In addition to marking Xs in squares, the user can issue two other commands at any time. The first quits the game, and the other clears the board and begins a new game.

Real projects will often have a more complete and formal description, but this is a simple program. The brief description above leaves a lot to the imagination, but it should be enough to get us started designing the game.

## 4.2    Finding the Objects

Let's begin the design process by trying to determine what objects will be needed by TicTacToe. As discussed in Chapter 3, one way to get started is to go through the description given above, and underline all the nouns or noun phrases. We can also mark the verbs at the same time. In the following description, all nouns are underlined and all verbs are *italicized*. With some experience, we could undoubtedly eliminate many that couldn't possibly be potential objects, but for now, let's try the process blindly, and simply mark everything.

---

[1]  In a book like this, it would be very easy to contrive a description of requirements such that all the nouns magically map to the objects we need in the system. All that would be needed is to do the design (or the implementation!) first and then write the requirements to fit the design. However, I promise that this was not done here. I did have some idea of where I wanted to go before writing the description, but hopefully that will always be the case - it would be silly not to use all your experience at all stages of the design. However, the problem description remains as it was first written. It is perhaps not even a very good description. That is all right. The point is to use the description as a starting point for thinking about the objects and classes in the system, not to get it perfect the first time.

TicTacToe *is* an interactive computerized <u>version</u> of the familiar <u>game, tic-tac-toe</u>. The <u>game</u> *displays* a 3 by 3 <u>grid</u> of <u>squares</u>. Each <u>square</u> in the <u>grid</u> can *display* an "<u>X</u>" or an "<u>O</u>". The <u>user</u> can *mark* an <u>X</u> in any unmarked <u>square</u> by *selecting* the <u>square</u> with the <u>mouse</u>. Each <u>time</u> the <u>user</u> *selects* an X <u>square</u>, the <u>program</u> *responds* by *displaying* an "<u>O</u>" in a different <u>square</u>. The first <u>player</u> (the <u>user</u> or the <u>program</u>) to *get* three <u>Xs</u> or <u>Os</u> in a straight <u>line</u> *wins* the game. The <u>program</u> should *prompt* the <u>user</u> to *make* a <u>move</u> when it is his or her <u>turn</u>, and also *report* the <u>winner</u> when either <u>player</u> *gets* three <u>marks</u> in a <u>row</u>. In addition to *marking* <u>Xs</u> in <u>squares</u>, the <u>user</u> can *issue* two other <u>commands</u> at any <u>time</u>. The first *quits* the <u>game</u>, and the other *clears* the <u>board</u> and *begins* a new <u>game</u>.

The description contains the following nouns, which, according to the approach presented in Chapter 3, may suggest objects and classes that could be used to implement the TicTacToe game:

| | | | | |
|---|---|---|---|---|
| TicTacToe | version | game | grid | square |
| X | O | user | mouse | program |
| player | line | move | turn | winner |
| command | mark | row | board | time |

The description also contains the following verbs, which should indicate actions that might be taken by the objects in the system.

| | | | | |
|---|---|---|---|---|
| display | mark | select | respond | wins |
| prompt | report | clear | start | quit |
| begins | issue | is | make | marking |
| gets | get | displaying | | |

These lists contain many verbs and nouns that do not seem very useful. Others might or might not be useful as objects and classes, and it seems likely that several radically different designs could be developed, all based on this list of nouns and verbs. Going through the entire list is a tedious task (and this is a small example!), but fortunately we can let intuition and experience weed out most of the list quickly.

For example, the noun <u>TicTacToe</u> is the name of the game, and it doesn't seem useful to model the entire game as an object. Modeling each <u>X</u> and <u>O</u> as an object is a possibility, but seems like overkill for a project of this size, so we can remove those as well. Similarly, modeling <u>moves</u> and <u>turns</u> as objects would require more work than we need to do for a simple game, although such objects might be very useful in a more complex game. We can also eliminate <u>version</u> as a relatively unimportant noun[2], and <u>mouse</u> as being an unnecessary entity to model, given X's event-driven model.

---

2  "Version" actually seems like a very good candidate object in a real system, although not in the context in which the word is used in this description. A Version object that records information about the current release of a system can be useful in supporting a piece of software. The Version object could be responsible for maintaining an identifying "stamp" of some kind, and also for checking versions of anything the program depends on, such as the operating system. The Version object could check all relevant dependencies at start-up time and report any problems to the user: "Sorry, you must upgrade your system to at least OS 17.2 before running this program," and so on. We don't need anything this sophisticated for the simple example discussed here. Such decisions represent a typical part of the design process, of course. Anything *could* be represented as an object. The goal is to split the problem into slices that make sense, that work together, and that meet the needs of the project.

Continuing to consider each noun in the description, we can narrow the list of potential objects to the following:

- grid
- square(s)
- commands
- board

This doesn't seem like an adequate list, but let's leave it for now and move on to the actions. Looking at the list of verbs, we see several items that indicate user actions and others that indicate actions performed by the game. It appears that the user should be able to *quit* the game, and *start* or *begin* a new game. These are types of commands, and may be related to the command object already tentatively identified as an object. Let's assume for now that we need such an object, and name it the Command object.

We also see that the user needs to be able to *select* squares, and that an appropriate mark must be displayed on the game board. It seems likely that the tic-tac-toe grid, listed as an object above could be modeled as an object that supports methods for displaying Xs or Os in the squares in the grid. The grid also serves as an input area that allows the user to select and mark a square. We also see from the description that we need a way for the user to clear the board when a new game is started. That could also be a responsibility of the grid object.

There are two other interesting verbs in our list. The first one is the verb *responds*. Who responds? Because TicTacToe is to be a computer game in which the user plays the computer, there must be a "brain" somewhere that plays against the user. Perhaps the brain is indicated by the <u>game</u> and <u>TicTacToe</u> nouns we threw away so quickly. Who responds? The game responds. But it isn't really the entire game, it is the other player in the game, the computer. So, let's pick a new name, and refer to the intelligent part of the program as the Engine object. The Engine is the part of the program that drives everything, determines the computer's next move, and so on.

The other interesting verb is *reports*. Who reports the winner? The Engine object could do it, or perhaps a separate object watches the game to determine the winner. Another question is "*How* is the winner reported to the user?" Related to this question, we see another verb, *prompt*. The program is supposed to prompt the user for the next move. How? Perhaps we need an object to handle messages to the user, popping up dialogs, or whatever is appropriate to convey information to the user. We could tentatively identify this object as the Message object, which is responsible for communication with the user.

## 4.3  Developing Initial Class Cards

At this point, let's start to put together a few CRC-style class cards and see what we have. Like the lists of verbs and nouns, these class cards need not be perfect. They serve as a way of getting started quickly, and focusing attention on the kinds of objects that could be used to model the problem. It is more important to get started than for everything to be correct the first time.

## The GameBoard Class

First, we know we have a tic-tac-toe grid. In fact, three of the four nouns in the list of potential objects seem to indicate a grid (grid, squares, and board). Let's call this object the GameBoard, and create a class card for it. We can assume that GameBoard is a concrete class. Because the TicTacToe grid is a visible portion of the game, we can also anticipate that the GameBoard class will be derived from the UIComponent class, although such details are relatively unimportant at this point in the design.

The previous section listed several responsibilities for the GameBoard class. The GameBoard displays the familiar tic-tac-toe grid, and is also responsible for displaying Xs and Os. For now, we can assume that, like the pencil and paper version of tic-tac-toe, moves are entered directly in the playing area. This implies that the GameBoard class is responsible for handling input, and for accepting the user's moves.

It is reasonable to expect the GameBoard to interact with the Engine object (also identified during the examination of verbs and nouns) in some way, because the Engine needs to be able to communicate the computer's moves to the user and to determine the user's moves. The first of these interactions represents a one-way collaboration in which the Engine uses the GameBoard as an output device. This indicates that the GameBoard is a collaborator of the Engine class, which can be listed on the Engine class card.

The second interaction involves passing information from the GameBoard to the Engine for further handling. This means the GameBoard must collaborate with the Engine class to record each of the user's moves, which should be indicated on the GameBoard class card.

These initial ideas produce the GameBoard class card in Figure 4.1.

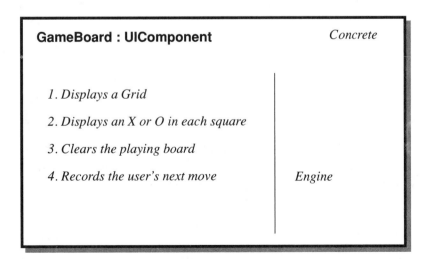

**Figure 4.1** The initial GameBoard class card.

## The Engine Class

Next, we can look at the Engine class. So far, we know that the Engine is responsible for picking the computer's move. It seems likely that the Engine will need to maintain some information about the internal state of the game to accomplish this task, so we can add "maintains state of game" as another responsibility. Because the Engine must keep track of the moves and the progress of the game, it also seems reasonable to make the Engine class responsible for prompting the user for the next move. The Engine class should also notify the user when either side wins the game.

The Engine object needs to collaborate with the GameBoard object to specify and display moves. The Engine object also needs to communicate with the user, but we have not firmly established how that is to be done. For example, we stated above that the Engine class should prompt the user for the next move. However, it does not seem right for the Engine to be involved in creating or displaying messages in windows. More likely, the Engine should only initiate or control these actions; some other object should handle the actual communication. For now, we can say that the Engine object collaborates with the Message object, tentatively identified earlier, to accomplish these goals.

These decisions result in the Engine class card shown in Figure 4.2.

| **Engine** | *Concrete* |
|---|---|
| *1. Picks computer's next move* | |
| *2. Informs user of computer's move* | *GameBoard* |
| *3. Maintains state of game* | |
| *4. Determines winner* | |
| *5. Reports winner* | *Message?* |
| *6. Prompts user for a move* | *Message?* |

**Figure 4.2**  The initial Engine class card.

## The Command Class

Now we can turn our attention to the Command class. We know that the user must be able to exit the game, and that the Command class should provide some way for the user to issue an exit command. Exiting an application is a simple thing, so perhaps we should make the Command class responsible for accepting the command from the user and actually exiting as well.

Next, the Command class must accept a "new game" command from the user. Carrying out this command involves resetting the state of the game board, which is maintained by the Engine class. Therefore, the Engine class is a collaborator.

When a new game begins, the GameBoard also needs to be cleared, so the Command object might also collaborate with the GameBoard. However, this implies that two separate messages, one to the GameBoard and one to the Engine, must be sent to accomplish one logical operation. This is an example of a "wide interface," which is best avoided. Such situations often lead to code that is difficult to maintain and should normally be avoided. It seems better for the Command object to simply notify the Engine object that a new game should be started. The Engine object can then reset its own state and, in so doing, request the GameBoard to clear itself. This identifies yet another collaboration between the Engine class and the GameBoard class and further establishes the Engine class's role as the central controller or "traffic cop" of the system. Making the Engine class responsible for resetting the game also simplifies the design and implementation of the Command class, which now interacts with only one other class instead of two.

Figure 4.3 shows the Command class card.

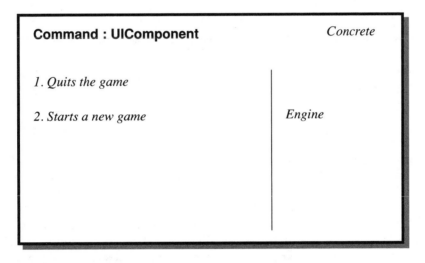

**Figure 4.3**  An initial Command class card.

## The Message Class

Earlier, we identified the need for a Message object that somehow displays messages to the user. The Message object fulfills the function indicated by the verb *reports* in the initial description. We decided earlier that the Engine was responsible for initiating various messages to the user, but that the Message class would provide the interface for the communication.

Let's create a card for the Message class as well. It apparently has only one responsibility: to display messages. Only the Engine class interacts with the Message class, because that is the only object we have identified as needing to report information to the user. So, the Message class does not need to collaborate with any other class. It can simply accept messages from any class. The Message object's class card is shown in Figure 4.4.

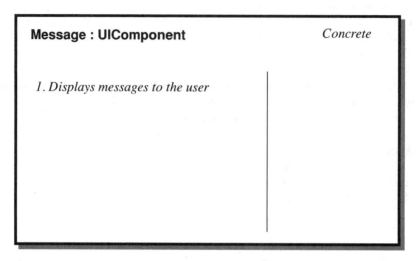

**Figure 4.4**  The initial Message class card.

# 4.4    Finalizing the Design

We have now identified four objects in the TicTacToe program, and have a rough idea of the responsibilities of each object, or class. We also have identified some collaborations between objects and have speculated a bit about how the objects fit together to form the system. We can now begin to examine this information in more detail.

The primary goal at this stage is to make sure the responsibilities have been assigned correctly and that the objects identified so far are adequate and represent a workable design. Before implementing the system we should also be comfortable with the overall structure of the application. It may be useful at this point to develop a collaboration graph that shows how all the pieces fit together to define the architecture of the program. Although we are not yet ready to begin implementing these classes, we can begin to consider some implementation issues as well. For example, we can begin to look for opportunities for inheritance and other forms of reuse.

## A Collaboration Graph

Let's begin by examining a collaboration graph based on the class cards identified in the previous section. Figure 4.5 shows a simple collaboration graph created by simply connecting all collaborating classes in the system. We see that the Engine plays a central role, and is connected in one way or another to the other three objects, which are all user interface components. The Command class collaborates with the Engine class to allow the user to start the game. The Engine uses the Message class to provide information to the user, while the GameBoard class and the Engine class collaborate with each other to provide input and display both the user's moves and the computer-generated moves.

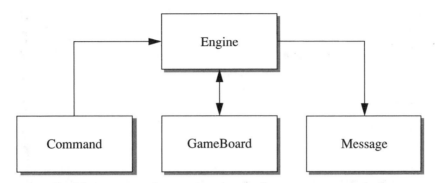

**Figure 4.5** A simple TicTacToe collaboration graph.

With this vague view of how the system fits together, let's revisit each of the classes we have specified so far. The goal is to make sure the responsibilities assigned to each class make sense, according to our current understanding of the system. In some cases, responsibilities may need to be reassigned or reorganized. In other cases, some minor changes in wording may help clarify the design.

## The Command Class

Earlier, we decided that the Command class is a user interface component that allows the user to issue a quit command and a new game command. So far, we have not decided the exact form of the interface used to issue these commands. The class could be implemented as popup or pulldown menus, or perhaps a set of command buttons. The class might not even be a visible component. It could just be an object that responds to commands typed in by the user.

According to the original class card shown in Figure 4.3, the Command class handles each of its commands differently. In one case, it assumes the responsibility of fulfilling the quit command itself, by exiting the game. In the other case, the new game command must be handled elsewhere, and the Command object simply forwards the request to the Engine class. In retrospect, this seems like a poor division of responsibilities. The Command class's responsibility should be to accept commands from the user and to route them to the appropriate entity in the program, not to fulfill commands itself. For example, other objects might need to perform some cleanup before the program exits. If the Command class handles exiting the application by itself, other objects will not have an opportunity to perform any required actions before the program exits.

It seems more appropriate for the Command class to collaborate with the Engine class to exit the application. The Command class simply passes the command from the user on to the Engine class. This is more suitable for the Engine class's role as the central coordinator for the game. Figure 4.6 shows the revised Command class card.

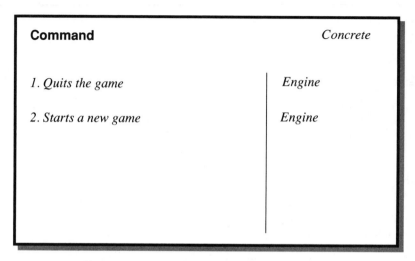

**Figure 4.6**  The revised Command class card.

## The GameBoard Class

The GameBoard class seems to have a reasonable set of responsibilities. Like the Command class, we are not sure exactly how the GameBoard functions, or precisely how it appears on the screen. However, we expect the GameBoard to display a tic-tac-toe grid, accept input, and display output. As an input device, the GameBoard passes the user's moves on to the Engine class, which records and responds to them. As an output device, the GameBoard object is completely under the control of the Engine, which displays the computer-generated moves, and clears the board when a new game is started.

## The Message Class

The Message class is the only other user interface component. This class simply provides a way for the Engine to communicate with the user. There is some potential for overlap with the GameBoard class because both function as output devices. It seems possible that the functionality supported by the Message class could be assumed by the GameBoard at some point. However, because we have not yet considered the user interface to TicTacToe, it seems better to abstract the facility used to display messages for the user in the Message class for now.

Because the Message class has no collaborators, it has some potential as a generally reusable component. We might be able to use an existing dialog class or other simple display component. We can address these ideas when we get closer to implementation. For now, the Message class card shown in Figure 4.4 is adequate.

## The Engine Class

The Engine class is a very important part of the TicTacToe program because the Engine controls the action of the game. It warrants closer examination because it has many responsibilities and plays a crucial role in the game. In fact, it seems that we may have overloaded the Engine class on the first pass, simply throwing everything that wasn't part of the user interface into the Engine class.

As defined on page 138, the Engine class is responsible not only for the flow of the game, (keeping track of who moves when), but also maintaining an internal version of the state of the board, and choosing the computer's responses to the user's moves. It might make more sense to reassign some of these responsibilities and redesign the Engine to play a more coordinating role.

Maintaining the state of the board separately from the GameBoard object seems redundant, and perhaps we could just use the GameBoard object to keep the state of the game. However, this might prove to be cumbersome in some situations. For example, we might want to experiment with the board, trying out future moves, and so on. One way to determine the game's moves would be to create a game tree, and use a min-max approach to find the best possible move [McDermott85]. This approach involves generating a version of the board for nearly every permutation of moves and evaluating each position. Because the GameBoard creates a visible user interface component, it does not seem likely that we would want to make this process visible by instantiating many GameBoard objects, complete with a tic-tac-toe grid for each possible move.

However, it does seem useful to define a lightweight Board class that can be instantiated as many times as necessary to create off-screen representations of the game. One instance of the Board class can be used to track the current state of the visible board, while additional instances might be used to try out future moves. So, let's remove the responsibility of maintaining the state of the board from the Engine class, but add the Board class as a collaborator. Even if TicTacToe creates only a single Board object, the design will be more modular.

Next, we need to consider the way the game chooses moves. There are several strategies for choosing moves in a tic-tac-toe game. In fact, we might at some point wish to change the algorithm used to determine moves, or even to change the rules of the game itself. Rather than grouping the decision-making process with the mechanics of playing the game, it might be best to pull the this component out of the Engine object and create a new MoveGenerator object.

What is left for the Engine class? It fills a coordinating role. For example, it must remember whose move is next so that it can arrange the appropriate action at each step. This seems to be an internal responsibility, because it does not directly involve any other class. Also, in the discussion on page 141 we removed the responsibility of exiting the game from the Command class and moved it to the Engine class. The Engine class should now perform the steps needed to close down the game.

The two newly-identified collaborators, Board and MoveGenerator, as well as a set of revised responsibilities, are shown on the final Engine class card in Figure 4.7. In many cases, the responsibilities listed on the original Engine class card have been reworded to indicate that the Engine relies on other objects to accomplish its goals. The class card in Figure 4.7 attempts to convey the external responsibilities of the Engine class, without implying that it performs these actions itself.

The Engine class still supports an unusually large number of responsibilities. However, most of these responsibilities are simply delegated to other objects. For now, we can proceed, keeping an eye on the complexity of the Engine class.

| Engine | Concrete |
|---|---|
| *1. Determines computer's next move* | *MoveGenerator* |
| *2. Presents computer's move* | *GameBoard* |
| *3. Records moves* | *Board* |
| *4. Determines the winner* | *Board* |
| *5. Reports the winner* | *Message* |
| *6. Resets to initiate new game* | *Board, GameBoard* |
| *7. Prompts user for next move* | *Message* |
| *8. Cleans up and exits game* | |

**Figure 4.7**  The Engine class card.

## The Board Class

As discussed in the previous section, the Board class represents the current state of a game. One Board object maintains the current state of the game being played. The Board class must support some representation of the game board, but the choice of representation is an implementation issue and can be kept private. The Board class must allow both the user and the TicTacToe game to record moves. The user enters moves via the GameBoard. The GameBoard passes each move to the Engine class, which records the move with a Board object. The computer-generated moves are chosen by the MoveGenerator class, although the Engine is responsible for seeing that a move is generated and recorded with a Board.

For the MoveGenerator to generate a valid move, it will need to be able to determine what moves are available. Because the Board class maintains the current state of the board, the Board class needs to provide a way for the GameBoard to retrieve this information. Some move generators might want to have additional information about the state of a Board object as well. For example, the MoveGenerator probably needs some way to evaluate any given situation to allow it to generate "good" moves. For many approaches to choosing moves, it is sufficient to know whether a particular board contains a winning X state, a winning O state, or no winning state. Because a Board object can perform this task without exposing the actual implementation of the board representation, we can assign the responsibility of determining the winning state of the board to the Board class.

Figure 4.8 shows the Board class card, with the responsibilities discussed so far. The Board class is used by the Engine and MoveGenerator classes, but Board does not refer to any other classes itself. Therefore the Board class card lists no collaborators.

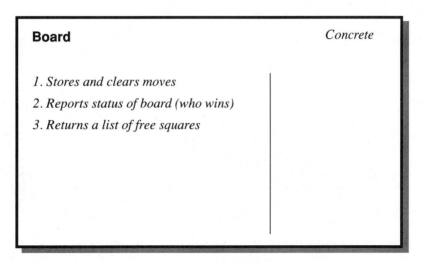

**Figure 4.8**  The Board class card.

## The MoveGenerator Class

The MoveGenerator object has a single, simple responsibility. Given a Board object that represents any particular state, the MoveGenerator should choose the computer's next move. To select a move, the MoveGenerator needs access to a Board object. In addition, the MoveGenerator needs to be able to determine what moves are available, and who, if anyone, has won, given any particular board configuration.

There are several algorithms that could be chosen to determine the next move. The game tree approach mentioned earlier works well for simple games like tic-tac-toe. This technique evaluates all possible moves and chooses only moves that lead to a win or draw for the computer, which leads to a game that is hard to beat. At the other end of the spectrum, the MoveGenerator could simply choose a square at random. Or, the MoveGenerator could choose moves at random during early phases of the game and switch to a more aggressive strategy later in the game.

It even seems possible that the game could support several different types of move generators. Perhaps the user could choose which type of object is used by selecting between novice, intermediate, and expert modes. We could support this capability by designing a single MoveGenerator class that supports each of these modes, or by allowing the Engine to install different move generators to accommodate each level.

In any event, these are lower-level details that do not need to be fully considered at this point. The only thing we need to specify right now is the external behavior of a GameBoard object. We know that the Engine is in charge of the progress of the game, and that the Engine object relies on a MoveGenerator to compute the next move. The MoveGenerator depends on a Board object to determine the current state of the board, which allows the MoveGenerator to pick a "good" move.

The resulting MoveGenerator class card is shown in Figure 4.9. The MoveGenerator class is a concrete class whose only responsibility is to pick the computer's next move. The GameBoard class must collaborate with the Board class to fulfill this responsibility.

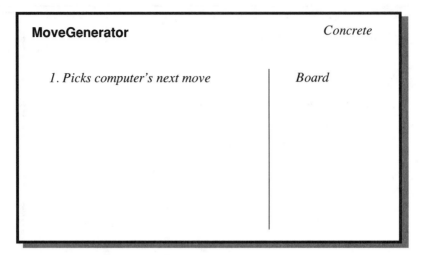

**Figure 4.9**  The MoveGenerator class card.

## The TicTacToe Inheritance Graph

Figure 4.10 shows an inheritance graph for classes identified as part of the TicTacToe program. Three of these classes are clearly user interface components, and as such, we expect them to be derived from the UIComponent class described in Chapter 2. The remaining classes have no particular inheritance relationship.

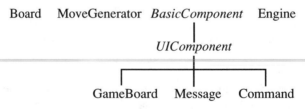

**Figure 4.10**  The TicTacToe inheritance hierarchy.

## The Collaboration Graph

We have now identified and described the objects in the system in a fair amount of detail. Once the main classes and the various relationships between them have been solidified, we can  draw a more detailed collaboration graph. The complete graph provides more information about how these pieces fit together than the simpler collaboration graph shown in Figure 4.5.

For purposes of the collaboration graph, we can consider the Engine, the Board, and the MoveGenerator to be grouped into an "Engine Subsystem." Recall that we originally identified the functionality of these three objects as belonging to a single Engine object. Although these responsibilities have now been distributed throughout multiple objects, it is still useful to think of a single "brain" as doing the work. In fact, the Board and MoveGenerator have no interactions (collaborations) except between themselves and the Engine class, which reinforces the idea that these classes are really a single, cohesive subsystem.

It is also useful to think of the entire game as a subsystem that contains all the other objects. This certainly matches the user's view. To the user, there are only two objects: the user and the game. Choosing to show the entire game as a composite object, or a subsystem, can help us to see how cohesive the structure is (or isn't).

Figure 4.11 shows a collaboration graph for the objects discussed in the previous sections. The numbers in the semi-circles in each object refer to the responsibilities identified on each class card.

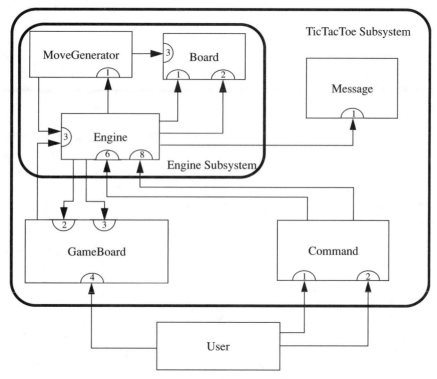

**Figure 4.11**  The TicTacToe collaboration graph.

The collaboration graph in Figure 4.11 makes the overall architecture of the system quite clear. For example, we can see exactly how the user interacts with the system. The Engine Subsystem is the most cluttered looking area of the graph, but this is to be expected because the Engine is the heart of the system.

The design exercise has now provided a set of classes that implement the basic features of the program, an inheritance hierarchy for these classes, and a fairly detailed picture of the overall architecture of the system. The design may need to be adjusted as we proceed, but the design exercise has provided a firm foundation from which the game can evolve.

# 4.5    Designing the TicTacToe User Interface

So far, the design process described in this chapter has considered only the internal structure of the TicTacToe program. However, designing the user interface is an equally important part of developing any interactive program. Of course, we have already assumed several things about the interface. We assumed from the beginning that TicTacToe is mouse-driven, and that the user has some way to issue simple commands.

There is also a lot we do not know. Exactly what does the game look like? How are the "quit" and "new game" commands issued? What feedback does the game provide and how is this information communicated to the user? Before we begin implementing, we need to answer some of these questions.

The answers to these questions will certainly have an impact on the implementation of the program, but they may also influence the design stage as well. Although this case study discusses the user interface after the internal design, we could have started the user interface design before even thinking about the internal architecture. The interface design generally occurs in parallel with the other parts of the design.

Because the interface is such an important part of an interactive program, the requirements of the interface can often drive the design. Thinking about the physical layout or the user model of the interface can even help identify objects in the system. Discussing how the user interacts with a system should be an integral part of a CRC-based design discussion. It is fair to say that many of the choices we made earlier in this chapter were influenced by preconceived ideas about how the final interface might look or behave. Such decisions might have been more difficult if we had been inventing a completely new game.

The TicTacToe user interface presents a surprisingly interesting challenge for such a simple game. Many computer programs have no parallels outside the computer environment in which they run. However, tic-tac-toe is a well known game and users are sure to approach an electronic version with certain expectations. It seems important for the game to make the transition from a simple pencil and paper game to the computer in a natural way.

The traditional tic-tac-toe game is very easy to play. It requires no special setup and can be played almost anywhere. All that is necessary is that the players be able to make simple marks on some surface. It has virtually no overhead of any kind, which may be one reason the game has remained popular for so long. It would be very easy to destroy the game's simplicity by developing a program that is too "computer-like," and thereby lose the essential appeal of the game.

On the other hand, literally trying to duplicate the original game on the computer is likely to fail. The computer screen is a different medium than pencil and paper. Often, techniques that work well on paper do not seem natural when transferred unchanged to the computer screen. Besides, if the computer version is truly the same as the original game, the user will have no reason to use relatively expensive computing resources instead of a scratch-pad.

With these concerns in mind, let's start by specifying some overall design goals for the interface:

- TicTacToe should be designed so that a player does not have to learn new ways to perform simple functions. The player should be able to apply his or her experience with the original tic-tac-toe game to this version.

- Controls should be immediately understandable. Tic-tac-toe is a simple game; the user should not be confused by a complex layout or controls.

- While drawing on the heritage of the original game, the game should take advantage of the fact that it is running on a computer.

- Because we have already decided that the game will be implemented in Motif, the visual design and interaction style should be consistent with Motif guidelines.

- The visual design should exploit the capabilities of Motif and provide a pleasing appearance for the program.

- The game should incorporate transition effects and otherwise respond in a way that provides an enjoyable experience for the user. The game should be fun to play.

## Handling Input

The biggest difference between playing tic-tac-toe on paper and on a computer lies in the way input must be handled. On paper, the players simply make moves by drawing Xs and Os with a pencil. A new game can be started by simply drawing a new grid, and the players can stop playing by crumpling the paper and throwing it in the trash. So, the first major issue to be resolved is to determine how these actions, or their equivalents, should be handled in the computerized version.

The original problem statement suggested that the user should be able to make a move by clicking on a square. While this approach seems reasonable, there are other possibilities that are worth considering. For example we could place two buttons below each square in the tic-tac-toe grid, one to mark the square as an X and the other to mark the square as an O. Allowing the user to select the type of mark they wish to make would allow the program to support a multi-player game, something we have not considered so far.

Figure 4.12 shows a proposed visual layout based on this idea, using a *storyboard* format. A storyboard is a sequence of drawings that shows different states of the program, much like the panels of a cartoon. Storyboards attempt to convey the actions that take place between the program and the user, and can be thought of as a simple movie script. The figure on the left shows the game as the user would first see it. The picture on the right shows how the user can make a move by pushing a button below the desired square.

The interface shown in Figure 4.12 is inadequate in many ways. The screen looks very cluttered, with many small duplicate buttons. The large number of buttons detracts from the overall look. In fact, this layout seems to have lost the familiar look of the traditional tic-tac-toe game. The board is not immediately recognizable as tic-tac-toe. The Xs and Os are also very close together, and the user could accidently choose the wrong one. Worse, it is difficult to be sure whether the middle row of buttons applies to the squares above or below.

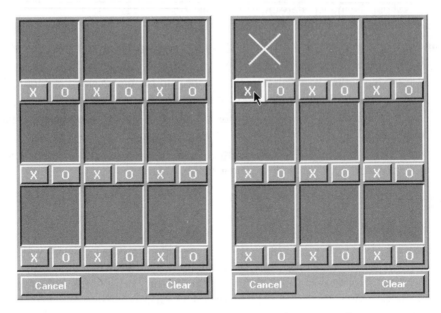

**Figure 4.12**  An early interface design that uses buttons to choose moves.

Another possible approach that addresses some of these problems is to use a "drag and drop" user interface model. The rows of buttons in the previous interface could be replaced by a pair of icons along the bottom of the playing area. The user could make a move by pressing the mouse over the icon that represents the desired mark, dragging the object to the desired square and releasing.

Figure 4.13 shows an artist's conception of this interface, using another simple storyboard.In the figure on the left, the user selects an X from a "bin" of Xs. The user then drags the X to the desired square, as shown on the right, causing an "X" to be displayed in that square (lower left).

This interface has some potential. Drag and drop interfaces can be fun to use, which meets one of the original goals. If one of the players is the computer itself, the game could display a simple animation to allow the user to watch the opposing move taking place. The drag and drop interface also solves several of the problems found in the previous design. For example, there is less ambiguity about which square is being marked. The layout of the game board is also more recognizable as tic-tac-toe.

However, this approach has several problems, too. Perhaps the most fundamental problem is that the model is quite different from the way the traditional game is played. Many games involve picking up pieces to be placed on a board, but tic-tac-toe is not one of them.[3] A first-time user would probably not know how to make the first move. Furthermore, because the version of Motif used in this book does not support drag and drop, this interface would require a relatively large amount of effort to implement.

---

[3]  Days before completing this book, I received a tic-tac-toe game as a Christmas gift. As if to deliberately contradict the statement above, the game consists of a board with nine recessed holes and a bin that contains two colors of marbles. Players must pick the pieces from the bin and place them on the board, just like a drag and drop interface.

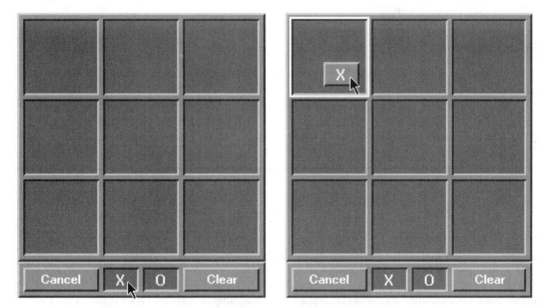

**Figure 4.13**  A drag and drop model.

Another common user model is an explicit selection model. When using an explicit selection interface, the user is expected to select an object, and then choose an operation to be performed on that object. This can be done in one of two ways. If we choose the *noun-verb* model, the user chooses the object (the "noun") first, and then chooses the action (the "verb") to be performed on that object. The other model is the *verb-noun* approach. Here, the user chooses the action using buttons, a menu, or some other mechanism, and then chooses the object to which that action is to apply. Motif, as well as most other popular user interface styles, tends to favor the noun-verb model.

Applying the explicit selection model to TicTacToe, the user could select a square using the mouse, and then mark that square by selecting a menu item or clicking on a button. The noun-verb explicit selection interface model works well in many situations. However, after some consideration, it does not seem right for tic-tac-toe. The process seems time-consuming and clumsy compared to the non-computerized version.

While all of these approaches are feasible, and all have been used in various applications, they all seem too clumsy for TicTacToe. The most straightforward interface would allow the user to simply click on a square to make a move. In this model, selecting a square would be similar to the action of pressing a button. Motif allows users to abort a command by moving the sprite outside an armed button before releasing the mouse button. The action of selecting a square should follow the same model. Providing feedback that a square is "armed" and about to be selected would be useful as well. In this respect, the squares should mimic Motif buttons, and could perhaps be implemented as Motif pushbutton widgets.

## Providing User Feedback

It is important for any interactive program to provide effective feedback to the user about the program's current state, the effect (or potential effect) of user actions, and so on. The previous section already raised some issues about feedback and presentation in TicTacToe, but there are still more issues to be addressed.

One question involves feedback about which squares are still available for moves. What should happen if the user tries to select a square that has already been marked? One simple approach is to just ignore the move and issue a warning. The warning could be a printed message, an error dialog, or maybe just a "beep." Another approach is to disable input in squares that have already been marked. If input is disallowed, the game should provide some indication that the squares cannot be chosen. Some interfaces highlight available input areas in some way as the mouse cursor moves over the command area. Notice the difference between these two approaches. The first allows incorrect moves, but tries to recover afterwards. The second tries to prevent the user from making an illegal move from the beginning.

It is interesting to realize that the program already provides one type of feedback. We can assume that marked squares already display an X or an O. Why is it necessary to provide any other additional feedback? In traditional tic-tac-toe, there is nothing other than common sense (and the other player's watchful eye!) to prevent a player from erasing or writing over the top of an already-marked square.

There are several reasons why additional feedback might be desirable. First, all programs need to anticipate deliberate or accidental illegal moves. If a programmer ignores the possibility of incorrect input, the application may become confused and crash. At a minimum, "user friendly" programs should detect an error, inform the user, and proceed. Second, it is often useful to give the user redundant feedback to reinforce the fact that only unmarked squares can be marked. Providing feedback about available moves allows the program to guide and advise about the rules of the game. Finally, providing this type of feedback helps fulfill one of the original goals: the program should be fun to use. A program that is responsive and provides constant feedback to the user is usually more enjoyable to use than a more passive program.

We also need to decide how to provide feedback when one player wins the game. In traditional tic-tac-toe, the winner draws a line through the winning squares. Should the computer version do the same? It seems reasonable, but there are alternatives. One approach would be to change the background color of the winning squares. This would only work correctly on color displays, although inverse video could be used on monochrome displays. An alternative would be to highlight the squares by drawing a border around each square. All Motif widgets support `XmNborderColor` and `XmNborderWidth` resources that could be used to indicate the winning squares. This approach could be used with both color and monochrome displays. Displaying the winning squares automatically, using some type of highlight seems like a simple enhancement to the pencil and paper version of the game that could be more visually appealing.

## Conclusions

Let's recap the decisions made in the previous sections. We decided that the interface should be mouse driven, and that the user indicates a move by clicking on a square. The squares should offer the ability to abort a move, in a manner consistent with Motif button widgets. We also decided that the game should provide some form of additional feedback about which squares are still available for future moves. The game should either not allow illegal moves, or report an error after the illegal move occurs. Finally, the game should use Motif's ability to highlight widget borders to indicate the appropriate sequence of squares when a player wins the game. An audible indication might be used to announce a winner as well.

Some of these decisions identify additional responsibilities for various objects in the game, and the class cards should be updated to reflect these. However, some of the issues considered in this section go beyond the scope of the class cards. These are either too detailed to fit on a card, or can be more properly categorized as implementation details.

Figure 4.14 shows an artist's conceptual drawing of the final TicTacToe interface in a storyboard format.

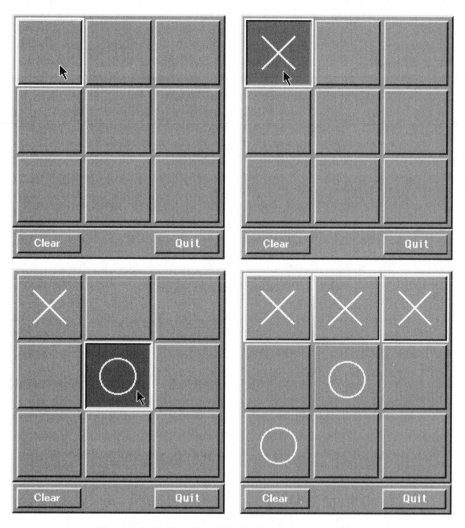

**Figure 4.14** The final TicTacToe interface design.

In this design, the TicTacToe grid consists of raised buttons that depress when selected. The "undo" capability, suggested by the Cancel button shown in earlier designs has been eliminated. The two command buttons are now labeled "Clear" and "Quit". The first command clears the board and starts a new game, while the second exits the game. Finally, the area between the two command buttons seems like a reasonable place to display messages to the user, if needed.

The upper right panel in Figure 4.14 shows the game as it first appears on the screen. All squares are selectable, and the user gets to make the first move. As the user moves the mouse cursor over the available squares, a highlighted border appears to indicate that the square is available. The image in the upper right shows a square as it is being selected and marked with an X. The square appears to be pushed into the screen as the user selects the square. The lower left image shows the game as an O is being marked. This storyboard assumes that the game can support two players, although a single-player game would be similar. According to the original plan for a single-player game, the O squares would be marked by the game itself. Finally, the figure in the lower right shows the game after X has won. The row of Xs is highlighted by a white border around the squares.

The discussion in this section is far from being a complete analysis and design of the visual and interactive characteristics of the TicTacToe user interface. Although we have identified several issues and made some basic decisions, the final test of any interface is how it feels once it is completed. The next step is to build the program, and then re-evaluate the interface. Sometimes, decisions that sound good on paper simply don't work in the final program. Also, it is likely that additional ideas and issues will emerge during implementation. Like software, good user interfaces usually require many rounds of design, testing, and evaluation and even more issues will become apparent once an initial prototype is available. For best results, the evaluation should include people trained in user interface design, and perhaps even more important, a cross-section of typical users.

## 4.6  Summary

This chapter presented a design for a simple computer version of the well known tic-tac-toe game. The exercise began with a simple problem statement, and used the simple object-oriented design approach introduced in Chapter 3 to identify objects and design a suitable collection of classes.

Designing the user interface is an important part of developing an interactive application. This chapter examined a few of the issues raised while designing TicTacToe's user interface, and explored a series of user models that could be used. The design of the user interface can influence the internal design of a system, and often provides clues about what objects and classes are needed.

Chapter 5 presents an implementation of TicTacToe based on the design developed in this chapter.

# TicTacToe: Implementation

This chapter presents an implementation of a tic-tac-toe game based on the design developed in the previous chapter. The task consists of implementing C++ classes that meet the requirements discussed in Chapter 5, and determining exactly how these classes fit together to create a working program. Before discussing the implementation of each class in TicTacToe, let's look at some issues related to the overall structure of the game. The collaboration graph in Chapter 4 showed all classes in the program as part of a TicTacToe subsystem. Chapter 4 described the subsystem as just a convenient and useful way to view the system for the purposes of the design. However, now that we are ready to begin implementing these classes, is there any reason to consider implementing a class that encapsulates the entire game? Perhaps.

Following the approach introduced in Chapter 2, each user interface object in the game is derived from the UIComponent class and forms a widget subtree. The question of how to tie these various subtrees together naturally arises. Each component manages its own collection of widgets, but what manages all the components? The main body of the game could create the necessary container widgets to manage all the various components. But an equally attractive idea is to create a single component that creates the widget infrastructure that ties all the components together.

We also need to decide how the various objects communicate with each other. For example, the GameBoard object needs to be able to call the Engine object's member functions. To do this, the GameBoard object needs a pointer to an Engine object. In the Stopwatch example described in Chapter 2, we connected the various components by passing pointers to objects in the various constructors. We could use the same approach for TicTacToe as well. Another approach is to make the objects in TicTacToe globally accessible. The main body of the program could instantiate an

Engine object that is globally available as `theEngine`, a GameBoard object referred to as `theGameBoard`, and so on. However, in some systems, we might wish to have two or more collections of objects that work independently. For example, consider the program with two Stopwatch panels shown in Chapter 2. In such a system, we cannot connect both subsystems using global variables.

Even in TicTacToe, it would not be hard to imagine an enhanced version of the program that supports multiple games that run simultaneously. Each instance of the game would need to refer to its own Engine object, which could not be handled by a global variable. Also, hard-coding a reference to `theEngine` inside the GameBoard class would compromise any potential for reuse this class might have. The GameBoard class could potentially be useful in other games, and it would not be wise to make the class require a particular global variable.

The approach used here is to define a TicTacToe class that encapsulates all the major objects in the system, and establishes the various connections between objects. The TicTacToe class provides access functions that allow the various objects to retrieve other objects indirectly. For example, when the GameBoard object needs to call an Engine member function, it refers to the Engine object contained by the TicTactoe object. This approach does not solve all problems, as there are still dependencies between classes. However, this approach at least defines a central location through which all connections are made.

We can now look at the implementation of each class in TicTacToe. The number of classes has already grown by at least one, the TicTacToe class, and responsibilities or additional classes that were not anticipated during the design phase may also be discovered during the implementation.

## 5.1    The TicTacToe Class

The previous section suggested a new TicTacToe class that serves two purposes: to provide a widget framework that groups and manages all the other components, and to serve as a central connection point between all objects in the system. The TicTacToe class can be declared as follows:

```
1    ////////////////////////////////////////////////////////////////
2    // TicTacToe.h: TicTacToe subsystem that encapsulates all
3    //              major components of the game
4    ////////////////////////////////////////////////////////////////
5    #ifndef TICTACTOE_H
6    #define TICTACTOE_H
7    #include "UIComponent.h"
8
9    class GameBoard;
10   class Message;
11   class Command;
12   class Engine;
13
14   class TicTacToe: public UIComponent {
```

```
15
16      protected:
17
18          // Pointers to the major UIComponents of TicTacToe
19
20          GameBoard    *_gameBoard;
21          Message      *_msgArea;
22          Command      *_commandArea;
23          Engine       *_engine;
24
25      public:
26
27          TicTacToe ( Widget, char * );
28          virtual ~TicTacToe();
29
30          // Access functions for each object in the game
31
32          GameBoard    *gameBoard()    const { return ( _gameBoard );    }
33          Message      *messageArea()  const { return ( _msgArea );      }
34          Command      *commandArea()  const { return ( _commandArea ); }
35          Engine       *engine()       const { return ( _engine );       }
36          virtual const char* const className() { return  ( "TicTacToe" ); }
37      };
38      #endif
```

The TicTacToe class is derived from UIComponent. In addition to the inherited members of UIComponent, the TicTacToe class supports a pointer to an instance of each major object in the game. Objects encapsulated by an instance of TicTacToe can access the other components of the game through inline member functions that return the appropriate instance.

The file TicTacToe.C contains the TicTacToe member function definitions. The constructor instantiates each of the objects used in the game. It also creates an XmForm widget that serves as a parent widget for all other components and manages the overall layout of the game. The constructor is somewhat lengthy because of the many XmForm constraint resources that must be specified.

```
1   ///////////////////////////////////////////////////////////////
2   // TicTacToe.C: TicTacToe subsystem that encapsulates all
3   //              major components of the game
4   ///////////////////////////////////////////////////////////////
5   #include "TicTacToe.h"
6   #include "GameBoard.h"
7   #include "Engine.h"
8   #include "Command.h"
9   #include "Message.h"
10  #include <Xm/Form.h>
11  #include <Xm/Separator.h>
12
13  TicTacToe::TicTacToe ( Widget parent, char *name ) : UIComponent( name )
14  {
```

```
15      // Create the driving engine for the game
16
17      _engine = new Engine ( this );
18
19      // Create a form to hold all other widgets
20
21      _w = XtCreateWidget ( _name,
22                            xmFormWidgetClass,
23                            parent, NULL, 0 );
24
25      installDestroyHandler();
26
27      // Separate the commands from the message area
28
29      Widget sep = XtCreateManagedWidget ( "commandSeparator",
30                                           xmSeparatorWidgetClass,
31                                           _w,
32                                           NULL, 0 );
33
34      // Create the widgets for the UI Components
35
36      _msgArea     = new Message ( _w, "messages" );
37      _commandArea = new Command ( _w, this, "commands" );
38      _gameBoard   = new GameBoard ( _w, this, "gameBoard" );
39
40      // Set up all constraints
41
42      // The GameBoard is attached to the parent XmForm widget
43      // on the top and sides; to an XmSeparator on the bottom
44
45      XtVaSetValues ( _gameBoard->baseWidget(),
46                      XmNtopAttachment,    XmATTACH_FORM,
47                      XmNleftAttachment,   XmATTACH_FORM,
48                      XmNrightAttachment,  XmATTACH_FORM,
49                      XmNbottomWidget,     sep,
50                      XmNbottomAttachment, XmATTACH_WIDGET,
51                      NULL );
52
53      // Attach a separator widget to the top of the message area
54
55      XtVaSetValues ( sep,
56                      XmNtopAttachment,    XmATTACH_NONE,
57                      XmNleftAttachment,   XmATTACH_FORM,
58                      XmNrightAttachment,  XmATTACH_FORM,
59                      XmNbottomWidget,     _msgArea->baseWidget(),
60                      XmNbottomAttachment, XmATTACH_WIDGET,
61                      NULL );
62
63      // Attach the Message component to the separator,
```

```
64        // and span the width of the Form widget
65
66        XtVaSetValues ( _msgArea->baseWidget(),
67                        XmNtopAttachment,    XmATTACH_NONE,
68                        XmNleftAttachment,   XmATTACH_FORM,
69                        XmNrightAttachment,  XmATTACH_FORM,
70                        XmNbottomWidget,     _commandArea->baseWidget(),
71                        XmNbottomAttachment, XmATTACH_WIDGET,
72                        NULL );
73
74        // Attach the Command component to the top, left, and right
75        // sides of the form, so it floats along the top
76
77        XtVaSetValues ( _commandArea->baseWidget(),
78                        XmNtopAttachment,    XmATTACH_NONE,
79                        XmNleftAttachment,   XmATTACH_FORM,
80                        XmNrightAttachment,  XmATTACH_FORM,
81                        XmNbottomAttachment, XmATTACH_FORM,
82                        NULL );
83
84        // Manage the widgets for all subcomponents, so that managing
85        // the TicTacToe base widget displays everything
86
87        _commandArea->manage();
88        _gameBoard->manage();
89        _msgArea->manage();
90        _gameBoard->clear();
91
92    }
```

The TicTacToe constructor creates and connects four major objects used in TicTacToe, along with several supporting widgets. The first object to be created is an Engine. The Engine object does not have a user interface, but needs a pointer to a TicTacToe object to allow it to access the other objects in the game. The `this` pointer for the TicTacToe object is passed to the Engine constructor to provide a single connection point between the Engine object and the user interface components in the game.

The TicTacToe constructor creates an XmForm widget to contain and position all other components of the interface. These components, which are instances of the Message, Command, and GameBoard classes identified in the previous chapter, support independent widget trees. The TicTacToe constructor simply positions each component's base widgets to determine the overall layout of the game. Each of these components expect a pointer to the TicTacToe object as a way to tie them all together and bind them to the other objects in the game.

In Chapter 4, we suggested several layouts for the TicTacToe interface. The final interface design placed the command buttons and message area below the playing area, set off by a separator. The TicTacToe constructor tries to follow the suggested layout as closely as possible. The constraints specified in the constructor attach the GameBoard to the top, left, and right sides of the form, and attach an XmSeparator widget below the game board. This is exactly as decided in Chapter 4.

The proposed layout of the command and message areas poses a slight problem. There is a basic conflict between the visual layout specified in Chapter 4 and the implementation strategy based on the UIComponent class. To place the message area (implemented by the Message class) between the two buttons in the command panel (implemented by the Command class), the Message object would have to be part of the Command widget tree. Classes derived from UIComponent, as described in Chapter 2, represent subtrees within the widget hierarchy. It isn't possible to have UIComponent objects that cross widget trees.

So, how can the Message component exist in the middle of the Command component? There are several solutions. One approach would be to attach the Message object to the bottom of the Form, and attempt to float it in the middle of the two buttons. This layout could be made to work by carefully specifying the fonts and controlling the length of the messages displayed in the message area. But this is a very questionable approach. Depending on various user-definable resources, the message area could overlap the buttons, or vice versa.

Another solution is to encapsulate the Message object inside the Command object. This would tie these two classes together, which seems like a debatable decision. Currently, the Message class is completely self-sufficient, making it a highly reusable class. Establishing a link between the Command and Message classes would reduce the modularity of the design, which seems like a great price to pay just to achieve a specific screen layout. On the other hand, many applications need to issue commands and display status messages. We could reconsider the original design and create a CommandPanel class that supports not only buttons, but also an area for messages.

However, there are other simple alternatives. We can attach the Command object to the bottom of the TicTacToe form widget, and place the Message object between the Command object and the XmSeparator widget. This differs only slightly from the final layout specified in Chapter 4, and maintains the separate identity of the Command and Message objects. This layout also provides more room for messages.

Figure 5.1 shows the layout of TicTacToe at the component level. An XmForm widget serves as a container for the other components of the game. The GameBoard occupies the upper portion of the window. The Message and Command components are located at the bottom of the XmForm, separated from the GameBoard by an XmSeparator widget.

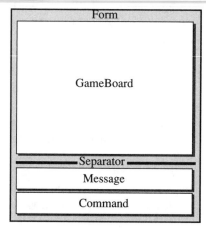

**Figure 5.1** TicTacToe's component layout.

The TicTacToe destructor simply deletes the objects created by the constructor. The UIComponent destructor destroys the XmForm widget, which destroys the XmSeparator widget created by the TicTacToe constructor as well.

```
93   TicTacToe::~TicTacToe()
94   {
95       delete _gameBoard;
96       delete _msgArea;
97       delete _commandArea;
98       delete _engine;
99   }
```

## 5.2   The GameBoard Class

The GameBoard class is derived from the UIComponent class. It creates the familiar tic-tac-toe grid and implements the responsibilities listed on the GameBoard class card in Figure 4.1. The GameBoard component is the most complex part of the TicTacToe user interface. It acts as both an input and an output device. It not only displays Xs and Os, but according to the interface design in Chapter 4, provides additional visual feedback about available moves, winning moves, and so on.

The file GameBoard.h contains the GameBoard class declaration:

```
1   ///////////////////////////////////////////////////////////
2   // GameBoard.h: A tic-tac-toe board
3   ///////////////////////////////////////////////////////////
4   #ifndef GAMEBOARD_H
5   #define GAMEBOARD_H
6
7   #include <Xm/Xm.h>
8   #include "UIComponent.h"
9
10   class TicTacToe;
11
12   class GameBoard: public UIComponent {
13
14     private:
15
16       void mark ( int ); // Handle user marking a square
17
18       // Callbacks registered with widgets in the grid
19
20       static void markCallback ( Widget, XtPointer, XtPointer );
21       static void drawXCallback ( Widget, XtPointer, XtPointer );
22       static void drawOCallback ( Widget, XtPointer, XtPointer );
23
```

```
24    protected:
25
26      Widget      _grid[9];             // 3 X 3 square of buttons
27      GC          _gc;
28      int         _gridSize;            // Size of each square
29      TicTacToe * _game;
30      Pixel       _highlightColor;      // Color of border when in
31                                        // an active square
32      Pixel       _noHighlightColor;    // Border color of inactive squares
33      Dimension   _shadowThickness;     // Default shadow width of a square
34
35      // Methods for refreshing the squares and getting input
36
37      virtual void drawX ( Widget );
38      virtual void drawO ( Widget );
39
40      // Override destruction hook, so we can free the GC if needed
41
42      void widgetDestroyed();
43
44    public:
45
46      GameBoard ( Widget, TicTacToe *, char * );
47      virtual ~GameBoard();
48      void highlightSquare ( int square );     // Highlight single square
49      void deemphasizeSquare ( int square );   // Fade square to 2D
50      void activateSquare ( int square );      // Allow input to square
51      void deactivateSquare ( int square );    // Shut off input
52      virtual void markO ( int square );       // Put an X in the square
53      virtual void markX ( int square );       // Put an O in the square
54      void clear();                            // Clear and reset board
55      virtual const char *const className() { return ( "GameBoard" ); }
56    };
57
58    #endif
```

The GameBoard class' public interface includes functions for marking a square as an X or an O, highlighting an individual square, and clearing the entire board. It also supports member functions that activate and deactivate squares to indicate whether or not they can accept input. The protected and private portions of the class define various callbacks and member functions that display and maintain the Xs and Os on the screen, and also handle input from the user.

One of the first decisions that must be made before implementing the GameBoard class is what widgets to use to implement a grid. There are several possible choices. For example, we could draw the tic-tac-toe grid on a single window. Because a tic-tac-toe grid consists of only four lines, drawing the grid would be very easy. However, input handling would be more complex because we would have to determine compute which square corresponds to various *x,y* positions. In addition, the visual design in Chapter 4 described a more visually complex grid than just four crossing lines. It is usually easier to implement different input areas with individual widgets. Using individual widgets for each square in the tic-tac-toe grid also makes the output easier, because each square can just display a single X or an O.

Possible widget choices include the various button widgets, the XmLabel widget, or even the XmDrawingArea widget. The XmLabel widget supports an `XmNlabelPixmap` resource, which could be used to display an X or O pixmap. However, the XmLabel widget does not support input except through event handlers. The XmPushButton widget can also be used the same way, and it supports various callbacks that could be used for input. The XmDrawingArea also supports various input callbacks, and provides callbacks that allow programs to redraw the contents of the XmDrawingArea widget when the widget receives an `Expose` event.

All of these choices seem like reasonable possibilities. However, the visual design discussion in Chapter 4 indicates the need for a very flexible display. The squares need to be able to respond like buttons, display symbols like an XmDrawingArea, and also provide support for different visual effects. One of the most flexible Motif widgets that fits this description is the XmDrawnButton widget. The XmDrawnButton widget behaves much like the XmPushButton widget, but allows the program to display arbitrary images in the widget. The XmDrawnButton widget also supports several different types of shadows, which can be used to provide different visual effects.

Next, we need to choose a manager widget to arrange the XmDrawnButton widgets into the tic-tac-toe grid. The XmRowColumn widget seems like a natural choice because the tic-tac-toe game board consists of rows and columns. The XmRowColumn widget is a good choice for this type of layout whenever all children are the same height.

Other possibilities include the XmForm widget and the XmBulletinBoard widget. The XmForm widget would allow the board to be resized dynamically - something the XmRowColumn widget does not support. However, setting up various constraint resources to create a tic-tac-toe grid would be complicated. The XmBulletinBoard forces the program to specify the precise position of each child, and also does not handle resizing. The XmRowColumn widget seems to be the simplest choice.

The GameBoard constructor takes three arguments, a widget to be used as the parent of this component's base widget, a pointer to a TicTacToe object, and a name, which is passed to the UIComponent constructor. The constructor creates an XmRowColumn widget and nine XmDrawn-Button widgets. The XmRowColumn widget is configured to manage the XmDrawnButton widgets in a square 3 by 3 grid. The constructor is written as:

```
1    ////////////////////////////////////////////////////////////
2    // GameBoard.C: A tic-tac-toe board
3    ////////////////////////////////////////////////////////////
4    #include "TicTacToe.h"
5    #include "GameBoard.h"
6    #include "Engine.h"
7    #include <Xm/RowColumn.h>
8    #include <Xm/DrawnB.h>
9
10   GameBoard::GameBoard ( Widget      parent,
11                          TicTacToe *game,
12                          char       *name' ) : UIComponent ( name )
13   {
14       int      i;
```

```
15        XGCValues values;
16
17        _game     = game;
18        _gridSize = 100;
19
20        // Create an XmRowColumn widget to manage a 3 X 3
21        // grid of widgets
22
23        _w = XtVaCreateWidget ( name, xmRowColumnWidgetClass, parent,
24                                 XmNnumColumns, 3,
25                                 XmNpacking,    XmPACK_COLUMN,
26                                 XmNadjustLast, FALSE,
27                                 NULL );
28        installDestroyHandler ();
29
30        // Create a grid of 9 XmDrawnButton widgets
31        // Store the index of each widget's position in the grid
32        // so it can be used to identify the widget's position later
33
34        for ( i = 0; i < 9; i++ )
35        {
36            _grid[i] = XtVaCreateWidget ( "xo",
37                                          xmDrawnButtonWidgetClass, _w,
38                                          XmNuserData,            i,
39                                          XmNrecomputeSize,       FALSE,
40                                          XmNpushButtonEnabled, TRUE,
41                                          XmNshadowType,   XmSHADOW_OUT,
42                                          XmNwidth,         _gridSize,
43                                          XmNheight,        _gridSize,
44                                          NULL );
45
46            // Get user input to mark a square
47
48            XtAddCallback ( _grid[i],
49                            XmNactivateCallback,
50                            &GameBoard::markCallback,
51                            ( XtPointer ) this );
52        }
53
54        XtManageChildren ( _grid, 9 );
55
56        // Get the background color of the rowcolumn widget,
57        // to be used to effectively shut off highlight-on-enter
58
59        XtVaGetValues ( _w, XmNbackground, &_noHighlightColor, NULL );
60
61        // Get the GC needed to display the Xs and Os
62        // and retrieve and save the normal highlight color
63        // Use the color of the first widget in the grid
```

```
64      XtVaGetValues ( _grid[0], XmNforeground,      &values.foreground,
65                                 XmNhighlightColor, &_highlightColor,
66                                 XmNshadowThickness, &_shadowThickness,
67                                 NULL );
68
69      _gc = XtGetGC ( _grid[0], GCForeground, &values );
70  }
```

The GameBoard constructor initializes a variable that determines the size of each square to 100 pixels, and stores a pointer to the TicTacToe object that encapsulates the GameBoard object. The constructor then creates an XmRowColumn widget configured to support a rectangular grid consisting of three columns and three rows. Setting the XmNadjustLast resource to FALSE prevents the XmRowColumn widget from stretching the last row of children when the widget is resized. The UIComponent::installDestroyHandler() function sets up the XmNdestroyCallback function for the XmRowColumn widget.

A for loop on line 34 creates each of the nine squares in the tic-tac-toe grid. Each square is implemented as an XmDrawnButton widget, set to be _gridSize pixels wide and _gridSize pixels high. The constructor also configures the given widget as a selectable square in the game board.

On line 48, the constructor registers a single XmNactivateCallback function with each XmDrawnButton widget. The markCallback() function will be called when the user clicks the mouse in any widget in the grid. Notice that the constructor specifies the GameBoard object's this pointer as client data for the callback, as usual. The callback needs a pointer to the instance to call the appropriate member functions. However, because the GameBoard uses a single callback for all squares in the grid, we also need some way to uniquely identify which square the user has activated. Ordinarily, passing the index as client data would be an easy way to identify the square. Because the client data argument is being used to pass the object pointer, this option is not available.

This can be handled in several different ways. We could register separate callback functions for each button, but this would require nine nearly identical callback functions. We could determine the square by searching the _grid array and compare each widget in the grid to the one passed to the callback, or we could store the corresponding index into the array in each widget's XmNuserData resource. We will use the latter approach here and simply retrieve the value of the XmNuserData resource from the widget for which the callback is invoked.

The constructor concludes by managing the widgets in the grid, and creating a *graphics context* (GC) that can be used when drawing the Xs and Os. A graphics context is a resource, maintained by the server, that describes various attributes to be used by X graphics functions. A graphics context describes the foreground and background colors, line width, font, and so on. (See [Scheifler90] for information about graphics contexts.)

The function

```
GC XtGetGC ( Widget widget, XtGCMask mask, XGCValues *values )
```

creates a cached graphics context, using the given widget to determine the screen with which the GC will be used. The mask argument specifies which members of the XGCValues structure contain valid data. Cached GCs should be freed when they are no longer needed, using the function:

```
XtReleaseGC ( Widget widget, GC gc )
```

The graphics context created by the GameBoard constructor uses the foreground of the first button in the grid, on the assumption that all squares in the grid will have the same color. The constructor also retrieves the background color of the GameBoard's base widget, as well as the shadow thickness and highlight color of the first widget in the grid. These values will be used to turn on and off the highlight-on-enter feature, and provide other visual effects as explained later.

The GameBoard destructor releases the graphics context, if the widget still exists.

```
71  GameBoard::~GameBoard()
72  {
73      if ( _w != NULL )
74          XtReleaseGC ( _w, _gc );
75  }
```

Notice that there is a potential problem if the GameBoard object's base widget is destroyed before the GameBoard object itself. Because XtReleaseGC() requires a widget as the first argument, the destructor cannot free the GC if the component's base widget has already been destroyed. We can solve this problem by overriding the widgetDestroyed() member function defined by the UIComponent base class. The GameBoard::widgetDestroyed() member function releases the graphics context while the widget still exists, just before setting the object's _w member to NULL.

```
76  void GameBoard::widgetDestroyed()
77  {
78      if ( _w != NULL )
79          XtReleaseGC ( _w, _gc );
80      _w  = NULL;
81  }
```

The markX() and markO() methods provide a programmatic interface that allows other objects to mark an X or an O in a square in the GameBoard grid. These methods are very similar. Both must be given a position in the grid (0 - 8) in which to display an X or an O. The appropriate mark is recorded by registering one of drawOCallback() or drawXCallback() as an XmNexposeCallback for the specified widget. Functions on this callback list are called whenever the XmDrawnButton widget's window needs to be redrawn, so once a callback is registered, that square will continue to display the corresponding mark.

Notice that before adding the callback, both methods remove any previously registered XmNexposeCallback functions. It is important to be very careful when using XtRemoveAll-Callbacks(). Removing all callbacks may remove callbacks installed elsewhere, perhaps even internally by the widget. In this case, the XmDrawnButton does not register any XmNexpose-Callback functions. In fact, it would be rare for any widget to register a callback to handle exposures. However, in other cases, carelessly removing all callback functions could lead to unexpected results

If the widget is realized, the appropriate figure must be displayed in the window immediately. The safest way to accomplish this task is to call XClearArea() to clear the widget's window and generate an `Expose` event. Calling the Xlib function `XClearArea()` with zero width and height (fifth and sixth arguments) clears the entire window. Setting the last argument to TRUE requests the X server to generate an `Expose` event for that window, which will cause the newly registered callback to be invoked.

The `markX()` and `markO()` functions also change the visual style of the XmDrawnButton widget that represents the given square. Unmarked squares look and act like Motif XmPushButton widgets, to indicate that they can be selected. When a square is marked as an X or an O, the `markX()` or `markO()` function disables pushbutton behavior by calling `deactivateSquare()`. This implements one of the goals established in Chapter 4. According to the user interface design, the game should provide additional feedback to the user about what squares are selectable, in addition to displaying an X or an O. Deactivated squares are no longer selectable, and therefore do not look like pushbuttons. The change in the visual appearance also adds some additional sense of animation to the interface.

```
82   void GameBoard::markX ( int position )
83   {
84       // Remove any previous callbacks, add one to draw
85       // an X and then trigger an Expose event to
86       // display the X in this square
87
88       XtRemoveAllCallbacks ( _grid[position], XmNexposeCallback );
89
90       deactivateSquare ( position );
91
92       XtAddCallback ( _grid[position],
93                       XmNexposeCallback,
94                       &GameBoard::drawXCallback,
95                       ( XtPointer ) this );
96
97       if ( XtIsRealized ( _grid[position] ) )
98          XClearArea ( XtDisplay ( _grid[position] ),
99                       XtWindow ( _grid[position] ),
100                       0, 0, 0, 0, TRUE );
101  }

102  void GameBoard::markO ( int position )
103  {
104      // Remove any previous callbacks, add one to draw
105      // an O and then trigger an Expose event to
106      // display the O in this square
107
108      XtRemoveAllCallbacks ( _grid[position], XmNexposeCallback );
109
110      deactivateSquare ( position );
111
112      XtAddCallback ( _grid[position],
113                      XmNexposeCallback,
```

```
114                              &GameBoard::drawOCallback,
115                              ( XtPointer ) this );
116
117        if ( XtIsRealized ( _grid[position] ) )
118            XClearArea ( XtDisplay ( _grid[position] ),
119                         XtWindow ( _grid[position] ),
120                         0, 0, 0, 0, TRUE );
121    }
```

The drawXCallback() and drawOCallback() member functions are called when
Expose events occur in the widgets within the tic-tac-toe grid. These static member functions
retrieve the object pointer from the client data, and call the corresponding drawX() and drawO()
member functions.

```
122    void GameBoard::drawXCallback ( Widget     w,
123                                    XtPointer clientData,
124                                    XtPointer )
125    {
126        // Retrieve the GameBoard object
127
128        GameBoard *obj = ( GameBoard * ) clientData;
129
130        obj->drawX ( w );
131    }


132    void GameBoard::drawOCallback ( Widget     w,
133                                    XtPointer clientData,
134                                    XtPointer )
135    {
136        GameBoard *obj = ( GameBoard * ) clientData;
137
138        obj->drawO ( w );
139    }
```

The drawX() member function computes a bounding box that spans the region from 20% to
80% of the size of a single widget in the grid and draws lines between opposite corners of the
bounding box. This member function is virtual to allow subclasses to change the appearance of the
X.

```
140    void GameBoard::drawX ( Widget square )
141    {
142        // Draw the X across the widget
143
144        int left   = ( int ) ( 0.2 * _gridSize );
145        int top    = ( int ) ( 0.2 * _gridSize );
146        int right  = ( int ) ( 0.8 * _gridSize );
147        int bottom = ( int ) ( 0.8 * _gridSize );
148
```

```
149        XDrawLine ( XtDisplay ( square ),
150                    XtWindow ( square ),
151                    _gc,
152                    left, top, right, bottom );
153        XDrawLine ( XtDisplay ( square ),
154                    XtWindow ( square ),
155                    _gc,
156                    right, top, left, bottom );
157    }
```

The drawO() member function computes a bounding box appropriate for a circle and calls
XDrawArc() to display a circle (an "O") in the specified widget. Like drawX(), drawO() is a
virtual member function which allows subclasses to redefine how the O is drawn.

```
158    void GameBoard::drawO ( Widget square )
159    {
160        // Draw a circle that occupies 80% of the widget
161
162        int left   = ( int ) ( 0.2 * _gridSize );
163        int top    = ( int ) ( 0.2 * _gridSize );
164        int width  = ( int ) ( 0.6 * _gridSize );
165        int height = ( int ) ( 0.6 * _gridSize );
166
167        XDrawArc ( XtDisplay ( square ),
168                   XtWindow ( square ),
169                   _gc,
170                   left, top, width, height, 0, 360 * 64 );
171    }
```

The clear() member function removes all Xs and Os from the GameBoard. The function
must remove all XmNexposeCallback functions registered for the widgets in the grid, and must
also call XClearArea() to erase any current contents of the windows.

We could also call the Xlib function XClearWindow() to erase the contents of each square.
However, the Motif XmDrawnButton widget draws a shadow inside its window. If we clear the
entire window, the shadow will also be erased. If we use XClearArea(), the widget will receive
an Expose event and redraw the shadow after the window is cleared.

```
172    void GameBoard::clear()
173    {
174        int i;
175
176        // Each element of the grid may have a callback for an X
177        // or an O, so all callbacks must be removed
178
179        for ( i = 0; i < 9; i++ )
180        {
181            XtRemoveAllCallbacks ( _grid[i], XmNexposeCallback );
182
```

```
183              activateSquare ( i );
184
185              // Use XClearArea with exposure events requested
186              // so that the widget's shadow is redrawn
187
188              if ( XtIsRealized ( _grid[i] ) )
189                  XClearArea ( XtDisplay ( _grid[i] ),
190                               XtWindow ( _grid[i] ),
191                               0, 0, 0, 0, TRUE );
192          }
193  }
```

The user needs to be able to select a square by clicking on a XmDrawnButton in the grid with the mouse. This is handled by the markCallback() function. The GameBoard constructor registers this function as an XmNactivateCallback for each widget in the grid. The markCallback() function retrieves the grid index of the selected widget, and just calls the mark() member function.

```
194  void GameBoard::markCallback ( Widget      w,
195                                 XtPointer clientData,
196                                 XtPointer )
197  {
198      GameBoard *obj = (GameBoard *) clientData;
199      int index;
200
201      XtVaGetValues ( w, XmNuserData, &index, NULL );
202
203      obj->mark ( index );
204  }
```

When used as an input mechanism, the GameBoard does not interpret the input itself. The mark() member function just passes the user's request to mark a square onto the Engine object. The GameBoard cannot mark the square itself because it does not know the current state of the game. The function accesses the appropriate Engine object through the TicTacToe object associated with a particular GameBoard object. The index of the square that the user wants to mark is sent to the Engine object as an argument to the Engine::recordMove() function.

```
205  void GameBoard::mark ( int index )
206  {
207      _game->engine()->recordMove ( index );
208  }
```

Chapter 4 discussed the need to make the interface feel responsive, and to provide feedback about what squares are selectable and which are not. The functions activateSquare() and deactivateSquare() provide feedback by changing the shadow style and other attributes of a button. The activateSquare() function enables pushbutton behavior for the XmDrawnButton widget used by the GameBoard component. If the XmDrawnButton widget's XmNpushButtonEnabled resource is set to TRUE, the XmDrawnButton widget behaves like a Motif XmPushButton widget.

The activateSquare() member function also sets a widget's shadow type to XmSHAD-OW_OUT, which is the normal appearance of a Motif XmPushButton widget. To be sure the shadow is visible, activateSquare() also sets the shadow widget to its original width. Other functions may change this value.

```
209  void GameBoard::activateSquare ( int position )
210  {
211      // Make the button look active by setting the shadow
212      // type to normal, enabling pushbutton behavior, and
213      // turning on highlights when the mouse enters the square
214
215      XtVaSetValues( _grid[position],
216                     XmNpushButtonEnabled, TRUE,
217                     XmNshadowType,        XmSHADOW_OUT,
218                     XmNshadowThickness,   _shadowThickness,
219                     XmNhighlightColor,    _highlightColor,
220                     NULL );
221  }
```

Recall from Chapter 4 that the user interface design calls for squares to provide some feedback when they are selectable. We speculated that this feature could be implemented by highlighting the border of a widget when the pointer entered a square, or the square received input focus. The XmDrawnButton widget supports an XmNhighlightOnEnter resource, which, if set to TRUE, automatically highlights a widget when it receives input focus. So, the most straightforward way to implement the desired behavior is to set XmNhighlightOnEnter to TRUE in the activateSquare() function and set it to FALSE when the square is deactivated.

Unfortunately, things are not that simple, and there are two problems with this solution. First, some users may dislike the highlighting effect. This behavior causes a great deal of flashing on the screen that some users like, and others find annoying. It seems better to allow users to control the XmNhighlightOnEnter resource. On the other hand, we could insist that we are justified in forcing the use of highlight-on-enter because the game uses this feature to communicate important information.

However, there is another, slightly more complex problem. The deactivateSquare() function is called when the user selects a button, while the pointer is in a square. Therefore, if XmNhighlightOnEnter is TRUE (which it would be if the square was active), the square is in a highlighted state when deactivateSquare() is called. The deactivateSquare() function would then use XtSetValues() to set XmNhighlightOnEnter to FALSE.

This appears to be the correct approach, except for one small problem. The logic used in the Motif code that controls the highlighting works like this: If XmNhighlightOnEnter is TRUE when the pointer enters a widget, the widget is highlighted. If XmNhighlightOnEnter is TRUE when the pointer leaves the widget, the border is unhighlighted. In the approach we have been discussing, XmNhighlightOnEnter will be set to FALSE before the pointer can leave the widget. So a widget that has been marked, and therefore deactivated, can never be unhighlighted!

One could debate about whether this is a bug or a feature in Motif, but the answer would be irrelevant. To continue to make progress with TicTacToe, we must find some other way to achieve the desired effect. One approach would be to work around the problem by registering a callback or an event handler to detect when the pointer leaves the widget's window and turn highlight-on-enter off at that time. However, this is a lot of work, and when combined with the usability issue raised earlier, it seems as if a better and simpler approach is called for.

Fortunately, there is an easy solution. First, we will not force `XmNhighlightOnEnter` to `TRUE`. It could be set to `TRUE` in the application's app-defaults file, if desired, but the user should be able to control the value of this resource. Then, assuming that `XmNhighlightOnEnter` is normally enabled for all widgets in the grid, we can simply change a widget's `XmNhighlight-Color` to effectively turn highlight-on-enter on and off. The `activateSquare()` function sets the widget's `XmNhighlightColor` to the default highlight color used by the widget (which can be controlled by the user). The `deactivateSquare()` function sets the `XmNhighlight-Color` resource to the color of the GameBoard's base widget background color. In this mode, even if the square's highlighting is on, the user cannot see it. From the user's perspective, a square is only highlighted when the `XmNhighlightColor` resource is not set to the widget's background color. If the user does not like this behavior, it can be turned off by setting the `XmNhighlightOnEnter` resource to `FALSE` in a resource file.

The `deactivateSquare()` function reverses the effect of `activateSquare()`. The function turns off the XmDrawnButton widget's pushbutton behavior, and changes the shadow style to make the button appear to be recessed into the screen. Finally, the highlight color is set to the value of `_noHighlightColor`, which was retrieved from the base widget in the GameBoard constructor. With these resources set, a button appears to be recessed into the screen, does not respond to input, and does not highlight when the mouse pointer enters the square.

```
222   void GameBoard::deactivateSquare ( int position )
223   {
224       // Change a button to appear inactive by setting the shadow
225       // type so the button is depressed, disabling pushbutton
226       // behavior, and turning off the highlight-on-enter feature
227
228       XtVaSetValues ( _grid[position],
229                       XmNpushButtonEnabled, FALSE,
230                       XmNshadowType,        XmSHADOW_IN,
231                       XmNhighlightColor,    _noHighlightColor,
232                       NULL );
233
234   }
```

The Gameboard also needs to provide some way to indicate that a player has won the game. In Chapter 4, we decided that a winning sequence could be shown by highlighting the winning set of widgets. To support this feature, we can add a `highlightSquare()` member function, which highlights a single square.

There are several ways to highlight a widget. For example, we could set all borders to some initial thickness, and simply change the color to highlight the widget. Another approach would be to use the same highlight mechanism Motif uses to implement highlight-on-enter. We could programmatically highlight the winning squares, even though they don't have input focus. However, the only programmatic interface for highlighting widgets is a set of undocumented, internal functions. Calling these functions directly seems unwise.

Perhaps it would be a good idea to rethink this aspect of the interface. Do we really want to indicate the winning squares by coloring their borders? Relying on color may mean that the program does not work well on monochrome displays. Furthermore, if we color the border of the winning squares, the same visual feedback used to indicate that a square is the currently active square will also indicate that this is a winning square. Using the same or similar feedback for different purposes may be confusing and is best avoided.

An alternate solution takes advantage of the different types of shadows supported by the XmDrawnButton widget. We have already used the XmSHADOW_IN and XmSHADOW_OUT styles, but the XmDrawnButton also supports an XmSHADOW_ETCHED_OUT style that looks very much like a border around an otherwise flat widget. We can take advantage of these multiple shadow styles to indicate the winning squares with an "etched out" appearance. The effect is similar to the original idea, but sufficiently distinctive to prevent any confusion with the highlight-on-enter mechanism.

```
235  void GameBoard::highlightSquare ( int position )
236  {
237      // Emphasize a square by changing the shadow type
238
239      XtVaSetValues ( _grid[position],
240                      XmNshadowType,       XmSHADOW_ETCHED_OUT,
241                      XmNshadowThickness, 2 * _shadowThickness,
242                      NULL );
243  }
```

To further enhance the effect, the GameBoard supports a second member function, deemphasizeSquare() that sets a widget's shadow thickness to zero, effectively flattening the widget. When used in conjunction with the highlightSquare() member function, the deemphasizeSquare() function allows the Engine to make all squares fade into the background and accent the winning moves with a raised border. The final implementation differs slightly from the plan in Chapter 4, but the result is still visually effective.

```
244  void GameBoard::deemphasizeSquare ( int position )
245  {
246      // Make a square fade into the background by shutting
247      // off the Motif 3-D effect
248
249      XtVaSetValues ( _grid[position], XmNshadowThickness, 0, NULL );
250  }
```

This completes the implementation of the GameBoard class. Figure 5.2 shows two views of the completed GameBoard panel. On the left, all buttons are in their activated state, and the board is clear. The figure on the right shows the gameboard after the user has recorded an X in the middle square. In addition to displaying the X, the center square is deactivated, and appears to be depressed into the screen, indicating that it can no longer be selected.

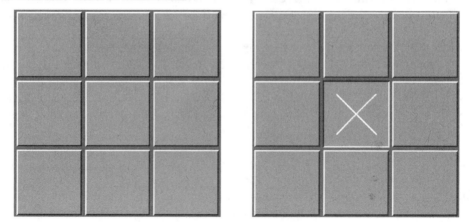

**Figure 5.2** The GameBoard user interface component

## 5.3   The Message Class

The Message class provides a way for messages to be posted to the user. This could be a non-trivial task. As discussed during the visual design of TicTacToe, there are many different types of messages that need to be displayed. Some need to be subtle and non-obtrusive, while others are important enough that we need to make sure the user sees and responds to them. However, for this implementation, the Message class is very simple. It creates a single XmLabel widget and displays strings in the widget upon request. Although the implementation is simple, we can replace the Message class with a more sophisticated mechanism later, if needed, because the implementation details of the class are completely hidden from the rest of the program.

In addition to the basic UIComponent protocol, the Message class supports two member functions: `postMessage()`, which displays a string, and `postAlert()`, which displays a string and also sounds a bell. The class structure is declared as:

```
1    /////////////////////////////////////////////////////////////
2    // Message.h: Display a string
3    /////////////////////////////////////////////////////////////
4    #ifndef MESSAGE_H
5    #define MESSAGE_H
6
7    #include "UIComponent.h"
8
9    class Message: public UIComponent {
10
11     public:
12
```

```
13      Message ( Widget, char * );
14      void postMessage ( char * );      // Display a simple string
15      void postAlert ( char *msg = NULL);
16      virtual const char * const className() { return ( "GameBoard" ); }
17    };
18    #endif
```

The Message constructor creates an XmLabel widget and installs the UIComponent's destruction handler function. It also calls its own `postMessage()` member function to initialize the message area to display an empty string. Without this step, the XmLabel widget would display the name of the widget when it first appears.

```
1     ///////////////////////////////////////////////////////
2     // Message.C: Manages a message panel
3     //             using an XmLabel widget
4     ///////////////////////////////////////////////////////
5     #include "Message.h"
6     #include <Xm/Xm.h>
7     #include <Xm/Label.h>
8     #include <assert.h>
9
10    Message::Message ( Widget parent, char * name ) : UIComponent( name )
11    {
12        _w = XmCreateLabel ( parent, _name, NULL, 0 );
13        installDestroyHandler();
14        postMessage ( " " );  // Clear the widget
15    }
```

The `postMessage()` member function creates a compound string from a character string passed as an argument and displays the string in the XmLabel widget.

```
16    void Message::postMessage ( char *msg )
17    {
18        assert ( _w );
19
20        // Convert the character string to a compound string for Motif
21
22        XmString xmstr = XmStringCreateSimple ( msg );
23
24        // Display the new label
25
26        XtVaSetValues ( _w, XmNlabelString, xmstr, NULL );
27
28        // XmLabel copies the string, so we can free our copy
29
30        XmStringFree ( xmstr );
31    }
```

When discussing the user interface in Chapter 4, we identified a need to notify the user that some messages were particularly important. One simple way to do this is to add a member function to the Message class that sounds a bell when displaying a message. The `postAlert()` member function calls the Xlib function `XBell()` to sound a short bell, and calls `postMessage()` to display the accompanying message, if one exists.

```
32   void Message::postAlert ( char *msg )
33   {
34       assert ( _w );   // Must have a widget to display message
35
36       if ( msg )
37           postMessage ( msg );   // Display the string
38
39       // Sound a bell as an alert.
40
41       XBell ( XtDisplay ( _w ), 100 );
42   }
```

# 5.4   The Command Class

The last user interface component to be implemented is the Command component. The Command class is a very simple component that creates two Motif XmPushButton widgets managed by an XmForm widget. Like the Message widget, the Command class has very few external dependencies, and could easily be re-implemented to present a different interface, or to add other commands.

The Command class defines the callback functions assigned to the pushbutton in the protected portion of the class, and also defines the member functions `quit()` and `newGame()`. The class is declared as follows:

```
1    //////////////////////////////////////////////////////////////
2    // Command.h
3    //////////////////////////////////////////////////////////////
4    #ifndef COMMAND_H
5    #define COMMAND_H
6
7    #include "UIComponent.h"
8
9    class TicTacToe;
10
11   class Command: public UIComponent {
12
13     private:
14
15       static void newGameCallback ( Widget, XtPointer, XtPointer );
```

```
16        static void quitCallback ( Widget, XtPointer, XtPointer );
17
18    protected:
19
20        Widget      _newGame;
21        Widget      _quit;
22        TicTacToe * _game;
23        virtual void newGame();
24        virtual void quit();
25
26    public:
27
28        Command ( Widget, TicTacToe *, char * );
29        virtual const char * const className() { return ( "Command" ); };
30    };
31    #endif
```

The Command constructor creates an XmForm base widget and two XmPushButton widgets.
The function registers the appropriate callbacks with each XmPushButton widget, and manages both
buttons.

```
1     /////////////////////////////////////////////////////////
2     // Command.C: Manage a set of command buttons
3     /////////////////////////////////////////////////////////
4     #include "stdlib.h"
5     #include "TicTacToe.h"
6     #include "Command.h"
7     #include "Engine.h"
8     #include <Xm/Form.h>
9     #include <Xm/PushB.h>
10
11    Command::Command ( Widget      parent,
12                       TicTacToe *game,
13                       char       *name ) : UIComponent ( name )
14    {
15        _game = game;
16
17        // Set up an XmForm widget to manage the buttons
18
19        _w = XmCreateForm ( parent, _name, NULL, 0 );
20
21        installDestroyHandler();
22
23        // Create the command buttons and attach callbacks
24
25        _newGame =
26            XtVaCreateManagedWidget ( "newGame",
27                                      xmPushButtonWidgetClass, _w,
```

```
28                                       XmNtopOffset,        5,
29                                       XmNbottomOffset,     5,
30                                       XmNleftOffset,       5,
31                                       XmNtopAttachment,    XmATTACH_FORM,
32                                       XmNleftAttachment,   XmATTACH_FORM,
33                                       XmNrightAttachment,  XmATTACH_NONE,
34                                       XmNbottomAttachment, XmATTACH_FORM,
35                                       NULL );
36
37      _quit = XtVaCreateManagedWidget ( "quit",
38                                        xmPushButtonWidgetClass, _w,
39                                        XmNtopOffset,        5,
40                                        XmNbottomOffset,     5,
41                                        XmNrightOffset,      5,
42                                        XmNtopAttachment,    XmATTACH_FORM,
43                                        XmNleftAttachment,   XmATTACH_NONE,
44                                        XmNrightAttachment,  XmATTACH_FORM,
45                                        XmNbottomAttachment, XmATTACH_FORM,
46                                        NULL );
47
48      XtAddCallback ( _newGame,
49                      XmNactivateCallback,
50                      &Command::newGameCallback,
51                      ( XtPointer ) this );
52
53      XtAddCallback ( _quit,
54                      XmNactivateCallback,
55                      &Command::quitCallback,
56                      ( XtPointer ) this );
57  }
```

The XmRowColumn widget would provide a simpler way to manage the buttons created in this component, but the XmRowColumn widget does not allow us to achieve the layout determined in Chapter 4. The constraints specified in the Command constructor attach the "New Game" button to the left side of the panel, and the Quit button to the right side.

The newGameCallback() function extracts the Command object pointer from the client data, and simply calls the newGame() member function.

```
58  void Command::newGameCallback ( Widget,
59                                  XtPointer clientData,
60                                  XtPointer )
61  {
62      Command *obj = ( Command * ) clientData;
63
64      obj->newGame();
65  }
```

The newGame() function retrieves the Engine object from the TicTacToe object and sends it the reset() message.

```
66  void Command::newGame()
67  {
68      _game->engine()->reset();
69  }
```

Finally, the quitCallback() member function calls the quit() member function, which forwards the request to the Engine object.

```
70  void Command::quitCallback ( Widget,
71                               XtPointer clientData,
72                               XtPointer )
73  {
74      Command *obj = ( Command * ) clientData;
75
76      obj->quit();
77  }

78  void Command::quit()
79  {
80      _game->engine()->quit();
81  }
```

This completes the user interface portion of TicTacToe. Figure 5.3 shows the widget tree created by the classes in TicTacToe. The light gray box outlines the widgets contained within the entire TicTacToe subsystem. The darker boxes outline each of the three user interface subcomponents, the Message, Command, and GameBoard classes. The root of the tree is an ApplicationShell widget, created by the main body of the program, which has not yet been discussed.

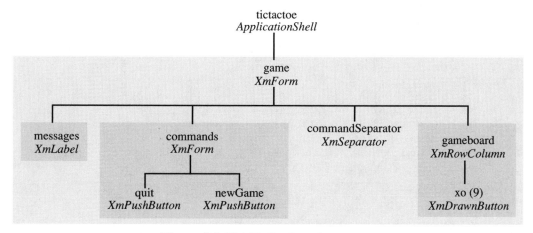

**Figure 5.3** The TicTacToe widget tree.

## 5.5     The Engine Subsystem

The Engine subsystem consists of three objects: a Board object, a MoveGenerator, and the Engine object itself. The following sections discuss the implementation of each of these classes.

### The Board Class

The Board class represents the current state of a TicTacToe game. Referring back to the class card in Figure 4.8, the Board class must provide methods to record moves, report the current status of the board, and provide a list of free squares. These are fairly high-level requirements and the Board class could be implemented many different ways.

In this implementation, the tic-tac-toe board is represented by a nine-element array of integers. The Board class also defines a second array used to report the indexes of all unmarked squares. The Board class defines methods that implement each external responsibility listed on the Board class card in Figure 4.8. The class also encapsulates an enumerated type used as a return value for the `recordMove()` member function, and another type used to specify different states of the game.

The user interface design in Chapter 4 identified the need to highlight the winning squares in some way. The Engine object must be able to determine what squares represent the winning pattern so this information can be passed along to the GameBoard. This responsibility was not identified in the initial class design. Because the Board class maintains the state of the game board, the information must come from the Board object. The `winningSquares()` member function provides a pointer to an array that indicates which squares contain the winning moves.

```
1   ///////////////////////////////////////////////////////////
2   // Board.h: Represent a TicTacToe board
3   ///////////////////////////////////////////////////////////
4   #ifndef BOARD_H
5   #define BOARD_H
6
7   class Board {
8
9     protected:
10
11        int  _state[9];        // Internal game state
12        int  _freeList[9];     // List used to report free squares
13        int  numFreeSquares();
14        int  *_winningPattern; // Pattern last tested when someone wins
15        static int  _winningBits[8][9];
16
17     public:
18
19        // Convenient values
20
```

```
21      enum MoveStatus { validMove, illegalMove };
22      enum markType { NOBODYYET, OO, XX, TIE };
23
24      Board();
25      MoveStatus recordMove ( int, markType ); // Record an X or an O
26
27      // Return number of available squares, and their indexes
28
29      int *const freeSquares ( int& );
30
31      // Public access for winning pattern of squares
32
33      int *const winningSquares() { return ( _winningPattern ); }
34
35      void clear();           // Clear and reset the board
36      markType whoHasWon();   // Return code for possible winner
37      virtual const char *const className() { return ( "Board" ); }
38    };
39    #endif
```

There are various ways to determine what player, if any, has won a game at any point. Because there are relatively few winning patterns in tic-tac-toe, this implementation defines a two-dimensional array of winning patterns in the file Board.C, as shown below. Each of the eight patterns in the array can be thought of as a mask. If all squares set to a 1 in the mask are Xs, or all are Os in the main Board object, that player has won.

The patterns are easier to see if written in rows of three. For example, the pattern

```
{ 1, 0, 0, 1, 0, 0, 1, 0, 0 }
```

can be rearranged to look like this:

```
{ 1, 0, 0,
  1, 0, 0,
  1, 0, 0 }
```

There are eight winning patterns in tic-tac-toe, as indicated in the _winningBits array. This array is not needed outside the class, and is declared as a static member of the Board class.

```
1    ///////////////////////////////////////////////////////////
2    // Board.C
3    ///////////////////////////////////////////////////////////
4    #include "Board.h"
5
6    // Array of all possible winning patterns (1 indicates a win)
7
8    int Board::_winningBits[8][9] = {
9      { 1, 0, 0, 1, 0, 0, 1, 0, 0 },
```

```
10    { 0, 1, 0, 0, 1, 0, 0, 1, 0 },
11    { 0, 0, 1, 0, 0, 1, 0, 0, 1 },
12    { 1, 1, 1, 0, 0, 0, 0, 0, 0 },
13    { 0, 0, 0, 1, 1, 1, 0, 0, 0 },
14    { 0, 0, 0, 0, 0, 0, 1, 1, 1 },
15    { 1, 0, 0, 0, 1, 0, 0, 0, 1 },
16    { 0, 0, 1, 0, 1, 0, 1, 0, 0 },
17    };
```

The Board constructor simply calls clear() to initialize the internal board.

```
18    Board::Board()
19    {
20        clear();   // Initialize the board
21    }
```

The clear() member function initializes the _state array to contain the value NOBODYYET, effectively clearing the board. The actual initial value is not particularly important so long as it is not an X or an O. The name NOBODYYET was chosen because it makes sense in the context of a yet-to-be-described member function.

```
22    void Board::clear()
23    {
24        // NOBODYYET doubles as an indication that no one has won
25        // and that no move has been recorded for a square
26
27        for ( int i = 0; i < 9; i++ )
28            _state[i] = NOBODYYET;
29    }
```

The recordMove() member function takes two parameters, a position on the board and an argument that indicates whether an X or an O should be recorded in that position. This function first checks to see if the specified square on the board is unmarked. If the square already has an X or an O in the specified position, the function returns illegalMove, indicating an error. Otherwise recordMove() marks the move in the _state array, and returns a value of validMove, indicating success.

```
30    MoveStatus Board::recordMove ( int position, markType mark )
31    {
32        if ( _state[position] != NOBODYYET ) // Make sure square is empty
33            return ( illegalMove );
34
35        // Record the move, and report it as legal
36
37        _state[position] = mark;
38        return ( validMove );
39    }
```

The freeSquares() member function loops through the _state array testing for squares that contain neither an X nor an O. The function stores the positions of all unmarked squares in a second array. The _freeList array is then returned to the caller, along with a reference to the number of unmarked squares in the list. The return value of the freeSquares() function is declared to be an array whose contents are declared to be const, to prevent the caller from modifying the contents of the _freeList array.

```
40  int *const Board::freeSquares ( int &numFree )
41  {
42      int i, j;
43
44      // Build up a list of the indexes (0-8) of free squares
45
46      for ( j = 0, i = 0; i < 9; i++ )
47          if ( _state[i] == NOBODYYET )
48              _freeList[j++] = i;
49      numFree = j;
50      return ( _freeList );
51  }
```

The numFreeSquares() member function is just a convenience routine used by the whoHasWon() member function to determine the number of squares that are still available. The function simply loops through all positions on the board, incrementing a counter for all unmarked positions, and returning the final value.

```
52  int Board::numFreeSquares()
53  {
54      int i, count;
55
56      // Look for and count unmarked squares
57
58      for ( count = 0, i = 0; i < 9; i++ )
59          if ( _state[i] == NOBODYYET )
60              count++;
61      return ( count );
62  }
```

The whoHasWon() member function is the most complex function supported by the Board class. It uses a double loop that tests each square of the board against each element in the _winningBits mask. For each winning combination, the function counts the number of Xs and Os that occur on squares that have a value of 1 in the _winningBits array. For each winning scenario, if there are three Xs or three Os counted, that player has won, and the function returns an XX or OO value as appropriate.

If neither X nor O has won, the function checks to see if any squares are still free. If all squares are marked, the game must be a tie, and whoHasWon() returns the value TIE. Otherwise the function returns NOBODYYET. Notice that the _winningPattern member is set to the current

pattern tested in each pass. If either player has won the game, this member will point to the winning
bit pattern in the _winningBits array.

```
63   markType Board::whoHasWon()
64   {
65       int i, j;
66
67       // Check the state of the board to see if anyone has won
68
69       for ( i = 0; i < 8; i++ )
70       {
71           int xcount = 0;  // Initialize to no Xs, no Os
72           int ocount = 0;
73
74           _winningPattern = _winningBits[i]; // Remember in case of a win
75
76           for ( j = 0; j < 9; j++ )       // Test each winning pattern
77               if ( _winningBits[i][j] )
78                   if ( _state[j] == OO )
79                       ocount++;            // Count Os in winning squares
80                   else if ( _state[j] == XX )
81                       xcount++;            // Count Xs in winning squares
82
83           if ( ocount == 3 )   // If either mark occupied 3 squares
84               return ( OO );   // then return the winner
85           if ( xcount == 3 )
86               return ( XX );
87       }
88
89       if ( numFreeSquares() > 0 )  // If no one won, report a tie or
90           return ( NOBODYYET );    // continue the game, as appropriate
91       else
92           return ( TIE );
93   }
```

## The MoveGenerator Class

The MoveGenerator class determines the computer's next move based on the current state of the
board. The MoveGenerator class has only one interesting member function, getNextMove().
This function takes a Board object as an argument, and computes and returns the position of the next,
presumably "best," move based on the current state of that Board.

The GameBoard class is declared as follows:

```
1    ///////////////////////////////////////////////////////
2    // MoveGenerator.h: Pick a move for TicTacToe
3    ///////////////////////////////////////////////////////
4    #ifndef MOVEGENERATOR_H
5    #define MOVEGENERATOR_H
```

```
6   class Board;
7
8   class MoveGenerator {
9
10    public:
11
12      MoveGenerator();
13      int getNextMove ( Board *board );  // Determine a good move
14      virtual const char *const className(){ return ( "MoveGenerator" ); }
15  };
16  #endif
```

There are many ways that we could compute the "best" move for any given state of the game board. For example, the game tree approach mentioned earlier traces the possible paths the game could take. Based on this information, one can determine which moves can lead to a win, and which can lead to a loss. TicTacToe is a reasonably deterministic game, which can only result in a tie between two players who have a reasonable strategy, so we may want to make the game easier for the user to win.

For this implementation, the MoveGenerator class simply chooses a square at random from the remaining free squares each time a move is requested. The MoveGenerator constructor calls srand48() to initialize the random number generator from the UNIX library. This function requires a seed value to initialize the random number sequence. To ensure that the game doesn't pick the same pattern of moves each time, the MoveGenerator uses the system call getpid() to retrieve the program's process id, which is used as a relatively unique seed.

```
1   ////////////////////////////////////////////////////
2   // MoveGenerator.C
3   ////////////////////////////////////////////////////
4   #include "MoveGenerator.h"
5   #include "Board.h"
6   #include "unistd.h"
7   #include "math.h"
8
9   MoveGenerator::MoveGenerator()
10  {
11      srand48( (long) getpid() );
12  }
```

The getNextMove() member function obtains the list of remaining free squares from the given Board object, and then generates a random number between zero and the number of squares remaining. It then returns the index of the chosen square as the new move.

```
13  int MoveGenerator::getNextMove ( Board *board )
14  {
15      int randomIndex, movesLeft;
16
17      // Get the list of free squares on the Board
```

```
18
19      int * const freeSquares = board->freeSquares ( movesLeft );
20
21      if ( movesLeft == 0 )
22          return ( -1 );
23
24      // Pick one of the free squares at random and return it
25
26      randomIndex = ( int ) ( movesLeft * drand48() );
27      return ( freeSquares[randomIndex] );
28  }
```

## The Engine Class

The Engine class plays a coordinating role and acts as the "traffic cop" of the TicTacToe game. The final design of the Engine class pulled most of the knowledge about the game out of the Engine class. We placed the representation of the game board in a separate class, and the responsibility for choosing a move in yet another class. The goal was to make the Engine simpler and more general, handling only the mechanism of switching between the user's moves and the moves generated by the game.

The final design also used an Engine subsystem object to encapsulate the Engine, MoveGenerator and Board classes, as shown in Figure 4.11. While this is a useful way to visualize the architecture of the system, notice that all interactions between other components in the game and the Engine subsystem actually go through the Engine object. As a matter of implementation, it seems easier to just encapsulate the other components of the Engine subsystem in the Engine itself. So, the Engine class, as implemented here, supports pointers to a Board object and a MoveGenerator object. The class defines a protected function, checkForWin(), which is used internally, while the public functions recordMove(), reset(), and quit() implement the corresponding responsibilities defined on the Engine class card in Chapter 4.

In addition to the class declaration, the file Engine.h defines several string constants used to report the state of the game to the user.

```
1  ///////////////////////////////////////////////////////////
2  // Engine.h: The brains of the TicTacToe game
3  ///////////////////////////////////////////////////////////
4  #ifndef ENGINE_H
5  #define ENGINE_H
6  #include "Board.h"
7
8    class TicTacToe;
9    class MoveGenerator;
10
11  class Engine {
12
13    protected:
14
15      TicTacToe       * _game;
```

```
16        markType            _whoseMove;       // Remember whose turn it is
17        Board             * _board;           // Internal game state
18        MoveGenerator     * _moveGenerator;   // Picks next move
19        int                 _gameOver;        // True if game has ended
20        void    checkForWin();                // Check and report the winner
21
22      public:
23
24        Engine ( TicTacToe * );
25        virtual ~Engine();
26        void recordMove ( int square );
27        void reset();                         // Start over
28        void quit();
29        virtual const char *const className() { return ( "Engine" ); }
30    };
31    #define NEWGAMEMSG      "New Game. Choose an X square"
32    #define ILLEGALMOVEMSG  "Illegal Move, Choose another X square"
33    #define USERSMOVEMSG    "Choose an X square"
34    #define XWINSMSG        "X Wins!"
35    #define OWINSMSG        "O Wins!"
36    #define TIEGAMEMSG      "Tie Game"
37    #define GAMEISOVERMSG   "Sorry, game is over"
38    #endif
```

The Engine class constructor sets the initial state of several internal instance variables, including setting the _whoseMove member to indicate that X (the user) gets the first move. This instance variable always indicates the current move, X or O. The constructor also instantiates a Board and a MoveGenerator object.

```
1     //////////////////////////////////////////////////////////
2     // Engine.C: The brains of the TicTacToe game
3     //////////////////////////////////////////////////////////
4     #include "TicTacToe.h"
5     #include "Engine.h"
6     #include "GameBoard.h"
7     #include "MoveGenerator.h"
8     #include "Message.h"
9     #include "Board.h"
10    #include <stdlib.h>  // Needed for exit()
11
12    Engine::Engine ( TicTacToe* game )
13    {
14        _game       = game;
15        _gameOver   = FALSE;
16        _whoseMove = Board::XX; // Start with X as the first move
17        _board = new Board(); // Create the Engine subcomponents
18        _moveGenerator = new MoveGenerator();
19    }
```

The Engine destructor simply deletes the Board and MoveGenerator objects when the Engine object is destroyed.

```
20  Engine::~Engine()
21  {
22      delete _board;
23      delete _moveGenerator;
24  }
```

The reset() member function resets the _whoseMove and _gameOver variables to their initial states, and sends a clear() message to the GameBoard object associated with this Engine object. The reset() member function also requests the Message object to display a "new game" message.

```
25  void Engine::reset()
26  {
27      _whoseMove = Board::XX;
28      _gameOver  = FALSE;
29      _board->clear();
30      _game->gameBoard()->clear();
31      _game->messageArea()->postMessage ( NEWGAMEMSG );
32  }
```

The recordMove() function is the heart of the Engine class. This function is called each time the user or the game makes a move. If the current game is over, the member function posts a message to warn the user, and returns. Otherwise, it tries to register the move with the internal Board object, by sending it a recordMove() message. If the Board recordMove() member function returns the value validMove, the Engine calls the GameBoard's markX() or markO() function to display the move in the appropriate square. Otherwise, the function returns, after posting an illegal move message for the user.

Before proceeding, recordMove() checks to see if the current move wins the game. If so, the game is over, and the function simply returns after issuing a warning. Finally, depending on whose move it is, recordMove() prompts the user for the next move, or calls the MoveGenerator object to choose a new move. If it is TicTacToe's turn to choose a move, the function simply calls itself recursively, after toggling the _whoseMove data member.

```
33  void Engine::recordMove ( int position )
34  {
35      if ( _gameOver ) // Don't accept moves if the game is over
36      {
37          _game->messageArea()->postAlert( GAMEISOVERMSG );
38          return;
39      }
40
41      // Record the move. If it is valid, display it on the board
42      // Otherwise ask the user to pick again
43
```

```
44        if ( _board->recordMove ( position, _whoseMove ) == Board::validMove)
45        {
46            if ( _whoseMove == Board::XX )
47                _game->gameBoard()->markX ( position );
48            else
49                _game->gameBoard()->markO ( position );
50        }
51        else
52        {
53            _game->messageArea()->postAlert ( ILLEGALMOVEMSG );
54            return;
55        }
56
57        // See if this move wins the game for the user
58
59        checkForWin();
60
61        if ( _gameOver )
62            return;
63
64        // If this is the game's move, change to Xs move and ask the
65        // user to choose a square
66        // If it is the user's move, change to game's move and pick a move
67        // Call this function recursively to record the game's choice
68
69        if ( _whoseMove == Board::OO )
70        {
71            _whoseMove = Board::XX;
72            _game->messageArea()->postMessage ( USERSMOVEMSG );
73        }
74        else
75        {
76            _whoseMove = Board::OO;
77            recordMove ( _moveGenerator->getNextMove ( _board ) );
78        }
79   }
```

The checkForWin() member function calls the Board member function, whoHasWon(), to determine the current state of the board. The function posts a message to the user and sets the _gameOver flag to TRUE if the game is over for any reason.

```
80   void Engine::checkForWin()
81   {
82        int     i, *winningSquares;
83        markType winner;
84
85        // If no one has won yet, just keep playing
86
```

```
87      if( ( winner = _board->whoHasWon() ) == Board::NOBODYYET )
88          return;
89      else if ( winner == Board::TIE )
90      {
91          // If it's a tie, end the game and notify the user
92
93          _gameOver = TRUE;
94
95          for ( i = 0 ; i < 9; i++ )
96              _game->gameBoard()->deemphasizeSquare ( i );
97
98          _game->messageArea()->postAlert( TIEGAMEMSG );
99      }
100     else // Someone won
101     {
102         _gameOver = TRUE;
103
104         // Get the mask for the wining pattern
105
106         winningSquares = _board->winningSquares();
107
108         // Deactivate each square to prevent input
109         // Highlight winning squares, fade others into the background
110
111         for ( i = 0 ; i < 9; i++ )
112         {
113             _game->gameBoard()->deactivateSquare ( i );
114
115             if ( winningSquares[i] )
116                 _game->gameBoard()->highlightSquare ( i );
117             else
118                 _game->gameBoard()->deemphasizeSquare ( i );
119         }
120
121         // Finally, alert the user that someone has won
122
123         if ( winner  == Board::XX )
124             _game->messageArea()->postAlert ( XWINSMSG );
125         else
126             _game->messageArea()->postAlert ( OWINSMSG );
127     }
128 }
```

The quit() member function simply exits the application when called.

```
129 void Engine::quit()
130 {
131     exit ( 0 );
132 }
```

## 5.6    Putting It All Together

To complete the TicTacToe program, we simply need to write a driver that creates an instance of the TicTacToe class. The TicTacToe subsystem instantiates and ties together the other components of the game. Figure 5.4 shows how all these classes fit together in the TicTacToe subsystem.

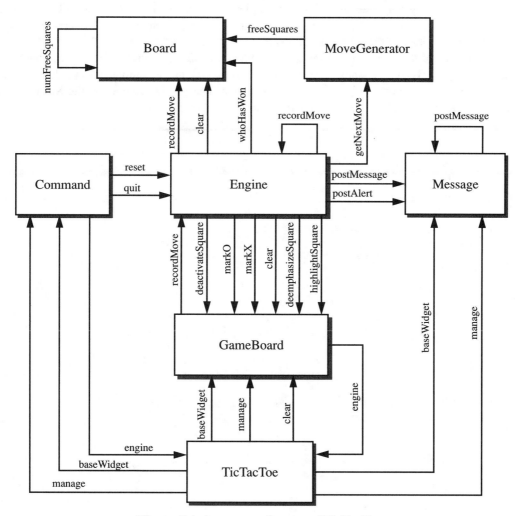

**Figure 5.4**  A message diagram of TicTacToe.

This message diagram includes most messages sent between objects, and a few internal member functions as well. However, the diagram is not complete. For example, it does not include calls to the UIComponent class, such as `installDestroyHandler()`. The diagram also neglects constructors and destructors for simplicity. The diagram could also be simplified by removing those messages that are merely mechanical, such as all calls to `manage()`, TicTacToe's `engine()` access function, the `baseWidget()` access function, and so on.

It is interesting to compare Figure 5.4 with the collaboration graph in Chapter 4. In general, both diagrams show the same relationships. However, the collaboration graph in Chapter 4 gives a cleaner view of the system. It is easier to see which components have dependencies on others, and which are part of logical subsystems. Figure 5.4, on the other hand, provides a more realistic and detailed look at the system. Because it includes implementation details, such as the calls to various components' `baseWidget()` and `manage()` member functions, the message diagram provides a more accurate picture of the interconnections in the system.

Let's complete the game by writing a driver that instantiates a single TicTacToe subsystem. Because the TicTacToe class handles the task of connecting the game components and defining the widget layout, the main body of the game is very simple. The program initializes the Xt Intrinsics and then creates a TicTacToe object to construct the rest of the game.

```
1    ////////////////////////////////////////////////////////////
2    // tictactoe.C: A simple tic-tac-toe game using Motif and C++
3    ////////////////////////////////////////////////////////////
4    #include <Xm/Xm.h>
5    #include "TicTacToe.h"
6
7    main ( unsigned int argc, char **argv )
8    {
9        XtAppContext   app;
10       Widget         toplevel;
11
12       // Initialize the Intrinsics
13
14       toplevel = XtAppInitialize ( &app, "Tictactoe", NULL, 0,
15                                    &argc, argv, NULL, NULL, 0 );
16
17       // Create the game widget tree as a child of the shell widget
18
19       TicTacToe *game = new TicTacToe ( toplevel, "game" );
20
21       game->manage();
22
23       // Realize all widgets and enter the event loop
24
25       XtRealizeWidget ( toplevel );
26       XtAppMainLoop ( app );
27   }
```

We can build the TicTacToe program by compiling all seven classes, plus the main routine and linking the results with the X and Motif libraries as well as the binaries for the UIComponent and BasicComponent classes:

```
cc -o tictactoe tictactoe.o TicTacToe.o Message.o Command.o \
     GameBoard.o Engine.o Board.o MoveGenerator.o \
     UIComponent.o BasicComponent.o -lXm -lXt -lX11
```

Figure 5.5 shows a storyboard that demonstrates TicTacToe in action.

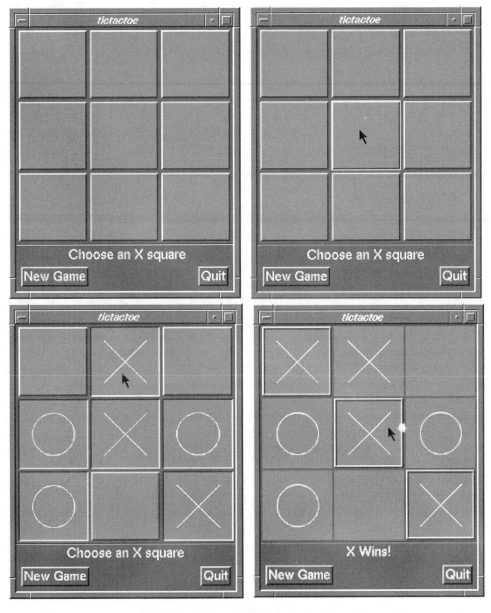

**Figure 5.5** A typical TicTacToe game.

The first figure, at the upper left shows the game as it initially appears. The board is clear, all squares look like pushbuttons and the message area displays a message that prompts the user to make the first move. The second scene, at the upper right of Figure 5.5, shows a square as the user positions the mouse cursor to make a move. The square under the mouse cursor is highlighted with a light border to indicate that it is active and available to be selected.

The third scene, at the lower left, shows the game after several moves have been made. The squares that have already been selected are depressed into the screen, and are not highlighted when the mouse cursor enters the square. Those squares that still represent valid moves maintain the appearance of a Motif XmPushButton widget, and highlight when the user moves the mouse cursor into the square.

The last scene, at the lower right corner of Figure 5.5, shows a game after a player has won. All squares have been faded into the background by removing all shadows. All squares are also inactive and do not highlight when the mouse cursor enters a square. The winning squares are accented using the etched-out shadow style supported by the XmDrawnButton. Finally, the message area confirms the game status by reporting the winner.

## 5.7  Summary

This chapter completes an exercise that began in the previous chapter. Chapter 4 stated the basic problem and developed a high-level design. This chapter presented the implementation of that design, using C++ and Motif. Now that TicTacToe is finished, it should be worthwhile to review the entire process and decide what worked well, and what didn't. For the most part, the implementation adheres closely to the design detailed in Chapter 4. The classes identified in the initial design phase are all present, and for the most part, they perform the functions identified during the design. The overall structure of the game has changed very little, and the architecture visible in the message diagram in Figure 5.4 resembles the organization in the collaboration graph in Chapter 4.

However, not everything went smoothly and there were a few surprises. For example, implementing a mechanism to highlight the winning squares was not as straightforward as originally anticipated. The command buttons and message area could not be laid out exactly as planned. A few new responsibilities were identified during the development phase and several additional member functions were required.

One of the claims made for object-oriented programming is that classes tend to be reusable. We paid some attention to reusability both in the design and the implementation, by trying to provide clean interfaces and minimize outside references. In spite of this, few of these classes are really reusable in a general sense. The Message class could be reused easily, because it has no dependencies. But the Message class is very simple, and is little more than a wrapper around a Motif XmLabel widget. The others are closely tied to their role within the TicTacToe program. The classes are modular, and self-contained, but not really reusable.

Of course, the primary goal of the TicTacToe exercise was not to create a set of general purpose classes. Another evaluation criteria is "how easy is it to maintain or add enhancements to this program?" We can't really know the answer to this question without attempting to modify the program. However, it seems as if the program is well modularized, and that at least minor changes could be made easily. For example, the MoveGenerator class could be replaced by a class that supports a better algorithm for selecting moves without affecting other parts of the program. The internal representation used by the Board class could easily be altered. The interaction style and presentation supported by the GameBoard class could also be modified in some ways without requiring changes to the rest of the program.

One test of the value of an object-oriented approach is to see how easy it would be to add some new features. The main questions here are "To what degree does a change to one part of the program affect other parts of the program? Does changing the internal details of one class require all classes to change? Can the program be extended without changing the external protocol of one or more classes? If not, what effect does that have on other classes?"

For example, how hard would it be to add a score-keeping facility? Aside from individual implementation challenges presented by each new class or classes, the primary issue is "how hard would it be to make this new feature work with the other existing classes?" Does the existing protocol support the new feature, or will one or more existing classes need to be altered? If existing classes must be changed to support enhancements to the game, can the changes be made by creating new derived classes, or must the original classes be modified? These questions are harder to answer without proof.

We need to evaluate the user interface as well. User interface development tends to be iterative by nature. We can't really know if the interface proposed in the design phase is effective, until the program has been built. The "feel" of a program is so difficult to predict beforehand, and so subject to personal taste, that the results can only be judged by having the intended audience try the program.

Several of the features provided in TicTacToe need to be tested and verified with users. For example, we tried to make the program very responsive and implemented several types of feedback. But will the users understand the various ways shadows are used with squares? Will they find this feedback helpful, essential, distracting, or annoying? The game uses highlight-on-enter to reinforce what squares are selectable, and to give the game a lively, responsive feel. This mechanism seems particularly appropriate for a game, but may annoy some users.

The TicTacToe interface has one particularly interesting problem that was not anticipated until the game was played in its final form. The computer picks its moves so quickly, that the game's O move seems to show up at almost exactly the same time as the corresponding X square chosen by the user. In fact, the "O" appears so quickly that the user may not even notice that the game has chosen its move. The speed of the game's moves keeps the user from feeling as if he or she is playing against a real opponent. Possible solutions to this problem include adding a delay before the game responds or adding some type of transition effect to simulate the computer's "thinking" time. Also, because the user has no indication that the game is picking a square until the O appears, perhaps the most recently picked square should be indicated in some way.

Although we do not yet have enough information to judge the success of the user interface design, it seems that this effort was also worthwhile. For a simple problem, a surprising number of user interface-related issues arose during both the design and the implementation phases. Regardless of the final quality of the interface and how it is received by users, it seems fair to say that the program was improved by the attention to the user interface at an early stage.

# Application Frameworks

The first part of this book concentrated on the mechanics of using C++ and Motif. Chapters 1 through 5 also focus on ways to identify useful objects and construct corresponding classes that can be used to implement an application. Part II continues to develop the ideas begun in Part I, but with a slightly different emphasis. Instead of focusing on the process of developing classes suitable for an individual application, the remaining chapters explore ways to create a *framework* of reusable classes designed to support many applications.

Although earlier chapters discussed ways to make classes more general, most of the classes examined so far have been designed to support a specific application. Reusability was a secondary consideration, and very few of the classes discussed in earlier chapters are useful in situations other than those for which they were designed. The UIComponent and BasicComponent classes are notable exceptions. These abstract classes were designed from the beginning to provide foundations for other classes.

In contrast with earlier examples, most of the classes discussed in Part II are designed primarily to provide a foundation for other classes. Developing classes that can be reused in many different situations is somewhat different from designing classes to be used only in a specific application. When designing a single application, the emphasis is on identifying objects that perform a specific function, or fulfill a particular role in that application. When reusability is the foremost goal, the programmer has to identify classes that address the needs of many applications, often without knowing in advance what these applications do.

The primary reason to develop reusable classes is to improve programmer productivity by reducing the amount of code a programmer must write for each new application. The goal is to provide programmers with a body of pre-existing, pre-tested code that can be combined to form a complete application. There are at least two ways to reduce the amount of code a programmer must write to complete an application. The first, and most traditional, approach is to provide collections of functions or classes that implement common components needed by many programs. Motif is a typical example of a *toolkit* based on this approach. Programmers who use Motif can choose from a collection of off-the-shelf user interface components. Without a toolkit like Motif, programmers would have to develop buttons, scrollbars, and so on for each new application. Toolkits are a very effective and widely-used form of reusable software.

Another approach is to pay less attention to individual components needed by various applications, and to focus instead on the *structure* and control flow within a particular *type* of application. Here, the goal is to spare the programmer from having to define the architecture of each new application. An *application framework* provides a way to capture the characteristics, particularly organizational characteristics, common to many applications.

Like a toolkit, an application framework is a library that provides various components needed by programs. However, unlike traditional toolkits, an application framework also defines most of the connections between these components, and defines the overall control structure of applications built on the framework. One common approach used in application frameworks is to provide an Application class that captures the essential behavior of all applications built from the framework. In this type of framework, programmers write new applications by deriving a new subclass of Application that handles application-specific details.

Application frameworks often support the idea of a *generic application*. The generic application is the simplest possible program that can be written using the framework. It can usually be written simply by creating an instance of the Application class, or by declaring and instantiating a trivial subclass. The resulting generic application usually serves no useful purpose, but follows all rules and conventions supported by the framework. Depending on the framework, the generic application may create windows and a basic set of menus, open files, connect to databases or other services, and so on.

More importantly, the generic application defines the flow of control used by all similar applications. The programmer doesn't have to worry about how to connect the various components of the program – the framework makes the connections automatically. To create a new application, the programmer implements only those parts of the program that are unique. Application-specific elements can be provided by adding a few new components, defining a few methods, or by deriving new classes from those provided by the framework. In this sense, writing an application using a framework is very similar to deriving a new class from an existing class. In both cases, a new entity can be created by specifying only how the new entity is different from the existing one.

It is sometimes difficult to differentiate between an application framework and an object-oriented library. For example, we noted earlier that Xt has a strong impact on the structure of an application. All Motif programs use the Xt dispatch mechanism, which effectively manages the control flow within the application. So, can Xt be considered an application framework? There are similarities, but Xt is closer in spirit to a traditional toolkit library.

When a library can be called an application framework instead of a toolkit often depends on the philosophy of how the library is meant to be used. A toolkit typically provides a flexible set of components. The programmer is free to combine these components in all sorts of ways. Traditional toolkits could be compared to a set of toy blocks. A set of blocks has very little inherent structure; the blocks can be combined in ways limited only by the imagination. Application frameworks tend to be more restrictive, but provide more structure. A framework is more like a coloring book, in which the outlines of the pictures have already been drawn. The programmer simply has to add the final details to complete the application.

Another way of thinking about application frameworks is to observe that the roles of the application and the framework library are reversed. When using traditional toolkit libraries, one normally considers the application code to be in charge. The application is the focus of attention, while libraries provide collections of useful routines, which are controlled by the program. In an application framework, the framework *is* the application. The framework is in control, and may even implement the bulk of the code. When necessary, the framework calls the routines provided by the application programmer to provide application-specific behavior.

An application framework is most effective when supporting applications with significant similarities. However, most applications, even those that appear to be quite different, usually have one or more elements in common. For example, all Xt-based programs follow approximately the same structure. They must all initialize the Xt Intrinsics, open a connection to the X server, create assorted widgets, and enter an event loop. The Motif Style Guide also recommends many features that should be supported by all Motif applications. All applications that are fully Motif compliant need to provide help facilities, and other features that are not directly provided by Motif. Many of these features could be supported in a framework, so that every programmer doesn't need to implement them for each individual application.

Applications that share a similar purpose or interact in some way may have even more in common. For example, imagine a collection of programs that provide a complete environment for a medical facility. Perhaps each program has access to various databases containing doctors' schedules, patients' medical histories, inventories, medical diagnostics, case studies, and so on. Some of the programs might need to communicate with each other to work together effectively. Such programs might also coordinate the way they present information throughout the system. For example, color could be used consistently across the set of related tools. An application framework provides a way to support such a family of related programs and to provide consistency throughout the environment.

Most frameworks do not support all applications equally well. One challenge when designing an application framework is to find a balance between power and flexibility. In general, the power of an application framework is inversely proportional to its flexibility. Frameworks provide power by correctly anticipating the needs of a particular type of application and performing various functions automatically. Flexibility, in this context, means that the framework must allow applications to define or alter the framework's default behavior as needed. Object-oriented programming makes it possible to achieve both these goals to some extent, because (at least in theory) applications can use inheritance to override features of the framework, when necessary. In practice, the more powerful the framework, the harder it is to write applications that don't fit into the framework's predefined structure. However, an application framework provides many advantages over the toolkit approach, for applications that fit the model supported by the framework.

In addition to providing a reusable structure for applications, an application framework can provide an effective base for writing reusable classes. Instead of struggling to create classes that have no external dependencies, a framework allows the programmer to develop classes that depend on the existence of the framework. Although encapsulation and self-sufficiency are worthwhile goals, many classes can be written more easily when the programmer can assume a supporting infrastructure. Of course, classes that refer to other parts of a framework are only reusable within the context of the framework.

# A Framework for Motif Applications

The following chapters describe a simple application framework that encapsulates a structure that can be useful to applications based on X and Motif. This framework, which we will call MotifApp, captures many characteristics of typical Motif applications. Motif applications provide a good domain for an application framework, in spite of the fact that "all Motif applications" represents a wide range of programs.

The framework described in the following chapters is very simple, and falls far short of capturing *all* the elements common to all Motif applications. The primary focus is on developing a basic architecture, which can be enhanced and expanded with additional classes to form a more powerful framework, if desired. The following chapters describe one collection of classes that provide support for some Motif-based applications. Of course, not all applications fit into the mold assumed by the MotifApp framework, and not all programmers would choose the same set of classes to form the base framework.

Chapter 6 introduces the core of the MotifApp framework, which includes an Application class and a MainWindow class. Chapter 7 discusses some techniques for using dialogs, and examines some classes that support dialogs in the MotifApp framework. Chapter 8 introduces some abstract base classes that allow applications to represent commands as objects, and Chapter 9 describes a menu system based on the command object model.

Chapter 10 presents a collection of classes that support applications that need to perform tasks that take a long time to complete. Although frameworks predominately focus on classes that define the structural elements of a program, most frameworks also provide user interface components. It is particularly appropriate for a framework to provide large-scale components that behave consistently across all applications based on the framework. As an example of such a component, Chapter 11 describes a user interface component that allows a user to select a color interactively. Finally, Chapter 12 ties the previous chapters together with a complete example program that uses the MotifApp framework. This program demonstrates the use of command objects, menus, dialogs, the color editor, and assorted C++ user interface components. However, the main purpose of this example is to demonstrate how a typical Motif application can take advantage of a framework like MotifApp.

Part II continues to use the graphical notations introduced in Chapter 3, when they are useful. However, the following chapters emphasize the structure supported by an example application framework, and the design decisions associated with the development of individual classes are of less interest than they were in earlier chapters. Class cards continue to provide a useful way to summarize the key responsibilities of various classes. Inheritance and message diagrams are also used when they provide useful information about the framework, but collaboration graphs are not used. A collaboration graph is a useful tool during early stages of design. In most cases, message diagrams provide a better way to visualize the relationships between classes once they are completed.

# Chapter 6
# The MotifApp
# Application Framework

This chapter introduces a simple application framework that supports typical Motif applications written in C++. The framework, which we will call *MotifApp*, supports features common to many Motif applications, including menus, dialogs, multiple top-level windows, and so on. Most of the classes in MotifApp are based on the UIComponent class described in Chapter 2, and use the techniques introduced in Part I of this book. Although the MotifApp classes include some common user interface components, the main purpose of this framework is to define the overall structure of an application. As with most frameworks, the way classes fit together is more important that the functionality of any one class.

Applications based on MotifApp must be written in a very stylized way to allow the framework to handle most of the connections between major components. To the extent possible, applications based on MotifApp need only implement application-specific parts of the user interface. The framework provides those parts that are common between typical Motif applications, and defines how the major elements of a MotifApp program fit together.

This chapter introduces two key classes, Application and MainWindow, which form the core of the MotifApp framework. Section 6.1 provides an overview of the MotifApp application framework. Section 6.2 presents the Application class and Section 6.3 describes the MainWindow class. Sections 6.4 and 6.5 show how these classes fit together to form the foundation of a MotifApp library. Section 6.6 reimplements the "Hello World" example originally described in Chapter 1 using the classes described in this chapter. This example demonstrates the differences between applications based on the MotifApp framework and those written using a more traditional approach. Later chapters develop additional classes for the framework and discuss individual components in more detail.

# 6.1   An Overview

The primary purpose of the MotifApp framework is to simplify the task of writing a Motif application by capturing structural elements common to most Motif applications. Although Xt and Motif provide a much higher-level interface than Xlib, most Motif and Xt applications contain a surprising amount of duplicate code. For example, all Motif applications must initialize the Xt Intrinsics, open a connection to the X server, enter an event loop, and so on. There is very little reason for each application to duplicate the code that implements these steps. Instead, we can capture these steps in a class that all applications can reuse.

It is also possible to capture part of the control structure of typical Motif applications, even though many specific details vary from application to application. For example, many applications support menus that allow a user to issue commands and perform operations. Although the content of any given menu depends on the specific application, it is possible to provide more support for constructing menus and issuing the associated commands than that provided by the basic Motif widget set.

Let's begin by listing some characteristics common to all Motif applications. Considering only the minimum features common to all Motif applications, we can say that all programs must:

- Initialize the Xt Intrinsics
- Open a connection to the X server
- Create an application context (`XtAppContext`)
- Create a shell widget that serves as a parent for other widgets
- Create one or more widgets that define the user interface
- Handle events by entering an event loop.

This list provides a good start toward defining the features of a framework for Motif applications. In fact, the steps above are common to nearly every Xt program, regardless of the widget set. Looking back at the examples in earlier chapters, it is easy to see that the body of `main()` in most Motif programs is remarkably similar. Most programs perform all the steps listed above with very little variation. In fact, if we ignore small differences between various applications, we can see that nearly every Xt application contains the same statements and follows the same form, which could be written as follows:

```
1   /////////////////////////////////////////////////////////
2   // Generic form of a typical Motif application
3   /////////////////////////////////////////////////////////
4   #include <Xm/Xm.h>
5
6   #define APPLICATIONCLASS   "<fill in your classname here>"
7
8   main ( unsigned int argc, char **argv )
9   {
10      Widget        toplevel;
```

```
11      XtAppContext app;
12
13      // Initialize the Intrinsics
14
15      toplevel = XtAppInitialize ( &app, APPLICATIONCLASS, NULL, 0,
16                                   &argc, argv, NULL, NULL, 0 );
17
18      //////////////////////////////////////////////////////
19      // APPLICATION-SPECIFIC CODE
20      //////////////////////////////////////////////////////
21
22      // Realize the shell widget and enter the main event loop
23
24      XtRealizeWidget ( toplevel );
25      XtAppMainLoop ( app );
26  }
```

The code shown above varies so little from program to program that it seems a waste of time to type these statements repeatedly for each program. Programmers often start new programs by copying an existing program, and one way to start writing a new Motif application quickly is to save this template in a file and use a copy as the basis of each new program. If these few lines were the only elements common to most Motif applications, copying this template might be a reasonable approach. However, we will be identifying many features in this and the following chapters that are not so easy to capture in a simple text template.

A more powerful approach is to capture an application skeleton like that shown above in a class. Applications can reuse the common code segment by instantiating the class, or by creating a new class derived from the original. Using a class to capture the common features of an application has several advantages over copying the template shown above. First, once a programmer makes a copy of a template, he or she loses the ability to track changes to the original. Imagine that after using a template like the one shown above for many different programs, someone discovers a bug in the template. Because the template has been copied, and the copies have probably been edited many times, there is no easy way to fix the bug in all programs based on the template. Each programmer will need to go through his or her programs, one at a time, and fix the same bug over and over. However, programs that simply instantiate an object that encapsulates this code can benefit from bug fixes or improvements by simply relinking with a fixed version.

There are other advantages as well. Suppose an application requires slightly different behavior than that implemented in the template. Once a programmer changes a copy of the template, it becomes more difficult to go back to the original. For example, imagine that as the program grows, a bug develops in the new program. The programmer may suspect that an error has been introduced in the code originally copied from the template, and may wish to compare the buggy program to the original (correct) template. However, by this time, the copy may have been modified so extensively that it may be difficult to see the relationships between the program and the original template.

Applications based on the object-oriented approach suggested here can modify the behavior of the generic code by deriving a new class. Because changes are made only to a derived class and not to the original, it is easier to revert to the original behavior. It is also easier to be sure that any new errors introduced during development are completely contained within new code. Programmers are unlikely to introduce accidental errors in the existing code, because the original code is encapsulated in a class, and changes are made only to a derived class.

The template shown on the previous page is so simple that it may not seem worthwhile to capture it in a class. The power of this approach becomes more evident when we begin to identify more complex features common to the types of applications we wish to support. Although the characteristics listed earlier represent the minimum feature set common across all Xt applications, most Motif applications share many more characteristics. For example:

- **Most Motif applications support menus**. Many Motif applications have a menubar that spans the top of the application's main window.

- **Most Motif applications are interactive and allow the user to execute commands**. These commands might be issued by selecting an item from a menu, pushing a button, selecting an item on a list, or simply by typing or clicking a mouse button.

- **Many Motif applications consist of more than one window**. All have at least one window that can be considered to be the application's main window. Many support multiple, independent top-level windows, or collections of secondary windows.

- **Most use popup dialogs to display information to the user, request input, report errors, and so on**.

Using just the two lists of features discussed so far, it is possible to define a collection of classes that support applications that fit within this model. Not every application requires all the features listed, but many do. It would be possible to identify more features if we could pick a specific application domain. For example, if we chose to support only drawing editors and paint programs, we could say that all such programs allow the user to select from palettes of colors and patterns, are able to read and save files in various formats, and much more. However, the features listed above are sufficient to demonstrate the benefits of an application framework for a relatively wide range of typical Motif applications.

The MotifApp framework described in the rest of this book includes the following core classes:

- **Application**. This class captures the initialization and general overhead required of every Motif or Xt application. The Application class provides the equivalent of the application template just discussed, plus some additional features.

- **MainWindow and MenuWindow**. The MainWindow class encapsulates those elements common to most independent top-level windows. This class supports a shell widget and a Motif XmMainWindow widget. Derived classes are responsible only for an application-specific work area, which contains the other widgets in the application. The MenuWindow class is derived from the MainWindow class and adds a menubar.

- **Cmd**. The MotifApp framework supports an object-oriented approach to issuing commands within an application. All commands and tasks can be modeled as objects that can be executed by calling an `execute()` member function. The effect of a command can be reversed (or undone) by calling the object's `undo()` member function. The Cmd class and several derived classes provide the basis of this mechanism.

- **MenuBar**. The MenuBar class constructs menu panes from lists of Cmd objects. The MenuWindow class creates a MenuBar object automatically, but the MenuBar class can also be used independently.

- **DialogManager**. Most Motif applications use one or more dialogs. The DialogManager class, along with several derived classes, provides an easy-to-use central facility that supplies dialogs for the entire application.

The MotifApp framework also contains several other supporting or special-purpose classes. For example, the framework provides a CmdList class that handles lists of Cmd objects, a PixmapCycler class for cycling through sequences of images, and a ColorChooser class that allows a user to select or edit a color. There are also many special classes designed to solve common problems encountered when developing X applications. For example, one challenge programmers often encounter when developing Motif applications involves performing tasks that require a long time to complete. The InterruptibleCmd class is a subclass of Cmd that supports applications that perform time-consuming operations. This class allows the program to provide constant feedback to the user about the current state of the task, and also allows the user to interrupt the command before it has completed.

Figure 6.1 shows a class hierarchy of the MotifApp library, formed by the collection of classes described in this and the following chapters.

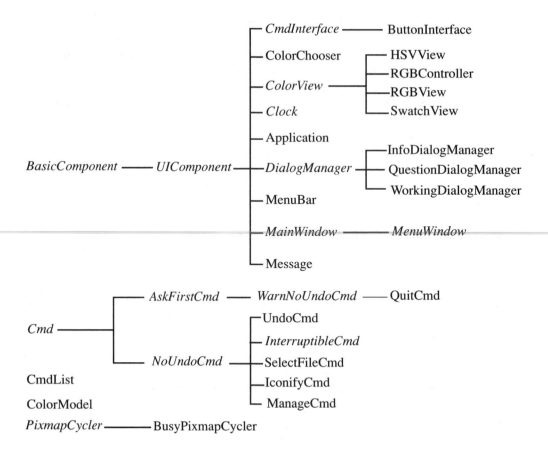

**Figure 6.1** The MotifApp class hierarchy.

Earlier chapters already presented several of these classes, including the UIComponent and BasicComponent classes. The UIComponent class, along with the concept of a user interface component, is the basis of much of the framework. The core of the framework is the Application class, described in detail in the following section. The MainWindow class, which works closely with the Application class, is described in Section 6.3. Chapters 7 though 12 discuss the remaining classes, which provide additional facilities needed by Motif applications. Most of these additional classes interact with or depend on the Application or MainWindow classes in some way.

# 6.2   The Application Class

The Application class handles the initialization and event-handling steps that are common to all Xt-based applications. Instead of calling Xt functions like `XtAppInitialize()` or `XtApp-MainLoop()`, MotifApp applications simply instantiate an Application object. Programs can derive new classes from Application, if necessary, but most of the time, the Application class can be instantiated directly. The Application class is derived from the UIComponent class, although it is somewhat unique, and does not follow the UIComponent model precisely. The most apparent difference is that the Application class does not create any widgets in the constructor, as we will see shortly.

The Application class described in this chapter is very simple. However, most programmers will quickly find that there are other facilities that can be supported in the Application class. For example, if all applications of interest must connect to a server or a database, the connection could be supported in the framework. The Application class provides the essential services required by a Motif application. Additional features can be added easily by creating subclasses. Figure 6.2 shows a class card that summarizes the responsibilities of the Application class.

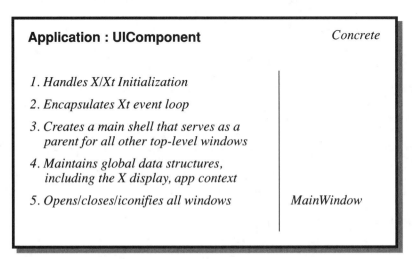

**Application : UIComponent**                                                        *Concrete*

*1. Handles X/Xt Initialization*

*2. Encapsulates Xt event loop*

*3. Creates a main shell that serves as a*
     *parent for all other top-level windows*

*4. Maintains global data structures,*
     *including the X display, app context*

*5. Opens/closes/iconifies all windows*                              *MainWindow*

**Figure 6.2**  The Application class card.

The Application class provides a place to store some data that may be needed throughout an application. This includes a pointer to the X `Display` structure associated with the application's connection to the server, the `XtAppContext` required by many Xt functions, the name of the application, and the class name of the application. This information is maintained in the protected portion of the class and is available to other classes via public access functions. The protected part of the class also includes two member functions, `initialize()` and `handleEvents()`. These member functions are called from `main()`, which is declared as a friend of the Application class. Because only `main()` calls these functions, they do not need to be public. These functions are protected, instead of private, to allow derived classes to override them.

The public portion of the Application class includes the constructor and destructor and various access methods that return the values of private data members. The public protocol also includes the `manage()` and `unmanage()` member functions, which override those inherited from UIComponent, and an `iconify()` member function. These member functions provide a way to manage, unmanage, or iconify all windows in a multi-window application with a single command.

The private portion of the class includes two member functions that can be used to register and unregister MainWindow objects with an Application object. The Application uses this information to manipulate all the windows in an application as a group. These member functions are completely hidden by declaring them in the private section of the class. The MainWindow class can call these functions to register a new MainWindow object, because MainWindow is declared to be a friend.

The Application class is declared as follows:

```
1   ////////////////////////////////////////////////////////////
2   // Application.h:
3   ////////////////////////////////////////////////////////////
4   #ifndef APPLICATION_H
5   #define APPLICATION_H
6   #include "UIComponent.h"
7
8   class Application : public UIComponent {
9
10      // Allow main and MainWindow to access protected member functions
11
12      friend void main ( unsigned int, char ** );
13
14      friend class MainWindow;   // MainWindow needs to call
15                                 // private functions for registration
16    private:
17
18      // Functions for registering and unregistering top level windows
19
20      void registerWindow ( MainWindow * );
21      void unregisterWindow ( MainWindow * );
22
23    protected:
24
25      // Support commonly needed data structures as a convenience
26
```

```
27        Display      *_display;
28        XtAppContext _appContext;
29
30        // Functions to handle Xt interface
31
32        virtual void initialize ( unsigned int *, char ** );
33        virtual void handleEvents();
34
35        char   *_applicationClass;    // Class name of this application
36        MainWindow **_windows;        // Top-level windows in the program
37        int           _numWindows;
38
39   public:
40
41        Application ( char * );
42        virtual ~Application();
43
44        // Functions to manipulate application's top-level windows
45
46        void manage();
47        void unmanage();
48        void iconify();
49
50        // Convenient access functions
51
52        Display      *display()    { return ( _display ); }
53        XtAppContext appContext()  { return ( _appContext ); }
54        const char   *applicationClass()  { return ( _applicationClass ); }
55
56        virtual const char *const className() { return ( "Application" ); }
57   };
58
59   // Pointer to single global instance
60
61   extern Application *theApplication;
62
63   #endif
```

The Application header file exports a pointer to an instance of the Application class, theApplication, which is available to any class that includes the Application.h header file. Each application must create a single instance of the Application class, which can be accessed throughout the program as theApplication.

The file Application.C contains the implementation of the Application class member functions. This file includes the required header files and then defines a pointer to an instance of the Application class, initialized to NULL.

```
1   /////////////////////////////////////////////////////////
2   // Application.C:
3   /////////////////////////////////////////////////////////
4   #include "Application.h"
5   #include "MainWindow.h"
6   #include <assert.h>
7   #include <stdlib.h>
8
9   Application *theApplication = NULL;
10
11  Application::Application ( char *appClassName ) :
12                                          UIComponent ( appClassName )
13  {
14      // Set the global Application pointer
15
16      theApplication = this;
17
18      // Initialize data members
19
20      _display     = NULL;
21      _appContext  = NULL;
22      _windows     = NULL;
23      _numWindows  = 0;
24      _applicationClass = strdup ( appClassName );
25  }
```

The Application class constructor is different than the constructors defined by other user interface classes in this book, because the constructor does not create any widgets. (The reason for this will become clear later in this chapter.) The constructor simply assigns the this pointer to the global variable theApplication, and initializes the class's data members. The constructor takes a single argument, which specifies the class name of the application.

Notice that the constructor also passes the appClassName argument to the UIComponent constructor as the name of the instance. Ideally, the argument passed to UIComponent should be the name of the program, as indicated by argv[0]. As we will see shortly, the Application class is used in such a way that the program name is not available when the Application object is instantiated. The value of appClassName serves as a temporary instance name, because the UIComponent constructor requires a name argument, until the correct name of the application can be determined.

The initialize() member function initializes the Xt Intrinsics and creates the Application object's base widget. The initialize() member function begins by calling XtApp-Initialize() to initialize the Xt Intrinsics, create an application context, and open a connection to the X server. The shell widget returned by XtAppInitialize() is assigned as the Application's base widget.

```
26  void Application::initialize ( unsigned int *argcp, char **argv )
27  {
28      _w = XtAppInitialize ( &_appContext, _applicationClass, NULL, 0,
29                             argcp, argv, NULL, NULL, 0 );
```

```
30
31          // Extract and save a pointer to the X display structure
32
33          _display = XtDisplay ( _w );
34
35          // The Application class is less likely to need to handle
36          // "surprise" widget destruction than other classes, but
37          // install a callback to be safe and consistent
38
39          installDestroyHandler();
40
41          // Center the shell, and make sure it isn't visible
42
43          XtVaSetValues ( _w,
44                          XmNmappedWhenManaged, FALSE,
45                          XmNx, DisplayWidth ( _display, 0 ) / 2,
46                          XmNy, DisplayHeight ( _display, 0 ) / 2,
47                          XmNwidth,  1,
48                          XmNheight, 1,
49                          NULL );
50
51          // The instance name of this object was set in the UIComponent
52          // constructor, before the name of the program was available
53          // Free the old name and reset it to argv[0]
54
55          delete _name;
56          _name = strdup ( argv[0] );
57
58          // Force the shell window to exist so dialogs popped up from
59          // this shell behave correctly
60
61          XtRealizeWidget ( _w );
62
63          // Initialize and manage any windows registered
64          // with this application.
65
66          for ( int i = 0; i < _numWindows; i++ )
67          {
68              _windows[i]->initialize();
69              _windows[i]->manage();
70          }
71  }
```

After creating a shell widget, `initialize()` extracts a pointer to the `Display` structure from the base widget as a convenience to applications based on the MotifApp framework. This structure is often needed in many different parts of an application. The Application class provides this structure through an inline access function, primarily for parts of an application that may not have access to a widget but need a pointer to a `Display` structure.

The UIComponent's destruction-handling mechanism is intended to handle cases where widgets are destroyed before a class's destructor is called. Because the base widget of an Application object is the root of an application's widget tree, it is less likely to be destroyed in this way. However, applications can destroy the widget, accidently or intentionally, by calling `XtDestroyWidget()` on the value returned by the Application's `baseWidget()` member function. To handle this case and to maintain consistency, the `initialize()` function calls `installDestroyHandler()` on line 39.

The MotifApp framework supports applications with multiple top-level windows. There are several possible models for multi-window applications in Xt. One approach is to create a single top-level window used as the main window of the application. All other windows should then be popup shells whose parent is the main window. Another approach is to create a single shell, which never appears on the screen. All other windows must then be popup children of the main shell. In this model, all top-level windows are treated equally, as siblings. One window may logically be the top-level window of the application, but as far as Xt is concerned, all windows are equal. (See [Asente90] for more information about various ways to use multiple top-level shells.)

The Application class supports the second model and creates a single widget that serves as the parent of all top-level windows created by the program. The Application's base widget does not appear on the screen. All other shells in the application must be created using `XtCreatePopupShell()` and displayed using `XtPopup()`. These shell widgets are created by the MainWindow class, discussed in the next section.

The resources specified on line 43 are necessary to support some classes, discussed in Chapter 7, that cache dialogs. One problem with caching dialogs is that every dialog must have a parent. If every dialog to be displayed can potentially have a different parent, caching can become very complex. MotifApp avoids this problem by using the Application class's base widget as the parent of all cached dialogs.

The Motif window manager centers each dialog over its parent widget, if that parent has a window. Normally, the Application class's base widget would not need to be realized to serve as the parent of popup shells. However, it is necessary to realize this widget to support the dialog mechanisms described in Chapter 7 because Motif dialogs must be associated with a window to work correctly with window managers. To prevent the Application class's base widget from appearing on the screen when it is realized, `initialize()` sets the shell's `XmNmappedWhenManaged` resource to `FALSE`. With this resource set, realizing the shell creates an X window for the widget, but does not map the window. The `initialize()` function also positions the shell widget in the center of the screen so dialogs created as children of this widget appear centered on the screen by default.

The Application class sets the value of the `_name` member to the name of the program, as indicated by `argv[0]`. By the time `initialize()` is called, the BasicComponent constructor has already allocated a string and assigned it to `_name`. Therefore, this string is deleted on line 55, before assigning a copy of `argv[0]` to `_name`.

Once the application's main shell has been created and realized, the `initialize()` function loops through a list of MainWindow objects that have been registered with the Application, calling each object's `initialize()` and `manage()` member functions. The MainWindow class, which is discussed in Section 6.3, also creates its widgets in an `initialize()` member function instead of the constructor.

The Application destructor frees the string allocated in the `initialize()` member function and deletes the list of windows. The BasicComponent destructor destroys both the string assigned to _name and the base widget.

```
72  Application::~Application()
73  {
74      delete _applicationClass;
75      delete _windows;
76  }
```

The `handleEvents()` member function calls `XtAppMainLoop()` and never returns.

```
77  void Application::handleEvents()
78  {
79      // Just loop forever
80
81      XtAppMainLoop ( _appContext );
82  }
```

The Application class supports several operations that can be performed on all top-level windows in a multi-window application. To perform operations on all windows, the Application class must maintain a list of all top-level windows in the application. In the MotifApp framework, top-level windows are implemented as instances of the MainWindow class, discussed later in this chapter. The Application member functions, `registerWindow()` and `unregister-Window()` allow each instance of the MainWindow class to register itself with the Application class when it is created, and to unregister itself when the MainWindow object is destroyed.

The function `registerWindow()` adds a single MainWindow object to the Application's list of windows. This function creates a new list of the appropriate size each time it is called. The contents of the old list are copied to the new, and the MainWindow object is added to the end of the list. The previous list is deleted, and the new list is assigned to the _windows member.

```
83  void Application::registerWindow ( MainWindow *window )
84  {
85      int i;
86      MainWindow **newList;
87
88      // Allocate a new list large enough to hold the new
89      // object, and copy the contents of the current list
90      // to the new list
91
92      newList = new MainWindow*[ _numWindows + 1];
93
94      for ( i = 0; i < _numWindows; i++ )
95          newList[i] = _windows[i];
96
97      // Install the new list and add the window to the list
98
```

```
99      delete []_windows;
100      _windows =  newList;
101      _windows[_numWindows] = window;
102
103      _numWindows++;
104   }
```

The function `unregisterWindow()` removes a MainWindow object from the list of top-level windows supported by an Application object. When a MainWindow object is to be removed from an Application object's list of windows, `unregisterWindow()` creates a new, smaller list of MainWindow objects. The contents of the previous list are copied to the new list, skipping the object to be removed. Then the new list is assigned to the `_windows` member.

```
105   void Application::unregisterWindow ( MainWindow *window )
106   {
107       int i, index;
108       MainWindow **newList;
109
110       // Allocate a new, smaller list
111
112       newList = new MainWindow*[_numWindows - 1];
113
114       // Copy all objects, except the one to be
115       // removed, to the new list
116
117       index = 0;
118       for ( i = 0; i < _numWindows; i++ )
119           if ( _windows[i] != window )
120               newList[index++] = _windows[i];
121
122       // Install the new list
123
124       delete []_windows;
125       _windows =  newList;
126
127       _numWindows--;
128   }
```

The Application class uses its list of MainWindow objects to apply many operations to all windows in an application. These operations might include popping up and down all windows, iconifying all windows, or perhaps setting a busy cursor in each window when the application is busy performing some lengthy task. The Application class supports `manage()`, `unmanage()`, and `iconify()` member functions. Derived classes can implement additional operations, if needed. The `manage()` and `unmanage()` member functions override the corresponding UIComponent members.

```
129  void Application::manage()
130  {
131      // Manage all application windows
132      // This will pop up iconified windows as well
133
134      for ( int i = 0; i < _numWindows; i++ )
135          _windows[i]->manage();
136  }

137  void Application::unmanage()
138  {
139      // Unmanage all application windows
140
141      for ( int i = 0; i < _numWindows; i++ )
142          _windows[i]->unmanage();
143  }
```

The iconify() member function closes each registered MainWindow object.

```
144  void Application::iconify()
145  {
146      // Iconify all top-level windows
147
148      for ( int i = 0; i < _numWindows; i++ )
149          _windows[i]->iconify();
150  }
```

Section 6.6 demonstrates how to use the Application class. But first, we must discuss the MainWindow class, which works closely with the Application class to display a top-level window.

# 6.3  The MainWindow Class

The MainWindow class provides the basic layout of an application's top-level window. The MainWindow class creates a popup shell widget that contains a Motif XmMainWindow widget. The XmMainWindow widget is a container widget that handles the layout of a work area and a menubar, in addition to some other widgets. The work area is the application-specific part of a top-level window. It must be a single widget, which is often a container widget that manages other widgets.

Applications that use the MainWindow class only need to create the widgets that appear in the work area. All other widgets and all connections between other objects are handled by the MainWindow class. Figure 6.3 shows a class card that outlines the MainWindow class's responsibilities.

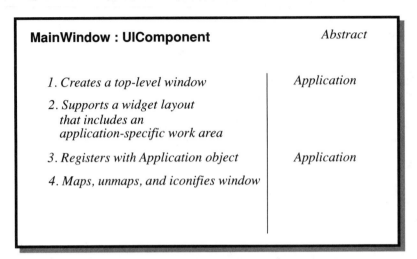

**Figure 6.3**  The MainWindow class card.

The MainWindow class is an abstract class derived from UIComponent. The MainWindow class's public protocol consists of a constructor, destructor, and the `manage()`, `unmanage()`, and `iconify()` member functions. The public portion also includes an `initialize()` member function. Like the Application class, the MainWindow class does not create widgets in its constructor, but uses the `initialize()` member function instead. This allows the MainWindow class to be instantiated before the application is ready to begin creating widgets.

The protected portion of the class defines the protocol between the MainWindow class and derived classes. This protocol includes a pure virtual function that must be overridden by derived classes. The `createWorkArea()` member function is called by the MainWindow class, and is expected to create the window's primary work area. The protected part of the class also allows derived classes to access the widgets created by the MainWindow class, if necessary.

The MainWindow class is declared as follows:

```
1   /////////////////////////////////////////////////////
2   // MainWindow.h: Support a top-level window
3   /////////////////////////////////////////////////////
4   #ifndef MAINWINDOW_H
5   #define MAINWINDOW_H
6   #include "UIComponent.h"
7
8   class MainWindow : public UIComponent {
9
10    protected:
11
12      Widget    _main;        // The XmMainWindow widget
13      Widget    _workArea;    // Widget created by derived class
14
```

```
15      // Derived classes must define this function to
16      // create the application-specific work area
17
18      virtual Widget createWorkArea ( Widget ) = 0;
19
20   public:
21
22      MainWindow ( char * );    // Constructor requires only a name
23      virtual ~MainWindow();
24
25      // The Application class automatically calls initialize()
26      // for all registered main window objects
27
28      virtual void initialize();
29
30      virtual void manage();    // Pop up the window
31      virtual void unmanage(); // Pop down the window
32      virtual void iconify();
33   };
34   #endif
```

The MainWindow constructor calls the UIComponent class constructor and then registers the new object with the program's Application object. An `assert()` statement checks that theApplication exists.

```
1    ////////////////////////////////////////////////////////////////
2    // MainWindow.C: Support a top-evel window
3    ////////////////////////////////////////////////////////////////
4    #include "Application.h"
5    #include "MainWindow.h"
6    #include <Xm/MainW.h>
7    #include <assert.h>
8
9    MainWindow::MainWindow ( char *name ) : UIComponent ( name )
10   {
11       _workArea = NULL;
12       assert ( theApplication ); // Application object must exist
13                                  // before any MainWindow object
14       theApplication->registerWindow ( this );
15   }
```

The `initialize()` member function creates the widgets used by the MainWindow object. Recall from Section 6.2 that the Application class's `initialize()` member function calls the `initialize()` function for each registered MainWindow object. If a program creates a MainWindow object after the Application's `initialize()` member function has been executed, the `MainWindow::initialize()` member function can also be called directly.

The MainWindow class's `initialize()` member function creates a popup shell, specifying the shell widget created by the Application class as the parent. After installing the UIComponent destruction handler, initialize() creates a Motif XmMainWindow widget. This widget provides a convenient layout for top-level windows, and supports a "work area," a menubar, and a command area. The MainWindow class is very simple and only uses the work area, but derived classes can take advantage of the additional features of the XmMainWindow widget.

Once the XmMainWindow widget exists, initialize() calls the createWorkArea() member function, which must be defined by a derived class, to create the application-specific work area widget. This function must return a single widget, and initialize() uses an assert() statement to confirm that createWorkArea() has a valid return value. If create-WorkArea() returns a valid widget, initialize() uses XtVaSetValues() to establish this widget as the XmMainWindow widget's work area widget. Finally, initialize() manages the work area widget if it is not already managed.

```
16   void MainWindow::initialize( )
17   {
18        // All top-level windows in the MotifApp framework are
19        // implemented as a popup shell off the Application's
20        // base widget

21

22        _w = XtCreatePopupShell ( _name,
23                                  applicationShellWidgetClass,
24                                  theApplication->baseWidget(),
25                                  NULL, 0 );
26        installDestroyHandler();

27

28        // Use a Motif XmMainWindow widget to handle window layout

29

30        _main = XtCreateManagedWidget ( "mainWindow",
31                                        xmMainWindowWidgetClass,
32                                        _w,
33                                        NULL, 0 );

34

35        // Called derived class to create the work area

36

37        _workArea = createWorkArea ( _main );
38        assert ( _workArea );

39

40        // Designate the _workArea widget as the XmMainWindow
41        // widget's XmNworkArea widget

42

43        XtVaSetValues ( _main,
44                        XmNworkWindow, _workArea,
45                        NULL );

46

47        // Manage the work area if the derived class hasn't already

48

49        if ( !XtIsManaged ( _workArea ) )
50            XtManageChild ( _workArea );
51   }
```

The MainWindow destructor removes the deleted object from the Application object's list of windows. The base class destructor destroys the shell widget, which triggers the destruction of the other widgets.

```
52  MainWindow::~MainWindow( )
53  {
54      // Unregister this window with the Application object
55
56      theApplication->unregisterWindow ( this );
57  }
```

The MainWindow class overrides the UIComponent manage() member function because popup shells must be made visible with XtPopup() instead of XtManageChild(). Like the manage() member function defined by UIComponent, this function uses the assert() macro to be sure the component's base widget exists when this member function is called. The manage() member function also calls the Xlib function XMapRaised() to raise the window to the top. This function also opens the window if it is currently in an iconic state.

```
58  void MainWindow::manage()
59  {
60      assert ( _w );
61      XtPopup ( _w, XtGrabNone );
62
63      // Map the window, in case the window is iconified
64
65      if ( XtIsRealized ( _w ) )
66          XMapRaised ( XtDisplay ( _w ), XtWindow ( _w ) );
67  }
```

The MainWindow class also overrides the unmanage() member function, because the MainWindow class needs to call XtPopdown() to remove the popup shell from the screen, instead of calling XtUnmanageChild() as the inherited member function does. The new unmanage() function is written as:

```
68  void MainWindow::unmanage()
69  {
70      assert ( _w );
71      XtPopdown ( _w );
72  }
```

Finally, the iconify() member function provides a way to iconify a window programmatically.

```
73  void MainWindow::iconify()
74  {
75      assert ( _w );
76
```

```
77        // Set the widget to have an initial iconic state
78        // in case the base widget has not yet been realized
79
80        XtVaSetValues ( _w, XmNiconic, TRUE, NULL );
81
82        // If the widget has already been realized,
83        // iconify the window
84
85        if ( XtIsRealized ( _w ) )
86            XIconifyWindow ( XtDisplay ( _w ), XtWindow ( _w ), 0 );
87    }
```

This completes the implementation of the MainWindow class. The MainWindow class provides the minimum set of features needed to allow an application to create only the "work area" portion of the user interface. The MainWindow class works closely with the Application class to provide some basic window manipulation functions. MotifApp applications are expected to use subclasses of MainWindow as the basis of each top-level window in an application.

# 6.4    The MotifApp main() Function

One of the most interesting aspects of MotifApp is that applications based on this framework do not need to define main(). The function main() is defined as part of the framework and handles calling the Application::initialize() member function and entering the event loop. Hiding main() allows the framework to handle even more of the routine initialization all applications must perform and encourages the view that each program is an instance of the Application class. MotifApp applications are created simply by instantiating an Application object.

MotifApp defines main() in the file Main.C. This function is written as follows:

```
1   ////////////////////////////////////////////////////////
2   // Main.C: Generic main program used by all applications
3   ////////////////////////////////////////////////////////
4   #include "Application.h"
5   #include <assert.h>
6
7   // We can implement main() in the library because the
8   // framework completely encapsulates all Xt boilerplate
9   // and all central flow of control
10
11  void main ( unsigned int argc, char **argv )
12  {
13      // Make sure the programmer has remembered to
14      // instantiate an Application object
15
```

```
16      assert ( theApplication );
17
18      // Init Intrinsics, build all windows, and enter event loop
19
20      theApplication->initialize ( &argc, argv );
21
22      theApplication->handleEvents();
23  }
```

Notice that `main()` does not create an instance of the Application class, but expects it to exist when the program begins. Each program must instantiate an Application object as a global variable. If the application does this correctly, `theApplication` will be initialized before the first statement in `main()` is executed. The function `main()` uses the `assert()` macro to make sure applications actually instantiate a global Application object.

Figure 6.4 shows a message diagram that documents the relationships between the MainWindow class, the Application class, and `main()`. It also shows the role of a class derived from MainWindow.

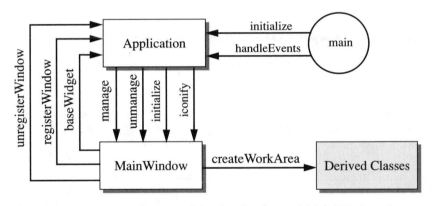

**Figure 6.4** A message diagram of the Application and MainWindow classes.

The MainWindow and Application classes work together to form a simple, but somewhat unusual, way to write programs. After briefly discussing how to build the MotifApp library, Section 6.6 demonstrates how these classes are used to write a MotifApp program.

# 6.5    The MotifApp Library

The examples in the remainder of this book assume the existence of a MotifApp library. This library includes the BasicComponent and UIComponent classes discussed earlier in this book, in addition to the Application and MainWindow classes described in this chapter. The library also includes the function `main()`, which is defined by the framework instead of by individual applications. Most of the classes introduced in later chapters belong in this library as well.

An initial version of the MotifApp library can be built by compiling the classes mentioned so far, and archiving them into a library, as follows:

```
CC -c Main.C BasicComponent.C UIComponent.C Application.C MainWindow.C

ar ruv libMotifApp.a Main.o BasicComponent.o UIComponent.o \
                     Application.o MainWindow.o
```

It is, of course, unusual to have the function `main()` built into a library. Linking `main()` into the MotifApp library means that all applications that use classes from this library must follow certain conventions. In particular, programs must not define `main()`, because `main()` already exists in libMotifApp.a, and only one function named `main()` can exist in any program.

The following section shows how this library is used in conjunction with application-specific files to create a MotifApp program.

## 6.6    Using the Application Framework

Although we have not yet discussed many other classes in the MotifApp framework, the Application and MainWindow classes provide an adequate base for simple applications. This section demonstrates how to use these classes to implement a version of the "Hello World" example, first presented in Chapter 1.

The first step is to create a subclass of MainWindow, to be used as the application's top-level window. This class only needs to create the "work area" part of the window. For the "Hello World" example, the work area is a label widget that displays the string "Hello World." The class Hello-Window can be declared as follows:

```
1   /////////////////////////////////////////////////////////////////
2   // HelloWindow.C: "Hello World" main window
3   /////////////////////////////////////////////////////////////////
4   #ifndef HELLOWINDOW_H
5   #define HELLOWINDOW_H
6
7   #include "MainWindow.h"
8
9   class HelloWindow : public MainWindow {
10
11      protected:
12
13          virtual Widget createWorkArea ( Widget ); // Creates the label
14
```

```
15    public:
16
17      // Empty, inline constructor
18
19      HelloWindow ( char *name ) : MainWindow ( name ) { }
20    };
21    #endif
```

The file HelloWindow.C contains the implementation of the `createWorkArea()` member function. This function simply creates a compound string that represents the character string "Hello World," and creates an XmLabel widget to display the string. The function concludes by freeing the compound string and returning the label widget.

```
1     /////////////////////////////////////////////////////////////
2     // HelloWindow.C: "Hello World" main window
3     /////////////////////////////////////////////////////////////
4     #include "HelloWindow.h"
5     #include <Xm/Label.h>
6
7     Widget HelloWindow::createWorkArea ( Widget parent )
8     {
9         // Create a compound string to display the Hello message
10
11        XmString xmstr = XmStringCreateSimple ( "Hello World" );
12
13        // Create a label widget to display the string
14
15        Widget label = XtVaCreateWidget ( "label",
16                                          xmLabelWidgetClass,
17                                          parent,
18                                          XmNlabelString, xmstr,
19                                          NULL );
20
21        // Free the compound string when it is no longer needed
22
23        XmStringFree ( xmstr );
24        return ( label );
25    }
```

Once a class derived from MainWindow has been defined, we can complete the application by creating the body of the application. MotifApp's notion of a "main application body" is very different from that of more traditional programs. The file HelloApp.C is considered to be the main body of the "Hello World" example. This file includes the Application.h and HelloWindow.h header files, and then declares two objects, an Application object and a HelloWindow object. This is the entire program.

```
1    ////////////////////////////////////////////////////////////
2    // HelloApp.C: "Hello World" program,
3    //             using the MotifApp framework
4    ////////////////////////////////////////////////////////////
5    #include "Application.h"
6    #include "HelloWindow.h"
7
8    // Instantiate an application object and a MainWindow
9
10   Application *helloApp = new Application ( "Hello" );
11   MainWindow  *window   = new HelloWindow ( "Hello" );
```

Let's look at the sequence of events that occur when this program runs. First, the program evaluates the global statements contained in HelloApp.C. These statements create an instance of the Application class, followed by an instance of the HelloWindow class. The MainWindow constructor registers the new HelloWindow object with the Application object, which can now be referenced though the variable `theApplication`. After these objects have been instantiated, the program enters `main()`, which calls the Application object's `initialize()` member function. `Application::initialize()` opens a connection to the X server, creates a shell widget, and then calls the HelloWindow object's `initialize()` member function. `MainWindow::initialize()` creates a shell and an XmMainWindow widget, and then calls the HelloWindow class's `createWorkArea()` member function to create the label widget. Finally, the Application object manages the HelloWindow object, causing it to appear on the screen. The framework enters the event loop when `main()` calls `Application::handleEvents()`, completing the process.

Notice that most of this process is hidden from applications based on MotifApp. MotifApp applications need only to derive a new class from MainWindow. This derived class provides any application-specific widgets that appear in the window. Once this class has been written, the body of the application simply creates an instance of the Application class, along with whatever MainWindow objects the applications wishes to display when the application runs.

To build the HelloApp program, the file HelloApp.C must be compiled and linked with the HelloWindow class and the MotifApp library. For example, the executable "hello" can be built like this:

```
CC -c HelloApp.C HelloWindow.C

CC -o hello HelloApp.o HelloWindow.o libMotifApp.a -lXm -lXt -lX11
```

Some caution is necessary when instantiating the global objects expected by MotifApp. The Application class must exist before the first line of `main()` is executed and also before any MainWindow object is created. Both the provided `main()` function and the MainWindow class use `assert()` statements to catch programs that do not do this correctly. For any given file, the order of initialization of non-local static objects occurs in the same order as the objects appear in the file. However, C++ does not guarantee the order of initialization for global objects in different files. Therefore, applications must instantiate the Application object and all initial MainWindow objects in the same file, in the order demonstrated above, because MainWindow depends on an instance of the Application class.

Applications in this book follow the convention just demonstrated. Every application has a file that serves as the main body of the program. By convention, examples in this book use a file name that ends with the letters "App" (for example, HelloApp.C) for this main file. This file creates one instance of the Application class, or a derived class, and then creates one or more MainWindow objects.

Although each application must create a single Application object, programs can create as many MainWindow objects as needed. For example, the following program creates two instances of the HelloWindow class, which creates two windows that display the "Hello World" message.

```
1   ////////////////////////////////////////////////////////////
2   // HelloApp.C: "Hello World" program,
3   //              using the MotifApp framework
4   ////////////////////////////////////////////////////////////
5   #include "Application.h"
6   #include "HelloWindow.h"
7
8   // Instantiate an application object and a MainWindow
9
10  Application *myApp   = new Application ( "Hello" );
11  MainWindow  *window  = new HelloWindow ( "Window1" );
12  MainWindow  *window2 = new HelloWindow ( "Window2" );
```

Figure 6.5 shows the widget tree created by this multi-window example. The Application class creates the root of the tree, but this window does not appear on the screen. The only widget directly created by the program is the XmLabel widget shown in each window. All other widgets are created by the application framework.

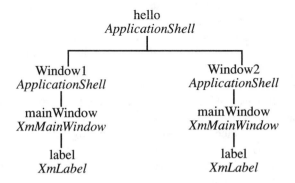

**Figure 6.5**  Widget tree formed by multi-window "Hello World" program.

Figure 6.6 shows the multi-window version of "Hello World" as it appears on the screen. Each window can be manipulated independently.

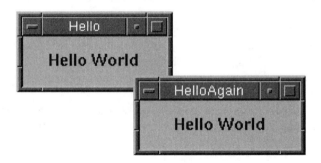

**Figure 6.6** "Hello World" with multiple MainWindow objects

## 6.7  Summary

This chapter introduces the foundation of an application framework that defines the basic architecture of a typical Motif application. The heart of the framework is the Application class. This simple class encapsulates the Xt initialization code required by all applications. Applications based on the MotifApp framework must create an instance of the Application class as a non-local variable at the beginning of a file.

The Application class works closely with the MainWindow class. This abstract class creates a shell and a Motif XmMainWindow widget. Concrete classes derived from MainWindow must define a single member function that creates the application-specific widgets that form the program's interface. Every MotifApp application is expected to create an instance of a class derived from MainWindow, immediately after creating an instance of the Application class. In addition, the MotifApp library defines `main()` instead of expecting applications to define this function.

The simple Application and MainWindow classes presented here provide only the minimum set of features that could be supported by such classes. Application frameworks are particularly effective when working with a family of related applications. In such cases, it is usually easy to identify many common features that can be supported in the framework, rather than being implemented in each program. It is usually best to add such features to the framework by creating new classes derived from the simpler base classes, like Application. By keeping the Application class as simple as possible, this class can meet the needs of a broad range of applications. Applications that require additional features and enhancements can define new classes derived from Application.

The following chapters examine other parts of the MotifApp framework, building on the simple architecture introduced in this chapter.

# Dialogs

Dialog windows that appear on the screen for a relatively short amount of time for some special purpose are a common feature of many interactive applications. Dialogs allow applications to ask questions, display important information, or provide access to functionality that does not always need to be accessible from the application's main window. Because most applications contain a significant amount of code dedicated to handling such dialogs, dialog-related facilities make good candidates for C++ classes. Although Motif provides many ready-to-use dialog widgets, it is still useful to consider some C++ classes that capture some higher-level mechanisms that help manage dialogs.

This chapter begins by discussing some general architectural considerations for X-based applications that use dialogs. Section 7.2 presents an abstract DialogManager class that supports a caching mechanism for Motif dialog widgets. Sections 7.3 and 7.4 discuss two classes derived from DialogManager that convey information to the user and ask questions that require responses.

## 7.1   Using Dialogs

Most interactive applications support many ways to get input from users. For many applications, the normal mode of operation requires continuous real-time input. For example, the TicTacToe game described in Chapter 5 allows the user to interact directly with the program through its main window. This type of input needs to be quick and simple for the user.

Consider the window in Figure 7.1. This hypothetical application provides a graph of some information that changes over time. The user can control the range of time over which the graph is displayed by changing the "From" or "To" fields. Presumably, the graph changes immediately to display the new range. The user can also use the toggle button in the lower left corner of the window to alter the way the information is displayed.

This window allows the user to see and manipulate all available parameters directly. For a simple program, it is reasonable to place all commands in the main window. However, as a program's complexity grows, so does the number of commands the program supports. Displaying all available operations in a single window quickly produces an application with an unmanageable number of buttons, menus, and other input areas. Such an interface can be overwhelming to the user because it is difficult to tell which input areas and controls are essential and which are merely options. Such interfaces are often large and clumsy looking, because of the large number of controls in the main window.

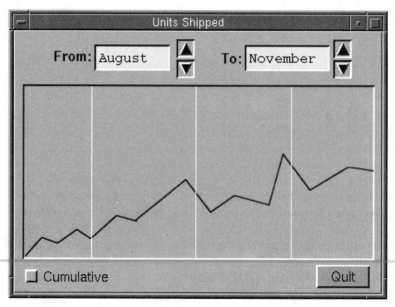

**Figure 7.1** A fully interactive user interface.

One way to handle applications with many inputs, controls, or options, is to place seldom-used portions of the user interface in separate dialog windows that are not displayed unless needed. Dialog windows can be used in several different ways. For example, applications often use dialogs to convey information to the user. Once the user has seen this type of dialog, either the user or the application usually removes it from the screen. Dialogs can also be used to request specific information from the user. Such dialogs usually disappear once the user has supplied the needed information.

Applications can also use dialogs as optional control panels that can stay on the screen as long as the user needs them. For example, Figure 7.2 shows a variation of the interface shown in Figure

7.1. In Figure 7.2, the controls for manipulating the range and format of the data displayed in the graph have been removed from the main window. These controls are not visible unless the user needs them. Clicking on the "Select Range" button displays a dialog that contains the controls previously located in the main window.

There are several ways this dialog could be used. One approach is to allow the controls to affect the graph display in real time, just as in the earlier version of the program. When used this way, the dialog usually stays on the screen as long as the user needs it. Once the user has finished using the dialog, he or she can dismiss the dialog or leave it on the screen for later use. The dialog could also be designed to allow the user to change the values in the dialog without immediately affecting the data displayed in the main window. When the user presses an OK button on the dialog, the dialog usually disappears and the graph is updated.

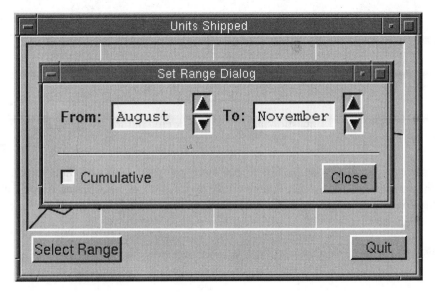

**Figure 7.2**  Putting seldom-needed controls in a dialog.

The example shown in Figure 7.2 demonstrates a dialog that allows the user to input data at any time. While the dialog is displayed, the user can usually continue to interact with the application in other ways. This dialog simply provides a way to reduce the clutter in the main window by putting the controls in a separate optional window.

Applications can also use dialogs to request information from the user that the application requires before proceeding. Figure 7.3 shows a dialog that asks the user to confirm a "quit" command. This type of question normally requires an immediate answer. The application cannot carry out the current command, "quit," without an answer.

Dialogs that ask questions present a challenge to X programmers because X applications must always continue to handle events, even when waiting for a response to a question. Organizing an application to handle events while waiting for such a response requires careful attention to the program's structure.

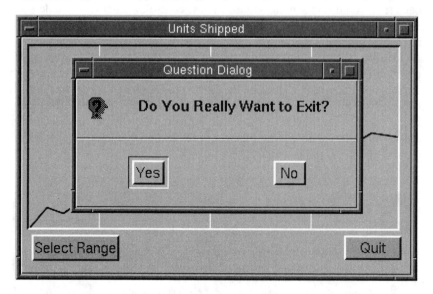

**Figure 7.3**  A question that must be answered before proceeding.


Consider the example shown in Figure 7.3. Here, the user selects a "Quit" button to exit an application. Attempting to be "user friendly," the application posts a dialog asking the user to confirm the command. A naive way to write the callback routine for the quit button might look something like this:

```
void quitCallback ( Widget w, XtPointer, XtPointer )
{
    // WRONG!!

    if ( confirmExitCommand() )
        exit ( 0 );
}
```

Here, the function `confirmExitCommand()` is expected to post a confirmation dialog, wait until the user responds, and return `TRUE` if the user confirms, or `FALSE` otherwise. However, this is difficult to do in an X application. In general, X applications cannot simply block while waiting for input. One way to simulate blocking in such situations is for the `confirmExitCommand()` function to enter its own event loop and handle events until the user responds. This loop can watch for events in the dialog widget and leave the loop when the user answers the question and dismisses the dialog. However, creating a secondary event loop is not usually recommended because this approach can lead to problems if code is not re-entrant. Secondary event loops can be used safely, but only if the programmer is aware that the program is not really blocked, but is actually continuing to handle events. (See [Sklar91] for a discussion of this approach to dialogs.)

The approach normally used in Motif applications requires the application to be restructured slightly to take advantage of the Xt callback mechanism, and to allow the application to continue to check the event queue for input. To continue handling events, we must move the actual call to exit() into a callback function registered with the "yes" (or "OK") button on the dialog. Using this approach, the quitCallback() function simply displays the confirmation dialog box, and registers additional functions to be called when the user answers the question.

The new quitCallback() function could be written as follows:

```
void quitCallback ( Widget w, XtPointer, XtPointer )
{
    Widget    dialog;
    XmString xmstr;

    // Declare callback functions, implemented elsewhere

    extern void reallyQuitCallback ( Widget, XtPointer, XtPointer );
    extern void destroyDialogCallback ( Widget, XtPointer, XtPointer );

    // Create a compound string version of the desired message

    xmstr = XmStringCreateSimple ( QUITMESSAGE );

    // Create a Motif QuestionDialog to display the message

    dialog = XmCreateQuestionDialog ( w, "confirm", NULL, 0 );

    // Set the string and mode of the dialog

    XtVaSetValues ( dialog,
                    XmNmessageString, xmstr,
                    XmNdialogStyle,    XmDIALOG_FULL_APPLICATION_MODEL,
                    NULL );

    // Register callback routines for ok and cancel

    XtAddCallback ( dialog,
                    XmNokCallback,
                    reallyQuitCallback,
                    NULL );
    XtAddCallback ( dialog,
                    XmNcancelCallback,
                    destroyDialogCallback,
                    NULL );
}
```

In this example, QUITMESSAGE is assumed to be defined as an appropriate message, such as "Do you really want to exit?", and reallyQuitCallback() is presumed to be a callback function that simply calls `exit()`. The `destroyDialogCallback()` function calls `XtDestroyWidget()` to destroy the dialog when it is no longer needed.

Figure 7.4 shows the sequence of events that would occur when the user tries to exit an application that implements this approach. Each arrow represents an event, or flow of control, and each box represents a function or module in the program. The sequence begins when the user clicks on the quit button, causing an event (shown as the vector marked A) which is read and dispatched by the application's event loop. The function `quitCallback()` is called as a result of this event (vector B). The `quitCallback()` function posts a dialog (a Motif QuestionDialog) to ask the user to confirm the command, and registers two callbacks. Next, `quitCallback()` returns, allowing the application to continue to handle events. Although the user has issued a quit command, the application is still running. While waiting for the user to confirm the command, the application is still handling events, responding to resize notifications, `Expose` events, and so on.

Eventually, the user will select one of the buttons on the confirmation dialog, either the "OK", or the "Cancel" button. Depending on which button is selected, the `reallyQuitCallback()` (vector E) will be called, or the `destroyDialogCallback()` (vector F) will be called. In the first case, the application exits. In the second case, the `destroyDialogCallback()` simply destroys the dialog, which removes it from the screen, and returns control (vector G) to the event loop, which waits for the next user input.

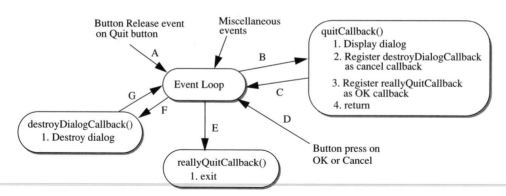

**Figure 7.4** Implementing a "safe quit" mechanism.

Notice that during this entire scenario the application is never actually blocked while waiting for a response. The application is continually handling events, including `Expose` events, window configuration events, and so on. There is one potential problem with this approach. The application can also handle device events, which means that the user can push buttons, pop up menus and so on, to issue additional commands. This can lead to many problems, and is not what the user expects.

Fortunately, there is a simple way to force the user to answer the question before moving on. Notice that the `quitCallback()` function shown on the previous page sets the dialog's `XmNdialogStyle` resource to `XmDIALOG_FULL_APPLICATION_MODAL`. This resource configures the dialog in such a way that Xt ignores any device events for the application except those that occur in the posted dialog. The remainder of the application can still receive and process exposure and configuration events, but mouse or keyboard input is ignored. The user can choose the OK or Cancel buttons on the dialog, but nothing else. Therefore the application appears to the user to be waiting for a reply to a question, even though the program is not blocked in the traditional sense.

The scenario above involves a relatively straightforward use of dialogs and dynamically-installed callbacks. This approach can also be extended to handle much more complex situations. For example, Figure 7.4 shows an expanded sequence of events that represents an application that performs one additional check in its exit routine. In this scenario, the application not only asks the user to confirm the quit command, but also checks if the program has data that should be saved before exiting. If the program has unsaved data, the program asks the user if the data should be saved before exiting.

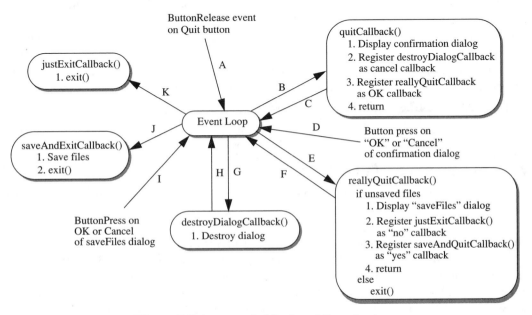

**Figure 7.5** An extended "safe quit" mechanism.

There are several possible scenarios in this example. Each sequence starts when the user initiates an event (vector A) that causes the program to invoke the `quitCallback()` function (vector B). The `quitCallback()` function posts a dialog and registers callbacks for the OK and Cancel buttons, and then returns (vector C). Eventually the user selects an OK or Cancel button on the confirmation dialog (vector D), which results in either the `reallyQuitCallback()` function (vector E) or the `destroyDialogCallback()` function (vector G) being called.

If the `destroyDialogCallback()` function is called, it simply destroys the confirmation dialog and returns, ending the sequence. If the `reallyQuitCallback()` function is invoked, the next phase of the sequence begins. The `reallyQuitCallback()` function checks whether any files need to be saved. If unsaved files exist, the function does not exit, but simply posts another dialog and registers two callbacks for the OK and Cancel buttons on this dialog. The new dialog displays a question: "Do you wish to save files before exiting?" and then returns control to the dispatch loop (vector F).

Eventually, the user will select one of the OK or Cancel buttons on the new dialog (vector I). When this happens, the dispatch mechanism will call either `justExitCallback()` (vector K), or `saveAndExitCallback()` (vector J), as appropriate. Both of these functions exit, ending the sequence, although `saveAndExitCallback()` saves all files first.

It is easy to imagine extending this sequence even further before exiting. For example, the routine responsible for saving the files might encounter an error while saving a file (the disk could be full, or the application might not have permission to write the file). Additional dialogs might be required to ask the user to make additional choices, or to allow the user to abort the exit sequence.

Motif provides many dialog widgets that can be used to implement mechanisms such as those described above. However, while Motif provides the raw pieces, most applications need to write a considerable amount of code, much of which is redundant, to manage these dialogs effectively. This makes a class or classes that manage dialogs an attractive idea. For example, the sequence of events described above could be encapsulated in a QuitHandler class, so that every application would not have to implement this mechanism. The following section looks at a general class that supports applications that use dialogs. The remainder of this chapter, together with Chapters 8 and 9, describe additional classes that make it easier to implement commands that involve complex sequences of user interaction, such as the scenarios discussed in this section.

## 7.2  The DialogManager Class

There are several issues that must be resolved in any substantial application that uses dialogs. For example, how does the application deal with many distinct messages to the user? Does each separate message use its own dialog? If so, are all dialogs created at startup, or only when needed? If an application creates all dialogs at start-up, the program will take a longer time to display the first window. These dialogs, which may never be used, consume memory and tie up server resources. If dialogs are not created until they are used, programs will be smaller and have a faster initial startup time. However, depending on the performance of the system being used, there may be an unacceptable delay in posting each dialog, because the application must create a new dialog for each message.

One reasonable compromise is to create only a single dialog widget, and reuse it for all messages. This is an efficient approach, because only one dialog widget must be created. Once the dialog has been created, later uses are very fast. However, there are some problems to solve when using this approach. For example, what happens if the dialog is already in use, and the application needs to display a second message? The new message could replace the previous message in the displayed dialog, but this might make the first message flash by so quickly that the user cannot read it.

One effective approach is to create a dialog cache. If the cache contains an unused dialog when the application needs to post some information, an existing dialog can be posted quickly. Otherwise the application can create additional dialogs as needed. These dialogs can be added to the cache, or destroyed when they are no longer needed. This mechanism is an ideal candidate for a C++ class that encapsulates the details and provides an easy-to-use interface.

This section presents a DialogManager class that encapsulates a simple dialog caching mechanism. The Dialog Manager is an abstract class that serves as a base class for several other, more specific, dialog classes that can be used by programs based on the MotifApp framework.

Before we can look at the DialogManager class, we must introduce an auxiliary class, the DialogCallbackData class. The DialogManager needs to pass several types of client data to various callbacks. The DialogCallbackData class provides a container for this information. The DialogCallbackData class is declared as follows:

```
1  ///////////////////////////////////////////////////////////////
2  // DialogCallbackData.h: Auxiliary class used by DialogManager
3  ///////////////////////////////////////////////////////////////
4  #ifndef DIALOGCALLBACKDATA
5  #define DIALOGCALLBACKDATA
6
7  class DialogManager;
8
9  typedef void ( *DialogCallback )( void * );
10
11  class DialogCallbackData {
12    private:
13
14      DialogManager  *_dialogManager;
15      DialogCallback  _ok;
16      DialogCallback  _help;
17      DialogCallback  _cancel;
18      void           *_clientData;
19
20    public:
21
22      DialogCallbackData ( DialogManager *dialog,
23                           void          *clientData,
24                           DialogCallback ok,
25                           DialogCallback cancel,
26                           DialogCallback help)
27      {
28          _dialogManager = dialog;
29          _ok            = ok;
30          _help          = help;
31          _cancel        = cancel;
32          _clientData    = clientData;
33      }
34      DialogManager  *dialogManager() { return ( _dialogManager ); }
35      DialogCallback  ok() { return ( _ok ); }
36      DialogCallback  help() { return ( _help ); }
37      DialogCallback  cancel() { return ( _cancel ); }
38      void           *clientData() { return ( _clientData ); }
39  };
40  #endif
```

The DialogCallbackData class declares a function pointer type, DialogCallback, which represents a function that has no return value and expects an untyped pointer as its only argument. The class supports several private members, including a pointer to a DialogManager object, several function pointers, and a `clientData` field. The constructor is declared inline and simply initializes the private members. There is no implementation file, because the complete DialogCallbackData class can be completely implemented in the header file using inline functions. We will see how this class is used shortly.

The DialogManager class handles the details of displaying and caching arbitrary types of dialogs. The DialogManager is an abstract class that provides a supporting infrastructure for derived classes, which must create the actual dialog widgets. For example, Section 7.3 describes an InfoDialogManager class used to display simple messages and Section 7.4 describes a QuestionDialogManager class that can be used to ask the user a question. The MotifApp framework supports a single instance of each of these classes. Applications that need to display dialogs can simply send a message to the appropriate DialogManager object.

The DialogManager class defines the external protocol followed by all dialog manager classes. Applications can display a dialog by calling the `post()` member function for the appropriate dialog manager object. This member function allows the caller to specify a message to be displayed and also allows the caller to provide some optional callback functions to be called if the user selects one of the various buttons supported by Motif dialogs. For example, all dialogs support an OK button and a help button; many also support a cancel button. Applications can simply provide a function of type DialogCallback, as defined in DialogCallbackData.h, to be called when the user clicks on one of these buttons.

Figure 7.6 shows a class card that outlines the primary responsibilities of the DialogManager class.

| **DialogManager: UIComponent** | *Abstract* |
|---|---|
| *1. Posts a dialog* | *Application* |
| *2. Caches dialogs for efficiency* | |
| *3. Handles dialog callbacks* | |

**Figure 7.6**  The DialogManager class card.

The DialogManager class relies on the Application class because Motif dialogs require a parent widget. We could force applications to pass a widget to the post() method to be used as a parent, but allowing different parents would complicate the caching mechanisms. Also, Motif dialogs tend to center over their parent, and applications may not always have an appropriate widget available at the point in the program at which the dialog is posted. For example, some dialogs may be posted from callbacks called from a menu item where the only available widget is the button widget in the menu. Centering the dialog over a button in a menu does not normally provide the best position.

The DialogManager class uses the unmapped shell supported by the Application class as the parent of all dialogs. Using the Application class's shell widget ensures that all dialogs have the same parent, which simplifies the caching, and centers the dialog on the screen. The center of the screen is not always the best place for a dialog, but it is a reasonable compromise between usability and ease of implementation in this simple example.

The DialogManager class is derived from UIComponent. The DialogManager class is declared as:

```
1    ////////////////////////////////////////////////////////
2    // DialogManager.h: A base class for cached dialogs
3    ////////////////////////////////////////////////////////
4    #ifndef DIALOGMANAGER_H
5    #define DIALOGMANAGER_H
6
7    #include "UIComponent.h"
8    #include "DialogCallbackData.h"
9
10   class DialogManager : public UIComponent {
11
12     private:
13
14       Widget getDialog();
15
16       static void destroyTmpDialogCallback ( Widget,
17                                              XtPointer,
18                                              XtPointer );
19       static void okCallback ( Widget,
20                                XtPointer,
21                                XtPointer );
22
23       static void cancelCallback ( Widget,
24                                    XtPointer,
25                                    XtPointer );
26
27       static void helpCallback ( Widget,
28                                  XtPointer,
29                                  XtPointer );
30
31       void cleanup ( Widget, DialogCallbackData* );
32
```

```
33    protected:
34
35      // Called to get a new dialog
36
37      virtual Widget createDialog ( Widget ) = 0;
38
39    public:
40
41      DialogManager ( char * );
42
43      virtual Widget post ( char *,
44                            void *clientData      = NULL,
45                            DialogCallback ok     = NULL,
46                            DialogCallback cancel = NULL,
47                            DialogCallback help   = NULL );
48  };
49  #endif
```

The DialogManager class has a very simple public protocol. The constructor expects a single argument, which is used as the name of all dialogs. Applications that need to display a dialog simply call the post() member function, providing a message to be displayed and various optional callback functions to be called when the user selects the OK, Cancel, or Help buttons on the dialog. Notice that not all Motif dialog widgets have all of these buttons, but the DialogManager class supports all three for those cases in which they apply.

The protected section of the class declaration defines the subclass protocol. All derived classes must implement a createDialog() member function. This member function must create and return a dialog widget of the type supported by the derived class. This widget must be a Motif XmMessageBox widget, or a subclass of XmMessageBox. The private portion of the class contains various callbacks used to manage the dialogs.

The DialogManager constructor just calls the UIComponent constructor to initialize the component's name.

```
1   ////////////////////////////////////////////////////////
2   // DialogManager.C: Support cached dialog widgets
3   ////////////////////////////////////////////////////////
4   #include "DialogManager.h"
5   #include "Application.h"
6   #include <Xm/MessageB.h>
7   #include <assert.h>
8
9   DialogManager::DialogManager ( char    *name ): UIComponent ( name )
10  {
11      // Empty
12  }
```

The function getDialog() is called whenever a DialogManager object needs a dialog widget. This member function provides a very simple caching mechanism. The function first checks to see if the component's base widget exists. If it exists, and is not currently being displayed, the function simply returns the existing base widget. Otherwise, getDialog() calls the create-Dialog() member function defined by derived classes to create a new dialog widget. This createDialog() member function expects a parent widget, which getDialog() specifies as the base widget of the global Application object. If the new widget is a temporary dialog, created because the base widget is already in use, getDialog() registers the destroyTmpDialog-Callback() function to destroy the dialog once it has served its purpose. If, on the other hand, the base widget has not yet been created, getDialog() assigns the newly created dialog widget to the _w member, which then serves as the permanently cached dialog widget.

```
13  Widget DialogManager::getDialog()
14  {
15      Widget newDialog = NULL;
16
17      // If the permanent widget exists and is not in use,
18      // just return it
19
20      if ( _w && !XtIsManaged ( _w ) )
21          return ( _w );
22
23      // Get a widget from the derived class
24
25      newDialog = createDialog ( theApplication->baseWidget() ) ;
26
27      // If this is a temporary dialog, install callbacks to
28      // destroy it when the user pops it down.
29
30      if ( _w )
31      {
32          XtAddCallback ( newDialog,
33                          XmNokCallback,
34                          &DialogManager::destroyTmpDialogCallback,
35                          ( XtPointer ) this );
36
37          XtAddCallback ( newDialog,
38                          XmNcancelCallback,
39                          &DialogManager::destroyTmpDialogCallback,
40                          ( XtPointer ) this );
41      }
42      else                    // If this is the first dialog to be
43          _w = newDialog;    // created, save it to be used again
44
45      return ( newDialog );
46  }
```

The destroyTmpDialogCallback() function is called when the user pops down a temporary dialog. This function simply destroys the dialog widget for which the callback was called. Notice that this callback function is called in addition to any other callbacks registered with the dialog.

```
47   void DialogManager::destroyTmpDialogCallback ( Widget w,
48                                                  XtPointer,
49                                                  XtPointer )
50   {
51       XtDestroyWidget ( w );
52   }
```

The `post()` member function displays a dialog widget on the screen. The `post()` function begins by calling the private member function `getDialog()`, which returns a dialog widget. This widget may be a cached dialog that already exists, or it may be a new dialog, if the cached dialog is not available. The `post()` member function requires a string to be displayed in the dialog, and may also take an optional `clientData` parameter and several optional callback functions, which are treated in much the same way as Motif callback functions. The `clientData` parameter is an untyped pointer that can be used to pass data back to the caller when callbacks are invoked.

```
53   Widget DialogManager::post ( char           *text,
54                                void           *clientData,
55                                DialogCallback ok,
56                                DialogCallback cancel,
57                                DialogCallback help)
58   {
59       // Get a dialog widget from the cache
60
61       Widget dialog = getDialog();
62
63       // Make sure the dialog exists, and that it is an XmMessageBox
64       // or subclass, since the callbacks assume this widget type
65
66       assert ( dialog );
67       assert ( XtIsSubclass ( dialog, xmMessageBoxWidgetClass ) );
68
69       // Convert the text string to a compound string and
70       // specify this to be the message displayed in the dialog
71
72       XmString xmstr = XmStringCreateSimple ( text );
73       XtVaSetValues ( dialog, XmNmessageString, xmstr, NULL );
74       XmStringFree ( xmstr );
75
76       // Create an object to carry the additional data needed
77       // to cache the dialogs
78
79       DialogCallbackData *dcb = new DialogCallbackData( this,
80                                                         clientData,
81                                                         ok, cancel,
82                                                         help );
83       // Install callback function for each button
84       // supported by Motif dialogs
85       // If there is no help callback, unmanage the
```

```
86          //  corresponding button instead, if possible
87
88          XtAddCallback ( dialog,
89                          XmNokCallback,
90                          &DialogManager::okCallback,
91                          ( XtPointer ) dcb );
92
93          XtAddCallback ( dialog,
94                          XmNcancelCallback,
95                          &DialogManager::cancelCallback,
96                          ( XtPointer ) dcb );
97
98          if ( help )
99              XtAddCallback ( dialog,
100                             XmNhelpCallback,
101                             &DialogManager::helpCallback,
102                             ( XtPointer ) dcb );
103         else
104         {
105             Widget w = XmMessageBoxGetChild ( dialog,
106                                               XmDIALOG_HELP_BUTTON );
107             XtUnmanageChild ( w );
108         }
109
110         // Post the dialog
111
112         XtManageChild ( dialog );
113
114         return ( dialog );
115  }
```

The `post()` function does not install the provided callback functions directly. Instead, `post()` installs callbacks defined by DialogManager, which invoke the caller's callback functions with the appropriate client data. To manage the dialog widgets effectively, the DialogManager needs to pass its `this` pointer to all callbacks. Applications that use the DialogManager classes may also need to provide client data as well. To allow both types of data to be available within a callback, the DialogManager instantiates a DialogCallbackData object to store both the DialogManager instance and any client data. This object also contains pointers to the callback functions provided by the caller.

After all callbacks have been installed, `post()` displays the dialog and returns the widget to the calling application. This allows applications to manipulate the dialog widget directly if desired. Notice that, although the DialogManager class is derived from UIComponent, applications cannot normally use the `baseWidget()` member function to access the dialog widget encapsulated by the class, because `baseWidget()` always returns the cached dialog. There is no way to access a particular dialog widget, other than retaining the widget returned by `post()`.

The three callbacks installed by `post()` are all very similar. Each callback retrieves the DialogCallbackData object from the `clientData` argument and then extracts the DialogManager object and the associated application-defined callback functions from the DialogCallbackData object. The application's callback function is then called, if it exists. The application's client data is passed as the only argument. Before returning, each callback function calls the `cleanup()` member function to remove the callbacks from the current widget.

```
116  void DialogManager::okCallback ( Widget      w,
117                                   XtPointer clientData,
118                                   XtPointer )
119  {
120      DialogCallbackData *dcd = ( DialogCallbackData * ) clientData;
121      DialogManager      *obj = ( DialogManager * ) dcd->dialogManager();
122      DialogCallback      callback;
123
124      // If caller specified an ok callback, call the function
125
126      if ( ( callback = dcd->ok() ) != NULL )
127          ( *callback )( dcd->clientData() );
128
129      // Reset for the next time
130
131      obj->cleanup ( w, dcd );
132  }

133  void DialogManager::cancelCallback ( Widget      w,
134                                       XtPointer clientData,
135                                       XtPointer )
136  {
137      DialogCallbackData *dcd = ( DialogCallbackData * ) clientData;
138      DialogManager      *obj = ( DialogManager * ) dcd->dialogManager();
139      DialogCallback      callback;
140
141      if ( ( callback = dcd->cancel() ) != NULL )
142          ( *callback )( dcd->clientData() );
143
144      obj->cleanup ( w, dcd );
145  }

146  void DialogManager::helpCallback ( Widget      w,
147                                     XtPointer clientData,
148                                     XtPointer )
149  {
150      DialogCallbackData *dcd = ( DialogCallbackData * ) clientData;
151      DialogManager      *obj = ( DialogManager * ) dcd->dialogManager();
152      DialogCallback      callback;
153
154      if ( ( callback = dcd->help() ) != NULL )
155          ( *callback )( dcd->clientData() );
156
```

```
157        obj->cleanup ( w, dcd );
158   }
```

The cleanup() member function simply removes the callbacks registered by post(), and then deletes the DialogCallbackData instance associated with this widget. This ensures that the cached widget is ready for the next time a dialog is needed.

```
159   void DialogManager::cleanup ( Widget w, DialogCallbackData *dcd )
160   {
161        // Remove all callbacks to avoid having duplicate
162        // callback functions installed
163
164        XtRemoveCallback ( w,
165                           XmNokCallback,
166                           &DialogManager::okCallback,
167                           ( XtPointer ) dcd );
168
169        XtRemoveCallback ( w,
170                           XmNcancelCallback,
171                           &DialogManager::cancelCallback,
172                           ( XtPointer ) dcd );
173
174        XtRemoveCallback ( w,
175                           XmNhelpCallback,
176                           &DialogManager::helpCallback,
177                           ( XtPointer ) dcd );
178
179        // Delete the DialogCallbackData instance for this posting
180
181        delete dcd;
182   }
```

The DialogManager class's primary responsibility is to support a set of derived classes. The rest of this chapter describes two typical subclasses. The InfoDialogManager provides a facility for posting informative dialogs, and the QuestionDialogManager serves applications that need to ask users a question.

Figure 7.7 shows a message diagram of the DialogManager and related classes. The Dialog-Manager and all derived classes use the global Application object's shell widget as a parent. Notice that, unlike many other message diagrams in this book, this diagram includes both the abstract DialogManager class and two derived classes. This diagram documents the interface between the base class and derived classes, and also illustrates the different role each of these classes play. The interface between the DialogManager and its subclasses consists of the single member function, createDialog(). Because the InfoDialogManager and QuestionDialogManager classes inherit the characteristics of the DialogManager class, they also inherit many of the other messages shown in this diagram.

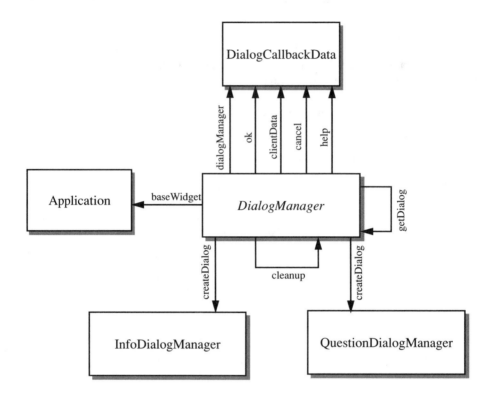

**Figure 7.7**  A message diagram for the DialogManager and related classes.

## 7.3   The InfoDialogManager Class

Programmers often need to display simple messages to the user. A message might be a warning, such as "Disk almost full," or simply a status report, such as "Compilation completed." This type of dialog is one of the simplest to use, and provides a first test case for the DialogManager class described in the previous chapter. The InfoDialogManager class is derived from DialogManager and displays a Motif InformationDialog in response to a `post()` message. The MotifApp framework includes a single instance of the InfoDialogManager class, declared as `theInfoDialog-Manager`. Any part of the application can access this object by simply including the file InfoDialogManager.h.

The InfoDialogManager class defines only a constructor and a `createDialog()` member, which is defined as a pure virtual function by the DialogManager base class. In addition to the class declaration, the header file also declares a pointer to an instance of the InfoDialogManager class, `theInfoDialogManager`. The InfoDialogManager class is declared as follows:

```
1   ///////////////////////////////////////////////////////////
2   // InfoDialogManager.h
3   ///////////////////////////////////////////////////////////
4   #ifndef INFODIALOGMANAGER_H
5   #define INFODIALOGMANAGER_H
6   #include "DialogManager.h"
7
8   class InfoDialogManager : public DialogManager {
9
10    protected:
11
12      Widget createDialog ( Widget );
13
14    public:
15
16      InfoDialogManager ( char * );
17
18  };
19  extern DialogManager *theInfoDialogManager;
20  #endif
```

The file InfoDialogManager.C contains the implementation of the InfoDialogManager class. The file begins by defining a pointer to a DialogManager object, theInfoDialogManager and instantiating an InfoDialogManager object. The constructor is empty, and simply calls the Dialog-Manager constructor.

```
1   ///////////////////////////////////////////////////////////
2   // InfoDialogManager.C:
3   ///////////////////////////////////////////////////////////
4   #include "InfoDialogManager.h"
5   #include <Xm/Xm.h>
6   #include <Xm/MessageB.h>
7
8   DialogManager *theInfoDialogManager =
9                       new InfoDialogManager ( "InformationDialog" );
10
11  InfoDialogManager::InfoDialogManager ( char    *name ) :
12                                          DialogManager ( name )
13  {
14      // Empty
15  }
```

The DialogManager class calls the InfoDialogManager class's createDialog() member function when a new dialog is needed. This function creates and returns a Motif InformationDialog.

```
16  Widget InfoDialogManager::createDialog ( Widget parent )
17  {
18      Widget dialog = XmCreateInformationDialog ( parent, _name, NULL, 0 );
```

```
19
20     return ( dialog );
21  }
```

Notice that this class does not have to deal with the cache mechanism. It merely provides a particular type of dialog. The base class handles all the details of caching dialogs, posting dialogs, setting up callbacks, and so on.

This completes the InfoDialogManager class. Now let's look at a very simple program that tests the InfoDialogManager class. The program uses the MotifApp framework, and simply displays a pushbutton. The button has a single callback, which posts a dialog each time it is called.

First we need to create a subclass of the MainWindow class to contain the button widget. This class can be declared as follows:

```
1   ///////////////////////////////////////////////////////
2   // DialogTestWindow.h: Test the InfoDialogManager class
3   ///////////////////////////////////////////////////////
4   #ifndef DIALOGTESTWINDOW_H
5   #define DIALOGTESTWINDOW_H
6   #include "MainWindow.h"
7
8   class DialogTestWindow : public MainWindow {
9
10    protected:
11
12      virtual Widget createWorkArea ( Widget );
13
14    public:
15
16      DialogTestWindow ( char *name ) : MainWindow ( name ) { }
17  };
18  #endif
```

The createWorkArea() member function creates a single XmPushButton widget and installs a callback to post a dialog when the user clicks on the button.

```
1   ///////////////////////////////////////////////////////
2   // DialogTestWindow.C: Test the InfoDialogManager class
3   ///////////////////////////////////////////////////////
4   #include "DialogTestWindow.h"
5   #include "InfoDialogManager.h"
6   #include <stdio.h>
7   #include <Xm/PushB.h>
8
9   void postDialogCallback ( Widget, XtPointer, XtPointer );
10
11  Widget DialogTestWindow::createWorkArea ( Widget parent )
12  {
13      Widget button = XtCreateManagedWidget ( "push_to_test",
```

```
14                                              xmPushButtonWidgetClass,
15                                              parent,
16                                              NULL, 0 );
17
18       XtAddCallback ( button,
19                       XmNactivateCallback,
20                       postDialogCallback,
21                       NULL );
22       return ( button );
23  }
```

The postDialogCallback() function uses a static local variable to produce a sequence of numbered dialogs. Each time this callback is called, the function increments the counter variable and displays a message by calling the InfoDialogManager object's post() member function.

```
24  void postDialogCallback ( Widget, XtPointer, XtPointer )
25  {
26       static int counter = 1;
27       char buf[100];
28
29       // Generate a unique message for each dialog
30
31       sprintf ( buf, "Information Dialog Number %d\n", counter++ );
32
33       // Display the message
34
35       theInfoDialogManager->post ( buf );
36  }
```

The file InfoDialogTestApp.C instantiates an Application object and a DialogTestWindow object to complete the program.

```
1   ////////////////////////////////////////////////////////
2   // InfoDialogTestApp.C: test the InfoDialogManager class
3   ////////////////////////////////////////////////////////
4   #include "Application.h"
5   #include "DialogTestWindow.h"
6
7   Application *myApp = new Application ( "DialogTest" );
8   MainWindow *window = new DialogTestWindow ( "DialogTest" );
```

To build this test program, we must compile the files InfoDialogTestApp.C and DialogTestWindow.C and link the results with the MotifApp library. (Both the DialogManager class and the InfoDialogManager class need to be added to the MotifApp library first.) Figure 7.8 shows the test program after posting several dialogs.

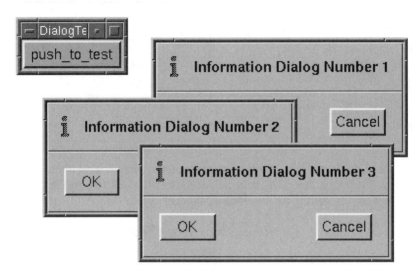

**Figure 7.8**  The InfoDialogManager test program.

## Instantiating Global Objects Safely

MotifApp provides several services in the form of objects that can be accessed throughout an application. These objects are instantiated as non-local, statically-initialized objects, and can be used by any part of a program by simply including the appropriate header file. For example, MotifApp supports an instance of the InfoDialogManager class, identified as `theInfoDialogManager`. This object can be used as a central resource by including InfoDialogManager.h. The object itself is instantiated in the file InfoDialogManager.C as a global object.

Providing commonly-used services as well-known global objects is a useful technique, particularly for libraries like MotifApp. However, there are several difficulties that one can encounter when relying on global objects, and this technique should not be used carelessly. MotifApp already relies on programs to create a global Application object as well as global MainWindow objects. This chapter adds several more global objects. It is important to understand the relationships between these objects and establish some guidelines for their use.

First, from a strict software engineering perspective, overuse or misuse of global objects can lead to code that is difficult to maintain. The fact that objects *can* be created as globals does not mean that all objects *should* be created this way. We should not forget the advantages of encapsulation. However, when it is apparent that an object is intended to provide a system-wide service, and that there can only be one such object in an application, a global object is sometimes useful. For example, the primary reason the DialogManager classes described in this chapter exist is to provide a central caching service for dialogs. If every part of a program that needs to post a dialog has to instantiate a new DialogManager object, the entire point of these classes would be lost.

Second, it is necessary to address the issue of initialization order when using global objects. As discussed in Chapter 6, C++ does not guarantee the order of initialization of non-local objects declared in different files. This means that it is not generally feasible to create a global object in one file whose constructor references a global object in another file. The globally-instantiated classes described in this book are carefully constructed in such a way that the constructors of these classes only initialize each object, and do not depend on any other objects. The one exception is the MainWindow class; this class must be instantiated *after* an Application object, and in the same file, to ensure the proper initialization order.

## 7.4    The QuestionDialogManager Class

Applications often use dialogs to ask questions that must be answered before the program can proceed. For example, an application may need to ask a user to confirm an exit command, or to ask if the user really wants to perform a potentially destructive operation. Section 7.1 describes the programming model that must be used to handle such questions. This section describes a simple QuestionDialogManager class that supports this model within MotifApp.

The QuestionDialogManager class is a subclass of the DialogManager class and, like the InfoDialogManager class, is meant to be used as an application-wide resource within the MotifApp framework. Applications are expected to have only one instance of the QuestionDialogManager class, and to send the post() message to this global object whenever a question needs to be answered. The DialogManager base class provides the basic dialog management. The QuestionDialogManager class defines the type of dialog to be displayed and creates a global instance, theQuestionDialogManager, which can be used throughout applications based on the MotifApp framework.

The QuestionDialogManager class defines only a constructor and then overrides the Dialog-Manager class's pure virtual createDialog() member function. The QuestionDialogManager class is declared as follows:

```
1   ///////////////////////////////////////////////////////////
2   // QuestionDialogManager.h
3   ///////////////////////////////////////////////////////////
4   #ifndef QuestionDIALOGMANAGER_H
5   #define QuestionDIALOGMANAGER_H
6   #include "DialogManager.h"
7
8   class QuestionDialogManager : public DialogManager {
9
10      protected:
11
12          Widget createDialog ( Widget );
13
14      public:
15
16          QuestionDialogManager ( char * );
17   };
18
```

```
19   extern QuestionDialogManager *theQuestionDialogManager;
20
21   #endif
```

The file QuestionDialogManager.C contains the implementation of the QuestionDialog-
Manager class. The beginning of the file defines the variable `theQuestionDialogManager`
and creates this object. The constructor is empty and simply calls the base class constructor.

```
1    //////////////////////////////////////////////////////////
2    // QuestionDialogManager.C:
3    //////////////////////////////////////////////////////////
4    #include "QuestionDialogManager.h"
5    #include <Xm/Xm.h>
6    #include <Xm/MessageB.h>
7
8    // Define an instance to be available throughout the framework
9
10   QuestionDialogManager *theQuestionDialogManager =
11                        new QuestionDialogManager ( "QuestionDialog" );
12
13   QuestionDialogManager::QuestionDialogManager ( char    *name ) :
14                                            DialogManager ( name )
15   {
16       // Empty
17   }
```

The `createDialog()` member creates a Motif QuestionDialog widget each time it is called.
The widget's dialog style is set to "full application modal," which means that while a dialog is
displayed, the application does not process device events for any widgets except those in the dialog.
This forces the user to answer the question and simulates blocking behavior, as discussed in Section
7.1. Applications can modify this behavior by changing the value of the `XmNdialogStyle`
resource of the widget returned by `post()`.

```
18   Widget QuestionDialogManager::createDialog ( Widget parent )
19   {
20       Widget dialog = XmCreateQuestionDialog ( parent, _name, NULL, 0);
21
22       XtVaSetValues ( dialog,
23                       XmNdialogStyle, XmDIALOG_FULL_APPLICATION_MODAL,
24                       NULL );
25
26       return ( dialog );
27   }
```

Now we can write a short program to test the QuestionDialogManager. This program is very
similar to the test program described in the previous section. The QuestionTestWindow class is
declared as:

```
1   ////////////////////////////////////////////////////////////////////
2   // QuestionTestWindow.h: Test the QuestionDialogManager class
3   ////////////////////////////////////////////////////////////////////
4   #ifndef QUESTIONTESTWINDOW_H
5   #define QUESTIONTESTWINDOW_H
6   #include "MainWindow.h"
7   #include <stream.h>
8
9   class QuestionTestWindow : public MainWindow {
10
11    protected:
12
13      virtual Widget createWorkArea ( Widget );
14
15    public:
16
17      QuestionTestWindow ( char *name ) : MainWindow ( name ) { }
18  };
19  #endif
```

The `createWorkArea()` member function creates an XmPushButton widget and registers a callback function that posts a question dialog when the user clicks on the button.

```
1   //////////////////////////////////////////////////////////////////
2   // QuestionTestWindow.C: Test the QuestionDialogManager class
3   //////////////////////////////////////////////////////////////////
4   #include "QuestionTestWindow.h"
5   #include "QuestionDialogManager.h"
6   #include <Xm/PushB.h>
7
8   void postDialogCallback ( Widget, XtPointer, XtPointer );
9   void cancelCallback ( void *data );
10  void okCallback ( void * );
11
12  Widget QuestionTestWindow::createWorkArea ( Widget parent )
13  {
14      Widget button = XtCreateManagedWidget ( "push_to_test",
15                                              xmPushButtonWidgetClass,
16                                              parent,
17                                              NULL, 0 );
18
19      XtAddCallback ( button,
20                      XmNactivateCallback,
21                      postDialogCallback,
22                      NULL );
23      return ( button );
24  }
```

The `postDialogCallback()` function uses the central QuestionDialogManager object to post a dialog that asks a question. The `okCallback()` function is to be called if the user answers the question affirmatively, while the `cancelCallback()` is to be called otherwise.

```
25  void postDialogCallback ( Widget, XtPointer, XtPointer )
26  {
27      theQuestionDialogManager->post ( "Can you answer the question?",
28                                       (void *) NULL,
29                                       okCallback,
30                                       cancelCallback );
31  }
```

The `cancelCallback()` and `okCallback()` functions print simple messages to confirm which function has been called.

```
32  void cancelCallback ( void * )
33  {
34      cout << "No" << "\n" << flush;
35  }

36  void okCallback ( void * )
37  {
38      cout << "Yes" << "\n" << flush;
39  }
```

The file QuestionTestApp.C completes the application. This file just instantiates the Application object and a QuestionTestWindow object.

```
1  //////////////////////////////////////////////////////////
2  // QuestionTestApp.C:
3  //////////////////////////////////////////////////////////
4  #include "Application.h"
5  #include "QuestionTestWindow.h"
6
7  Application *myApp  = new Application ( "QuestionTestApp" );
8  MainWindow  *window = new QuestionTestWindow ( "QuestionTest" );
```

Classes like InfoDialogManager and QuestionDialogManager, along with the DialogManager base class, offer several advantages for the developer. For example, the DialogManager automatically creates new dialogs as they are needed, and destroys dialogs when they are no longer required, freeing the application from this responsibility. By supporting globally-available facilities that can be used from anywhere in the system, these classes free parts of the application from dealing with widgets. Often applications need to display information, issue warnings, or ask questions in parts of the program that are unrelated to the user interface. The DialogManager class provides an interface that hides its widget-based application, allowing these class to be used easily from any part of an application.

However, the simple implementation presented here has several deficiencies. In particular, there are several problems with creating dialogs as children of the Application class's unmapped shell. Usually, it is preferable to position dialogs over one of the application's top-level windows, instead of always placing them in the center of the screen. Also, by making dialogs children of the unmapped shell, dialogs will not raise, lower, or iconify with the application's visible windows, as dialogs are usually expected to do. One solution to both these problems would be to associate dialogs with a MainWindow instead of the Application. Multi-window applications could have a dialog manager class for each top-level window, as implemented by the MainWindow class. Another solution would be to continue to support only a single DialogManager object, but to make the DialogManager cache dialogs on a per-window basis. Both approaches require a more complex approach than that described in this chapter, and these issues are ignored in the interest of simplicity.

# 7.5   Summary

This chapter presents a DialogManager class that supports cached dialogs. The implementation is very simple, but defines a protocol that can support more complex implementations. For example, the DialogManager class could be altered to cache more than one dialog if desired, without requiring any changes to derived classes or to applications that use the MotifApp dialog classes. One value of the DialogManager, along with its related classes, is that applications can display a dialog with a single call. The DialogManager interface does not expose the widget-based implementation, which allows portions of a program that have no user interface component to post messages or ask questions. Because the DialogManager caches widgets, dialogs will often appear on the screen more quickly than if the program has to create a new Motif widget each time a dialog is needed.

Chapter 10 discusses another dialog class, the BusyDialogManager. This class is also derived from DialogManager, but serves a significantly different purpose than the classes described in this chapter. The BusyDialogManager class supports applications that are expected to be "busy" for extended periods of time, and is designed to be used in conjunction with several other MotifApp classes.

Chapter 8 introduces another facility provided by the MotifApp framework: a set of classes that support a general architecture for issuing and executing commands. Many of these classes depend on the DialogManager classes described in this chapter. For example, the QuitCmd class described in Chapter 9 collaborates with the QuestionDialogManager class to provide a "safe quit" facility much like that described in Section 7.1.

# Command Classes

---

Nearly every user action in an interactive application can be thought of as a "command." For example, most word processors support simple commands like "insert character" as well as more complex commands, like "reformat paragraph" and "save file." The user may not think of inserting a character as issuing a command, but to a programmer, there is little difference between a user action that inserts a character and one that reformats a paragraph. Programmers typically implement such commands as functions (callback functions, for example) that are invoked as a result of some user action. This chapter explores an approach in which each command in a system is modelled as an object.

Representing commands as objects has many advantages. Many commands have some state or data associated with the command, while others may involve a set of related functions. In both cases, a class allows the data and functions associated with a single logical operation to be encapsulated in one place. Because command objects are complete and self-contained, they can be queued for later execution, stored in "history" lists, re-executed, and so on.

One advantage of representing commands as objects is that it becomes relatively easy to "undo" a command. Although some operations are inherently difficult to reverse, others can be undone by simply implementing a function that reverses the effect of the function that originally performed the command. A class provides a straightforward way to associate the function that performs an action with the function that reverses that same action. Also, to prepare to undo a command, it may be necessary to save some state before executing the command. When commands are modeled as objects, this information can be stored in data members.

This chapter presents several classes that can be used to represent commands. The primary responsibility of each command class is to provide a way to perform some action and also to undo, or reverse the effects of, that action. Section 8.1 describes an abstract Cmd class that serves as the basis of all other command classes. This section also describes some auxiliary classes, including a class that provides an abstract interface between command objects and Motif widgets, which are often used to issue commands. The remaining sections describe additional abstract classes that support special-purpose commands, including commands whose effects cannot be undone and commands that should be confirmed by the user before being executed.

# 8.1  The Cmd Class

All commands in the MotifApp framework are represented by classes derived from an abstract Cmd class. The Cmd class defines the primary interface to all derived classes and provides a supporting infrastructure that makes new command classes simple to implement.

The Cmd class is based on the idea that every command object should support an action and also a way to reverse, or undo, that action. The Cmd class provides a public interface for each of these operations. The execute() member function initiates an action, and an undo() member function reverses that action. The Cmd class also supports member functions that can be used to enable and disable a command, along with any user interface associated with the command. Each command object also supports a list of other commands that need to be enabled or disabled when this command is executed. This feature makes it easy to set up dependencies between commands.

The Cmd class provides support for a central undo facility that allows applications based on the MotifApp framework to undo the most recent command. The Cmd class supports an undo facility by maintaining a pointer to the most recently executed command in a static data member. This member is shared by all classes derived from Cmd, but is not visible to other classes.

Figure 8.1 shows a class card that summarizes the Cmd class's primary responsibilities.

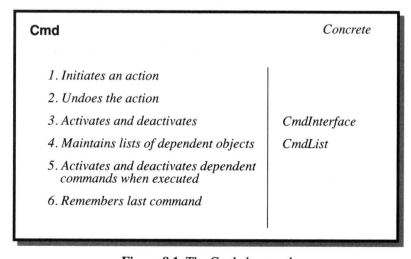

**Figure 8.1** The Cmd class card.

## The CmdList Class

The Cmd class and related classes often need to deal with lists of Cmd objects. Before looking at the implementation of the Cmd class, let's create a simple class that makes it easier to deal with these lists of objects. The CmdList class maintains a list of pointers to Cmd objects, and allows a list to be constructed dynamically by adding objects to the list one by one. The CmdList class is used internally by the Cmd class, and can also be useful to other classes that use Cmd objects.

Figure 8.1 shows the CmdList class card.

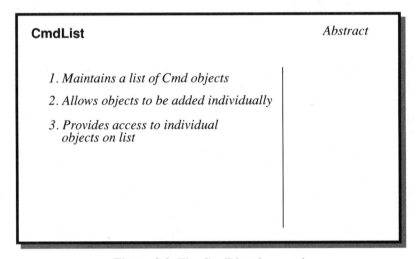

**Figure 8.2**  The CmdList class card.

The CmdList class is declared as follows:

```
1    /////////////////////////////////////////////////////////////
2    // CmdList.h: Maintain a list of Cmd objects
3    /////////////////////////////////////////////////////////////
4    #ifndef CMDLIST_H
5    #define CMDLIST_H
6    class Cmd;
7
8    class CmdList {
9
10      private:
11
12        Cmd **_contents;     // The list of objects
13        int   _numElements;  // Current size of list
14
15      public:
16
17        CmdList();           // Construct an empty list
```

```
18        virtual ~CmdList();   // Destroys list, but not objects in list
19
20        void add ( Cmd * );   // Add a single Cmd object to list
21
22        Cmd **contents() { return ( _contents ); } // Return the list
23        int size() { return ( _numElements ); }    // Return list size
24        Cmd *operator[] ( int );          // Return an element of the list
25   };
26   #endif
```

The CmdList constructor simply initializes the data members of the object to start with an empty list.

```
1    ///////////////////////////////////////////////////////////
2    // CmdList.C: Maintain a list of Cmd objects
3    ///////////////////////////////////////////////////////////
4    #include "CmdList.h"
5
6    class Cmd;
7
8    CmdList::CmdList()
9    {
10       // The list is initially empty
11
12       _contents    = 0;
13       _numElements = 0;
14   }
```

The CmdList destructor deletes the _contents array, which may contain pointers to other Cmd objects.

```
15   CmdList::~CmdList()
16   {
17       // free the list
18
19       delete []_contents;
20   }
```

Cmd objects can be added one by one to the CmdList, using the add() member function. This function allocates a new array of Cmd pointers each time it is called. This new array is always large enough to hold the previous list plus the new object. After copying the contents of the previous _contents array to the new array, the original array is deleted, and the new list is installed. The new Cmd object is appended to the end of the list.

```
21   void CmdList::add ( Cmd *cmd )
22   {
23       int i;
```

```
24        Cmd **newList;
25
26        // Allocate a list large enough for one more element
27
28        newList = new Cmd*[_numElements + 1];
29
30        // Copy the contents of the previous list to
31        // the new list
32
33        for( i = 0; i < _numElements; i++)
34            newList[i] = _contents[i];
35
36        // Free the old list
37
38        delete []_contents;
39
40        // Make the new list the current list
41
42        _contents =  newList;
43
44        // Add the command to the list and update the list size
45
46        _contents[_numElements] = cmd;
47
48        _numElements++;
49    }
```

The Cmd class needs access to the objects contained by a CmdList object. The inline member function, size(), allows callers to determine the number elements in a CmdList object, and the [] operator provides access to individual objects in the list.

```
50    Cmd *CmdList::operator[] ( int index )
51    {
52        // Return the indexed element
53
54        return ( _contents[index] );
55    }
```

C++ allows operators to be overloaded, using the operator keyword. In this case, creating a member function named operator[] defines the meaning of the [] operator when applied to a CmdList object. This operator allows the CmdList object to be treated much like an array. For example, the following code segment creates a list of Cmd objects and then executes each one in sequence:

```
    // ...
    Cmd *one, *two, *three;
    CmdList *execList = new CmdList();
```

```
// Create Cmd objects (Cmd is abstract, so objects belong to a subclass)
// ...
execList->add ( one );
execList->add ( two );
execList->add ( three );
for ( int i = 0; i < execList->size(); i++ )
    ( *execList )[i]->execute();
```

Notice that, as shown in this example, the [ ] operator must be applied to an object, not a pointer to an object. This example uses a pointer to a CmdList object, which must be de-referenced before the [ ] operator can be applied.

## The Cmd Implementation

Now we can examine the implementation of the Cmd class. The Cmd class is an abstract class that supports six essential public member functions. These member functions correspond to the responsibilities listed on the class card in Figure 8.1.

- The execute() member function initiates the action or actions supported by the command. This function provides the public interface through which any command is executed. However, execute() relies on other methods to perform the action supported by the command.

- The undo() member function causes the action initiated by the execute() member function to be reversed. Like execute(), this function provides the public interface, but relies on other methods to reverse the command.

- The activate() member function enables the command and enables any user interface component associated with the object. Command objects can only be executed if they are currently enabled.

- The deactivate() member function disables the command and disables any user interface component associated with the object.

- The addToActivationList() member function adds a Cmd object to a list of objects to be automatically activated when an object is executed.

- The addToDeactivationList() member function adds a Cmd object to a list of objects to be automatically deactivated when an object is executed.

The Cmd class also provides a way to register interface components with a command object, and provides several access member functions. These include a member function that reports whether or not an object is active, and a member function that can be used to determine if a particular object supports an undo() member function.

The Cmd class is declared as follows:

```
1  ////////////////////////////////////////////////////
2  // Cmd.h: A base class for all command objects
3  ////////////////////////////////////////////////////
4  #ifndef CMD_H
5  #define CMD_H
```

```
6
7    class CmdList;
8    class CmdInterface;
9
10   class Cmd {
11
12       friend CmdInterface;
13
14     private:
15
16       // Lists of other commands to be activated or deactivated
17       // when this command is executed or "undone"
18
19       CmdList        *_activationList;
20       CmdList        *_deactivationList;
21       void            revert();    // Reverts object to previous state
22       int            _active;      // Is this command currently active?
23       int            _previouslyActive; // Previous value of _active
24       char          *_name;                // Name of this command
25       CmdInterface **_ci;
26       int            _numInterfaces;
27
28     protected:
29
30       int           _hasUndo;      // True if this object supports undo
31       static Cmd   *_lastCmd;      // Pointer to last Cmd executed
32
33       virtual void doit()   = 0;   // Specific actions must be defined
34       virtual void undoit() = 0;   // by derived classes
35
36     public:
37
38       Cmd ( char *,  int );               // Protected constructor
39
40       virtual ~Cmd ();                    // Destructor
41
42       // Public interface for executing and undoing commands
43
44       virtual void execute();
45       void    undo();
46
47       void    activate();    // Activate this object
48       void    deactivate();  // Deactivate this object
49
50       // Functions to register dependent commands
51
52       void    addToActivationList ( Cmd * );
53       void    addToDeactivationList ( Cmd * );
54
```

```
55     // Register a UIComponent used to execute this command
56
57     void    registerInterface ( CmdInterface * );
58
59     // Access functions
60
61     int active () { return ( _active ); }
62     int hasUndo() { return ( _hasUndo ); }
63     const char *const name () { return ( _name ); }
64     virtual const char *const className () { return ( "Cmd" ); }
65  };
66  #endif
```

Classes derived from Cmd must implement the pure virtual `doit()` and `undoit()` member functions defined in the protected portion of the class. In addition to the `doit()` and `undoit()` member functions, the protected section of the Cmd class declares a static member, `_lastCmd`, which points to the most recently executed cmd. Because it is static, this member is shared by all objects belonging to classes derived from Cmd. The `_lastCmd` member always points to the most recently executed command, to allow the command to be undone easily. The Cmd class also supports a Boolean member, `_hasUndo`. This flag specifies whether or not a command can be successfully reversed. Derived classes must set this flag to `FALSE` if they don't support undo.

The private portion of the Cmd class maintains a list of objects to be activated and deactivated when a command is executed. Because the supporting mechanism is implemented entirely by the Cmd class, these CmdList objects do not need to be accessible to derived classes. Similarly, the Cmd class supports two private flags that indicate the current and previous active state of the command. These, along with a name and a function for reverting the state, should not be needed by derived classes. The private portion of the Cmd class also defines a pointer to a list of CmdInterface objects. This list allows command objects to activate and deactivate any associated user interface according to whether the object is currently enabled or disabled.

The file Cmd.C includes the header files for the CmdList class as well as the CmdInterface class which has not yet been discussed. The file also declares an external command object known as `theUndoCmd`. This object provides a convenient way to undo the most recent command. Applications that need to undo a command can simply execute `theUndoCmd`. Section 8.4 describes `theUndoCmd` in more detail.

The Cmd constructor initializes the data members, setting the `_activationList` and `_deactivationList` members to NULL, and the `_name` and `_active` to values specified by the constructor's arguments. The constructor initializes the `_hasUndo` flag to TRUE, because all derived classes are expected to implement undo, by default.

```
1   /////////////////////////////////////////////////////
2   // Cmd.C
3   /////////////////////////////////////////////////////
4   #include "Cmd.h"
5   #include "CmdList.h"
6   #include "CmdInterface.h"
7
```

```
8    extern Cmd *theUndoCmd;   // External object that reverses the
9                              // most recent Cmd when executed
10   Cmd *Cmd::_lastCmd = NULL;   // Pointer to most recent Cmd
11
12   Cmd::Cmd ( char *name, int active )
13   {
14       // Initialize all data members
15
16       _name               = name;
17       _active             = active;
18       _numInterfaces      = 0;
19       _ci                 = NULL;
20       _activationList     = NULL;
21       _deactivationList   = NULL;
22       _hasUndo            = TRUE;
23   }
```

The Cmd destructor simply deletes the two CmdList objects and the list of CmdInterface objects.

```
24   Cmd::~Cmd()
25   {
26       delete _activationList;
27       delete _deactivationList;
28       delete _ci;
29   }
```

The Cmd class supports a public member function, registerInterface(), that registers a user interface component with a Cmd object. Each Cmd object can be associated with more than one user interface component. Once a CmdInterface object is registered with a Cmd object, the Cmd object can change the sensitivity of the interface based on whether or not the command is active. As each CmdInterface component is registered, registerInterface() updates the component according to the current active state of the command. The CmdInterface class is discussed in Section 8.2.

```
30   void Cmd::registerInterface ( CmdInterface *ci )
31   {
32       // Make a new list, large enough for the new object
33
34        CmdInterface **newList = new CmdInterface*[_numInterfaces + 1];
35
36       // Copy the contents of the previous list to
37       // the new list
38
39       for ( int i = 0; i < _numInterfaces; i++)
40           newList[i] = _ci[i];
41
42       // Free the old list
```

```
43
44      delete []_ci;
45
46      // Install the new list
47
48      _ci = newList;
49
50      // Add the object to the list and update the list size
51
52      _ci[_numInterfaces] = ci;
53
54      _numInterfaces++;
55
56      if ( ci )
57          if ( _active )
58              ci->activate();
59          else
60              ci->deactivate();
61  }
```

The activate() member function enables a command object. This member function sets the protected data member, _active to TRUE, after saving the current value in the _previously-Active variable. If there are interface components associated with this command, this function calls each CmdInterface object's activate() member function.

```
62  void Cmd::activate()
63  {
64      // Activate the associated interfaces
65
66      for ( int i = 0; i < _numInterfaces; i++ )
67          _ci[i]->activate ();
68
69      // Save the current value of active before setting the new state
70
71      _previouslyActive = _active;
72      _active = TRUE;
73  }
```

The deactivate() member function disables a command. This function saves the previous state of the objects, and then sets the protected data member, _active to FALSE. The function also deactivates all associated interface components.

```
74  void Cmd::deactivate()
75  {
76      // Deactivate the associated interfaces
77
78      for ( int i = 0; i < _numInterfaces; i++ )
79          _ci[i]->deactivate ();
```

```
80
81      // Save the current value of active before setting the new state
82
83      _previouslyActive = _active;
84      _active = FALSE;
85   }
```

The `revert()` member function is a private member function that returns a Cmd object to its previous active or inactive state, as stored in the `_previousState` member.

```
86   void Cmd::revert()
87   {
88      // Activate or deactivate, as necessary,
89      // to return to the previous state
90
91      if ( _previouslyActive )
92          activate();
93      else
94          deactivate();
95   }
```

The Cmd class supports two CmdList objects – a list of Cmd objects that should be activated when a command is executed, and a list of Cmd objects that should be deactivated when a command is executed. A Cmd object can automatically activate or deactivate all objects on these lists when it is executed. This feature can be useful when there are dependencies between certain commands. For example, in a text editor, it may be reasonable to assume that a command to paste some text is not valid until a cut or copy command has been issued. In a system that supports an undo command, the undo command can be disabled until a command that can be undone is executed.

The function `addToActivationList()` takes a pointer to another Cmd object and adds it to the list of objects to be activated when the command is executed.

```
96   void Cmd::addToActivationList ( Cmd *cmd )
97   {
98       if ( !_activationList )
99           _activationList = new CmdList();
100
101       _activationList->add ( cmd );
102   }
```

The function `addToDeactivationList()` is similar to `addToActivationList()`, except that it adds Cmd objects to a list of objects to be deactivated when the command is executed.

```
103   void Cmd::addToDeactivationList ( Cmd *cmd )
104   {
105       if ( !_deactivationList )
106           _deactivationList = new CmdList();
107
```

```
108        _deactivationList->add ( cmd );
109    }
```

The public member function `execute()` provides the external interface used to execute any command. Unless a command object has been disabled, `execute()` calls the object's `doit()` member function, which must be defined by derived classes, to actually perform the action the command supports. Next, if this object supports undo, `execute()` activates the `theUndoCmd` object and saves the current command object in the `_lastCmd` variable. If a command does not support undo, `execute()` deactivates `theUndoCmd` and sets `_lastCmd` to NULL.

Finally, `execute()` calls `activate()` for each object on the `_activationList` and the `deactivate()` member function for each object on the `_deactivationList`. The `execute()` function is written as:

```
110   void Cmd::execute()
111   {
112        int i;
113
114        // If a command is inactive, it cannot be executed
115
116        if ( !_active )
117            return;
118
119        // Call the derived class's doit member function to
120        // perform the action represented by this object
121
122        doit();
123
124        // Activate or deactivate the global theUndoCmd,
125        // and remember the last command, as needed
126
127        if ( _hasUndo )
128        {
129            Cmd::_lastCmd = this;
130            theUndoCmd->activate();
131        }
132        else
133        {
134            Cmd::_lastCmd = NULL;
135            theUndoCmd->deactivate();
136        }
137
138        // Process the commands that depend on this one
139
140        if ( _activationList )
141            for ( i = 0; i < _activationList->size(); i++ )
142                ( *_activationList )[i]->activate();
143
144        if ( _deactivationList )
```

```
145              for ( i = 0; i < _deactivationList->size(); i++ )
146                  ( *_deactivationList )[i]->deactivate();
147  }
```

The undo() member function provides the external interface for reversing the effects of the execute() member function. First, undo() calls undoit(), which must be implemented by a derived class. It then deactivates the theUndoCmd object, because the Cmd architecture only supports a single level of undo. Finally, the undo() member function invokes the revert() member function for each dependent object to return these objects to their previous state:

```
148  void Cmd::undo()
149  {
150      int i;
151
152      // Call the derived class's undoit() member function
153
154      undoit();
155
156      // The system only supports one level of undo, and this is it,
157      // so deactivate the undo facility
158
159      theUndoCmd->deactivate();
160
161      // Reverse the effects of the execute() member function by
162      // reverting all dependent objects to their previous states
163
164      if ( _activationList )
165          for ( i = 0; i < _activationList->size(); i++ )
166              ( *_activationList )[i]->revert();
167
168      if ( _deactivationList )
169          for ( i = 0; i < _deactivationList->size(); i++ )
170              ( *_deactivationList )[i]->revert();
171  }
```

The next section describes the CmdInterface class, which provides a connection between a Cmd object and a user interface component. Later sections describe specialized derived classes that provide additional functionality. The Cmd class does the bulk of the work required to support command objects, and most derived classes are far simpler.

# 8.2   The CmdInterface Class

The Cmd class described in the previous section is completely independent of any user interface. Command objects can be instantiated and executed programmatically, and do not necessarily require a user interface component. However, it is common for a command object to represent an action initiated by the user through some user interface component, such as a button widget or an entry in a menu. This section describes a CmdInterface class that supports interaction between Cmd objects and widgets or other user interface components.

The CmdInterface class is an abstract class derived from UIComponent. The class does not create any widgets itself, but simply adds some features to those provided by UIComponent to support interactions with Cmd objects. For example, the CmdInterface class accepts `activate()` and `deactivate()` messages from Cmd objects. These member functions change the sensitivity of the component's base widget to match the state of the associated Cmd object. Each CmdInterface object also automatically registers itself with a Cmd object, which must be specified in the CmdInterface constructor. Finally, the CmdInterface class supports a callback function that can be used to execute the associated Cmd object. The CmdInterface class does not create a widget, so it cannot register the callback, but derived classes can register this callback function with the appropriate widget.

Figure 8.1 shows a class card for the CmdInterface class, which summarizes its responsibilities.

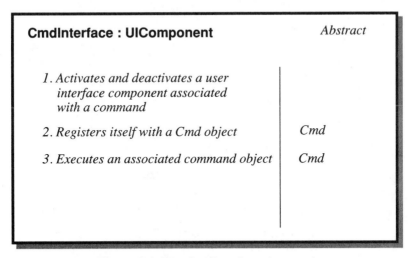

**Figure 8.3** The CmdInterface class card.

The CmdInterface class is declared in the file CmdInterface.h. The class supports a protected `_active` flag that maintains the current active status of the component. This information is needed because a CmdInterface object can be deactivated before any widgets are created. By maintaining this state, derived classes can activate or deactivate widgets, as needed, when they are created. The constructor is declared in the protected portion of the class to force the CmdInterface class to be treated as an abstract class.

The CmdInterface class maintains a pointer to a Cmd object. Each CmdInterface object is associated with a single Cmd object, although each Cmd object may be associated with multiple CmdInterface objects.

The CmdInterface class also supports two virtual member functions, activate() and deactivate(). These functions activate and deactivate the widget or widgets supported by a CmdInterface object. Only a Cmd object should activate or deactivate a CmdInterface object. Therefore, these member functions are declared in the protected portion of the class. In fact, the CmdInterface class has no public protocol. The entire CmdInterface protocol is protected, and accessible only to derived classes and the Cmd class (because the Cmd class is declared as a friend). Applications that need to disable a command should deactivate the appropriate Cmd object, not the user interface component associated with the Cmd.

The CmdInterface class is declared as follows:

```
1    ///////////////////////////////////////////////////
2    // CmdInterface.h
3    ///////////////////////////////////////////////////
4    #ifndef CMDINTERFACE
5    #define CMDINTERFACE
6    #include "UIComponent.h"
7
8    class Cmd;
9
10   class CmdInterface : public UIComponent {
11
12       friend Cmd;
13
14     protected:
15
16       Cmd     * _cmd;
17
18       static void executeCmdCallback ( Widget,
19                                        XtPointer,
20                                        XtPointer );
21       int _active;
22
23       CmdInterface ( Cmd * );
24       virtual void activate();
25       virtual void deactivate();
26   };
27   #endif
```

The CmdInterface constructor expects a Cmd object as its only argument. It passes the name of the Cmd object to the UIComponent constructor, to be used as the name of the object's widget. The CmdInterface constructor initializes the _active member to TRUE, saves a pointer to the specified Cmd object, and then registers itself with that Cmd object.

```
1   ///////////////////////////////////////////////////////
2   // CmdInterface.C
3   ///////////////////////////////////////////////////////
4   #include "CmdInterface.h"
5   #include "Cmd.h"
6
7   CmdInterface::CmdInterface ( Cmd *cmd ) : UIComponent( cmd->name() )
8   {
9       _active = TRUE;
10      _cmd    = cmd;
11      cmd->registerInterface ( this );
12  }
```

The CmdInterface class provides a callback function as a convenience to derived classes. This callback executes the Cmd object associated with the CmdInterface that invokes the callback. Derived classes can register the callback, if desired. The callback is most suitable for button widgets, although it could be used with some other widgets as well.

```
13  void CmdInterface::executeCmdCallback ( Widget,
14                                                XtPointer clientData,
15                                                XtPointer )
16  {
17      CmdInterface *obj = ( CmdInterface * ) clientData;
18      obj->_cmd->execute();
19  }
```

Notice that this callback does not follow the convention used in many other examples in this book, because it performs a task directly, rather than calling a CmdInterface virtual function. This function is so simple that it does not seem necessary to call yet another function. Furthermore, derived classes have the option of registering or not registering the callback, so there is little reason to provide a virtual function for derived classes to override, as done in other examples.

The `activate()` and `deactivate()` member functions are very simple. If the `_w` widget has already been created, `XtSetSensitive()` is used to set the widget's sensitivity accordingly. Each function also updates the value of the `_active` flag. If these functions are called before the object's widget has been created, the derived class constructor can use this value to initialize the widget appropriately.

```
20  void CmdInterface::activate()
21  {
22      if ( _w )
23          XtSetSensitive ( _w, TRUE );
24      _active = TRUE;
25  }

26  void CmdInterface::deactivate()
27  {
28      if ( _w )
```

```
29           XtSetSensitive ( _w, FALSE );
30      _active = FALSE;
31  }
```

This completes the CmdInterface class. Chapter 9 describes a ButtonInterface class, which is derived from CmdInterface. The ButtonInterface class uses a Motif XmPushButton widget to execute a Cmd object.

# 8.3   The NoUndoCmd Class

Some commands are difficult, or even impossible to undo, for one reason or another. For example, an action that deletes a file cannot be undone (unless the deletion does not really take place until a later time). The Cmd class forces all derived classes to support undo by declaring the undoit() member function as a pure virtual. However, derived classes can implement an empty undoit() member function that does not really provide undo, but satisfies the C++ compiler. The Cmd class depends on the value of the _hasUndo member to specify whether a class really has the capability to undo its actions, or just defines an empty member function.

The NoUndoCmd class is a very simple abstract class that defines an empty undoit() member function and ensures that the _hasUndo flag is set correctly for all classes that cannot support undo. Therefore, the easiest way to implement a class that cannot support undo is to derive the class from NoUndoCmd.

The file NoUndoCmd.h contains the class declaration. The NoUndoCmd class supports only an empty undoit() member function and a constructor. The constructor expects a name and a flag that specifies the initial state of the object.

```
1   ///////////////////////////////////////////////////////
2   // NoUndoCmd.h: Base class for all commands without undo
3   ///////////////////////////////////////////////////////
4   #ifndef NOUNDOCMD_H
5   #define NOUNDOCMD_H
6   #include "Cmd.h"
7
8   class NoUndoCmd : public Cmd {
9
10    protected:
11
12      virtual void undoit();
13
14    public:
15
16      NoUndoCmd ( char *, int );
17  };
18  #endif
```

The NoUndoCmd constructor calls the Cmd class constructor and then overrides the value of _hasUndo.

```
1    /////////////////////////////////////////////////////////
2    // NoUndoCmd.C: Base class for all commands without undo
3    /////////////////////////////////////////////////////////
4    #include "NoUndoCmd.h"
5
6    #define FALSE 0
7
8    NoUndoCmd::NoUndoCmd ( char      *name,
9                          int        active ) :  Cmd ( name, active )
10   {
11       _hasUndo = FALSE; //  Derived classes have no undo
12   }
```

The undoit() member function is an empty stub, defined because the Cmd class requires derived classes to implement this function. Classes derived from NoUndoCmd do not need to implement an undo() member function.

```
13   NoUndoCmd::undoit()
14   {
15       // Empty
16   }
```

## 8.4  The UndoCmd Class

When any command is executed, the object activates and deactivates a central command object named theUndoCmd, depending on whether or not the executed object supports undo. This object is an instance of UndoCmd, a class whose only responsibility is to call the undo() member function for the most recently executed command object. Because theUndoCmd itself cannot be undone, the UndoCmd class is derived from the NoUndoCmd class.

The file UndoCmd.h contains the declaration of the UndoCmd class. This class supports a constructor and a single doit() member function. The header file declares a pointer to an external object named theUndoCmd. The MotifApp framework contains only a single instance of UndoCmd, which is available to any part of the program that includes UndoCmd.h.

```
1    /////////////////////////////////////////////////////////
2    // UndoCmd.h: An interface for undoing the last command
3    /////////////////////////////////////////////////////////
4    #ifndef UNDOCMD_H
5    #define UNDOCMD_H
6    #include "NoUndoCmd.h"
```

```
7
8    class UndoCmd : public NoUndoCmd {
9
10     protected:
11
12       virtual void doit();
13
14     public:
15
16       UndoCmd ( char * );
17   };
18
19   extern UndoCmd *theUndoCmd;
20
21   #endif
```

The file UndoCmd.C creates an instance of UndoCmd that can be used throughout any MotifApp program. The UndoCmd constructor is empty and simply calls the base class constructor.

```
1    //////////////////////////////////////////////////////////
2    // UndoCmd.C: An interface to undoing the last command
3    //////////////////////////////////////////////////////////
4    #include "UndoCmd.h"
5
6    #define NULL   0
7    #define FALSE 0
8    // Declare a global object: theUndoCmd
9
10   UndoCmd *theUndoCmd = new UndoCmd ( "Undo" );
11
12   UndoCmd::UndoCmd ( char *name ) : NoUndoCmd ( name, FALSE )
13   {
14       // Empty
15   }
```

The UndoCmd class's doit() member function is responsible for undoing the most recent command. If the _lastCmd member inherited from the Cmd class is non-NULL, doit() calls the undo() member function for the most recently executed command object. Because a command can only be undone once, the function then sets _lastCmd to NULL.

```
16   void UndoCmd::doit()
17   {
18       // If there is a current command, undo it
19
20       if ( _lastCmd != NULL )
21       {
22           // Undo the previous command
23
```

```
24              _lastCmd->undo();
25
26              _lastCmd = NULL; // Make sure we can't undo twice
27         }
28    }
```

## 8.5    The AskFirstCmd Class

Some commands may have serious consequences that cannot be reversed (for example, deleting a file or exiting a program). Many programs ask the user for confirmation before actually executing such commands. This functionality is often difficult to provide, or at least tedious to implement, and is sometimes neglected.

The Cmd structure described in this chapter provides an easy way to capture a mechanism for checking with the user before executing a command. We can implement the basic facility once and for all in a base class. Cmd classes that represent commands that should be confirmed before being executed can simply be derived from the AskFirstCmd class.

The abstract AskFirstCmd class is derived from Cmd, and adds one important feature. The AskFirstCmd class posts a dialog to ask the user to confirm a command before actually executing it. Figure 8.4 shows an AskFirstCmd class card that outlines this class's additional responsibilities.

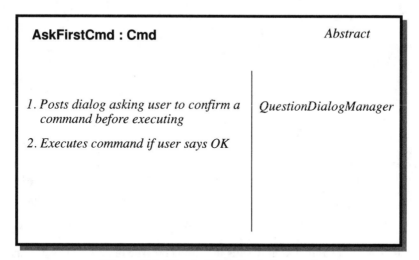

**Figure 8.4**  The AskFirstCmd class card.

The AskFirstCmd class defines an `execute()` member function that overrides the `Cmd::execute()` member function. Following the approach described in Section 7.1, `AskFirstCmd::execute()` just displays a dialog instead of invoking the `doit()` member function. AskFirstCmd uses the MotifApp framework's QuestionDialogManager class to display and manage the dialog. A single callback is provided, to be called if the user confirms the command.

Programmers may want to change the message displayed in the dialog, depending on the nature of the specific command. AskFirstCmd supports different messages, or questions, by providing a setQuestion() member function, which sets a protected _question member. Derived classes or applications that use an AskFirstCmd object can call the setQuestion() member function to control the question to be displayed.

The AskFirstCmd class is declared in the file AskFirstCmd.h as follows:

```
1    ///////////////////////////////////////////////////////////////
2    // AskFirstCmd.h: Base class for Cmds that ask for confirmation
3    ///////////////////////////////////////////////////////////////
4    #ifndef ASKFIRSTCMD_H
5    #define ASKFIRSTCMD_H
6    #include "Cmd.h"
7
8    class AskFirstCmd : public Cmd {
9
10     private:
11
12       // Callback for the yes choice on the dialog
13
14       static void yesCallback ( void * );
15
16       // Derived classes should use setQuestion to change
17       // the string displayed in the dialog
18
19       char *_question;
20
21     public:
22
23       AskFirstCmd ( char *, int );
24       void setQuestion ( char *str );
25
26       virtual void execute(); // Overrides the Cmd member function
27       virtual const char *const className () { return ( "AskFirstCmd" ); }
28    };
29
30    #endif
```

The AskFirstCmd constructor simply calls the Cmd constructor and initializes _question to a default string. The setQuestion() function makes a copy of the string given as its argument and deletes the previous value. Therefore, the constructor sets _question to NULL before calling the setQuestion() function with the default question.

```
1   ///////////////////////////////////////////////////////////
2   // AskFirstCmd.C
3   ///////////////////////////////////////////////////////////
4   #include "AskFirstCmd.h"
5   #include "QuestionDialogManager.h"
6
7   #define DEFAULTQUESTION "Do you really want to execute this command?"
8
9   AskFirstCmd::AskFirstCmd ( char *name, int active ) : Cmd ( name, active )
10  {
11      _question = NULL;
12      setQuestion ( DEFAULTQUESTION );
13  }
```

The setQuestion() member function deletes any previous string and creates a copy of its argument.

```
14  void AskFirstCmd::setQuestion ( char *str )
15  {
16      delete _question;
17      _question = strdup ( str );
18  }
```

The AskFirstCmd class overrides the virtual execute() member function implemented by Cmd. Instead of calling the doit() member function directly, this function uses the MotifApp framework's theQuestionDialogManager object to post a dialog. The current value of the _question member is used as the string to be displayed in the dialog. The action supported by this command is delayed until the user answers the question in the dialog.

```
19  void AskFirstCmd::execute()
20  {
21      theQuestionDialogManager->post ( _question, ( void * ) this,
22                                       &AskFirstCmd::yesCallback );
23  }
```

If the user confirms the command, the yesCallback() function is invoked. This function calls the Cmd::execute() member function to execute the doit() member function and handle the other details involved in executing the command.

```
24  void AskFirstCmd::yesCallback ( void *clientData )
25  {
26      AskFirstCmd *obj = (AskFirstCmd *) clientData;
27
28      obj->Cmd::execute();   // Call the base class execute()
29                             // member function to do all the
30                             // usual processing of the command
31  }
```

If the user selects the cancel button on the dialog, the dialog simply disappears and the command is not executed.

## 8.6    The WarnNoUndoCmd Class

One common use for classes like AskFirstCmd is to warn the user that there is no undo available for a particular command. This section describes a derived class that provides an appropriate warning message and initializes the _hasUndo member to FALSE. The WarnNoUndoCmd class is similar to the NoUndoCmd class, but provides the benefit of warning the user before it is too late.

The WarnNoUndoCmd class is simple to implement and contains only a constructor and an empty undoit() member function.

```
1   ////////////////////////////////////////////////////////
2   // WarnNoUndoCmd.h: Warns user before executing a command
3   ////////////////////////////////////////////////////////
4   #ifndef WARNNOUNDOCMD_H
5   #define WARNNOUNDOCMD_H
6
7   #include "AskFirstCmd.h"
8
9   class WarnNoUndoCmd : public AskFirstCmd {
10
11     protected:
12
13        virtual void undoit();
14
15     public:
16
17        WarnNoUndoCmd ( char *, int );
18        virtual const char *const className (){ return ( "WarnNoUndoCmd" ); }
19   };
20
21   #endif
```

The WarnNoUndoCmd constructor sets the _hasUndo member to FALSE to indicate that the class has no undo ability. It also provides a more specific default question to be displayed by the QuestionDialogManager when the command is executed. This question can still be changed by derived classes, or by the application that instantiates a WarnNoUndoCmd object. The WarnNoUndoCmd class's undoit() member function is empty, but must be implemented because Cmd declares it to be a pure virtual function.

```
1   //////////////////////////////////////////////////////////
2   // WarnNoUndoCmd.C: Warns user before executing a command
3   //////////////////////////////////////////////////////////
4   #include "WarnNoUndoCmd.h"
5
6   #define DEFAULTWARNING "This command cannot be undone. Proceed anyway?"
7   #define FALSE 0
8
9   WarnNoUndoCmd::WarnNoUndoCmd ( char *name, int active) :
10                                       AskFirstCmd ( name, active )
11  {
12      _hasUndo = FALSE;      // Specify that there is no undo
13      setQuestion ( DEFAULTWARNING );
14  }
15
16  void WarnNoUndoCmd::undoit()
17  {
18      // Empty
19  }
```

This completes a core set of abstract base classes that support command objects in the MotifApp framework. Figure 8.5 shows the inheritance graph that includes the classes discussed in this chapter. Most of the classes are abstract, with the exception of the supporting CmdList class and the UndoCmd class.

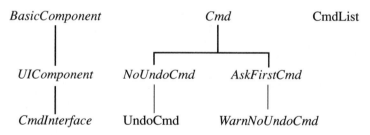

**Figure 8.5** The command inheritance hierarchy.

Figure 8.6 provides a view of the connections between many of these classes. The Cmd class interacts closely with the CmdList, CmdInterface, and UndoCmd classes to provide an infrastructure on which derived classes can be built. Figure 8.6 also shows some of the messages supported by the AskFirstCmd class. This class also inherits all the messages and connections of the Cmd class, and interacts with the QuestionDialogManager class.

For the most part, the command classes described in this chapter are independent of the rest of the MotifApp framework. None of the command classes have direct dependencies on the Application or MainWindow classes. In fact, the Cmd class is not even dependent on Motif, because the user interface aspect of each command is abstracted in a CmdInterface class. However, the AskFirstCmd and WarnNoUndoCmd classes are indirectly dependent on the Application class and the structure of the MotifApp framework because these classes use the DialogManager class to post dialogs. The DialogManager class is dependent on the Application class. In any case, the Cmd class and derived classes are intended for use in the MotifApp framework and should be added to the MotifApp library.

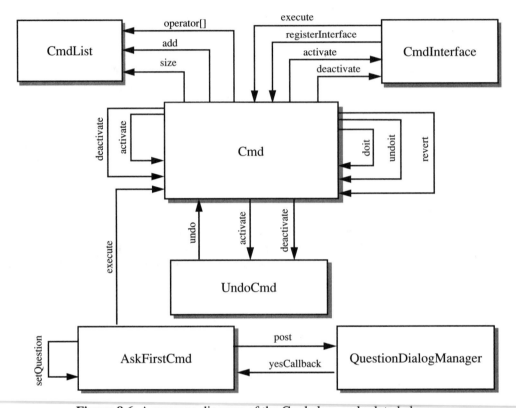

**Figure 8.6**  A message diagram of the Cmd class and related classes.

## 8.7    Summary

This chapter describes a collection of classes used to represent commands or actions to be taken within a program. These classes allow each command in a system to be modeled as an individual object. Representing commands as objects offers several advantages. First, applications can support an undo facility that applies to all commands. Second, certain complex but often-needed operations are supported in base classes for all to use. For example, operations that require confirmation before being executed can be handled merely by deriving a class from the AskFirstCmd class.

Chapter 9 describes a menu system based on the Cmd classes described in this chapter, and demonstrates how the Cmd classes might be used in a typical program.

Chapter 9

# A Simple Menu System

Motif provides a flexible set of widgets and gadgets that can be used to construct many types of menus. Although Motif provides all the necessary pieces, putting these pieces together can be somewhat tedious. Each item in a Motif menu is a separate widget. The programmer normally creates each widget separately and registers callbacks to be invoked when the user selects an item in the menu. The construction of even a modest menu along with the various callbacks needed for each item can easily require hundreds of lines of code. Motif provides a convenience function, `XmCreateSimpleMenu()` that makes some menus easier to build. However this function still does not address many of the common issues programmers face when implementing menus and the commands that appear in menus.

More importantly, the interactions between the various actions on a menu are often very complex. For example, some entries in a menu may need to enable or disable other menu items when they are executed. This requires maintaining relationships between the actions involved and the various widgets in a menu, so the correct menu widgets can be made sensitive and insensitive. Many programs also provide the ability to "undo" the previous command. Although Motif and other widget sets provide the components to build menus, they do not directly define an architecture that allows applications to do such things easily.

This chapter presents a menu package based on the Cmd class and derived classes discussed in Chapter 8. This menu system supports a menubar with multiple pulldown menu panes, an automatic undo facility, and an easy way to activate and de-activate groups of menu items. Section 9.1 describes a ButtonInterface class, which the MenuBar class uses to provide an interface between a menu item and a Cmd object. Section 9.2 describes the MenuBar class and Section 9.3 introduces the MenuWindow class, a subclass of MainWindow that supports a menubar. Finally, Section 9.4 describes a simple program that demonstrates the menu system and the Cmd class along with its various derived classes introduced in the previous chapter.

# 9.1    The ButtonInterface Class

The MenuBar class discussed in the following section creates menu panes that consist of Motif XmPushButton widgets. Each item in a menu pane corresponds to a Cmd object. The interface between each widget in a menu and its associated Cmd object is provided by instances of the ButtonInterface class. This class, which is derived from the CmdInterface class described in the previous chapter, creates a Motif XmPushButton widget and registers the `CmdInterface::execute-Callback()` function as an `XmNactivateCallback` function, to be called when the user selects an item from a menu.

The ButtonInterface class is declared as follows:

```
1   /////////////////////////////////////////////////////////////
2   // ButtonInterface.h: A pushbutton interface to a Cmd object
3   /////////////////////////////////////////////////////////////
4   #ifndef BUTTONINTERFACE
5   #define BUTTONINTERFACE
6   #include "CmdInterface.h"
7
8   class ButtonInterface : public CmdInterface {
9
10    public:
11
12      ButtonInterface ( Widget, Cmd * );
13  };
14  #endif
```

The ButtonInterface class defines only a constructor. All other facilities are inherited from CmdInterface. The constructor expects a parent widget and a pointer to a Cmd object. The constructor creates an XmPushButton widget and installs a callback to handle unexpected widget destruction, using the convenience function defined by UIComponent. Once the widget has been created, the constructor sets the widget's sensitivity according to the current value of the _active flag, which is initialized when the object is registered with a Cmd object. Finally, the constructor installs the `executeCallback()` function, which executes the associated Cmd object when the base widget is activated.

```
1   /////////////////////////////////////////////////////////////
2   // ButtonInterface.C: A pushbutton interface to a Cmd object
3   /////////////////////////////////////////////////////////////
4   #include "ButtonInterface.h"
```

```
5    #include <Xm/PushB.h>
6
7    ButtonInterface::ButtonInterface ( Widget parent,
8                                      Cmd *cmd ) : CmdInterface ( cmd )
9    {
10       _w = XtCreateWidget ( _name,
11                             xmPushButtonWidgetClass,
12                             parent,
13                             NULL, 0 );
14       installDestroyHandler();
15
16       // The _active member is set when each instance is registered
17       // with an associated Cmd object
18       // Now that a widget exists, set the widget's sensitivity
19       // according to its active state
20
21       if ( _active )
22           activate();
23       else
24           deactivate();
25
26       XtAddCallback ( _w,
27                       XmNactivateCallback,
28                       &CmdInterface::executeCmdCallback,
29                       (XtPointer) this );
30
31   }
```

The rest of the functionality of the ButtonInterface class is inherited from the CmdInterface class described in Chapter 8. The following section shows how the MenuBar class uses the Button-Interface class to construct a menu pane.

## 9.2  The MenuBar Class

The MenuBar class encapsulates the process of constructing a Motif menubar with multiple pulldown menu panes. The MenuBar class creates a pulldown menu from a list of Cmd objects, creating one menu entry for each command in the list.

The MenuBar class supports only one public member function in addition to the constructor. The addCommands() member function takes a CmdList object and a string and creates a menu pane with an entry for each Cmd object in the list. The second argument specifies a name for the pulldown pane.

The MenuBar class is derived from UIComponent and is declared as:

```
1    /////////////////////////////////////////////////////////
2    // MenuBar.h: A menubar, whose panes support items
3    //              that execute Cmd's
4    /////////////////////////////////////////////////////////
5    #ifndef MENUBAR_H
6    #define MENUBAR_H
7    #include "UIComponent.h"
8
9    class Cmd;
10   class CmdList;
11
12   class MenuBar : public UIComponent {
13
14     public:
15
16       MenuBar ( Widget, char * );
17
18       // Create a named menu pane from a list of Cmd objects
19
20       virtual void addCommands ( CmdList *, char * );
21       virtual const char *const className() { return ( "MenuBar" ); }
22   };
23   #endif
```

The MenuBar constructor creates a menubar widget by calling `XmCreateMenuBar()` and then installs the destruction handler provided by the UIComponent class. The menubar widget is the base widget of this component.

```
1    /////////////////////////////////////////////////////////
2    // MenuBar.C: A menubar whose panes support items
3    //              that execute Cmd's
4    /////////////////////////////////////////////////////////
5    #include "MenuBar.h"
6    #include "Cmd.h"
7    #include "CmdList.h"
8    #include "ButtonInterface.h"
9    #include <Xm/RowColumn.h>
10   #include <Xm/CascadeB.h>
11
12   MenuBar::MenuBar ( Widget parent, char *name ) : UIComponent ( name )
13   {
14       // Base widget is a Motif menubar widget
15
16       _w = XmCreateMenuBar ( parent, _name, NULL, 0 );
17
18       installDestroyHandler();
19   }
```

The member function addCommands() takes a CmdList object and a name and creates a pulldown menu pane containing a menu entry for each Cmd object on the list. Motif menu panes consist of a pulldown menu widget and an associated XmCascadeButton widget. The XmCascade-Button is the widget that appears in the menubar, and the pulldown menu is a menu pane that cascades from the menubar. The second argument to addCommands() specifies the name of the menu pane.

Once a new pane is created, addCommands() loops through the CmdList and creates a ButtonInterface object for each Cmd object. The pulldown menu pane serves as the parent widget of each ButtonInterface component.

```
20   void MenuBar::addCommands ( CmdList *list, char *name )
21   {
22       int     i;
23       Widget pulldown, cascade;
24
25       // Create a pulldown menu pane for this list of commands
26
27       pulldown = XmCreatePulldownMenu ( _w, name, NULL, 0 );
28
29       // Each entry in the menubar must have a cascade button
30       // from which the user can pull down the pane
31
32       cascade = XtVaCreateWidget ( name,
33                                    xmCascadeButtonWidgetClass,
34                                    _w,
35                                    XmNsubMenuId, pulldown,
36                                    NULL );
37       XtManageChild ( cascade );
38
39       // Loop through the cmdList, creating a menu
40       // entry for each command
41
42       for ( i = 0; i < list->size(); i++)
43       {
44           CmdInterface *ci;
45           ci  = new ButtonInterface ( pulldown, ( *list ) [i] );
46           ci->manage();
47       }
48   }
```

The MenuBar class has no direct dependencies on the rest of the MotifApp framework and can be used wherever a menubar is needed. However, because many applications need menubars, it is convenient to provide a top-level window as part of MotifApp that automatically creates a MenuBar object. The next section describes a MenuWindow class that automatically provides a menubar for applications that require one.

# 9.3   The MenuWindow Class

The MainWindow class described in Chapter 6 uses a Motif XmMainWindow widget to handle the layout of top-level windows. The MainWindow class is useful for applications that only require a work area. This section describes a MenuWindow class that extends the MainWindow class by adding a menubar along the top of the window. Applications that need a menubar should create a top-level window class derived from the MenuWindow class.

MenuWindow is an abstract class derived from MainWindow. Classes derived from MenuWindow must define both the `createWorkArea()` member function required by MainWindow, and a new pure virtual member function, `createMenuPanes()`. The MenuWindow class adds a pointer to a MenuBar object in its protected section and also overrides MainWindow's `initialize()` member function.

```
1    ///////////////////////////////////////////////////////////
2    // MenuWindow.h: Add a menubar to the features of MainWindow
3    ///////////////////////////////////////////////////////////
4    #ifndef MENUWINDOW_H
5    #define MENUWINDOW_H
6    #include "MainWindow.h"
7
8    class MenuBar;
9
10   class MenuWindow : public MainWindow {
11
12     protected:
13
14       MenuBar *_menuBar;
15
16       virtual void initialize();          // Called by Application
17       virtual void createMenuPanes() = 0; // Defined by derived
18                                           // classes to specify the
19                                           // contents of the menu
20     public:
21
22       MenuWindow ( char *name );
23       virtual ~MenuWindow();
24   };
25   #endif
```

The MenuWindow constructor initializes the `_menuBar` member to `NULL` and passes the `name` argument to the MainWindow constructor.

```
1    //////////////////////////////////////////////////////////////
2    // MenuWindow.C: Add a menubar to the features of MainWindow
3    //////////////////////////////////////////////////////////////
4    #include "MenuWindow.h"
5    #include "MenuBar.h"
6
7    MenuWindow::MenuWindow ( char *name ) : MainWindow ( name )
8    {
9        _menuBar = NULL;
10   }
```

The initialize() member function calls the MainWindow::initialize() member function to create an XmMainWindow widget, and to set up the work area. Then, MenuWindow::initialize() instantiates a MenuBar object and specifies the MenuBar object's base widget as the value of the XmMainWindow widget's XmNmenuBar resource. Finally, the virtual function createMenuPanes() is called to allow derived classes to add panes to the menubar before it is managed. The createMenuPanes() member function must be implemented by all derived classes.

```
11   void MenuWindow::initialize()
12   {
13       // Call base class to create XmMainWindow widget
14       // and set up the work area
15
16       MainWindow::initialize();
17
18       // Specify the base widget of a MenuBar object
19       // the XmMainWindow widget's menubar
20
21       _menuBar = new MenuBar ( _main, "menubar" );
22
23       XtVaSetValues ( _main,
24                       XmNmenuBar, _menuBar->baseWidget(),
25                       NULL);
26
27       // Call derived class hook to add panes to the menu
28
29       createMenuPanes();
30       _menuBar->manage();
31   }
```

The MenuWindow destructor frees the MenuBar object created by the initialize() member function.

```
32   MenuWindow::~MenuWindow()
33   {
34       delete _menuBar;
35   }
```

# 9.4    A MenuBar Example

This section presents a simple example that creates a menu, using some of the Cmd classes from Chapter 8 along with the classes described in this chapter. MotifApp applications that need a menubar do not have to create the menubar widget, nor the widgets in the menu. When using MotifApp, an application can simply define a new class derived from MenuWindow, and provide a list of Cmd objects to be included in each menu pane. Rather than worrying about the details of constructing a menu, programmers who use MotifApp concentrate on implementing the commands supported by the application. The framework handles the details of creating menus to execute these commands.

Before looking at an example program that uses a menubar, the following sections describe some command classes used by the example program. The program does very little except demonstrate the menu facilities. However, some classes described in the following sections, especially the QuitCmd, ManageCmd, and IconifyCmd classes, can be used by other programs.

## The QuitCmd Class

The QuitCmd class is derived from the WarnNoUndoCmd class described in Chapter 8. It provides a "user-friendly" way to exit an application, as described in the dialog discussion in Chapter 7. This class should be useful to many applications, and can be added to the MotifApp library. The QuitCmd class supports a constructor and a `doit()` member function. The class is declared in the file QuitCmd.h as:

```
1   ///////////////////////////////////////////////////////
2   // QuitCmd.h: Exit an application after checking with user
3   ///////////////////////////////////////////////////////
4   #ifndef QUITCMD_H
5   #define QUITCMD_H
6
7   #include "WarnNoUndoCmd.h"
8
9   class QuitCmd : public WarnNoUndoCmd {
10
11    protected:
12
13      virtual void doit();        // Call exit
14
15    public:
16
17      QuitCmd ( char *, int );
18      virtual const char *const className () { return ( "QuitCmd" ); }
19   };
20
21   #endif
```

The QuitCmd constructor simply calls the base class constructor to initialize the object before setting the default question to the string "Do you really want to exit?"

```
1   /////////////////////////////////////////////////////////
2   // QuitCmd.C: Exit an application after checking with user
3   /////////////////////////////////////////////////////////
4   #include "QuitCmd.h"
5   #include <stdlib.h>
6
7   #define QUITQUESTION "Do you really want to exit?"
8
9   QuitCmd::QuitCmd ( char *name, int active ) :
10                                  WarnNoUndoCmd ( name, active )
11  {
12      setQuestion ( QUITQUESTION );
13  }
```

The doit() member function calls exit(). This member function is called only if the user replies affirmatively to a dialog popped up by the AskFirstCmd class. The dialog and the associated details are all handled by the base classes provided by the MotifApp framework. The QuitCmd class only needs to implement the action to be taken if the command is actually performed.

```
14  void QuitCmd::doit()
15  {
16      // Just exit
17
18      exit ( 0 );
19  }
```

## The ManageCmd Class

The ManageCmd class provides a way for the user to invoke the manage() member function supported by the Application class. Recall that this member function manages all registered MainWindow objects in an Application. The ManageCmd class and the IconifyCmd class described in the next section provide simple ways to open or close all windows in an application with a single command. This class should be useful to many applications, and can be added to the MotifApp framework.

The ManageCmd class is derived from the NoUndoCmd class described in Chapter 8, and supports a doit() member function. It would be convenient if this class supported an undoit() member function as well. However, the doit() function simply relies on the Application class to manage all windows. The ManageCmd class cannot determine which windows were previously managed. Therefore, it cannot know which windows should be hidden, and which should be left alone when undoing the manage command. Without extending the Application class, it is not possible to undo the action correctly.

The ManageCmd class is declared in the file ManageCmd.h as:

```
1     ///////////////////////////////////////////////////////////
2     // ManageCmd.h: Manage all windows in a MotifApp application
3     ///////////////////////////////////////////////////////////
4     #ifndef MANAGECMD_H
5     #define MANAGECMD_H
6     #include "NoUndoCmd.h"
7
8     class ManageCmd : public NoUndoCmd {
9
10      protected:
11
12        virtual void doit();        // Manage all windows
13
14      public:
15
16        ManageCmd ( char *, int );
17        virtual const char *const className () { return ( "ManageCmd" ); }
18    };
19    #endif
```

The ManageCmd constructor simply calls the base class constructor to initialize the object.

```
1     ///////////////////////////////////////////////////////////
2     // ManageCmd.C: Manage all windows in a MotifApp application
3     ///////////////////////////////////////////////////////////
4     #include "ManageCmd.h"
5     #include "Application.h"
6
7     ManageCmd::ManageCmd ( char *name, int active ) :
8                                            NoUndoCmd ( name, active )
9     {
10        // Empty
11    }
```

The `doit()` member function calls the `manage()` member function for the program's global Application object.

```
12    void ManageCmd::doit()
13    {
14        theApplication->manage(); // Opens all top-level windows
15    }
```

## The IconifyCmd Class

The IconifyCmd class provides an interface to the `iconify()` member function supported by the Application class. This member function iconifies all MainWindow objects registered with Application. The IconifyCmd class provides a simple way to close all windows in an application. This class should be useful to many applications and can be added to the MotifApp framework.

The IconifyCmd class is derived from the NoUndoCmd class described in Chapter 8, and supports a doit() member function. Like the ManageCmd class, the IconifyCmd class has no way to determine which windows were already iconified, which makes it difficult to support undo.

The IconifyCmd class is declared in the file IconifyCmd.h as:

```
1   //////////////////////////////////////////////////////////////////
2   // IconifyCmd.h: Iconify all windows in a MotifApp application
3   //////////////////////////////////////////////////////////////////
4   #ifndef ICONIFYCMD_H
5   #define ICONIFYCMD_H
6   #include "NoUndoCmd.h"
7
8   class IconifyCmd : public NoUndoCmd {
9
10    protected:
11
12      virtual void doit();        // Iconify all windows
13
14    public:
15
16      IconifyCmd ( char *, int );
17      virtual const char *const className () { return ( "IconifyCmd" ); }
18  };
19  #endif
```

The IconifyCmd constructor simply calls its base class constructor to initialize the object.

```
1   //////////////////////////////////////////////////////////////////
2   // IconifyCmd.C: Iconify all windows in a MotifApp application
3   //////////////////////////////////////////////////////////////////
4   #include "IconifyCmd.h"
5   #include "Application.h"
6
7   IconifyCmd::IconifyCmd ( char *name, int active ) :
8                                       NoUndoCmd ( name, active )
9   {
10      // Empty
11  }
```

The doit() member function calls the iconify() member function for the program's global Application object.

```
12  void IconifyCmd::doit()
13  {
14      theApplication->iconify(); // Close all top-level windows
15  }
```

## The NoOpCmd Class

The NoOpCmd class is a simple command class that does nothing except report that its doit() or undoit() member functions have been called. The example program in the next section uses this class to demonstrate the undo facility and to show how dependencies can be specified between objects. The NoOpCmd class is derived from the Cmd class described in Chapter 8, and supports both doit() and undoit() member functions. The NoOpCmd class is declared in the file NoOpCmd.h as:

```
1   ////////////////////////////////////////////////////////
2   // NoOpCmd.h: Example, dummy command class
3   ////////////////////////////////////////////////////////
4   #ifndef NOOPCMD_H
5   #define MNOOPCMD_H
6   #include "Cmd.h"
7
8   class NoOpCmd : public Cmd {
9
10     protected:
11
12        virtual void doit();
13        virtual void undoit();
14
15     public:
16
17        NoOpCmd ( char *, int );
18        virtual const char *const className () { return ( "NoOpCmd" ); }
19   };
20
21   #endif
```

The NoOpCmd constructor simply calls the constructor of its base class to initialize the object.

```
1   ////////////////////////////////////////////////////////
2   // NoOpCmd.C: Example, dummy command class
3   ////////////////////////////////////////////////////////
4   #include "NoOpCmd.h"
5   #include "Application.h"
6   #include <stream.h>
7
8   NoOpCmd::NoOpCmd ( char *name, int active ) : Cmd ( name, active )
9   {
10       // Empty
11   }
```

The doit() member function reports the name of the object and the message "doit."

```
12   void NoOpCmd::doit()
13   {
14       // Just print a message that allows us to trace the execution
15
16       cout <<  name() << ":" << "doit\n" << flush;
17   }
```

The `undoit()` member function is similar, but prints the message "undoit."

```
18   void NoOpCmd::undoit()
19   {
20       // Just print a message that allows us to trace the execution
21
22       cout <<  name() << ":" << "undoit\n" << flush;
23   }
```

## The menuDemo Program

The menuDemo program uses the command classes described in the previous sections to demonstrate the MotifApp menu system, which is based on the command mechanism described in Chapter 8. This example displays three identical top-level windows. Each window supports a menubar with three menu panes. The first menu pane on each window contains commands that apply to the application as a whole. In this example, these commands are labeled "Quit", "Open", "Iconify", and "Undo".

The second menu pane in each window also contains three commands that also apply to the entire application. These commands are stubs, implemented by the NoOpCmd class described in the previous section. These commands are known merely as "X", "Y", and "Z". As instances of NoOpCmd, these command objects simply print a message when they are executed and undone. Although these commands appear in the second menu pane of all three top-level windows, there is only one Cmd object for each command. It makes no difference what menu the user uses to execute the command. The same NoOpCmd object is always executed. This demonstrates the Cmd class's ability to support multiple CmdInterface objects for a single Cmd object.

Finally, each window's menubar has a third menu pane, which contain the commands "A", "B", and "C". These commands are also implemented as instances of the NoOpCmd class. However, each top-level window has its own instance of each of these commands.

To support the application-wide commands, we can start by creating a subclass of the Application class. This derived class provides a convenient place to create and maintain the commands used throughout the application. The "X", "Y", and "Z" commands can be instantiated in the constructor and assigned to class data members. The "Quit", "Open," and "Iconify" commands can also be created by the Application subclass. These command objects are all assigned to protected data members, and can be retrieved by any MenuWindow object through inline access functions.

The MenuDemoApp class is declared as follows:

```
1   ////////////////////////////////////////////////////////////////
2   // MenuDemoApp.h: An application class for the menu demo program
3   ////////////////////////////////////////////////////////////////
4   #ifndef MENUDEMOAPP_H
5   #define MENUDEMOAPP_H
6   #include "Application.h"
7
8   class Cmd;
9
10   class MenuDemoApp : public Application {
11
12      protected:
13
14        // Maintain pointers to Cmd objects used throughout the application
15
16        Cmd *_quit;
17        Cmd *_manage;
18        Cmd *_iconify;
19        Cmd *_x;
20        Cmd *_y;
21        Cmd *_z;
22
23      public:
24
25        MenuDemoApp ( char * );
26        virtual ~MenuDemoApp();
27
28        // Provide access functions for all Cmd objects
29
30        Cmd *quitCmd()    { return ( _quit ); }
31        Cmd *manageCmd()  { return ( _manage ); }
32        Cmd *iconifyCmd() { return ( _iconify ); }
33        Cmd *xCmd() { return ( _x ); }
34        Cmd *yCmd() { return ( _y ); }
35        Cmd *zCmd() { return ( _z ); }
36
37        virtual const char *const className() { return ( "MenuDemoApp" ); }
38   };
39
40   // Classes that need to retrieve the MenuDemoApp's Cmd objects
41   // need a pointer to an Application object that supports
42   // MenuDemoApp's extended protocol
43
44   extern MenuDemoApp *theMenuDemoApp;
45   #endif
```

The file MenuDemoApp.C contains the implementation of the MenuDemoApp member functions, and also instantiates a MenuDemoApp object and three MenuDemoWindow objects. The

MenuDemoWindow class is the top-level window class defined for this example. The file includes the headers for the MenuDemoApp class, the MenuDemoWindow class, and for the Cmd classes instantiated by the MenuDemoApp class.

```
1   ////////////////////////////////////////////////////////////
2   // MenuDemoApp.C:
3   ////////////////////////////////////////////////////////////
4   #include "MenuDemoApp.h"
5   #include "QuitCmd.h"
6   #include "ManageCmd.h"
7   #include "IconifyCmd.h"
8   #include "NoOpCmd.h"
9   #include "MenuDemoWindow.h"
10
11  MenuDemoApp *theMenuDemoApp = new MenuDemoApp ( "MenuDemo" );
12  MainWindow  *window1 = new MenuDemoWindow ( "Window1" );
13  MainWindow  *window2 = new MenuDemoWindow ( "Window2" );
14  MainWindow  *window3 = new MenuDemoWindow ( "Window3" );
```

The MenuDemoApp constructor creates the Cmd objects for the first two menu panes that appear in each window. These Cmd objects cannot be added to a menu at this point, the menu must be constructed in the MenuDemoWindow class. However, because there is to be only one instance of each of these classes in the entire application, the "Quit", "Open", and "Iconify" objects are instantiated in the MenuDemoApp constructor.

```
15  MenuDemoApp::MenuDemoApp ( char * name ) : Application ( name )
16  {
17      // Create the application-wide commands that appear in all menus
18
19      _quit    = new QuitCmd ( "Quit" , TRUE );
20      _manage  = new ManageCmd ( "Open", TRUE );
21      _iconify = new IconifyCmd ("Iconify", TRUE );
22
23      // Create three NoOpCmd objects to demonstrate dependencies and
24      // to demo the support for multiple interfaces to a single Cmd
25      // Start X and Y as active, Z as inactive
26
27      _x = new NoOpCmd ( "X", TRUE );
28      _y = new NoOpCmd ( "Y", TRUE );
29      _z = new NoOpCmd ( "Z", FALSE );
30
31      // Specify relationships between the X, Y, and Z commands
32      // Activating any command deactivates itself and activates
33      // the other two commands
34
35      _x->addToActivationList ( _y );
36      _x->addToActivationList ( _z );
```

```
37        _x->addToDeactivationList ( _x );
38
39        _y->addToActivationList ( _x );
40        _y->addToActivationList ( _z );
41        _y->addToDeactivationList ( _y );
42
43        _z->addToActivationList ( _x );
44        _z->addToActivationList ( _y );
45        _z->addToDeactivationList ( _z );
46   }
```

The MenuDemoApp constructor also creates three NoOpCmd objects to be used in the menu panes of all three windows. These commands simply report when their doit() and undoit() member functions are called. Although the menus are constructed in the MenuDemoApp class, we can specify relationships between the Cmd objects when they are created. This is an important feature of MotifApp's command architecture. Applications do not need to worry about activating or deactivating user interface components. The application only determines what commands need to be active or inactive. The Cmd objects handle the interface components, regardless of how many interfaces are associated with any given command.

In this example, the "X" and "Y" commands are initially active, while "Z" is inactive. The MenuDemoApp constructor specifies relationships between these objects such that activating any command disables that command, and enables the other two. This arrangement demonstrates a fairly complex "two out of three" toggle behavior. The complexity of programming such behavior without support from the Cmd architecture is more apparent when we consider that each can be undone at any time, and that this example coordinates three simultaneous interfaces to these commands. This behavior is, of course, totally arbitrary, because the commands do nothing. The behavior of these menu items just demonstrates how dependencies between Cmd objects might be useful.

The MenuDemoApp destructor simply destroys the six command objects created in the constructor.

```
47   MenuDemoApp::~MenuDemoApp()
48   {
49        delete _quit;
50        delete _manage;
51        delete _iconify;
52        delete _x;
53        delete _y;
54        delete _z;
55   }
```

The top-level window in this example program is implemented as a class derived from the MenuWindow class. The MenuDemoWindow class adds three panes to the menubar provided by the MenuWindow class. The first two panes represent Cmd objects created by the MenuDemoApp class. The third menu pane is created by registering three Cmd objects created in the MenuDemoWindow constructor. Unlike the Cmd objects created in the MenuDemoApp class, these three objects are unique within each instance of the MenuDemoWindow class.

The file MenuDemoWindow.h declares the MenuDemoWindow class. The class contains pointers to three Cmd objects in the protected portion of the class. The class maintains a widget that might be used as a drawing area, and implements the two pure virtual member functions required by its base classes.

```
1   ///////////////////////////////////////////////////////////
2   // MenuDemoWindow.h: Demonstrate Cmd and MenuBar classes
3   ///////////////////////////////////////////////////////////
4   #ifndef MENUDEMOWINDOW_H
5   #define MENUDEMOWINDOW_H
6   #include "MenuWindow.h"
7
8   class Cmd;
9
10  class MenuDemoWindow : public MenuWindow {
11
12    protected:
13
14      // Support three window-specific command objects
15
16      Cmd * _a;
17      Cmd * _b;
18      Cmd * _c;
19
20      Widget _canvas;
21      Widget createWorkArea ( Widget );
22      void   createMenuPanes();
23
24    public:
25
26      MenuDemoWindow ( char * );
27
28  };
29  #endif
```

The MenuDemoWindow constructor instantiates three NoOpCmd objects named "A", "B", and "C", in much the same way as the "X", "Y", and "Z" commands are created in the MenuDemoApp constructor. Although these objects behave in the same way as their counterparts in the MenuDemoApp class, these objects are not shared among all windows in the program. Each MenuDemoWindow object creates three unique NoOpCmd objects.

```
1   ///////////////////////////////////////////////////////////
2   // MenuDemoWindow.C: Demonstrate Cmd and MenuBar classes
3   ///////////////////////////////////////////////////////////
4   #include "MenuDemoWindow.h"
5   #include "MenuBar.h"
6   #include "MenuDemoApp.h"
7   #include "NoOpCmd.h"
```

```
8   #include "UndoCmd.h"
9   #include "CmdList.h"
10  #include <Xm/DrawingA.h>
11
12  MenuDemoWindow::MenuDemoWindow ( char *name ) : MenuWindow ( name )
13  {
14      // Create three NoOpCmd objects to demonstrate relationships
15      // between objects, as well as MotifApp's undo facility
16
17      _a = new NoOpCmd ( "A", TRUE );
18      _b = new NoOpCmd ( "B", TRUE );
19      _c = new NoOpCmd ( "C", FALSE );
20
21      // Set up dependencies between objects
22      // Each command disables itself once it is executed,
23      // and enables the other two
24
25      _a->addToActivationList ( _b );
26      _a->addToActivationList ( _c );
27      _a->addToDeactivationList ( _a );
28
29      _b->addToActivationList ( _a );
30      _b->addToActivationList ( _c );
31      _b->addToDeactivationList ( _b );
32
33      _c->addToActivationList ( _a );
34      _c->addToActivationList ( _b );
35      _c->addToDeactivationList ( _c );
36  }
```

Every class derived from MainWindow must define a `createWorkArea()` member function. For this example, `createWorkArea()` simply creates and returns an XmDrawingArea widget. The example does not use this widget, but every MainWindow object must have a work area.

```
37  Widget MenuDemoWindow::createWorkArea ( Widget parent )
38  {
39      _canvas = XtCreateWidget ( "canvas",
40                                 xmDrawingAreaWidgetClass,
41                                 parent,
42                                 NULL, 0 );
43      return ( _canvas );
44  }
```

The `createMenuPanes()` member function is called by the MenuWindow class after the window's MenuBar object has been created. This function is expected to add menu panes to the window's MenuBar object by constructing a list of Cmd objects from which to create each menu pane. The MenuDemoWindow class creates three menu panes. The first pane in each menubar consists of an "Undo" command, provided by MotifApp's `theUndoCmd` object, and also the

"Quit", "Open", and "Iconify" objects instantiated by the MenuDemoApp constructor. The function `createMenuPanes()` adds each of these objects to a CmdList object and adds a menu pane named "Application" to the window's menubar.

Next, `createMenuPanes()` creates a new CmdList object and builds a list that contains the "X", "Y", and "Z" objects provided by the MenuDemoApp object. Finally, the third menu pane contains the "A, "B", and "C" command objects created by each instance of MenuDemoWindow.

```
45   void MenuDemoWindow::createMenuPanes()
46   {
47       CmdList *cmdList;
48
49       // Create an Application pane containing undo,
50       // and other application-wide commands
51
52       cmdList = new CmdList();
53       cmdList->add ( theUndoCmd );
54       cmdList->add ( theMenuDemoApp->manageCmd() );
55       cmdList->add ( theMenuDemoApp->iconifyCmd() );
56       cmdList->add ( theMenuDemoApp->quitCmd() );
57       _menuBar->addCommands ( cmdList, "Application" );
58
59       delete cmdList;
60
61       // Create a menu pane of NoOpCmd objects to demonstrate
62       // Cmd objects that have multiple interfaces
63
64       cmdList = new CmdList();
65       cmdList->add ( theMenuDemoApp->xCmd() );
66       cmdList->add ( theMenuDemoApp->yCmd() );
67       cmdList->add ( theMenuDemoApp->zCmd() );
68       _menuBar->addCommands ( cmdList, "XYZ" );
69
70       delete cmdList;
71
72       // Create a window-specific menu pane, containing
73       // commands that are independent within each window
74
75       cmdList = new CmdList();
76       cmdList->add ( _a );
77       cmdList->add ( _b );
78       cmdList->add ( _c );
79       _menuBar->addCommands ( cmdList, "ABC" );
80
81       delete cmdList;
82   }
```

This program can be built by compiling the files MenuDemoWindow.C, MenuDemoApp.C, and NoOpCmd.C, and linking the resulting object files with the MotifApp library:

```
CC -c MenuDemoApp.C MenuDemoWindow.C NoOpCmd.C

CC -o menuDemo MenuDemoApp.o MenuDemoWindow.o \
      NoOpCmd.o -lMotifApp -lXm -lXt -lX11
```

At this point, the MotifApp library is expected to contain all the reusable classes discussed so far, including the MenuWindow, MenuBar, QuitCmd, ManageCmd, and IconifyCmd classes described in this chapter.

Figure 9.1 shows the windows displayed by the menuDemo program. It is necessary to try the various menus to understand exactly how they work. The "Application" menu pane provides a way to test the `manage()` and `iconify()` member functions defined by the Application class, and a way to experiment with a "user-friendly" quit mechanism, similar to that described in Chapter 7. The "XYZ" menu pane in each window's menubar represents the same commands. Selecting an item from this menu pane in any one of the windows enables the other commands, which changes the sensitivities of the corresponding items in all three menus. Finally, each "ABC" menu pane works independently. Selecting one of the active items from an "ABC" menu pane changes the sensitivities of the other items in that pane, but does not affect items in other menus. Notice that the Undo entry in any "Application" menu pane can be used to reverse the effects of any command, regardless of the window from which it was executed.

This program is a contrived example, intended to demonstrate the capabilities of the MenuBar and Cmd classes. However, this example shows how real applications can take advantage of these facilities to build menus that control "undoable" commands that have complex dependencies, as well as multiple interfaces. Because the framework captures the underlying structure necessary to support these mechanisms in a collection of classes, the programmer is free to concentrate on the application-specific functions required by the program.

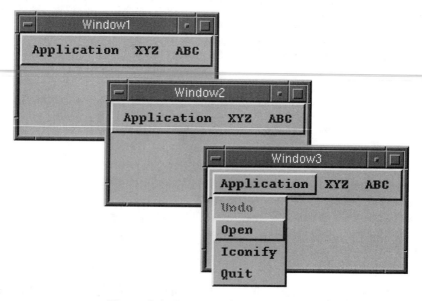

**Figure 9.1**  The menuDemo program.

# 9.5    Summary

This chapter describes a simple menu package based on the command classes discussed in Chapter 8. Although this system has some limitations, it offers an easy way to construct complex menus with a surprising number of features. All commands throughout the system can be undone through a single interface, which can easily be added to any menu. The command classes work with the DialogManager classes described in Chapter 7 to provide a simple way to handle commands that need to be confirmed before executing. These classes allow applications to implement complex commands, like the "safe quit" techniques described in Chapter 7 with a minimum amount of effort.

# Chapter 10
# Lengthy Tasks

Interactive applications that perform lengthy operations present a significant challenge to programmers. By their very nature, interactive applications must maintain a continuous dialogue with the user. They must be designed to accept user input at almost any time. For Motif applications, this means that programs must return to the event loop frequently. Unless an X application checks the event queue at regular intervals, the user will be unable to push buttons, pop up menus, move scrollbars, or interact with the application in any way.

However, most significant applications must do something besides process events, and often must perform operations that take a relatively long time to complete. For an interactive application, a "relatively long time" is any length of time that reduces the responsiveness of the application. Non-responsiveness is only one of many problems that can occur when a Motif application is too busy to handle events for even a brief period. If the contents of a program's windows are lost while the application is too busy to handle events, the program will be unable to restore the windows' contents until it is no longer busy. In this case, the user is left with a blank window; even Motif's three-dimensional shadows will not be redrawn. If the user resizes a top-level window while the program is busy, the window manager changes the top-level window's size, but the window's contents do not resize as the user may expect.

More serious problems can occur if the user doesn't understand what a program is doing and begins to click mouse buttons in random parts of the application's window or type at the keyboard, hoping to get the program to respond. If a busy program allows the X server to queue these events, the events will be reported to the application when it eventually returns to the event loop. The results may be unpredictable, and may even be disastrous.

There is also no general way for the user to interrupt an X application that is too busy to check the event queue. UNIX programmers know that they can type a Control-C in a terminal to interrupt most processes. Using Control-C as an interrupt character is a feature of the UNIX shell, which has little in common with X and Motif input handling. To the X server, a Control-C is just another set of keystrokes, which the server reports to the application as a sequence of `KeyPress` and `KeyRe-lease` events. If the application is too busy to check the event loop, it will not detect such a key sequence until the program is no longer busy.

This chapter discusses some ways to handle interactive applications that must perform time-consuming operations. Section 10.1 discusses some guidelines for applications that must perform lengthy non-interactive tasks, and presents several techniques for handling such situations. Sections 10.2 and 10.3 present several C++ classes that implement some of the solutions discussed in Section 10.1. Section 10.4 discusses an example program that uses the classes introduced in this chapter to handle a potentially lengthy operation.

# 10.1  Strategies for Busy Applications

Ideally, interactive applications should be designed to avoid operations that require longer than a few milliseconds to perform. Of course, this is not always possible and most real applications must perform tasks that can potentially take considerable amounts of time. Dealing gracefully with lengthy tasks usually requires the programmer to pay special attention to an application's structure; the program must be designed from the beginning to handle the lengthy task. Unlike non-interactive applications, X-based programs cannot simply call a potentially time-consuming function and wait for it to return.

The following paragraphs list a few guidelines for applications that expect to be busy for an extended period of time and present some techniques for implementing these guidelines. These guidelines are based on the user's view of the application, and the need to provide a responsive interface.

**Always let the user know when the application is busy.** The easiest way to show that an application is busy is to change the program's mouse cursor to a special "busy cursor," usually an hourglass or a watch. The Xlib function `XDefineCursor()` can be used to specify a cursor for an application's top-level shell. Multi-window applications should set the cursor in all top-level windows. A busy cursor is often adequate if a task is expected to be completed quickly (within a few seconds). For more time-consuming operations, it may also be useful to post a dialog to provide information about the task's progress.

**Disable user input while the application is busy.** There are several ways to prevent user input from being queued while an application is busy. An easy way to disable device events is to post a dialog whose `XmNdialogStyle` resource is set to `XmDIALOG_FULL_APPLICATION_MODAL`. This type of dialog disables input to all parts of an application except the dialog window itself, but allows the application to continue processing `Expose` and configuration events. Of course, if the application is too busy to check the event queue periodically, these events will not be processed until the application returns to the event queue. However, disabling user input prevents the X server from queuing device events (user input). If an application disables input, it will not be faced with a series of random user input when it completes the lengthy task and returns to the event loop, even if the user tries to type or use the mouse while the application is busy.

Another technique for preventing user input involves creating an *input-only* window as a child of an application's top-level shell. An input-only window is a region of the screen that accepts input, but is not visible to the user. This window can be mapped and raised to cover all descendents of the shell, and prevent user input to those windows while the application is busy. Each input-only window can prevent user input in the children of *one* shell widget. Applications with multiple top-level windows or dialog windows must create and map an input-only window for each visible window or dialog. (See [Schiefler90] for information about input-only windows.)

Ordinarily, handling an input-only window for each top-level window and dialog in a multi-window application could be a complex task. However, an application framework like MotifApp could support this technique and allow applications to simply call a busy() method to cover all visible windows in the application.

**Keep the user informed of progress.** Although displaying a busy cursor or posting a busy dialog provides a way to show the user that the application is busy, it is often more effective to let the user know exactly what is happening at any time. Even when an application displays a busy cursor, the user is likely to be concerned if the program remains busy for more than a few seconds. Informing the user when various milestones have passed can be very effective. If the operation has a known duration, the program can often use a dialog to report progress in terms of percentages, 10% done, 20% done, and so on. If this information cannot be computed, it can still be effective to tell the user what is happening at various stages. For example, an application might display messages like "Reading data," "Sorting," and so on.

Reporting the current state of a program takes time and can actually increase the total time required to perform a given task. However, the user often believes that a task that provides continuous feedback is completed more quickly than an equivalent task that provides no feedback. In many interactive applications, the user's perception is more important than the actual elapsed time.

**Keep the application's windows, including dialogs, refreshed**. Even if an application uses a dialog to provide progress reports, the user will be unable to read these messages unless the application continues to handle Expose events.[1] There are several ways to handle Expose events while an application is busy:

- Embed periodic calls to XmUpdateDisplay() in the busy code. XmUpdateDisplay() is a Motif utility function that checks the event queue for Expose events. Any pending

---

[1] The XmLabel widget class, as well as many other widget classes, relies on Expose events to update text displayed in the widget. This is a common source of problems in busy applications. Often, an application posts a dialog widget as recommended here, and periodically changes the text to report progress. However, when using XtSetValues() to change the text displayed in a widget, the XmLabel widget simply stores the new text and triggers an Expose event. When the application processes the event, the widget is redrawn using the new text. If the application is too busy to receive an Expose event, the dialog is not redrawn, and the text doesn't change.

`Expose` events are removed and dispatched; all other events remain in the queue. This technique works well with a dialog that reports an application's status. A program can simply call `XmUpdateDisplay()` each time it changes the message displayed in the dialog. Obviously, it is only possible to embed calls to `XmUpdateDisplay()` in source code that is available and can be modified. For example, this technique is not useful if an application is waiting for the result of a database query, where the database interface is a commercial database library whose source code is not available for modification.

- Implement the task as a subprocess. Some very lengthy operations are best performed in a separate process. Applications can initiate the task as a subprocess, disable user input using one of the techniques mentioned above, and then return to the event loop. The application can communicate with the subprocess using pipes or sockets. For example, if the subprocess produces data that the parent process needs, the function `XtAppAddInput()` can be used to watch for data written by the subprocess to a pipe. Because the application returns to the event queue between reading data from the subprocess, the contents of the application's windows can be maintained at all times.

- Applications can also use *work procedures* to simulate background tasks. A work procedure is a callback function registered with the Xt Intrinsics to be called whenever the event queue is empty. A work procedure must do a small amount of work and return quickly, to allow the application to continue to check the event queue. While not always possible, tasks can sometimes be broken into smaller chunks that can be performed in succession. For example, a ray-tracing function could be designed to trace only a few rays in each call. A function that performs an animation might render one frame.

- Some applications can use a timeout callback function to perform a lengthy task. A timeout callback is a function called by Xt when a specified amount of time has elapsed. Xt removes timeout callbacks once they are called. However, the timeout function can re-install itself to be called again, setting up a cycle of function calls. Timeout callbacks can be used to implement steady, periodic tasks while continuing to handle events. Typical applications for this approach include clocks, timers such as the Stopwatch example in Chapter 2, or any program that needs to perform periodic checks or measurements.

The primary goal of each technique just mentioned is to allow an application to return to the event loop periodically to handle `Expose` and configuration events. When using these techniques, it is important to remember to prevent user input. Allowing users to issue additional commands while the application is busy with one task adds greatly to the complexity of the program.

**Allow the user to interrupt the application.** Lengthy tasks can be very frustrating for the user if there is no way to interrupt the program. Unfortunately, there is no general way to interrupt an X application that is too busy to return to the event queue. It would be convenient if X could support some type of "interrupt event" that can be sent to an application when the user types an interrupt character, like Control-C. Unfortunately, X applications cannot be forced to receive any event. The X server can place an event on the application's event queue, but this does little good if the application is too busy to check the event queue. Interrupts in a UNIX environment are based on signals. The X server cannot send signals to an X application, because X applications may be running anywhere on a network, and may not be running on the same machine as the server.

It is possible to design an application to support interruptible tasks when using the techniques described above. If an application can return to the event queue periodically, it can check for user input to see if the user has tried to interrupt the program. Figure 10.1 demonstrates the flow of control in an application that combines a busy cursor, a modal "working" dialog, and a subprocess to handle a lengthy, interruptible operation. In this scenario, the application initiates a lengthy task in the `startTaskCallback()` function. This function displays a busy cursor and posts a dialog. Because the dialog uses the full application modal style, the dialog continues to accept user input, but locks out input to the rest of the application. Next, a callback, `interruptCallback()`, is installed. This function allows the user to interrupt the task by clicking on a button on the dialog. Finally, the real task is started, by calling `popen()` to fork a subprocess. The function concludes by registering an input handler to be called by the Xt main event loop when input is pending from the subprocess. At this point, the callback returns control to the event loop.

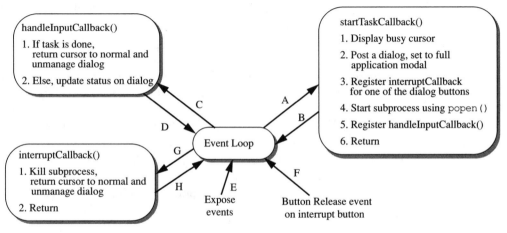

**Figure 10.1** Performing a lengthy task as a subprocess.

While the subprocess is running, the main application continues to monitor the event queue. The program ignores user input to all windows except the modal dialog, but handles `Expose` events and configuration events as they occur. As the subprocess performs its task, it occasionally communicates with the parent process by writing to the pipe created by `popen()`. Depending on the specific situation, the subprocess might provide progress reports, or supply data to be read by the main application. When input is available from the subprocess, Xt calls the `handleInputCallback()` function. In addition to handling the input from the subprocess, this callback function checks to see if the subprocess has completed its task. If the task has been completed, `handleInput-Callback()` removes the dialog and restores the application's normal cursor. Otherwise, it updates the status on the dialog.

With this approach, lengthy operations can be interrupted because the application continues to check the event queue for user input between handling `Expose` events and input from the subprocess. The application ignores all device events except those that occur within the dialog. However, if the user clicks on the dialog's interrupt button, the `interruptCallback()` function is called. This callback terminates the subprocess, removes the busy dialog, and restores the application's normal cursor.

This technique is not appropriate for every busy situation. For example, if an operation normally requires only a few seconds, spawning a separate process is a rather heavy-weight approach. However, a subprocess may be a reasonable way to implement a task that takes several minutes. One challenge for the programmer, of course, is knowing in advance whether a particular task will take seconds, minutes, or hours. Using subprocesses is also most suitable for tasks that can be cleanly separated from the rest of the application,. Obviously, some operations are difficult to implement as separate processes. For example, a task that requires continuous access to data maintained by the program could be difficult to implement as a separate process.

A work procedure provides a simple way to simulate a subprocess without the overhead of spawning a separate process. The technique for using a work procedure is very similar to that of using a separate process. However, work procedures are simply callback functions, executed within the application process. Xt calls all registered work procedures repeatedly when no other events are pending. A work procedure must perform a small part of some task and return quickly to allow the application to continue to check the event queue. The work procedure must be responsible for maintaining any necessary state between calls. Work procedures are only suitable for tasks that can be implemented as a sequence of repeated calls to a function.

Figure 10.2 shows the sequence of events that might occur when using a work procedure to perform a lengthy background task. Like the previous example, this approach allows the user to interrupt the task at any time, and allows the application to handle `Expose` and configuration events while the task is in progress.

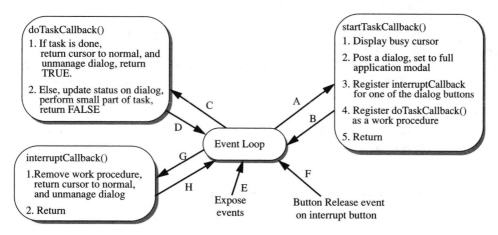

**Figure 10.2**  Performing a lengthy task as a subprocess.

In this scenario, an application initiates a task in the `startTaskCallback()` function. This function displays a busy cursor and posts a dialog that supports an interrupt callback function. Instead of starting a subprocess, `startTaskCallback()` registers the function `doTask-Callback()` with the Xt Intrinsics as a work procedure. The callback then returns control to the event loop (vector B).

The main application continues to monitor the event queue and handles `Expose` and configuration events as they occur. The program disregards all user input except events that occur within the dialog. Whenever the event queue is empty, Xt calls `doTaskCallback()` (vector C). This function first checks whether the task has finished normally. If the task has finished, the callback restores the application's normal cursor, removes the busy dialog, and returns `TRUE`. Xt automatically removes the work procedure. Otherwise, the function does a portion of the overall task and returns `FALSE` to indicate that the work procedure is not finished and that the callback should be called again. If the user interrupts the task, the `interruptCallback()` function removes the work procedure, restores the application's normal cursor, and dismisses the dialog.

This technique can be useful for some situations, but some tasks are difficult to implement as a series of repeated calls to a function. Performance may also be an issue, because the overhead of checking the event loop, and the repeated calls to the work procedure may represent a significant portion of the total time required to perform the task. However, as mentioned earlier, user perception is often more important than actual elapsed time in interactive applications. Time seems to pass more quickly when an application informs the user of its progress regularly, and when the user knows he or she can interrupt the task at any time.

Applications can also control the amount of overhead added by this technique by changing the amount of work performed by each call to the work procedure. For example, if the work procedure uses as much as a quarter to a third of a second (a long time in CPU terms) each time it is called, the user is unlikely to notice any lack of response to interrupts. In many situations, each call to the work procedure can use several seconds without any ill effects.

The following sections present several classes that support lengthy tasks within the MotifApp framework, based on the work procedure approach described here. The WorkingDialogManager class can be used to display a dialog that informs the user that the application is busy. This dialog class allows applications to change the message to notify the user as a task progresses. The WorkingDialogManager class also displays a simple animation to reassure the user that the application is busy working. The InterruptibleCmd class is designed to be used with the WorkingDialogManager. The abstract InterruptibleCmd class implements a general framework that supports the work procedure technique just described. Derived classes must implement a single function that can be called repeatedly to perform the task. Together, the WorkingDialogManager and InterruptibleCmd classes provide a way to perform lengthy operations that can be interrupted at any time, while providing continuous feedback to the user, and keeping the application's windows up-to-date.

# 10.2  The WorkingDialogManager Class

The WorkingDialogManager class is a subclass of the DialogManager class described in Chapter 7. The WorkingDialogManager class adds several unique features to the facilities provided by the DialogManager base class. First, the WorkingDialogManager class supports an `update-Message()` member function, which allows applications to change the text displayed in a dialog while the dialog is posted. Second, the WorkingDialogManager allows applications to remove the dialog programmatically by calling the `unpost()` member function. The dialog classes described in Chapter 7 must be dismissed by the user. The WorkingDialogManager reports the status of a busy application, and the application must remove it from the screen when the program is no longer busy.

Another unique feature of the WorkingDialogManager class is that it displays an animated image while the dialog is posted. This animation is implemented with the assistance of a BusyPixmap class that provides a continuous stream of pixmaps. For the animation to take place, the application must return to the event loop frequently while the dialog is displayed. The Working-DialogManager class is meant to be used with one of the approaches described in the previous section for performing a lengthy task in the background while continuing to handle events. When used with the InterruptibleCmd class, described in Section 10.3, the WorkingDialogManager can display a smooth series of images.

As mentioned in the previous section, it is important to lock out user input while the application is busy. It is particularly important to prevent user input when using the approach implemented in this chapter because the busy application continues to handle events. Allowing the user to issue additional commands while the application is busy is technically possible, but would add greatly to the complexity of the application. As recommended earlier, the WorkingDialogManager widget supports a full application modal dialog style that locks out user input while it is posted.

Figure 10.3 shows a WorkingDialogManager class card that summarizes these responsibilities.

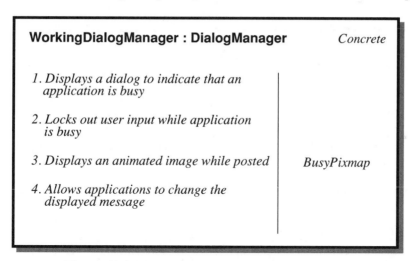

**Figure 10.3** The WorkingDialogManager class card.

The WorkingDialogManager class is declared as follows:

```
1   /////////////////////////////////////////////////////////
2   // WorkingDialogManager.h
3   /////////////////////////////////////////////////////////
4   #ifndef WORKINGDIALOGMANAGER_H
5   #define WORKINGDIALOGMANAGER_H
6   #include "DialogManager.h"
7
```

```
8   class PixmapCycler;
9
10  class WorkingDialogManager : public DialogManager {
11
12    protected:
13
14      Widget createDialog ( Widget );
15      PixmapCycler *_busyPixmaps; // Source of animated pixmap sequence
16
17      XtIntervalId _intervalId;   // ID of the last timeout
18
19      static void unpostCallback ( Widget, XtPointer, XtPointer );
20      static void timerCallback ( XtPointer, XtIntervalId * );
21
22      void timer();
23
24    public:
25
26      WorkingDialogManager ( char * );
27
28      virtual Widget post ( char *,
29                            void *clientData     = NULL,
30                            DialogCallback ok      = NULL,
31                            DialogCallback cancel = NULL,
32                            DialogCallback help   = NULL );
33
34      void unpost();    // Remove the dialog from the screen
35
36      void updateMessage ( char * );  // Change the text in the dialog
37  };
38
39  extern WorkingDialogManager *theWorkingDialogManager;
40
41  #endif
```

The WorkingDialogManager widget implements the pure virtual `createDialog()` member function required by the DialogManager class. The protected portion of the class also contains a pointer to a PixmapCycler class (an abstract base class for the BusyPixmap class, described in the following section), and several members that support an animated image. The public portion of the class overrides the `post()` member function and declares two new member functions, `unpost()` and `updateMessage()`.

Like the other dialog manager classes described in Chapter 7, the MotifApp framework supports a single, globally available instance of the WorkingDialogManager class. The file WorkingDialog-Manager.h declares a pointer to an external object named `theWorkingDialogManager`. Applications that wish to use the WorkingDialogManager class can simply include WorkingDialog-Manager.h and send messages to `theWorkingDialogManager`.

The file WorkingDialogManager.C begins by creating an instance of the WorkingDialog-Manager class. The WorkingDialogManager constructor simply initializes the two data members supported by the class to NULL.

```
1   //////////////////////////////////////////////////////////
2   // WorkingDialogManager.C:
3   //////////////////////////////////////////////////////////
4   #include "WorkingDialogManager.h"
5   #include "Application.h"
6   #include <Xm/Xm.h>
7   #include <Xm/MessageB.h>
8   #include "BusyPixmap.h"
9   #include <assert.h>
10
11  WorkingDialogManager *theWorkingDialogManager =
12                        new WorkingDialogManager ( "WorkingDialog" );
13
14  WorkingDialogManager::WorkingDialogManager ( char  *name ) :
15                                              DialogManager ( name )
16  {
17      _intervalId  = NULL;
18      _busyPixmaps = NULL;
19  }
```

The DialogManager base class calls createDialog(), which must be implemented by a derived class, when a new dialog widget is needed. The WorkingDialogManager's create-Dialog() member function creates a dialog and registers the function unpostCallback() to be called when the user clicks on either the dialog's OK button or Cancel button. The create-Dialog() member function also instantiates a BusyPixmap object, passing the newly-created dialog widget as an argument.

```
20  Widget WorkingDialogManager::createDialog ( Widget parent )
21  {
22      Widget dialog = XmCreateWorkingDialog ( parent, _name, NULL, 0 );
23
24      XtVaSetValues ( dialog,
25                      XmNdialogStyle, XmDIALOG_FULL_APPLICATION_MODAL,
26                      NULL );
27
28      XtAddCallback ( dialog,
29                      XmNokCallback,
30                      &WorkingDialogManager::unpostCallback,
31                      ( XtPointer ) this );
32
33      XtAddCallback ( dialog,
34                      XmNcancelCallback,
35                      &WorkingDialogManager::unpostCallback,
36                      ( XtPointer ) this );
```

```
37
38        if ( !_busyPixmaps )
39             _busyPixmaps = new BusyPixmap ( dialog );
40
41        return ( dialog );
42    }
```

The WorkingDialogManager class overrides the DialogManager's `post()` member function. The WorkingDialogManager is unique in that it supports only one dialog widget, and does not use the DialogManager's caching capability. The WorkingDialogManager class is based on the assumption that an application can only be busy doing one thing at a time. The `post()` function checks to see if the object's cached widget already exists and if it is currently displayed on the screen. If so, the function simply returns the displayed widget. This test prevents multiple dialog widgets from being created. If the widget does not exist, or if it is not currently being displayed, the `post()` member function calls the base class's `post()` function directly. Finally, `post()` calls `timer()` to start the animation before returning the dialog widget.

```
43   Widget WorkingDialogManager::post ( char            *text,
44                                       void            *clientData,
45                                       DialogCallback ok,
46                                       DialogCallback cancel,
47                                       DialogCallback help )
48   {
49
50        // If the the dialog already exists and is currently in use,
51        // just return this dialog
52        // The WorkingDialogManager only supports one dialog.
53
54        if ( _w && XtIsManaged ( _w ) )
55             return ( _w );
56
57        // Pass the message on to the base class
58
59        DialogManager::post ( text, clientData, ok, cancel, help );
60
61        // Call timer to start an animation sequence for this dialog
62
63        timer();
64
65        return ( _w );
66    }
```

The `timer()` member function registers a timeout callback with the Xt Intrinsics. The `timerCallback()` member function is a timeout callback function that uses the same technique as other callbacks in this book. It retrieves an instance of the WorkingDialogManager class from the client data specified when the callback was registered. Then it calls that object's `timer()` member function to update the image in the dialog and re-install the callback.

```
67   void WorkingDialogManager::timerCallback ( XtPointer clientData,
68                                               XtIntervalId * )
69   {
70       WorkingDialogManager *obj = ( WorkingDialogManager * ) clientData;
71
72       obj->timer();
73   }
```

The `timer()` member function installs the static member function `timerCallback()` to be called again in 250 milliseconds. Therefore, Xt calls `timer()` approximately every 250 milliseconds, once the initial callback is installed. In addition to re-installing the `timerCallback()` function, `timer()` installs the next available pixmap from the BusyPixmap object as the value of the displayed dialog's `XmNsymbolPixmap` resource.

```
74   void WorkingDialogManager::timer ()
75   {
76       if ( !_w )
77           return;
78
79       // Reinstall the timeout callback to be called again
80
81       _intervalId =
82           XtAppAddTimeOut ( XtWidgetToApplicationContext ( _w ),
83                             250,
84                             &WorkingDialogManager::timerCallback,
85                             ( XtPointer ) this );
86
87       // Get the next pixmap in the animation sequence and display
88       // it in the dialog's symbol area
89
90       XtVaSetValues ( _w,
91                       XmNsymbolPixmap, _busyPixmaps->next(),
92                       NULL );
93   }
```

The `unpostCallback()` function is called when the user clicks on the dialog widget's OK or Cancel buttons. This callback simply calls the `unpost()` member function.

```
94   void WorkingDialogManager::unpostCallback ( Widget ,
95                                               XtPointer clientData,
96                                               XtPointer )
97   {
98       WorkingDialogManager *obj = ( WorkingDialogManager* ) clientData;
99
100      obj->unpost();
101  }
```

The unpost() member function dismisses the dialog. This function may be called from the unpostCallback() function when the user closes the dialog, or called programmatically when an application is no longer busy. The function XtUnmanageChild() removes the dialog from the screen, in case unpost() is called programmatically. (The dialog is unmanaged automatically when the user clicks on one of the dialog's buttons.) If there is a current timeout callback installed, it is removed by calling the Xt function XtRemoveTimeOut(). This breaks the chain of repeated calls to timer() and stops the animation displayed in the dialog. The unpost() member function uses an assert() statement to detect programmatic calls to unpost() that occur before the dialog has been posted for the first time.

```
102  void WorkingDialogManager::unpost ()
103  {
104      assert ( _w );
105
106      // Remove the dialog from the screen
107
108      XtUnmanageChild ( _w );
109
110      // Stop the animation
111
112      if ( _intervalId )
113          XtRemoveTimeOut ( _intervalId );
114  }
```

The last function supported by the WorkingDialogManager class is the updateMessage() member function. This function converts a character string to a compound string and updates the text displayed in the dialog.

```
115  void WorkingDialogManager::updateMessage ( char *text )
116  {
117      if ( _w )  // Don't do anything unless the widget exists
118      {
119          // Just change the string displayed in the dialog
120
121          XmString xmstr = XmStringCreateSimple ( text );
122          XtVaSetValues ( _w, XmNmessageString, xmstr, NULL );
123          XmStringFree ( xmstr );
124      }
125  }
```

The next sections describe the PixmapCycler and BusyPixmap classes used by the WorkingDialog-Manager class to display a sequence of animated images.

## The PixmapCycler Class

The PixmapCycler class is an abstract class that supports a continuous cycle of pixmaps. In addition to a constructor and destructor, the PixmapCycler class provides a single public function, next(), which returns the next pixmap in a cycle. The class supports a list of Pixmaps, and a pointer to the current Pixmap. It also declares a pure virtual function, `createPixmaps()`, which must be implemented by all derived classes. Derived classes create pixmaps, and specify the size and number of pixmaps in a cycle. PixmapCycler provides a generic mechanism for managing the sequences of images created by derived classes.

The PixmapCycler class is declared as follows:

```
1   /////////////////////////////////////////////////////////////////////
2   // PixmapCycler.h: Abstract class that supports a continuous cycle
3   //                 of pixmaps for short animation sequences
4   /////////////////////////////////////////////////////////////////////
5   #ifndef PIXMAPCYCLER_H
6   #define PIXMAPCYCLER_H
7   #include <Xm/Xm.h>
8
9   class PixmapCycler {
10
11     protected:
12
13       int      _numPixmaps;      // Total number of pixmaps in cycle
14       int      _current;         // Index of the current pixmap
15       Pixmap   *_pixmapList;      // The array of pixmaps
16       Dimension _width, _height;  // Pixmap size
17       virtual void createPixmaps() = 0; // Derived class must implement
18       PixmapCycler ( int, Dimension, Dimension  );
19
20     public:
21
22       virtual ~PixmapCycler();
23       Dimension width()  { return ( _width ); }
24       Dimension height() { return ( _height ); }
25
26       Pixmap next();           // Return the next pixmap in the cycle
27   };
28   #endif
```

The PixmapCycler constructor takes three arguments. The first indicates the number of pixmaps in a single cycle, and the remaining arguments specify the width and height of the pixmaps. The constructor allocates an array of pixmaps large enough to hold `numPixmaps`, and initializes the `_current` member to indicate that the cycle has not yet begun. This constructor is declared in the protected portion of the class, and can only be called from derived classes.

```
1   /////////////////////////////////////////////////////////////////////
2   // PixmapCycler.C: Abstract class that supports a continuous cycle
3   //                 of pixmaps for short animation sequences
4   /////////////////////////////////////////////////////////////////////
5   #include "PixmapCycler.h"
6
```

```
7   #define INVALID -1
8
9   PixmapCycler::PixmapCycler ( int numPixmaps, Dimension w, Dimension h )
10  {
11       _numPixmaps = numPixmaps;
12       _current    = INVALID;
13       _pixmapList = new Pixmap[_numPixmaps];
14       _width      = w;
15       _height     = h;
16  }
```

The PixmapCycler destructor frees the list of pixmaps.

```
17  PixmapCycler::~PixmapCycler()
18  {
19       delete []_pixmapList;
20  }
```

The first time it is called, the next() member function calls createPixmaps() to create a series of pixmaps. After that, next() simply increments an index into the array of pixmaps and returns the next available pixmap. When all pixmaps have been used, the cycle begins over at the beginning.

```
21  Pixmap PixmapCycler::next()
22  {
23       // The first time, call the createPixmaps() function
24       // implemented by the derived class to create the pixmaps
25
26       if ( _current == INVALID )
27       {
28           createPixmaps();
29           _current = 0;     // Initialize to the first pixmap
30       }
31
32       // If the counter is larger than the index of the
33       // last pixmap, roll it over and restart with zero
34
35       if ( _current >= _numPixmaps )
36           _current = 0;
37
38       // Return the current pixmap and increment the counter
39
40       return ( _pixmapList[_current++] );
41  }
```

The function createPixmaps() must be implemented by all derived classes. This function must create a sequence of pixmaps and store them in the _pixmapList array. The derived class is also responsible for the content of the pixmaps.

## The BusyPixmap Class

The BusyPixmap class is a subclass of PixmapCycler. BusyPixmap provides a sequence of animated pixmaps for the WorkingDialogManager class. The BusyPixmap class implements the pure virtual `createPixmaps()` member function declared by the PixmapCycler class. This function creates the array of pixmaps expected by the PixmapCycler class.

The BusyPixmap class is declared as:

```
1   /////////////////////////////////////////////////
2   // BusyPixmap.h
3   /////////////////////////////////////////////////
4   #include "PixmapCycler.h"
5
6   class BusyPixmap : public PixmapCycler {
7
8     protected:
9
10       GC      _gc, _inverseGC; // Used to draw Pixmaps
11       Widget _w;               // Widget whose colors are to be used
12       void createPixmaps();    // Overrides base class's pure virtual
13       virtual Pixmap createBusyPixmap ( int, int );
14
15    public:
16
17       BusyPixmap ( Widget );
18   };
```

The BusyPixmap constructor requires a widget, which is used to create a graphics context. The colors used in the pixmaps match the foreground and background colors of this widget. The constructor initializes the _w member to the given widget, and calls the PixmapCycler constructor to create an array to hold eight pixmaps, 50 pixels high and 50 pixels wide.

```
1   /////////////////////////////////////////////////
2   // BusyPixmap.C
3   /////////////////////////////////////////////////
4   #include "BusyPixmap.h"
5   #include <Xm/Xm.h>
6
7   #define NUMPIXMAPS   8
8   #define PIXMAPSIZE   50
9
10  BusyPixmap::BusyPixmap ( Widget w ) :
11                      PixmapCycler ( NUMPIXMAPS, PIXMAPSIZE, PIXMAPSIZE )
12  {
13      _w = w;
14  }
```

There are several ways to create a pixmap containing a particular image. One simple way to produce a sequence of pixmap images is to draw each image interactively in an editor, like the bitmap editor included with the standard X distribution. The bitmap program creates ASCII files that can be included directly in a program and converted to a pixmap. Another way to produce a pixmap image is to create a blank pixmap and use X lib graphics functions to draw images in the pixmap.

The BusyPixmap class creates a sequence of bitmaps that are easier to render programmatically than to draw interactively. Each image consists of a circle with a filled arc drawn within the circle. As the sequence proceeds, the filled portion moves, clockwise, around the circle. Figure 10.4 shows the initial pixmap pattern provided by the BusyPixmap class.

**Figure 10.4** The basic BusyPixmap image.

The `createPixmaps()` member function creates two graphics contexts. The first corresponds to the foreground and background colors of the widget passed to the constructor, while the second is the inverse of the first. An auxiliary member function, `createBusyPixmap()`, uses these graphics contexts when creating and rendering each individual pixmap. The function `createPixmaps()` calls `createBusyPixmap()` in a loop that computes a starting angle for the "pie slice" drawn by each call to `createBusyPixmap()`. Finally, the graphics contexts are released when they are no longer needed.

```
15   void BusyPixmap::createPixmaps()
16   {
17       int angle, delta, i;
18       XGCValues  gcv;
19
20       // Create a graphics context used to draw each pixmap,
21       // based on the colors of the given widget
22
23       XtVaGetValues ( _w,
24                       XmNforeground, &gcv.foreground,
25                       XmNbackground, &gcv.background,
26                       NULL );
27
28       _gc = XtGetGC ( _w,  GCForeground | GCBackground, &gcv );
29
30       // Create a second GC used to fill the pixmap with
31       // the background color of the widget
32
33       XtVaGetValues ( _w,
34                       XmNforeground, &gcv.background,
```

```
35                        XmNbackground, &gcv.foreground,
36                        NULL );
37
38    _inverseGC = XtGetGC ( _w,  GCForeground | GCBackground, &gcv );
39
40    // Define the starting increment, and a slice of the pie
41    // The size of the pie slice depends on the number of pixmaps
42    // to be created
43
44    angle = 360;
45    delta = 360 / NUMPIXMAPS;
46
47    for ( i = 0; i < NUMPIXMAPS; i++)
48    {
49        // Create a pixmap for each slice of the pie
50        // X measures counterclockwise, so subtract the
51        // size of each slice so the sequence moves clockwise
52
53        _pixmapList[i] = createBusyPixmap ( angle, delta );
54        angle -= delta;
55    }
56
57    // Release the GCs after all pixmaps have been created
58
59    XtReleaseGC ( _w, _gc );
60    XtReleaseGC ( _w, _inverseGC );
61 }
```

The function `createBusyPixmap()` creates a single pixmap and draws an image similar to that in Figure 10.4 in the pixmap. This function requires the starting angle of the filled area and the size of the filled area, in degrees.

```
62 Pixmap BusyPixmap::createBusyPixmap ( int start, int end )
63 {
64    Pixmap    pm;
65    const int margin = 1;
66
67    // Create a pixmap
68    // Use the root window used by the widget,
69    // because the widget may not be realized, or may be a gadget
70
71    pm = XCreatePixmap ( XtDisplay ( _w ),
72                         RootWindowOfScreen ( XtScreen ( _w ) ),
73                         _width, _height,
74                         DefaultDepthOfScreen ( XtScreen ( _w ) ) );
75    // Pixmaps have to be cleared by filling them with a background color
76
77    XFillRectangle ( XtDisplay ( _w ),
```

```
78                       pm,
79                       _inverseGC,
80                       0, 0, _width, _height );
81
82      // Draw a complete circle just inside the bounds of the pxmap
83
84      XDrawArc ( XtDisplay ( _w ),
85                 pm, _gc,
86                 margin, margin,
87                 _width - 2 * margin,
88                 _height - 2 * margin,
89                 0, 360 * 64 );
90
91      // Draw the pie slice as a solid color
92
93      XFillArc ( XtDisplay ( _w ),
94                 pm, _gc,
95                 margin, margin,
96                 _width - 2 * margin,
97                 _height - 2 * margin,
98                 start * 64, end * 64 );
99
100     return ( pm );
101  }
```

After creating each pixmap, `createBusyPixmap()` uses `XFillRectangle()` and the `_inverseGC` graphics context to fill the pixmap with the background color of the widget. Then `XDrawArc()` and `XFillArc()` draw the image from Figure 10.4 in the pixmap. The `start` and `end` arguments to this function determine the position and size of the filled pie shape.

Figure 10.5 shows the WorkingDialogManager's dialog widget, displaying the animation produced by the BusyPixmap class.

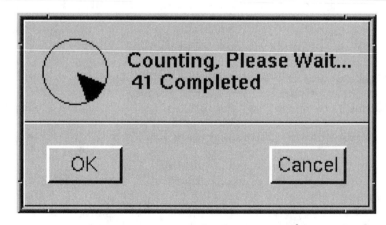

**Figure 10.5**  The WorkingDialogManager.

# 10.3 The InterruptibleCmd Class

The InterruptibleCmd class is a subclass of Cmd, and is designed to support commands that take a long time to execute. This class uses the work procedure strategy described in Section 10.1 to perform a task by splitting it into many small pieces. One challenge when using work procedures is that the function performing the task must often save some state between calls. By defining the work procedure as a member function of a class, the class's data members provide a natural way to maintain the current state between calls.

The InterruptibleCmd class is an abstract class that works much like other abstract classes derived from Cmd. New commands can be created by deriving a new class that implements the doit() member function. Unlike other command classes, the InterruptibleCmd doit() member function is called as often as necessary to complete the task. The doit() function must indicate that the task is completed by setting the _done data member supported by InterruptibleCmd to TRUE.

The InterruptibleCmd class uses the WorkingDialogManager class to display an animated dialog to indicate that the application is busy. The user can interrupt operations based on the InterruptibleCmd class at any time, by clicking on the dialog's Cancel button.

Figure 10.6 shows a class card that summarizes the responsibilities of the InterruptibleCmd class.

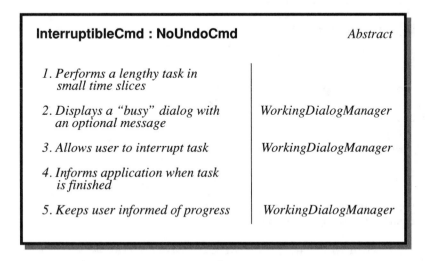

**InterruptibleCmd : NoUndoCmd**                     *Abstract*

1. *Performs a lengthy task in small time slices*

2. *Displays a "busy" dialog with an optional message*          *WorkingDialogManager*

3. *Allows user to interrupt task*          *WorkingDialogManager*

4. *Informs application when task is finished*

5. *Keeps user informed of progress*          *WorkingDialogManager*

**Figure 10.6**  The InterruptibleCmd class card.

The InterruptibleTask class is declared as follows:

```
1    ////////////////////////////////////////////////////////////
2    // InterruptibleCmd.h: Abstract class that supports lengthy,
3    //                       user-interruptible activities
4    ////////////////////////////////////////////////////////////
5    #ifndef INTERRUPTIBLECMD_H
6    #define INTERRUPTIBLECMD_H
7    #include <Xm/Xm.h>
8    #include "NoUndoCmd.h"
9
10   // Define a type for the callback invoked when the task is finished
11
12   class InterruptibleCmd;
13   typedef void ( *TaskDoneCallback ) ( InterruptibleCmd *,
14                                        Boolean,
15                                        void * );
16
17   class InterruptibleCmd : public NoUndoCmd {
18
19     private:
20
21       XtWorkProcId      _wpId;        // The ID of the workproc
22       TaskDoneCallback _callback;     // Application-defined callback
23       void            *_clientData;   // Provided by application
24
25       Boolean workProc ();
26       static Boolean  workProcCallback ( XtPointer );
27       static void     interruptCallback ( void * );
28       void interrupt();
29
30     protected:
31
32       Boolean       _done;          // TRUE if the task has been completed
33       virtual void cleanup();       // Called when task ends
34       virtual void updateMessage ( char * );
35
36       // Derived classes must implement doit(), declared by Cmd
37
38     public:
39
40       InterruptibleCmd ( char * , int );
41       virtual ~InterruptibleCmd();
42
43       virtual void execute();  // Overrides base class member function
44       virtual void execute ( TaskDoneCallback, void * );
45   };
46   #endif
```

The InterruptibleTask class supports both an external interface and an interface for derived classes. The public interface is similar to that supported by other command classes. An application initiates a task by creating an instance of a class derived from InterruptibleCmd and calling its `execute()` member function. The InterruptibleCmd class defines an overloaded version of `execute()` that allows the caller to specify a callback function. This callback function allows the application to be notified when the task is finished or has been interrupted. The callback must be a function of type `TaskDoneCallback`, defined in InterruptibleCmd.h as a function that takes a pointer to an InterruptibleCmd object, a Boolean value, and an untyped pointer.

The protected portion of the class defines the interface provided for derived classes. Derived classes must implement the `doit()` member function, declared as a pure virtual by the Cmd class. This member function must set the protected _done member to TRUE when the task is completed.

The `cleanup()` function is called when the task ends. This function can be overridden by derived classes to perform any cleanup required when the task is interrupted or completed. Finally, the protected portion of the InterruptibleCmd class provides a convenience function for updating the text in the WorkingDialogManager widget. The InterruptibleCmd class handles posting the WorkingDialog and removing it. The derived class's `doit()` function can use the `update-Message()` function to inform the user of progress by changing the text of the dialog, if desired.

The private portion of the InterruptibleCmd class provides the infrastructure needed to support the interruptible task. This includes interacting with the WorkingDialogManager class, installing the work procedures used to call the `doit()` function, handling interrupts, and so on. These supporting mechanisms can all be handled entirely within the InterruptibleCmd class, and the details do not need to be exposed to derived classes.

The InterruptibleCmd constructor simply initializes all data members.

```
1   ////////////////////////////////////////////////////////////
2   // InterruptibleCmd.C: Abstract class that supports lengthy,
3   //                     user-interruptible activities
4   ////////////////////////////////////////////////////////////
5   #include "InterruptibleCmd.h"
6   #include "WorkingDialogManager.h"
7   #include "Application.h"
8   #include <Xm/Xm.h>
9   #include <Xm/MessageB.h>
10  #include <assert.h>
11
12  InterruptibleCmd::InterruptibleCmd ( char *name, int active ) :
13                                      NoUndoCmd ( name, active )
14  {
15      _wpId       = NULL;   // There is no work procedure yet
16      _callback   = NULL;   // Callbacks are specified in execute()
17      _clientData = NULL;
18      _done       = FALSE;
19  }
```

The destructor removes the current work procedure, if one exists.

```
20  InterruptibleCmd::~InterruptibleCmd()
21  {
22      // Clean up by removing all callbacks
```

```
23
24      if ( _wpId)
25        XtRemoveWorkProc ( _wpId );
26   }
```

The InterruptibleCmd class defines two overloaded execute() member functions. The first allows the caller to provide a function to be called when the command is completed, while the second overrides the member function inherited from Cmd. The callback function passed to execute() must have the form:

```
void callback ( InterruptibleCmd *, Boolean interrupted, void * )
```

After saving a pointer to the provided callback function, the first execute() function calls the second InterruptibleCmd::execute() member function, which takes no arguments.

```
27   void InterruptibleCmd::execute ( TaskDoneCallback callback,
28                                    void             *clientData )
29   {
30       _callback   = callback;
31       _clientData = clientData;
32       execute();
33   }
```

The second execute() member function, which can be called directly if there is no callback to be registered, initializes the _done member to FALSE and calls the Cmd::execute() member function to initiate the command. The Cmd::execute() member function eventually calls doit(), which must be defined by all instantiable classes derived from InterruptibleCmd. The doit() member function must perform a small amount of work and return quickly. If the function completes the entire task, it must set the _done member to TRUE.

The execute() member function checks the _done flag before posting a message and installing a work procedure. If the task is already done, the function calls cleanup() to notify derived classes that the task is finished, and calls the _callback function to notify the application that initiated this command. If the task has not been completed, execute() posts a working dialog and installs a work procedure to complete the task. Notice that the post() function arguments specify a pointer to the current InterruptibleCmd instance and a pointer to the interrupt-Callback() member function, which will be registered as the BusyDialogManager's cancel callback.

```
34   void InterruptibleCmd::execute()
35   {
36       _done = FALSE;  // Initialize flag
37
38       // Call the Cmd execute function to handle the Undo, and other
39       // general mechanisms supported by Cmd
40       // (Execute calls doit())
41
```

```
42      Cmd::execute();
43
44      // If the task was completed in a single call,
45      // don't bother to set up a work procedure
46      // Just give derived classes a chance to cleanup and
47      // call the application's callback function
48
49      if ( _done )
50      {
51          cleanup();
52
53          if ( _callback )
54              ( *_callback )( this, FALSE, _clientData );
55      }
56
57      // If the task is not done, post a WorkingDialog and
58      // install a work procedure to continue the task
59      // as soon as possible
60
61      if ( !_done )
62      {
63      theWorkingDialogManager->post ( "" , (void *) this,
64                                  NULL,
65                                  &InterruptibleCmd::interruptCallback );
66
67      _wpId = XtAppAddWorkProc ( theApplication->appContext(),
68                                  &InterruptibleCmd::workProcCallback,
69                                  ( XtPointer ) this );
70      }
71  }
```

The `workProcCallback()` function is a static member function, registered with Xt as a work procedure. This function simply retrieves the instance pointer from the client data and calls the `workProc()` member function. A work procedure must return `FALSE` (indicating "not done") if it should be called again, and `TRUE` (indicating "task done") if it should be removed and not called again. The `workProcCallback()` function returns the value returned by the `workProc()` member function.

```
72  Boolean InterruptibleCmd::workProcCallback ( XtPointer clientData )
73  {
74      InterruptibleCmd *obj = ( InterruptibleCmd * ) clientData;
75
76      // The work procedure just returns the value returned by the
77      // workProc member function
78
79      return ( obj->workProc() );
80  }
```

The `workProc()` member function calls the `doit()` member function to perform the next part of the task. If the task has been completed following this call, `workProc()` removes the dialog from the screen and calls a virtual `cleanup()` member function. Finally, `workProc()` calls the application-defined callback function. The first argument to this function identifies the current InterruptibleCmd object, while the second indicates that the task completed normally.

Finally, `workProc()` returns `_done`. If this value is TRUE, Xt will remove the `workProc-Callback()` work procedure. Otherwise, Xt calls `workProcCallback()` again once it has cleared the event queue of any pending events.

```
81   Boolean InterruptibleCmd::workProc()
82   {
83       doit();
84
85       // If the task has been completed, hide the dialog,
86       // give the derived class a chance to clean up, and notify
87       // the application that instantiated this object
88
89       if ( _done )
90       {
91           theWorkingDialogManager->unpost();
92           cleanup();
93
94           if ( _callback )
95               ( *_callback )( this, FALSE, _clientData );
96       }
97
98       return ( _done );
99   }
```

The `cleanup()` function is empty. This virtual member function may be overridden by derived classes if needed. The InterruptibleCmd class calls this function when an operation has completed successfully, or when the user interrupts the operation. Derived classes can implement the `cleanup()` member function to perform any operations required to clean up after the task.

```
100  void InterruptibleCmd::cleanup()
101  {
102      // Empty
103  }
```

The `interruptCallback()` function is a static member function called when the user clicks the Cancel button on the working dialog. This function simply retrieves the object pointer provided as client data and calls `interrupt()`.

```
104  void InterruptibleCmd::interruptCallback ( void * clientData )
105  {
106      InterruptibleCmd *obj = ( InterruptibleCmd * ) clientData;
```

```
107
108        // Just set the _interrupt flag to TRUE.
109        // The workProc() function will notice the next time it is called
110
111        obj->interrupt();
112  }
```

The `interrupt()` function calls `XtRemoveWorkProc()` to remove the work procedure and end the task. If a callback was registered, `interrupt()` calls the function to inform the application that the user interrupted the command.

```
113  void InterruptibleCmd::interrupt()
114  {
115        // Remove the work procedure
116
117        XtRemoveWorkProc ( _wpId );
118
119        // Remove the working dialog and give derived
120        // classes a chance to clean up
121
122        theWorkingDialogManager->unpost();
123        cleanup();
124
125        // Notify the application that the task was interrupted
126
127        if ( _callback )
128            ( *_callback )( this, TRUE, _clientData );
129  }
```

The `updateMessage()` member function simply calls the WorkingDialogManager `updateMessage()` member function. Derived classes can call this function to change the message shown in the working dialog.

```
130  void InterruptibleCmd::updateMessage ( char * msg )
131  {
132        theWorkingDialogManager->updateMessage ( msg );
133  }
```

Figure 10.7 shows a message diagram that illustrates the connections between the InterruptibleCmd, PixmapCycler, BusyPixmap, and WorkingDialogManager classes. This diagram also shows the connections between the InterruptibleCmd class and a typical derived class.

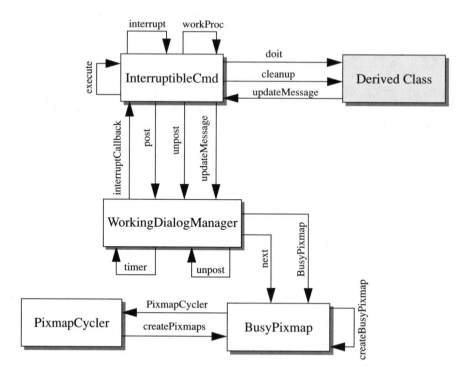

**Figure 10.7**  A message diagram of InterruptibleCmd and related classes.

# 10.4  An Example Program

This section demonstrates how the InterruptibleCmd and WorkingDialogManager classes can be used to perform a lengthy, interruptible task. The example program, called wordCount, constructs and displays a table that lists each word found in a text file and the number of times each word occurs. Figure 10.8 shows the window created by the wordCount program. A menubar supports two commands, a Quit command, and a Select File command. The Select File command displays an XmFileSelectionBox dialog that allows the user to choose a file to be processed. Once a file has been chosen, the program opens the file, counts the words, and displays the results in a scrolled list.

Although very simple, wordCount provides a good test case for the InterruptibleCmd class and the techniques described in this chapter. The time required to count the words in an arbitrary file may vary, depending on the size of the file, the load on the machine, the speed of the system, and perhaps even the nature of the text in the file.

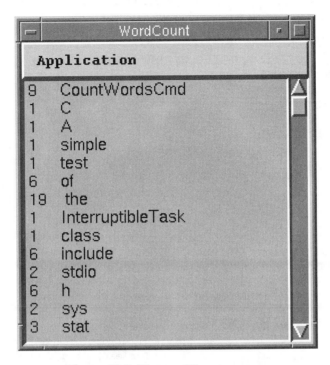

**Figure 10.8** The wordCount program.

The wordCount program requires four new classes. The program creates a subclass of MenuWindow, a subclass of InterruptibleCmd, a class that supports the XmFileSelectionBox dialog, and a class that represents a single word. The WordCountWindow class is derived from MenuWindow and creates the user interface shown in Figure 10.8. The CountWordsCmd class, which is derived from InterruptibleCmd, is responsible for collecting and counting the words in a text file. The CountWordsCmd class reads a text file and saves each unique word in an instance of the Word class. Because the CountWordsCmd class is a subclass of InterruptibleCmd, the user can interrupt the operation at any time, and the CountWordsCmd object can report its progress using the WorkingDialogManager dialog posted by the InterruptibleCmd class. The following sections discuss each new class used in this example.

## The WordCountWindow Class

The WordCountWindow class is a subclass of MenuWindow that creates a work area containing a scrolled list widget. The class's public protocol consists of only a constructor. The private and protected portions of the class include callbacks and member functions used to initiate the task and the `createWorkArea()` and `createMenuPanes()` member functions required of all MenuWindow subclasses.

The class is declared as follows:

```
1    /////////////////////////////////////////////////////////////
2    // WordCountWindow.h: Count the frequency of each word
3    //                    in a text file, as a test of the
4    //                    InterruptibleCmd class
5    /////////////////////////////////////////////////////////////
6    #ifndef WORDCOUNTWINDOW_H
7    #define WORDCOUNTWINDOW_H
8    #include "MenuWindow.h"
9
10   class InterruptibleCmd;
11   class CountWordsCmd;
12
13   class WordCountWindow : public MenuWindow {
14
15     private:
16
17       Widget _list;        // List of words found in file
18       Cursor _busyCursor;   // Displayed when application is busy
19       Cursor _normalCursor; // Cursor used when not busy
20
21       // Functions for interfacing with the word count Cmd
22
23       static void countWordsCallback ( void *, char * );
24       static void taskFinishedCallback ( InterruptibleCmd *,
25                                          Boolean, void * );
26       void taskFinished ( CountWordsCmd * );
27       void countWords ( char * );
28
29       // Utility functions for manipulating cursors
30
31       void setBusyCursor();
32       void setNormalCursor();
33
34     protected:
35
36       virtual void WordCountWindow::createMenuPanes();
37       virtual Widget createWorkArea ( Widget );
38
39     public:
40
41       WordCountWindow ( char * );
42   };
43   #endif
```

The WordCountWindow constructor is empty, and just calls the MenuWindow constructor.

```
1   ///////////////////////////////////////////////////////////
2   // WordCountWindow.C: Test the InterruptibleCmd class
3   ///////////////////////////////////////////////////////////
4   #include "Application.h"
5   #include "InfoDialogManager.h"
6   #include "WordCountWindow.h"
7   #include "CountWordsCmd.h"
8   #include "SelectFileCmd.h"
9   #include "QuitCmd.h"
10  #include "MenuBar.h"
11  #include "CmdList.h"
12  #include <Xm/List.h>
13  #include <X11/cursorfont.h>
14  #include <stdio.h>
15
16  WordCountWindow::WordCountWindow ( char *name ) : MenuWindow ( name )
17  {
18      // Empty
19  }
```

As in all classes derived from MenuWindow, WordCountWindow creates the widgets that implement its user interface in the `createWorkArea()` member function. This function simply creates an XmScrolledList widget, which provides a place to display the words found in the file, along with their frequency of occurrence. Notice that `createWorkArea()` returns the *parent* of the list widget. The Motif convenience function `XmCreateScrolledList()` creates an XmList widget as the child of an XmScrolledWindow widget, and returns the XmList widget. For most purposes, the XmScrolledWindow widget can be hidden. However, the MainWindow class installs the widget returned by `createWorkArea()` as the XmNworkArea widget used by its XmMain-Window widget. This must be a direct child of the XmMainWindow, not a grandchild. Therefore, `createWorkArea()` must return the XmScrolledWindow widget instead of the XmList widget.

```
20  Widget WordCountWindow::createWorkArea ( Widget parent )
21  {
22      _list = XmCreateScrolledList ( parent, "list", NULL, 0 );
23
24      XtManageChild ( _list );
25
26      return ( XtParent ( _list ) );
27  }
```

The `createMenuPanes()` member function sets up a single menu pane that contains a "Quit" command, provided by the QuitCmd class described in Chapter 9. The menu pane also includes a "Select File" command that allows a user to choose the file to be processed. This command is implemented as a SelectFileCmd class, described later in this chapter. The Select-FileCmd constructor requires a callback function that can be called when the user selects a file from an XmFileSelectionBox.

```
28  void WordCountWindow::createMenuPanes()
29  {
30      // Create the command objects for this menu
31
32      Cmd   *quit        = new QuitCmd ( "Quit" , TRUE );
33      Cmd   *selectFile =
34                  new SelectFileCmd ( "selectFile" ,
35                                       TRUE,
36                                       &WordCountWindow::countWordsCallback,
37                                       (void *) this );
38
39      // Create a list of commands and install it in a menu pane
40
41      CmdList   *cmdList = new CmdList();
42      cmdList->add ( selectFile );
43      cmdList->add ( quit );
44      _menuBar->addCommands ( cmdList, "Application" );
45  }
```

The function `countWordsCallback()` is called when the user selects a file to be counted. This function just calls the WordCountWindow object's `countWords()` member function.

```
46  void WordCountWindow::countWordsCallback ( void *clientData,
47                                               char *filename )
48  {
49      WordCountWindow *obj = ( WordCountWindow * ) clientData;
50
51      obj->countWords ( filename );
52  }
```

The `countWords()` member function initiates the task of counting the words in a file by creating a new CountWordsCmd object and calling its `execute()` member function. This example creates a new CountWordsCmd object for each command it executes. This is not strictly necessary; for many applications it may be more appropriate to create a single instance of a command object that can be used more than once. For this simple example, it is easiest to create a new object each time one is needed. The CountWordsCmd class is meant to be instantiated and destroyed for each individual task.

The `countWords()` function begins by checking that the specified filename is non-NULL. If the `filename` argument is NULL, there is no point in continuing. Next, this function instantiates a new CountWordsCmd object. Before executing the command, `countWords()` calls the WordCountWindow class's `setBusyCursor()` member function to display a busy cursor. Finally, `countWords()` clears the contents of the XmScrolledList widget and executes the CountWordsCmd object.

```
53  void WordCountWindow::countWords ( char * filename)
54  {
55      if ( !filename )   // Catch NULL filenames
```

```
56            return;
57
58       // Instantiate a Cmd object to count words in the given file
59
60       CountWordsCmd *task = new CountWordsCmd ( "countWords",
61                                                 TRUE, filename );
62
63       setBusyCursor();   // Display a busy cursor
64
65       XtVaSetValues ( _list,    // Remove any items currently in the list
66                       XmNitems,       NULL,
67                       XmNitemCount, 0,
68                       NULL );
69
70       // Execute the cmd, providing a function to be called when finished
71
72       task->execute ( &WordCountWindow::taskFinishedCallback ,
73                       ( void * ) this );
74  }
```

When the CountWordsCmd object has completed its task, it calls `taskFinished-Callback()`. The first argument to this function indicates the InterruptibleCmd object that called the function. The second argument indicates whether the command completed normally, or whether the user interrupted the command. The third argument provides any client data specified when the task was executed. The `countWords()` member function provides the `this` pointer as client data when registering the callback on line 72. Notice that the InterruptibleCmd object must be cast as a pointer to a CountWordsCmd object for further use by the WordCountWindow class. Once the results have been processed, `taskFinishedCallback()` restores the application's normal cursor and deletes the CountWordsCmd object.

```
75  void WordCountWindow::taskFinishedCallback ( InterruptibleCmd *cmd,
76                                               Boolean          interrupted,
77                                               void             *clientData)
78  {
79      CountWordsCmd    *cwObj = ( CountWordsCmd * )   cmd;
80      WordCountWindow *obj   = ( WordCountWindow * ) clientData;
81
82      // If the user interrupted the task, just confirm the interrupt
83      // Otherwise, call taskFinished() to process the results
84
85      if ( interrupted )
86          theInfoDialogManager->post ( "Interrupted!" );
87      else
88          obj->taskFinished ( cwObj );
89
90      // Complete the operation by restoring a normal cursor and
91      // freeing the InterruptibleCmd object
92
```

```
93        obj->setNormalCursor ();
94        delete cwObj;
95    }
```

The taskFinished() member function is called when the WordCountCmd finishes its task successfully. This function retrieves the words found by the WordCountCmd object and displays them in the program's list widget. The CountWordsCmd class supports several member functions that can be used to retrieve the results of the operation. The numWords() member function returns the total number of unique words found in the file. The getWord() member function returns a string containing a single word, and the getCount() member function returns the number of times a word occurs. The taskFinished() member function displays a dialog informing the user of the number of unique words in the file and then converts the results to an array of compound strings, to be displayed by the XmList widget.

```
96   void WordCountWindow::taskFinished ( CountWordsCmd *cwObj )
97   {
98        int        i;
99        char       buf[100];
100       XmString *xmstrList;
101
102       // Report the number of unique words
103
104       sprintf ( buf, "This file contains %d unique words.",
105                      cwObj->numWords());
106
107       theInfoDialogManager->post ( buf );
108
109       // Create an array of compound strings large
110       // enough to hold the results
111
112       xmstrList = new XmString[cwObj->numWords()];
113
114       // Retrieve each word, format the results, and
115       // add an entry to the compound string array
116
117       for ( i = 0; i < cwObj->numWords(); i++ )
118       {
119           char buf[BUFSIZ];
120
121           sprintf ( buf,
122                     "%-5d %s",
123                     cwObj->getCount ( i ), cwObj->getWord ( i ) );
124           xmstrList[i] = XmStringCreateSimple ( buf );
125       }
126
127       // Display the array of compound strings in the list
128
129       XtVaSetValues ( _list,
```

```
130                      XmNitems,      xmstrList,
131                      XmNitemCount, cwObj->numWords(),
132                      NULL );
133
134      // The XmList widget makes its own copy of the compound strings
135      // so free all local copies
136
137      for ( i = 0; i < cwObj->numWords(); i++ )
138          XmStringFree ( xmstrList[i] );
139
140      delete []xmstrList;
141  }
```

The WordCountWindow supports two utility functions that can be used to change the cursor displayed when the user moves the mouse into the WordCountWindow. The function setBusy-Cursor() calls the Xlib function XCreateFontCursor() to create a cursor shaped like a watch. XDefineCursor() installs the busy cursor for the WordCountWindow's base widget, the shell widget. All children inherit this cursor as well, unless they specifically override it. The symbol XC_watch is defined in the file cursorfont.h, which is included by WordCountWindow.C. (See [Scheifler90] for more information on cursors and related functions.)

```
142  void WordCountWindow::setBusyCursor()
143  {
144      // Do nothing if the widget has not been realized
145
146      if ( XtIsRealized ( _w ) )
147      {
148          // If this is the first time, create the busy cursor
149
150          if ( !_busyCursor )
151              _busyCursor = XCreateFontCursor ( XtDisplay ( _w ),
152                                                XC_watch );
153
154          // Install the busy cursor for this window's top-level shell
155
156          XDefineCursor ( XtDisplay ( _w ),
157                          XtWindow ( _w ),
158                          _busyCursor );
159      }
160  }
```

The setNormalCursor() function is similar, but creates and installs a left pointer cursor instead of the watch shape. Notice that this function assumes that the left pointer is the normal cursor, which may not actually be the case.

```
161  void WordCountWindow::setNormalCursor()
162  {
163      // Do nothing if the widget has not been realized
```

```
164      if ( XtIsRealized ( _w ) )
165      {
166          // If this is the first time, create the busy cursor
167
168          if ( !_normalCursor )
169              _normalCursor = XCreateFontCursor ( XtDisplay ( _w ),
170                                                  XC_left_ptr );
171
172          // Install the left pointer cursor as the normal
173          // cursor for this window's top-level shell
174
175          XDefineCursor ( XtDisplay ( _w ),
176                          XtWindow ( _w ),
177                          _normalCursor );
178      }
179  }
```

These last two member functions provide a general-purpose facility that really belongs at a higher level than the WordCountWindow class. All applications may need to display busy cursors and restore the normal cursor at various times. It is not unusual to discover that a member function implemented for a specific use has broader application. In this case, the setBusyCursor() and setNormalCursor() member functions, or something similar, should probably be supported by the MainWindow class.

## The CountWordsCmd and Word Classes

The CountWordsCmd class is a subclass of InterruptibleCmd that performs the task of counting the words in a file. The CountWordsCmd class reads a text file and separates the file into individual words. As each word is detected, the word is added to a table, which is composed of a list of objects that represent unique words. If the table already contains an object that represents the current word, a counter in that object is incremented. Otherwise, an object is created to represent the new word and the new object is added to the table.

Words are represented by a simple Word class, which can be implemented entirely using inline functions. The Word class supports public functions for incrementing the count associated with a particular word, and for comparing the string contained in a Word object to another character string.

The Word class is defined in the file CountWordsCmd.h, along with the CountWordsCmd class:

```
1   ///////////////////////////////////////////////////////////////
2   // CountWordsCmd.h: Count the frequency of words in a file
3   ///////////////////////////////////////////////////////////////
4   #ifndef COUNTWORDSCMD_H
5   #define COUNTWORDSCMD_H
6   #include <string.h>     // Needed for strcmp
7   #include <stdio.h>
8   #include "InterruptibleCmd.h"
9
10  // The Word class stores a string and maintains a count field
```

```
11   // used to record how many times the word has been encountered
12
13   class Word {
14
15     private:
16
17       char * _word;    // The "word" represented by this object
18       int    _count;   // Number of times this word has been found
19
20     public:
21
22       Word ( char *str ) { _word = strdup ( str ); _count = 1; }
23       ~Word() { delete _word; }
24
25       // Compare the character string stored in this object
26       // to another character string
27
28       int operator== ( char *str ) { return ( !strcmp ( _word, str ) ); }
29
30       // Increment the count associated with this word
31
32       void operator++() { _count++ ; }
33       char *word()  { return ( _word ); }
34       int   count() { return ( _count ); }
35   };
```

The CountWordsCmd class maintains a list of Word objects, along with information about the file being read, in the protected portion of the class. CountWordsCmd's public interface consists of a constructor and destructor, as well as several member functions that allow the results of the command to be retrieved.

Figure 10.9 summarizes the responsibilities of the CountWordsCmd class.

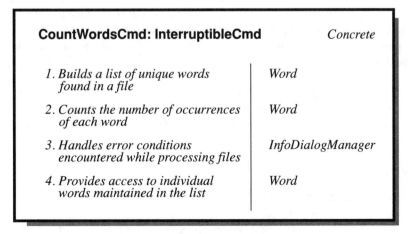

**Figure 10.9**  The CountWordsCmd class card.

The CountWordsCmd class is declared as follows:

```
36  class CountWordsCmd : public InterruptibleCmd {
37
38    private:
39
40      Word  ** _list;     // List of words found in the file
41      int     _numWords;  // Size of the _list
42      long    _fileSize;  // Total size of the file in bytes
43      int     _bytesRead; // How much of the file has been processed
44      FILE *  _fd;        // The file being read
45      int     _percentDone;
46
47      void saveWord ( char * );  // Add a word to the _list
48
49    protected:
50
51      void doit();        // The function that performs the work
52
53    public:
54
55      CountWordsCmd ( char *, int , char * );
56      virtual ~CountWordsCmd ();
57      int    numWords () { return ( _numWords ); }
58      char *getWord ( int i ) { return ( _list[i]->word() ); }
59      int    getCount ( int i ) { return ( _list[i]->count() ); }
60  };
61  #endif
```

The CountWordsCmd constructor initializes the class's various data members before opening the file specified in its third argument. If the given file cannot be opened for any reason, the constructor uses MotifApp's InfoDialogManager facility to post a warning to the user before it returns. Otherwise, the constructor uses stat() to determine the size of the file in bytes. This information can be used as the basis of progress reports as the command executes. If the file is empty, the constructor posts a warning, closes the file, and returns. Otherwise, the object is ready to begin executing the command.

```
1   ////////////////////////////////////////////////////////////////
2   // CountWordsCmd.C: A simple test of the InterruptibleCmd class
3   ////////////////////////////////////////////////////////////////
4   #include <stdio.h>
5   #include <sys/stat.h>
6   #include <sys/types.h>
7   #include "CountWordsCmd.h"
8   #include "InfoDialogManager.h"
9
10  CountWordsCmd::CountWordsCmd ( char *name,
11                                 int    active,
```

```
12                             char *filename ) :
13                                 InterruptibleCmd ( name, active )
14  {
15      struct stat statInfo;
16
17      // Initialize data members
18
19      _bytesRead = 0;
20      _fileSize  = 0;
21      _numWords  = 0;
22      _list      = NULL;
23      _percentDone = 0;
24
25      // Open the given file and post a warning in case of failure
26
27      if( ( _fd = fopen ( filename, "r" ) ) == NULL )
28      {
29          char buf[BUFSIZ];
30
31          sprintf ( buf, "Can't open %s", filename );
32
33          theInfoDialogManager->post ( buf );
34      }
35      else
36      {
37          // Check the size of the file, to use as a basis for
38          // reporting progress
39          // Don't bother counting if the file is empty.
40
41          char buf[BUFSIZ];
42
43          if ( stat ( filename, &statInfo ) == 0 )
44              _fileSize = statInfo.st_size;
45
46          if ( _fileSize == 0 )
47          {
48              sprintf ( buf, "%s is empty!", filename );
49
50              theInfoDialogManager->post ( buf );
51
52              fclose ( _fd );
53              _fd = 0;
54          }
55      }
56  }
```

The CountWordsCmd destructor is called when the WordCountWindow's `taskFinished-Callback()` function deletes the object. The destructor deletes the list of Word objects created as the command executes, and closes the file opened in the constructor.

```
57   CountWordsCmd::~CountWordsCmd ()
58   {
59       // Only close the file if it was successfully opened
60
61       if ( _fd )
62           fclose ( _fd );
63
64       for ( int i=0; i < _numWords; i++ )
65           delete _list[i];
66
67       delete _list;
68   }
```

The `doit()` member function is the heart of the CountWordsCmd class. This member function is called repeatedly until the task is completed or interrupted by the user. The mechanics of handling the work procedure, checking for interrupts, and so on, are all handled by the InterruptibleCmd base class. The `doit()` function just needs to perform a small subset of the complete task and return periodically to allow the InterruptibleCmd to do its job.

The `doit()` member function reads lines from the file opened in the constructor and separates the text into individual words. Here, a word is defined as any alphanumeric sequence of characters. The function `strtok()` provides an easy way to separate a string into individual tokens. Given a list of separators and a string, `strtok()` returns the next available token in the string each time it is called.

It is important to decide how much work the `doit()` member function should perform each time it is called. If the function does too little, the overhead of calling the work procedure repeatedly will be prohibitive. If the function does too much, the application will not be responsive to interrupts and exposure events. The animation displayed by the WorkingDialogManager class also depends on the application returning frequently to the event queue. In this example, the `doit()` function processes twenty lines of text each time it is called. Each time through the main loop, `doit()` uses `fgets()` to read a single line from the file. The `_bytesRead` member is updated by counting the number of bytes in the new line, to allow the function to report its progress to the user. As each word is extracted from the text, the `saveWord()` member function is called to add the word to the list of Word objects. Before returning, `doit()` computes how much of the task has been completed, based on the size of the file and the number of bytes read. If the resulting percentage has changed, `doit()` updates the working dialog.

```
69   void CountWordsCmd::doit()
70   {
71       char  buf[BUFSIZ];
72       char *sep = " !@#$%^&*()_+=-}{][|\';:\"?></.,`~\\\n\t";
73       int   percent;
74
```

```
75      // If the file has not been opened, indicate that the task
76      // is finished
77
78      if ( ! _fd )
79      {
80          _done = TRUE;
81          return;
82      }
83
84      // Read a few lines each time doit() is called
85
86      for ( int i = 0; i < 20; i++ )
87      {
88          char *result;
89          char *word;
90
91          // Read in one line of text, indicating that the
92          // task is done if we reach end-of-file
93
94          if ( ( result = fgets ( buf, BUFSIZ, _fd ) ) == NULL )
95          {
96              _done = TRUE;
97              return;
98          }
99
100          // Compute the total characters read for progress report
101
102          _bytesRead += strlen ( buf );
103
104          // Extract the first full word and save it in the word list
105
106          word = strtok ( buf, sep );
107
108          saveWord ( word );
109
110          // Continue to extract words until the line is exhausted
111
112          while ( ( word = strtok ( NULL, sep ) ) != NULL )
113              saveWord ( word );
114      }
115
116      // Update the busy dialog and report progress as
117      // the percentage of the file read so far
118      // Only report if the percent done has changed
119
120      percent =  ( int ) (( float ) _bytesRead / ( float ) _fileSize * 100);
121
122      if ( _percentDone != percent )
123      {
```

```
124                  _percentDone = percent;
125
126                  sprintf ( buf, "Counting, Please Wait...\n %d %% Completed",
127                              _percentDone );
128
129                  updateMessage( buf );
130          }
131  }
```

The saveWord() member function searches a table of Word objects for an existing object that represents a newly found word. If a word is already in the list, the object's count is incremented. Otherwise, saveWord() creates a new Word object, expands the list of Words, and adds the new Word to the list. For the purposes of this wordCount example, the extreme inefficiency of this implementation is unimportant.

```
132  void CountWordsCmd::saveWord ( char * word )
133  {
134      // Check for valid input
135
136      if ( !word )
137          return;
138
139      // Search for the word and increment the count if found
140
141      for ( int i = 0; i < _numWords; i++ )
142      {
143          if ( *_list[i] == word ) // Note use of overloaded operator==
144          {
145              ( *_list[i] )++;
146              return;
147          }
148      }
149
150      // If not found, create a new Word object and add it to the
151      // list, increasing the size of the list for each new word
152
153      Word *obj = new Word ( word );
154
155      Word **newList = new Word*[_numWords + 1];
156
157      for ( i = 0; i < _numWords; i++ )
158          newList[i] = _list[i];
159
160      newList[_numWords] = obj;
161      delete _list;
162      _list = newList;
163
164      _numWords++;
165  }
```

# The SelectFileCmd Class

The last class required to complete the wordCount example is a command class that allows the user to choose a file to be processed by CountWordsCmd. The SelectFileCmd class uses an XmFileSelectionBox widget to allow the user to select a file, and provides a way to report the selected file back to the WordCountWindow class. Like many classes described in this book, the SelectFileCmd hides some of the details of its Motif-based implementation. Applications that need to allow the user to select a file can simply instantiate a SelectFileCmd object, providing a function to be called when the user selects a file. The class handles the details of creating a Motif XmFileSelectionBox dialog, setting up callbacks, dealing with compound strings, and so on.

The SelectFileCmd class is derived from NoUndoCmd and is declared as follows:

```
1   /////////////////////////////////////////////////////////////////
2   // SelectFileCmd.h:  Allow the user to select a file interactively
3   /////////////////////////////////////////////////////////////////
4   #ifndef SELECTFILECMD_H
5   #define SELECTFILECMD_H
6   #include "NoUndoCmd.h"
7   #include <Xm/Xm.h>
8
9   typedef void (*FileCallback) ( void *, char * );
10
11  class SelectFileCmd : public NoUndoCmd {
12
13    private:
14
15      static void fileSelectedCallback ( Widget, XtPointer, XtPointer );
16
17    protected:
18
19      void doit();              // Called by base class
20      FileCallback _callback;   // Function to be called
21                                // when user selects a file
22      void         *_clientData; // Data provided by caller
23
24      Widget       _fileBrowser; // The Motif widget used to get file
25
26      virtual void fileSelected ( char * );
27
28    public:
29
30      SelectFileCmd ( char *, int , FileCallback, void * );
31  };
32  #endif
```

The SelectFileCmd constructor passes its name and active arguments on to its base class. It stores the values of the last two arguments in data members for later use.

```
1    ///////////////////////////////////////////////////////
2    // SelectFileCmd.C:
3    ///////////////////////////////////////////////////////
4    #include "SelectFileCmd.h"
5    #include "Application.h"
6    #include <Xm/FileSB.h>
7
8    SelectFileCmd::SelectFileCmd ( char          *name,
9                                   int           active,
10                                  FileCallback  callback,
11                                  void          *clientData ) :
12                                        NoUndoCmd ( name, active )
13   {
14       _callback   = callback;
15       _clientData = clientData;
16   }
```

The doit() member function creates an XmFileSelectionBox dialog widget. This dialog is created as a child of MotifApp's main shell widget, which eliminates the need for the SelectFileCmd class to require a widget as a parameter. This function registers a callback to be called when the user selects a file and then displays the dialog.

```
17   void SelectFileCmd::doit()
18   {
19       // Create a FileSelectionBox widget
20
21       _fileBrowser =
22               XmCreateFileSelectionDialog ( theApplication->baseWidget(),
23                                             name(),
24                                             NULL, 0 );
25
26       // Set up the callback to be called when the user chooses a file
27
28       XtAddCallback ( _fileBrowser,
29                       XmNokCallback,
30                       &SelectFileCmd::fileSelectedCallback,
31                       ( XtPointer ) this );
32
33       // Display the dialog
34
35       XtManageChild ( _fileBrowser );
36   }
```

The fileSelectedCallback() function is a static member function, called when the user has chosen a file. This function retrieves the SelectFileCmd object pointer from the client data, and casts the callData argument to type XmFileSelectionBoxCallbackStruct. This structure contains information about what file has been selected. The function XmString-GetLtoR() retrieves the data portion of a compound string, which is necessary because the

XmFileSelectionBox widget reports the selected file as a compound string and the CountWordsCmd callback expects a character string. After retrieving the name of the selected file, fileSelected-Callback() calls fileSelected() and destroys the dialog widget.

```
37  void SelectFileCmd::fileSelectedCallback ( Widget      w,
38                                             XtPointer clientData,
39                                             XtPointer callData )
40  {
41      SelectFileCmd * obj = ( SelectFileCmd * ) clientData;
42      XmFileSelectionBoxCallbackStruct *cb =
43                          ( XmFileSelectionBoxCallbackStruct * ) callData;
44      char      *name   = NULL;
45      XmString  xmstr  = cb->value;   // The selected file
46      int       status = 0;
47
48      if ( xmstr )    // Make sure a file was selected
49      {
50          // Extract the first character string matching the default
51          // character set from the compound string
52
53          status = XmStringGetLtoR ( xmstr,
54                                     XmSTRING_DEFAULT_CHARSET,
55                                     &name );
56
57          // If a string was successfully extracted, call
58          // fileSelected to handle the file
59
60          if ( status )
61              obj->fileSelected ( name );
62      }
63
64      XtDestroyWidget ( w );   // Destroy the file selection dialog
65  }
```

The fileSelected() member function calls the function specified when this command is executed, if the function is non-NULL.

```
66  void SelectFileCmd::fileSelected ( char *filename )
67  {
68      if ( _callback )
69          _callback ( _clientData, filename );
70  }
```

## The wordCount Program

Now we can put the classes described in previous sections together to form a complete program that demonstrates one way to deal with lengthy operations. As with most MotifApp programs, the main program is very simple. The file WordCountApp.C simply instantiates an Application object and creates a WordCountWindow object.

```
1   /////////////////////////////////////////////////////////////////
2   // WordCountApp.C: A program that tests the InterruptibleCmd
3   //                  class and related classes
4   /////////////////////////////////////////////////////////////////
5   #include "Application.h"
6   #include "WordCountWindow.h"
7
8   Application      *app    = new Application ( "WordCount" );
9   WordCountWindow *window = new WordCountWindow ( "WordCount" );
```

Figure 10.10 shows the inheritance relationships of the classes in the wordCount program, including the MotifApp classes used directly or indirectly by this example. Classes unique to the wordCount program are shown in bold. All other classes are part of MotifApp. The SelectFileCmd is shown as part of MotifApp, because it is a general purpose class that can be added to the library.

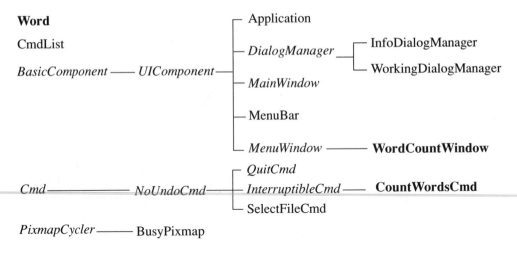

**Figure 10.10**  Hierarchy of classes in the wordCount program.

The message diagram shown in Figure 10.11 shows some of the connections between the major classes used in the wordCount example. This diagram does not show all classes involved; in particular, the Application, MainWindow, and MenuWindow classes are missing. Also, none of the abstract command classes are shown, nor is the DialogManager class. The classes shown boxed in light gray with bold lettering are the classes that a programmer writing a program like the wordCount example must implement. The others, in addition to many classes not shown here, are provided by the MotifApp framework.

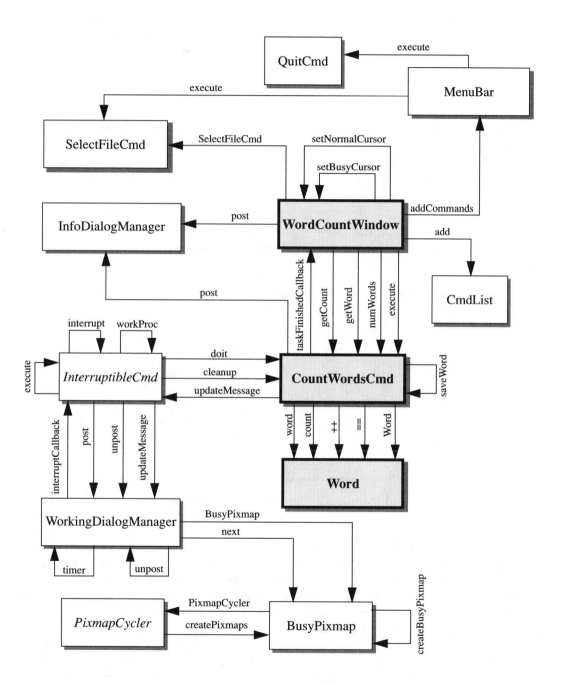

**Figure 10.11** A message diagram of the wordCount program.

To build wordCount, we must compile the files WordCountApp.C, WordCountWindow.C and CountWordsCmd.C and link the resulting binaries with the MotifApp library. The SelectFileCmd class is a useful command class independent of this example and should be added to the MotifApp library.

```
CC -o wordCount WordCountApp.C WordCountWindow.C CountWordsCmd.C \
      libMotifApp.a -lXm -lXt -lX11
```

To see how the CountWordsCmd class works, run the wordCount program, choose the "Select File" entry from the "Application" menu pane and select a file that contains ASCII text. A large file provides the best demonstration. In spite of several inefficiencies in the implementation of this example, the program processes most files very quickly. Figure 10.12 shows the wordCount program while it is busy counting words.

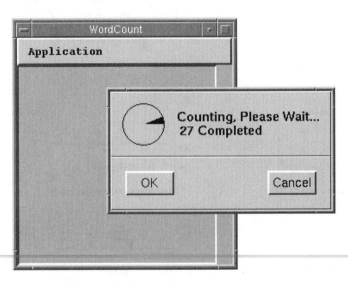

**Figure 10.12**  The wordCount program.

It is interesting to notice that with a large file, the dialog eventually reports that the task is 100% completed, and disappears, but the results do not appear immediately. This is because the XmList widget takes some time to display a large list. Adding items to the XmList widget is an example of a lengthy operation over which the application has very little control. Motif is busy, and there is little the application can do until the XmList widget returns. One possible approach is to add items to the list one at a time so the program can continue to provide progress reports. However, adding individual items is very inefficient and causes the scrollbar to resize as each item is added, which is visually distracting. The wordCount program adds the items to the list in the most efficient way possible and continues to display the busy cursor until the call to XtVaSetValues() returns.

When using the technique demonstrated in this chapter, it is important to consider the overhead of the work procedure. Each time Xt returns to the event loop, it must wait for a call to select()

to time out before calling the next work procedure. Each timeout consumes some time, and we must also consider the overhead of making a function call for each work procedure, as well as any overhead required to maintain the required state between calls. We must also expect some time to be spent updating the message displayed in the dialog, supporting the animation, and handling events.

It is possible to get some idea of the overhead added by this technique by measuring the time required for the wordCount program to process a large file. In one experiment, the `CountWords-Cmd::doit()` function was modified to loop 40,000 times before returning. When processing a file containing 40,000 lines or less, this effectively disables the work procedure mechanism. On the author's system, processing a 40,000-line file required 27 seconds (wall clock time). Changing `doit()` to read only 20 lines at a time increased the execution time to 38 seconds. This represents an increase of about 40%. Dividing the 11-second difference by 2000 calls to `doit()` shows that the overhead of each call, in this case, is approximately 5.5 milliseconds, in this particular case.

Eleven seconds out of thirty-eight seems like an acceptable price to pay for the added benefits of allowing the user to interrupt the command while in progress, keeping the user informed of progress, and so on. However, it is important to find an appropriate balance between the overhead of the work procedure mechanism and the amount of work done with each call. For example, modifying the `doit()` function to process only a single line of text with each call changes the total time required to process the same 40,000-line file to 5 minutes and 12 seconds. The average overhead per call remains approximately the same, but this time, the program must make 40,000 calls to `doit()`. The increased number of calls results in an increase in total time of over 1,100%, which is clearly too great a price to pay for the benefits offered by this approach.

# 10.5  Summary

The WorkingDialogManager and InterruptibleTask classes demonstrate how C++ classes can be used to provide fairly complex facilities needed by many programs. The classes that form a framework to support lengthy interruptible tasks are complicated, but writing a new interruptible command class is much easier. The CountWordsCmd class is straightforward; its implementation mostly consists of the details associated with the task it must perform. Behind the scenes, the MotifApp framework combines the InterruptibleCmd class, the BusyPixmap class, the WorkingDialogManager, and many other classes to support the command transparently.

The InterruptibleCmd mechanism described in this chapter demonstrates part of the power of an application framework. The amount of work required to implement all the mechanisms described in this chapter for each lengthy task a program needs to perform would be prohibitive. By capturing the basic flow of control in a set of cooperating classes within the framework, programmers need only implement a single class to perform the desired task.

# Chapter 11

# A Color Chooser

This chapter describes a reusable user interface component that allows users to select a color. Unlike other MotifApp classes described earlier, the ColorChooser class has little to do with the overall structure of the MotifApp framework. Although most MotifApp classes discussed so far are designed to provide architectural support for Motif applications, an application framework can also include user interface components. In MotifApp, the basic low-level user interface components are supplied by Motif. The ColorChooser class is an example of a high-level reusable user interface component designed to fit into the MotifApp framework.

The ColorChooser class demonstrates an effective way to structure interactive applications that feature multiple, synchronized presentations of some shared information. This technique is based on the Model-View-Controller (MVC) architecture supported by the Smalltalk environment. Section 11.1 introduces the fundamental concepts behind the MVC approach. Section 11.2 presents the ColorChooser user interface component, which is based on an MVC architecture.

## 11.1 Models and Views

Many applications provide multiple graphical views of the same information. For example, a statistical package may present bar charts, scatter plots, or pie charts of a data set. A spreadsheet may simultaneously present many cells whose contents are related by some formula. A word processor may present a document as both a formatted page and an outline view. In each of these cases, it is usually necessary to ensure that all views remain synchronized at all times. For example, if a user creates a new subheading in a word-processor's outline view, the new entry should also appear in the other views of the document. The user should be able to interact with any view of the document, and all other views should immediately reflect any changes.

The Model-View-Controller (MVC) architecture provides a powerful way to organize systems that support multiple presentations of the same information. This technique is used in the Smalltalk programming environment, and is particularly useful in interactive systems. MVC is based on three types of objects, Models, Views, and Controllers.

A Model object has no visual characteristics, but simply represents raw data. For example, consider a program that simulates a bank account. In such a system, a Model object might maintain the current balance of the account, a list of transactions, perhaps the current interest rate for an interest-bearing account, and so on. The Model might also support various operations that alter the state of the modeled data. For example, the Model object might support deposit() and withdraw() methods, as well as methods that retrieve the current balance and retrieve a list of recent transactions.

View objects present the current state of a Model to the user. Views must be able to retrieve the data in a Model, but should not care about the Model object's internal implementation. Views respond to an update() message that causes each View object to display the current state of a Model according to its abilities. Each type of View displays some aspect of the data maintained by the Model. For example, a banking program might provide one View object that always displays the current balance. Another might display a list of deposits, while yet another could display a list of recent withdrawals. Some views may be text-based, while others may provide information graphically.

The Model object is responsible for notifying all associated View objects when any aspect of the Model's data changes. Views simply format and display the current values maintained by the Model. Users sometimes manipulate Views to change the displayed data without affecting or interacting with the Model. For example, a user might choose to see a list of transactions sorted by date or sorted by the size of the transaction. The user might choose to filter the data to see only transactions between certain dates. The current balance could be displayed in different currencies, changing from US dollars to Swiss Francs, for example. None of these changes affect the underlying model. They are merely presentation options that determine how each View displays the data maintained by the Model.

The third type of object in the MVC approach is the Controller. Controller objects allow users to manipulate the data in a Model or alter the way a View displays that data. For example, the banking program mentioned earlier could provide a Controller that allows the user to enter a new balance, make deposits or withdrawals, change the interest rate, and so on. Views and Controllers often work closely. In some cases a single object may function as both a Controller and a View. For example, a banking simulation might allow the user to establish a new balance by typing directly into the window that displays the current balance.

Figure 11.1shows the relationships between several objects based on an MVC architecture. The Controller manipulates the Model and various Views by sending appropriate messages, represented in Figure 11.1 by "change" messages. The Model object responds to the Controller's requests and then notifies all dependent View objects that the Model has changed. Each View object responds to update messages by retrieving the information it needs from the Model object and updating its display.

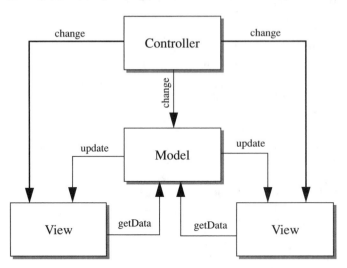

**Figure 11.1** Relationships between Model, View, and Controller objects.

In theory, it is possible to create reusable collections of generic Views and Controllers that function as user interface components that can be connected to different models to implement complex applications quickly. In practice, Models, Views, and Controllers tend to be closely associated. Although these three types of components should be designed to be as independent as possible, Views must know how to retrieve data from a Model, and Controllers must know the protocol through which a particular types of Models and Views can be manipulated. Strong type-checking, as implemented by C++, also tends to force programmers to create tightly-bound collections of Models, Views, and Controllers.

The MVC approach has many potential uses in interactive systems. Using a basic architecture like MVC can help programmers when designing object-oriented systems by providing a template that has proved effective in similar situations. Instead of starting from scratch, trying to identify objects as in the case study in Chapters 4 and 5, it is often easier to look for specific objects that match an architecture like MVC. Not all applications fit the MVC model. However, if it seems as if MVC might be the right approach, programmers can start the design process by trying to identify which parts of the program belong in the Model, and which are Views and Controllers.

There are similarities between the MVC architecture described here and some techniques demonstrated earlier in this book. For example, all command objects described in Chapter 8 support lists of dependent CmdInterface objects. In this sense, a CmdInterface object can be thought of as a view of a command object. Applications activate and deactivate commands by changing the state of a command object, which broadcasts this change to all dependent interface objects.

There is another effective way to use command objects that draws on the ideas of MVC. Programmers can set up command objects to be automatically activated and deactivated when other commands are executed. Although this is often useful, it may sometimes be more effective to think of each command as an object that combines the attributes of a Controller and a View. The command object can be associated with some part of an application, which functions as a Model.

For example, consider a SaveFileCmd object supported by a text editor. This object should be active when a file is loaded, when the text buffer has been modified, and when the corresponding file on disk is writable. The command should be inactive when no file has been loaded, the file has not been modified since the last time the user saved the file, or if the file cannot be written on disk for any reason. The mechanism described in Chapter 8 cannot handle all these situations easily. However, by representing a file as a Model object that has a "savable" attribute as part of its state, we could treat a SaveFileCmd object as a view of that model. The command should receive update messages whenever the state of the file model changes.

The MVC model can be used as the basis of entire systems, and can also be used to implement smaller subsystems within an application. The remainder of this chapter presents a moderately complex user interface component borrows its basic architecture from the MVC approach. The component is part of the MotifApp framework and allows the user to select the components of a color. The component allows the user to manipulate various parameters that affect a color, while viewing the color in several different ways. This component could be useful for drawing editors, paint programs, and so on, and provides another example of how a C++ class can combine Motif widgets to form a higher-level self-contained user interface component.

## 11.2  A ColorChooser Dialog

The following sections present several classes that collectively form a user interface component that allows a user to select a color. The ColorChooser class encapsulates a collection of objects and defines the external interface for this component. Each ColorChooser object supports a dialog that allows the user to choose a color by moving sliders that control its red, green, and blue (RGB) color components. Figure 11.2 shows the ColorChooser dialog as it appears on the screen.

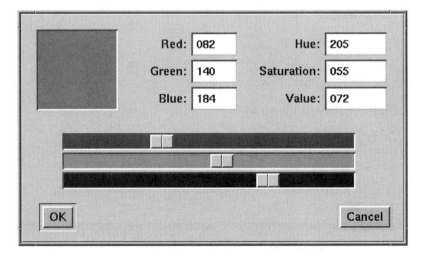

**Figure 11.2**  The ColorChooser dialog.

The dialog provides only one way to manipulate a color, but provides several different views, which update dynamically as the color is edited. The ColorChooser dialog displays the RGB components of a color as numeric values, and also shows the color's hue, saturation, and value (HSV) characteristics. The dialog also displays a "swatch" of color that shows how the chosen shade appears on the screen. When the user clicks an OK button, the dialog is dismissed and the Color-Chooser makes the selected color available to the application through a callback function.

The architecture of the ColorChooser component is based on an MVC model that separates the abstract representation of a color from the various presentations shown in the dialog. The following sections discuss the individual classes before examining the ColorChooser class that ties the pieces together into one logical component. The classes that make up the ColorChooser subsystem include the ColorModel class, the RGBController class, and the RGBView, HSVView, and SwatchView classes.

## The ColorModel Class

The ColorModel class provides an abstract representation of a single color. The views planned for the ColorChooser component display both RGB and HSV components of the color, but the Color-Model class can be based on any reasonable color model. X currently uses an RGB model, so it seems appropriate to use this approach in the ColorModel object as well.

The ColorModel object functions as the "model" in an MVC system. Each ColorChooser subsystem includes a single ColorModel object, which maintains the current state of a color. Each ColorModel object must allow other objects to retrieve various components of the color it represents to allow the color to be displayed. It must also provide an external interface that allows the color to be manipulated. Each ColorModel object also maintains a list of ColorView objects that depend on this ColorModel and notifies each dependent ColorView object when any aspect of the color model changes. Figure 11.3 shows a class card that summarizes the ColorModel class's responsibilities.

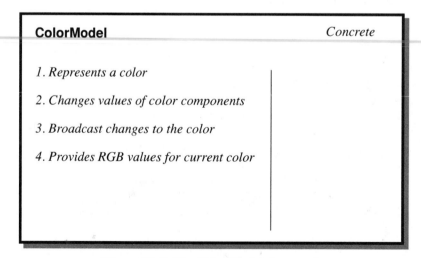

**Figure 11.3**  The ColorModel class card.

The ColorModel class defines three protected members that represent the red, green, and blue components of a color. The public portion of the class supports member functions for setting and retrieving RGB components of the color and for associating ColorView objects with the Color-Model.

The ColorModel class is declared as follows:

```
1    //////////////////////////////////////////////////////////
2    // ColorModel.h: An RGB color model for a single color
3    //////////////////////////////////////////////////////////
4    #ifndef COLORMODEL_H
5    #define COLORMODEL_H
6
7    class ColorView;
8
9    class ColorModel {
10
11     private:
12
13       int         _numViews;    // Number of dependent views
14       ColorView **_views;       // View objects that depend on this model
15
16       int       _red;           // RGB representation of a color
17       int       _green;
18       int       _blue;
19
20       // Called whenever the model's data changes
21
22       void      updateViews();
23
24     public:
25
26       ColorModel();
27
28       // Add dependent View objects
29
30       void attachView ( ColorView * );
31
32       // Functions that allow controllers to manipulate the Model
33
34       void setRgb    ( int, int, int );
35       void setRed    ( int r ) { setRgb ( r,    _green, _blue ); }
36       void setGreen ( int g ) { setRgb ( _red, g,     _blue ); }
37       void setBlue  ( int b ) { setRgb ( _red, _green, b    ); }
38
39       // Functions that allow views to retrieve the model's current state
40
41       int red()   { return ( _red );   }
42       int green() { return ( _green ); }
```

```
43       int  blue()   { return ( _blue );   }
44   };
45   #endif
```

The ColorModel constructor initializes all data values to NULL or zero.

```
1    /////////////////////////////////////////////////////////////
2    // ColorModel.C: A class that represents a single color, using
3    //               an RGB representation
4    /////////////////////////////////////////////////////////////
5    #include "ColorModel.h"
6    #include "ColorView.h"
7
8    ColorModel::ColorModel()
9    {
10       _numViews = 0;
11       _views    = NULL;
12       _red      = 0;
13       _green    = 0;
14       _blue     = 0;
15   }
```

Each ColorModel object maintains a list of objects that must be updated when any of the RGB components of the object's color changes. In the ColorChooser subsystem, all views are derived from the ColorView class. The attachView() member function adds a ColorView object to the list of dependent views supported by a ColorModel object.

```
16   void ColorModel::attachView ( ColorView *view )
17   {
18       int i;
19       ColorView **newViewList;
20
21       // Allocate a new list large enough for the new object
22       // and copy the old list to the new
23
24       newViewList = new ColorView*[_numViews + 1];
25
26       for ( i = 0; i < _numViews; i++ )
27           newViewList[i] = _views[i];
28
29       // Install the new list
30
31       delete _views;
32       _views =  newViewList;
33
34       // Add the new ColorView object to the list
35
36       _views[_numViews] = view;
```

```
37      _numViews++;
38
39      // Update the new view to synchronize it with this model
40
41      view->update ( this );
42  }
```

The updateViews() function sends an update() message to all ColorView objects registered with a ColorModel object. Notice that this function provides no information about the data maintained by the ColorModel. In general, a Model object cannot know what information a particular view may be interested in. All ColorView objects are responsible for retrieving information they need from the ColorModel and updating themselves appropriately.

```
43  void ColorModel::updateViews()
44  {
45      int i;
46      for ( i = 0; i < _numViews; i++ )
47          _views[i]->update ( this );
48  }
```

The setRGB() member function allows the ColorModel's red, green, and blue components to be altered. This function calls updateViews() to notify dependent views that the model has changed.

```
49  void ColorModel::setRgb ( int r, int g, int b )
50  {
51      _red   = r;
52      _blue  = b;
53      _green = g;
54      updateViews();
55  }
```

Notice that the ColorModel object is little more than a data structure with support for notifying other objects when the value of its data changes. The ColorModel does not allocate colors and does not depend on the X color model in any way. With the approach used here, the ColorModel class is independent of any particular type of hardware. The model uses an RGB color model, but could easily be changed to support any abstract color model. The internal representation is of no importance and should not matter to other classes in the ColorChooser system. For simplicity, the ColorModel class shown here presents an RGB external interface and also uses an RGB model internally. There is no reason the external interface must match the internal implementation, and the ColorModel could be changed to use any suitable color model. However, it must provide an external RGB interface for the views in the ColorChooser.

## The ColorView Class

All views in the ColorChooser are derived from a common ColorView class. The main purpose of this abstract class is to define a protocol for all objects that depend on the ColorModel object. The ColorView class is derived from UIComponent, because all "views" are visible user interface components. The class defines an inline constructor that calls the UIComponent base class and declares a pure virtual member function, update(), which must be implemented by all derived classes.

```
1   ////////////////////////////////////////////////////////////
2   // ColorView.h: Abstract base class. Defines protocol for
3   //              all views attached to the ColorModel
4   ////////////////////////////////////////////////////////////
5   #ifndef COLORVIEW_H
6   #define COLORVIEW_H
7   #include "UIComponent.h"
8
9   class ColorModel;
10
11  class ColorView : public UIComponent {
12
13    protected:
14
15      ColorView ( char *name ) : UIComponent ( name ) { }
16
17    public:
18
19      virtual void  update ( ColorModel * ) = 0;
20      virtual const char *const className() { return ( "ColorView" ); }
21  };
22  #endif
```

## The RGBController Class

The RGBController class is the only "controller" supported by the ColorChooser. The RGBController allows the user to change each red, green, or blue component of the ColorModel's color independently. Although the RGBController class's main responsibility is to manipulate a Color-Model object, this class also provides a view of a ColorModel. Each RGBController object supports a slider for each component of a color; the position of each of these sliders provides a measure of the relative contribution of each red, green, or blue value. Therefore, the RGBController class functions as both a controller and a view. To allow RGBController objects to receive update() messages from a ColorModel object, the RGBController class is derived from ColorView.

If the ColorModel class is changed programmatically, the ColorModel notifies all its dependent views, including the RGBController. This guarantees that the positions of the sliders displayed by the RGBController object always remain synchronized with the ColorModel object. The Color-Chooser could also support additional controllers based on different color models. For example, adding an HSVController object would allow the user to use either set of controls to manipulate the

ColorModel. Because the ColorModel sends `update()` messages to all views, including the RGBController, the RGBController's sliders would move to the appropriate RGB positions as the user manipulates the model using the HSVController. In this example, the ColorChooser supports only a single RGBController object.

Figure 11.4 shows the RGBController's user interface as it appears on the screen.

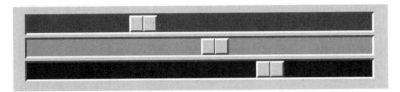

**Figure 11.4** The RGBController user interface component.

Figure 11.5 summarizes the responsibilities of the RGBController class.

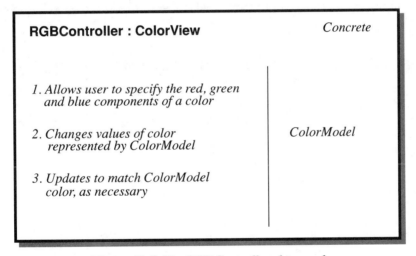

**Figure 11.5** The RGBController class card.

The public interface to the RGBController class consists of the constructor and an `update()` function. The constructor requires a pointer to the ColorModel on which this controller operates. Because the RGBController is also a user interface component that creates widgets, the constructor also requires a name and a widget to be used as a parent.

```
1    //////////////////////////////////////////////////////////
2    // RGBController.C: Control the ColorModel
3    //////////////////////////////////////////////////////////
4    #ifndef RGBCONTROLLER_H
5    #define RGBCONTROLLER_H
6    #include <Xm/Xm.h>
7    #include "ColorView.h"
8
9    class ColorModel;
10
11   class RGBController : public ColorView {
12
13     private:
14
15       Widget _redSlider;        // XmScale widgets for each color component
16       Widget _greenSlider;
17       Widget _blueSlider;
18
19       // Callbacks for when user moves any slider
20
21       static void redChangedCallback   ( Widget, XtPointer, XtPointer );
22       static void greenChangedCallback ( Widget, XtPointer, XtPointer );
23       static void blueChangedCallback  ( Widget, XtPointer, XtPointer );
24
25     protected:
26
27       ColorModel *_model;     // ColorModel controlled by this object
28
29       // Called when user moves sliders to change a color component
30
31       virtual void  redChanged ( int );
32       virtual void  greenChanged ( int );
33       virtual void  blueChanged ( int );
34
35     public:
36
37       RGBController ( Widget , ColorModel *, char * );
38       void update ( ColorModel * ); // Called when the ColorModel changes
39       const char *const className() { return ( "RGBController" );}
40   };
41   #endif
```

The RGBController constructor creates an XmRowColumn widget and the three sliders that control the three color components. The XmRowColumn widget is configured to stack the sliders vertically in a single column. Each slider controls a value between 0 and 255, and has a horizontal orientation. Once all widgets have been created, the RGBController constructor registers a pair of callbacks for each slider, to be called when the user moves any slider.

```
1   //////////////////////////////////////////////////////////
2   // RGBController.C: Control the ColorModel
3   //////////////////////////////////////////////////////////
4   #include "RGBController.h"
5   #include "ColorModel.h"
6   #include <Xm/Xm.h>
7   #include <Xm/RowColumn.h>
8   #include <Xm/Scale.h>
9
10  RGBController::RGBController ( Widget      parent,
11                                ColorModel *model,
12                                char       *name ) : ColorView ( name )
13  {
14      Arg wargs[10];
15      int n;
16
17      _model = model;   // Keep a pointer to the model
18
19      // Set up a manager for a single column of controls
20
21      _w = XtVaCreateWidget ( "rgbController",
22                              xmRowColumnWidgetClass,
23                              parent,
24                              XmNnumColumns,  1,
25                              XmNpacking,     XmPACK_COLUMN,
26                              XmNorientation, XmVERTICAL,
27                              NULL );
28
29      installDestroyHandler();
30
31      // Create an XmScale to control each color component
32      // Each widget needs to have the same configuration, so create
33      // a single Arg list and pass it to all three widgets
34
35      n = 0;
36      XtSetArg ( wargs[n], XmNminimum,       0 ) ; n++;
37      XtSetArg ( wargs[n], XmNmaximum,     255 ); n++;
38      XtSetArg ( wargs[n], XmNorientation,  XmHORIZONTAL ); n++;
39      _redSlider   = XtCreateManagedWidget ( "red",
40                                             xmScaleWidgetClass,
41                                             _w, wargs, n);
42      _greenSlider = XtCreateManagedWidget ( "green",
43                                             xmScaleWidgetClass,
44                                             _w, wargs, n);
45      _blueSlider  = XtCreateManagedWidget ( "blue",
46                                             xmScaleWidgetClass,
47                                             _w, wargs, n );
48
49      // Install callbacks for each widget, to be called if the
```

```
50        // scale moves suddenly or is dragged
51
52        XtAddCallback ( _redSlider,
53                          XmNvalueChangedCallback,
54                          &RGBController::redChangedCallback,
55                          ( XtPointer ) this );
56        XtAddCallback ( _redSlider,
57                          XmNdragCallback,
58                          &RGBController::redChangedCallback,
59                          ( XtPointer ) this );
60
61        XtAddCallback ( _greenSlider,
62                          XmNvalueChangedCallback,
63                          &RGBController::greenChangedCallback,
64                          ( XtPointer ) this );
65        XtAddCallback ( _greenSlider,
66                          XmNdragCallback,
67                          &RGBController::greenChangedCallback,
68                          ( XtPointer ) this );
69
70        XtAddCallback ( _blueSlider,
71                          XmNvalueChangedCallback,
72                          &RGBController::blueChangedCallback,
73                          ( XtPointer ) this );
74        XtAddCallback ( _blueSlider,
75                          XmNdragCallback,
76                          &RGBController::blueChangedCallback,
77                          ( XtPointer ) this );
78  }
```

The RGBController class registers one function for each slider's XmNdragCallback and XmNvalueChangedCallback callback lists. These callback functions simply retrieve the current value of the XmScale widget from the callData argument, and call the object's corresponding redChanged(), blueChanged(), or greenChanged() member functions.

```
79  void RGBController::redChangedCallback ( Widget,
80                                            XtPointer clientData,
81                                            XtPointer callData )
82  {
83      RGBController* obj = ( RGBController * ) clientData;
84      XmScaleCallbackStruct *cb = ( XmScaleCallbackStruct * ) callData;
85
86      obj->redChanged ( cb->value );
87  }
88
88  void RGBController::greenChangedCallback ( Widget,
89                                              XtPointer clientData,
90                                              XtPointer callData )
```

```
91  {
92       RGBController* obj = ( RGBController * ) clientData;
93       XmScaleCallbackStruct *cb  = ( XmScaleCallbackStruct * ) callData;
94
95       obj->greenChanged ( cb->value );
96  }

97  void RGBController::blueChangedCallback ( Widget,
98                                            XtPointer clientData,
99                                            XtPointer callData )
100 {
101      RGBController* obj = ( RGBController * ) clientData;
102      XmScaleCallbackStruct *cb  = ( XmScaleCallbackStruct * ) callData;
103
104      obj->blueChanged ( cb->value );
105 }
```

The redChanged(), blueChanged(), and greenChanged() member functions send the appropriate message to the ColorModel object, with the new value of the color component.

```
106  void  RGBController::redChanged ( int value )
107  {
108       _model->setRed ( value );
109  }

110  void  RGBController::greenChanged ( int value )
111  {
112       _model->setGreen ( value );
113  }

114  void  RGBController::blueChanged ( int value )
115  {
116       _model->setBlue ( value );
117  }
```

The RGBController responds to update() messages by setting the value of each slider to match the value currently represented by the ColorModel object.

```
118  void RGBController::update ( ColorModel *model )
119  {
120       // Update each slider with the current values in the model
121
122       XtVaSetValues ( _redSlider,   XmNvalue, model->red(),   NULL );
123       XtVaSetValues ( _greenSlider, XmNvalue, model->green(), NULL );
124       XtVaSetValues ( _blueSlider,  XmNvalue, model->blue(),  NULL );
125  }
```

## The SwatchView Class

The SwatchView displays a "swatch" of the color represented by a ColorModel by manipulating a widget's background color. Any widget could be used for this purpose, but the SwatchView class creates an XmDrawingArea widget. Besides creating the widget, the SwatchView class has only a single responsibility, which is to respond to update() messages from the ColorModel object.

The file SwatchView.h contains the declaration of the SwatchView class.

```
1   //////////////////////////////////////////////////////////
2   // SwatchView.h: Display a color "swatch" corresponding to
3   //                   the color in the ColorModel
4   //////////////////////////////////////////////////////////
5   #ifndef SWATCHVIEW_H
6   #define SWATCHVIEW_H
7   #include "ColorView.h"
8
9   class ColorModel;
10
11  class SwatchView : public ColorView {
12
13    protected:
14
15      Widget     _swatch;   // The widget that changes color
16      Pixel      _index;    // Background color of _swatch
17      Boolean    _enabled;  // TRUE if _index is an editable color cell
18
19    public:
20
21      SwatchView ( Widget,  char * );
22      virtual void update ( ColorModel * );
23      virtual const char *const className() { return ( "SwatchView" ); }
24  };
25  #endif
```

The SwatchView constructor creates an XmDrawingArea widget as a child of an XmFrame widget. The XmFrame widget places a three-dimensional frame around its child, which visually separates the color swatch from the rest of the ColorChooser window.

Like all classes derived from UIComponent, the SwatchView constructor begins by creating the base widget and installing the destruction callback provided by UIComponent. Next, the constructor calls XAllocColorCells() to allocate a single read-write color cell. (See [Scheifler90] for detailed information on allocating colors.) If this call is successful, the pixel value of the allocated color cell determines the value of the XmDrawingArea widget's XmNbackground resource. The members of this color cell, which determine the color displayed by the XmDrawingArea widget, are set in response to update() messages from the ColorModel.

```
1    ///////////////////////////////////////////////////////////
2    // SwatchView.C: Display a swatch of color
3    ///////////////////////////////////////////////////////////
4    #include <Xm/Xm.h>
5    #include <Xm/DrawingA.h>
6    #include <Xm/Frame.h>
7    #include "SwatchView.h"
8    #include "ColorModel.h"
9
10   SwatchView::SwatchView ( Widget parent, char *name ) : ColorView ( name )
11   {
12       int    status;
13       Pixel  pixels[1];
14
15       // Put the color swatch in a 3D frame to set it off from
16       // its surroundings
17
18       _w = XtCreateWidget ( _name, xmFrameWidgetClass,
19                             parent, NULL, 0 );
20
21       installDestroyHandler();
22
23       // Try to allocate a read-write color cell
24       // This function  is an array of pixels, of length 1.
25       // If sucessful, the allocated color cell will be in pixel[0].
26
27       status =
28           XAllocColorCells ( XtDisplay( _w ),
29                              DefaultColormapOfScreen ( XtScreen ( _w ) ),
30                              FALSE,
31                              NULL,
32                              0,
33                              pixels, 1 );
34
35       if ( status == FALSE )
36       {
37           // If the color allocation fails, use the parent's background
38           // color as the color of the swatch, and set the frame's
39           // shadow thickness to zero, effectively hiding this component
40
41           _enabled = FALSE;
42           XtVaGetValues ( parent, XmNbackground, &_index , NULL );
43           XtVaSetValues ( _w, XmNshadowThickness, 0, NULL );
44       }
45       else
46       {
47           // Flag this object as enabled, and store the allocated
48           // color cell for later use
49
```

```
50              _enabled = TRUE;
51              _index   = pixels[0];
52          }
53
54      // Create a widget whose background is set to the allocated color
55
56      _swatch = XtVaCreateManagedWidget ( "swatch",
57                                          xmDrawingAreaWidgetClass,
58                                          _w,
59                                          XmNbackground, _index,
60                                          NULL );
61  }
```

The SwatchView class is designed to work with displays that support a PseudoColor *visual*, in which applications reference colors through a pixel index into a color lookup table. If the entry in the color lookup table is writable, the program can change the contents of that entry in the table, which changes the color displayed by any object drawn using that pixel index. X supports several types of visuals, and the SwatchView will not work with all of them. However, the ColorChooser separates all dependencies on the X color models from the remaining components and the rest of the ColorChooser classes work with all color models. (See [Scheifler90] for information on the X color model and visual types.)

If a color cannot be allocated, the SwatchView constructor sets a flag, _enabled, to FALSE, to prevent future attempts to modify the color represented by the SwatchView. If the SwatchView is disabled, the XmDrawingArea widget managed by the SwatchView object is set to the background color of the component's parent. Then, the XmFrame widget's shadow width is set to zero to effectively hide the SwatchView component. A more complex implementation of this class could try to deal with the failure in a more sophisticated way. For example, the view could attempt to display dithered patterns that simulate the intensity of a color on monochrome screens.

The update() member function retrieves the RGB value maintained by the ColorModel. These values are placed in an XColor structure and passed to XStoreColor(). This Xlib function changes the values of the RGB components for the background pixel used by the XmDrawingArea widget. Notice that the 0-255 range used by the ColorModel must be converted to the 0-65535 range expected by the X server.

```
62  void SwatchView::update ( ColorModel *model )
63  {
64      // Don't update if the widget has not yet been
65      // created or if no color cell was allocated
66
67      if ( _swatch && _enabled )
68      {
69          XColor color;
70
71          // Convert from the 0-256 scale used by the ColorModel
72          // to the 0-65535 scale supported by X, and store
73          // the result in an XColor structure
74
```

```
75          color.red    = model->red()    * 256;
76          color.green  = model->green()  * 256;
77          color.blue   = model->blue()   * 256;
78          color.flags  = DoRed | DoBlue | DoGreen;
79          color.pixel  = _index;
80
81          // Change the values stored in the color cell, thereby
82          // changing the background color of the swatch widget
83
84          XStoreColor ( XtDisplay ( _w ),
85                        DefaultColormapOfScreen ( XtScreen ( _w ) ),
86                        &color );
87      }
88  }
```

## The TextView Class

The ColorChooser supports two views that consist of text fields: RGBView and HSVView. Because these views are very similar in function and appearance, it is convenient to implement a common base class that implements those features common to both classes. TextView is an abstract base class that creates the widget layout used by both the RGBView and HSVView classes. The class creates three labels and three text areas. Derived classes must provide the information displayed by each of these widgets.

The file TextView.h contains the TextView class declaration. The class supports six widgets: three labels and three output fields. These are identified generically as _label1, _label2, _label3, and _field1, _field2, _field3, because derived classes determine the exact function of these members.

```
1   /////////////////////////////////////////////////////////////
2   // TextView.C: Abstract base class for all text (numerical)
3   //             views of a ColorModel
4   /////////////////////////////////////////////////////////////
5   #ifndef TEXTVIEW_H
6   #define TEXTVIEW_H
7   #include "ColorView.h"
8
9   class TextView : public ColorView {
10
11    protected:
12
13      Widget _field1;     // An output area
14      Widget _field2;
15      Widget _field3;
16
17      Widget _label1;     // Labels for each output area
18      Widget _label2;
19      Widget _label3;
20
```

```
21    public:
22
23      TextView ( Widget,  char * );
24      virtual const char *const className() { return ( "TextView" ); }
25    };
26    #endif
```

The TextView constructor creates two columns of widgets: three labels and three corresponding output fields. The labels are implemented as XmLabel widgets, while the output areas are XmText-Field widgets. All six widgets are managed by a single XmRowColumn widget.

```
1    /////////////////////////////////////////////////////////////
2    // TextView.C: Abstract base class for all text (numerical)
3    //             views of a ColorModel
4    /////////////////////////////////////////////////////////////
5    #include "TextView.h"
6    #include <Xm/TextF.h>
7    #include <Xm/RowColumn.h>
8    #include <Xm/Label.h>
9
10    TextView::TextView ( Widget  parent,
11                          char   *name ) : ColorView ( name )
12    {
13        int n;
14        Arg args[10];
15
16        // A RowColumn widget manages a 3 by 2 grid of
17        // labels and text widgets
18
19        _w = XtVaCreateManagedWidget ( _name,
20                                       xmRowColumnWidgetClass,
21                                       parent,
22                                       XmNorientation,    XmHORIZONTAL,
23                                       XmNpacking,        XmPACK_COLUMN,
24                                       XmNnumColumns,     3,
25                                       XmNentryAlignment, XmALIGNMENT_END,
26                                       XmNadjustLast,     FALSE,
27                                       NULL );
28        installDestroyHandler();
29
30        // All text widgets need the same arguments, so set up one
31        // arg list to be used by all three
32
33        n = 0;
34        XtSetArg ( args[n], XmNcolumns,     5 ); n++;
35        XtSetArg ( args[n], XmNeditable,    FALSE );n++;
36        XtSetArg ( args[n], XmNcursorPositionVisible, FALSE ); n++;
37
```

```
38        // Create the labels and text output areas.
39        // Order is important if the widgets are to appear as:
40        //    label      text
41        //    label      text
42
43        _label1 = XtCreateManagedWidget ( "label1",
44                                          xmLabelWidgetClass, _w,
45                                          NULL, 0 );
46        _field1 = XtCreateManagedWidget ( "field1",
47                                           xmTextFieldWidgetClass, _w,
48                                           args, n );
49
50        _label2 = XtCreateManagedWidget ( "label2",
51                                          xmLabelWidgetClass, _w,
52                                          NULL, 0 );
53        _field2 = XtCreateManagedWidget ( "field2",
54                                          xmTextFieldWidgetClass, _w,
55                                          args, n );
56
57        _label3 = XtCreateManagedWidget ( "label3",
58                                           xmLabelWidgetClass, _w,
59                                           NULL, 0 );
60        _field3 = XtCreateManagedWidget ( "field3",
61                                          xmTextFieldWidgetClass, _w,
62                                          args, n );
63   }
```

The XmTextField widgets are used as output areas in this example. To be sure these widgets are not mistaken for editable text areas, each widget is configured as read-only by setting the XmNeditable resource to FALSE. Setting XmNcursorPositionVisible to FALSE removes the text insertion cursor from each widget.

Figure 11.6 shows how a component derived from TextView appears on the screen.

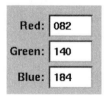

**Figure 11.6**  The layout supported by the TextView class.

## The RGBView Class

The RGBView class is derived from the TextView class. RGBView displays red, green, and blue values between 0 and 255, corresponding to the current values of the RGB components maintained by the ColorModel. Because the TextView class creates and arranges the widgets used by this view, the RGBView class is very simple. The RGBView just updates the information shown in the XmTextField widgets when its `update()` member function is called.

The File RGBView.h contains the declaration of the RGBView class.

```
1   ////////////////////////////////////////////////////////////
2   // RGBView.h: Display the contents of a ColorModel as
3   //             RGB color components
4   ////////////////////////////////////////////////////////////
5   #ifndef RGBVIEW_H
6   #define RGBVIEW_H
7   #include "TextView.h"
8
9   class RGBView : public TextView {
10
11    public:
12
13      RGBView ( Widget, char * );
14
15      virtual void update ( ColorModel * );
16      virtual const char *const className() { return ( "RGBView" ); }
17  };
18  #endif
```

The RGBView constructor just calls the TextView constructor to create the widgets used by this component.

```
1   ////////////////////////////////////////////////////////////
2   // RGBView.C: Display the contents of a ColorModel as
3   //             RGB color components
4   ////////////////////////////////////////////////////////////
5   #include "RGBView.h"
6   #include "ColorModel.h"
7   #include <Xm/Xm.h>
8   #include <Xm/TextF.h>
9   #include <stdio.h>
10
11  RGBView::RGBView ( Widget parent, char *name ) :
12                                        TextView ( parent, name )
13  {
14      // Empty
15  }
```

The `update()` member function retrieves the red, green, and blue color components of a color from the ColorModel object and displays each as a three digit integer in the appropriate output field.

```
16  void RGBView::update ( ColorModel *model )
17  {
18      char buf[100];
```

```
19
20       sprintf ( buf, "%3.3d", model->red() );    // Red
21       XmTextFieldSetString ( _field1, buf );
22       sprintf ( buf, "%3.3d", model->green() ); // Green
23       XmTextFieldSetString ( _field2, buf) ;
24       sprintf ( buf, "%3.3d", model->blue() );   // Blue
25       XmTextFieldSetString ( _field3, buf );
26   }
```

## The HSVView Class

The HSVView class is similar to the RGBView class, except that it displays a color's hue, saturation, and value components. The HSVView class uses the widgets created by the TextView class, and implements the update() member function and a member function that converts from the RGB to the HSV color models. This conversion is necessary because the ColorModel provides only RGB values.

The file HSVView.h contains the HSVView class declaration.

```
1    /////////////////////////////////////////////////////////////
2    // HSVView.h: Display the contents of a ColorModel as
3    //            HSV color components
4    /////////////////////////////////////////////////////////////
5    #ifndef HSVVIEW_H
6    #define HSVVIEW_H
7    #include "TextView.h"
8
9    class ColorModel;
10
11   class HSVView : public TextView {
12
13     protected:
14
15       void HSVView::RGBToHSV ( int, int, int, int&, int&, int& );
16
17     public:
18
19       HSVView ( Widget parent, char * );
20
21       virtual void update ( ColorModel * );
22
23       virtual const char *const className() { return ( "HSVView" ); }
24   };
25   #endif
```

Like the RGBView constructor, the HSVView constructor calls the TextView constructor to build the widgets used by the view.

```
1    /////////////////////////////////////////////////////////////
2    // HSVView.C: Display the contents of a ColorModel as
3    //             HSV color components
4    /////////////////////////////////////////////////////////////
5    #include "HSVView.h"
6    #include "ColorModel.h"
7    #include <Xm/Xm.h>
8    #include <Xm/TextF.h>
9    #include <stdio.h>
10
11   HSVView::HSVView ( Widget parent, char *name ) :
12                                           TextView ( parent, name )
13   {
14       // Empty
15   }
```

The update() member function retrieves the red, green, and blue values from the ColorModel and converts them to an HSV color model. The resulting hue, saturation, and value components are displayed in the corresponding XmTextField widgets.

```
16   void HSVView::update( ColorModel *model )
17   {
18       char     buf[100];
19       int      hue, value, saturation;
20
21       // Compute the hue, saturation, and value components
22       // of a color from its RGB values
23
24       RGBToHSV ( model->red(),
25                  model->green(),
26                  model->blue(),
27                  hue, saturation, value );
28
29       // Format and display each of the color components
30
31       sprintf ( buf, "%3.3d",    hue );        // Hue
32       XmTextFieldSetString ( _field1, buf );
33       sprintf ( buf, "%3.3d",    saturation ); // Saturation
34       XmTextFieldSetString ( _field2, buf );
35       sprintf ( buf, "%3.3d",    value );      // Value
36       XmTextFieldSetString ( _field3, buf );
37   }
```

RGBToHSV() is a protected member function that takes the RGB components of a color and computes the corresponding hue, saturation and value components. The following function is adapted from an algorithm that can be found in [Foley82]. In this implementation, the hue is computed as an angle that lies between 0 and 360 degrees, while the value and saturation components are expressed as percentages, and lie between 0 and 100.

Notice that the last three parameters to this function are passed by reference to allow these parameters to be used as return values.

```
38  #define MAX(a,b)  ((a) > (b) ? (a) : (b))
39  #define MIN(a,b)  ((a) > (b) ? (b) : (a))
40
41  void HSVView::RGBToHSV ( int     red,
42                           int     green,
43                           int     blue,
44                           int&    hue,          // Return value
45                           int&    saturation,   // Return value
46                           int&    value )       // Return value
47  {
48      float h, s, v;
49      float r, g, b;
50      float temp;
51
52      // Normalize the rgb values to lie between 0 and 1.0
53
54      r = ( float ) red   / 255.0;
55      g = ( float ) green / 255.0;
56      b = ( float ) blue  / 255.0;
57
58      // Compute the value
59
60      v = MAX ( MAX ( r, g ), b );
61
62      // Compute the saturation
63
64      temp = MIN ( MIN ( r, g ), b );
65
66      if ( v == 0.0 )
67          s = 0.0;
68      else
69          s = ( v - temp ) / v;
70
71      // If saturation is not zero, compute the hue
72
73      if ( s != 0.0 )
74      {
75          float Cr = ( v - r ) / ( v - temp );
76          float Cg = ( v - g ) / ( v - temp );
77          float Cb = ( v - b ) / ( v - temp );
78          if ( r == v )
79              h = Cb - Cg;
80          else if ( g == v )
81              h = 2.0 + Cr - Cb;
82          else if ( b == v )
83              h = 4.0 + Cg - Cr;
```

```
84
85            h = 60.0 * h;
86            if ( h < 0.0 )
87                 h += 360.0;
88        }
89        else
90            h = 0.0;
91
92        // Convert value and saturation to percentages
93
94        value      = ( int ) ( 100 * v );
95        saturation = ( int ) ( 100 * s );
96        hue = ( int ) h;
97    }
```

## The ColorChooser Class

The ColorChooser class ties the ColorModel, the RGBController, and all views described in previous sections together to form a single logical user interface component. The ColorChooser class creates and displays a dialog that allows an application to request a color from the user. The MVC objects form a subsystem that allows the user to view and manipulate a color; the ColorChooser defines the external programmatic interface for this subsystem.

The file ColorChooser.h contains the ColorChooser class declaration. The ColorChooser class supports members that represent each of the MVC components of the color editor. The public interface consists of the constructor plus a `pickColor()` member function that displays the dialog. This member function requires a pointer to a function to be called when the user selects a color and a second function to be called if the user cancels the selection. The `pickColor()` function also allows the caller to pass some client data to be passed to these callback functions. The type of the "ok" callback function must be `ColorSelectedCallback`, which is declared in the ColorChooser header file. The "cancel" callback function is expected to take a single untyped argument, which is used to return any client data to the application.

```
1    ///////////////////////////////////////////////////////////
2    // ColorChooser.h
3    ///////////////////////////////////////////////////////////
4    #ifndef COLORCHOOSER_H
5    #define COLORCHOOSER_H
6    #include "UIComponent.h"
7
8    // Function type to be passed to pickColor()
9
10   typedef void ( *ColorSelectedCallback ) ( int, int, int, void * );
11   typedef void ( *CancelCallback ) ( void * );
12
13   class ColorModel;
14   class ColorView;
15
```

```
16   class ColorChooser : public UIComponent {
17
18     private:
19
20       ColorModel    * _model;        // The abstract color model
21       ColorView     * _rgbSliders;   // Controls the model
22       ColorView     * _swatch;       // A patch of color
23       ColorView     * _rgbView;      // Text view of RGB components
24       ColorView     * _hsvView;      // Text view of HSV components
25
26       Widget _okButton;             // Selects the current color
27       Widget _cancelButton;         // Dismisses dialog
28
29       // Pointers to application-defined functions called
30       // when user selects a color or cancels the selection
31
32       ColorSelectedCallback _clientOkCallback;
33       CancelCallback        _clientCancelCallback;
34
35       void              * _clientData;
36
37       void   ok();                   // Called by click on "OK"
38       void   cancel();               // Called by click on "Cancel"
39       static void okCallback ( Widget,
40                                XtPointer,
41                                XtPointer );
42       static void cancelCallback ( Widget,
43                                    XtPointer,
44                                    XtPointer );
45
46     public:
47
48       ColorChooser ( Widget , char * );
49       virtual ~ColorChooser ();
50       void pickColor ( ColorSelectedCallback, CancelCallback, void * );
51
52       virtual const char *const className() { return ( "ColorChooser" ); }
53   };
54   #endif
```

The ColorChooser component is an example of a self-contained component that could be used in many different programs. Several widget resources must be set to achieve the layout shown in Figure 11.2. Rather than force every application that uses the dialog to include these resources in an application resource file, the ColorChooser uses the UIComponent setDefaultResources() member function to specify resources for this component. These resources include those required by various views as well as those required by the ColorChooser class.

The ColorChooser component uses an XmBulletinBoard widget as a base. This widget does not enforce any layout on its children, which means that the position of each component of the Color-

Chooser must be specified explicitly. Specifying individual positions for each component has some drawbacks, but is the only reasonable way to define the layout shown in Figure 11.2. Each component in the ColorChooser manages its own internal layout, so the ColorChooser only needs to specify the *x,y* position of each component. The size and location of each component is specified in the default resources provided by the class.

```
1    ///////////////////////////////////////////////
2    // ColorChooser.C:
3    ///////////////////////////////////////////////
4    #include "ColorModel.h"
5    #include "HSVView.h"
6    #include "SwatchView.h"
7    #include "RGBController.h"
8    #include "RGBView.h"
9    #include "ColorChooser.h"
10   #include <Xm/Xm.h>
11   #include <Xm/Form.h>
12   #include <Xm/BulletinB.h>
13   #include <Xm/Separator.h>
14   #include <Xm/PushB.h>
15
16   // Default resources needed by the ColorChooser component
17
18   static String colorChooserResources[] = {
19       "*rgbView.x:                     150",
20       "*rgbView.y:                      20",
21       "*rgbView*label1*labelString:    Red:",
22       "*rgbView*label2*labelString:    Green:",
23       "*rgbView*label3*labelString:    Blue:",
24       "*hsvView.x:                     300",
25       "*hsvView.y:                      20",
26       "*hsvView*label1*labelString:    Hue:",
27       "*hsvView*label2*labelString:    Saturation:",
28       "*hsvView*label3*labelString:    Value:",
29       "*rgbController.x:                50",
30       "*rgbController.y:               150",
31       "*rgbController*scaleWidth:      375",
32       "*rgbController*scaleHeight:      22",
33       "*colorView.x:                    20",
34       "*colorView.y:                    20",
35       "*swatch.width:                  100",
36       "*swatch.height:                 100",
37       "*colorView.shadowType:          shadow_in",
38       "*ok.x:                           20",
39       "*ok.y:                          240",
40       "*ok*labelString:                OK",
41       "*cancel.x:                      400",
42       "*cancel.y:                      240",
```

```
43       "*cancel*labelString:              Cancel",
44  //   Debatable use of color
45       "*rgbController*red*troughColor:   red",
46       "*rgbController*green*troughColor: green",
47       "*rgbController*blue*troughColor:  blue",
48       NULL,
49  };
```

The resources specified by the ColorChooser include three color specifications for the sliders created by the RGBController class. In general, it is best to avoid specifying colors in application resource files, and it is almost never appropriate to hard-code colors in a program. The user should be able to choose colors according to his or her taste. However, in this case, the three colors serve as labels for the controls on the ColorChooser, so the colors have an intrinsic meaning that the user should not alter. In addition, the resources that accompany the ColorChooser are only default values; the user can override them easily. Specifying colors in an application can also make the program non-portable; not all systems support color. However, the ColorChooser itself depends on a color system, so specifying these three colors as defaults should not pose a serious problem in this example.

The ColorChooser constructor instantiates a ColorModel object, a RGBController object, and the three ColorView objects. It also creates two Motif XmPushButton widgets. The first serves as an "OK" button. The user clicks on this button to end the selection process and choose the currently displayed color. The other button dismisses the dialog without selecting a color.

The ColorChooser's base widget is an XmBulletinBoard widget, managed by an XmDialog-Shell widget. Motif provides a convenience function, XmCreateBulletinBoardDialog() that creates and configures both widgets. The XmBulletinBoard widget provides support for Motif-style dialogs. For example, the constructor declares the _okButton to be the XmNdefault-Button for the dialog, and the _cancelButton widget to be the dialog's XmNcancelButton. Setting these resources informs the XmBulletinBoard widget of the function these widget perform. Once these buttons are registered, the _cancelButton automatically unmaps the dialog, with no action required by the program. The _okButton functions as the default button, which is activated when the user presses the <RETURN> key. The ColorChooser constructor registers the okCallback() function with the _okButton widget, to be called when the user clicks on the button.

```
50  ColorChooser::ColorChooser ( Widget parent, char *name ) :
51                                                UIComponent ( name )
52  {
53      _clientData = NULL;
54
55      // Load the ColorChooser component's resources into the
56      // resource database
57
58      setDefaultResources ( parent , colorChooserResources );
59
60      // The ColorChooser is a dialog, but no existing
61      // Motif dialog supports the required layout, so use
```

```
62      // a generic BulletinBoardDialog
63
64      _w = XmCreateBulletinBoardDialog ( parent, _name, NULL, 0 );
65
66      _okButton    = XtCreateManagedWidget ( "ok",
67                                                 xmPushButtonWidgetClass,
68                                                 _w, NULL, 0 );
69      _cancelButton = XtCreateManagedWidget ( "cancel",
70                                                 xmPushButtonWidgetClass,
71                                                 _w, NULL, 0 );
72
73      // Set up the Ok and Cancel buttons, so the BulletinBoard
74      // widget can handle them automatically
75
76      XtVaSetValues ( _w,
77                      XmNdefaultButton, _okButton,
78                      XmNcancelButton,  _cancelButton,
79                      NULL );
80
81      // The OK button allows the user to finalize the selected value
82
83      XtAddCallback ( _okButton,
84                      XmNactivateCallback,
85                      &ColorChooser::cancelCallback,
86                      (XtPointer) this );
87
88      // Create a ColorModel object, and instantiate one of each
89      // available ColorView class
90
91      _model      = new ColorModel();
92      _rgbSliders = new RGBController ( _w, _model, "rgbController" );
93      _swatch     = new SwatchView ( _w, "colorView" );
94      _rgbView    = new RGBView ( _w, "rgbView" );
95      _hsvView    = new HSVView ( _w, "hsvView" );
96
97      // Attach each ColorView to the ColorModel object
98
99      _model->attachView ( _swatch );
100     _model->attachView ( _rgbView );
101     _model->attachView ( _hsvView );
102     _model->attachView ( _rgbSliders );
103
104     // Manage each of the views
105
106     _rgbSliders->manage();
107     _swatch->manage();
108     _rgbView->manage();
109     _hsvView->manage();
110 }
```

The ColorChooser destructor simply deletes the various objects instantiated by the constructor. The UIComponent destructor destroys the widgets.

```
111  ColorChooser::~ColorChooser()
112  {
113      delete _model;
114      delete _rgbSliders;
115      delete _swatch;
116      delete _rgbView;
117      delete _hsvView;
118  }
```

The `pickColor()` member function provides the primary external interface to the Color-Chooser class. Applications that need to allow the user to choose a color call this member function, specifying a callback function to be invoked when the user makes his or her selection and a second callback to be called if the user cancels the selection. The `pickColor()` function stores a pointer to these callbacks for later use and displays the dialog.

```
119  void ColorChooser::pickColor ( ColorSelectedCallback okCB,
120                                  CancelCallback        cancelCB,
121                                  void                  *clientData; )
122  {
123      _clientOkCallback     = okCB;
124      _clientCancelCallback = cancelCB;
125      _clientData           = clientData;
126      manage();
127  }
```

The `okCallback()` function is called when the user clicks on the ColorChooser's `_okButton`. This function just retrieves the ColorChooser object from the `clientData` argument and calls the `ok()` member function.

```
128  void ColorChooser::okCallback ( Widget,
129                                  XtPointer clientData,
130                                  XtPointer )
131  {
132      ColorChooser *obj = ( ColorChooser * ) clientData;
133
134      obj->ok();
135  }
```

The `ok()` member function calls the "ok" callback function passed to `pickColor()`. The arguments to this function provide the current value of each color component, as well as the client data passed to `pickColor()`.

```
136   void ColorChooser::ok()
137   {
138       if ( _clientOkCallback )
139           ( *_clientOkCallback )( _model->red(),
140                                   _model->green(),
141                                   _model->blue(),
142                                   _clientData );
143   }
```

The `cancelCallback()` function is called when the user clicks on the ColorChooser's `_cancelButton`. This function just retrieves the ColorChooser object from the `clientData` argument and calls the `cancel()` member function.

```
144   void ColorChooser::cancelCallback ( Widget,
145                                       XtPointer clientData,
146                                       XtPointer )
147   {
148       ColorChooser *obj = ( ColorChooser * ) clientData;
149
150       obj->cancel();
151   }
```

The `cancel()` member function calls the "cancel" callback function passed to `pickColor()` to inform the application that the user has canceled the color selection without choosing a color. The arguments to this function provide the client data passed to `pickColor()`.

```
152   void ColorChooser::cancel()
153   {
154       if ( _clientCancelCallback )
155           ( *_clientCancelCallback )( _clientData );
156   }
```

Figure 11.7 shows the inheritance relationships between the classes used to create the Color-Chooser component.

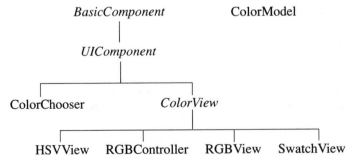

**Figure 11.7**  The ColorChooser inheritance tree.

Figure 11.8 shows a message diagram of the classes that make up the ColorChooser. This diagram is relatively complete, but does not include any abstract base classes.

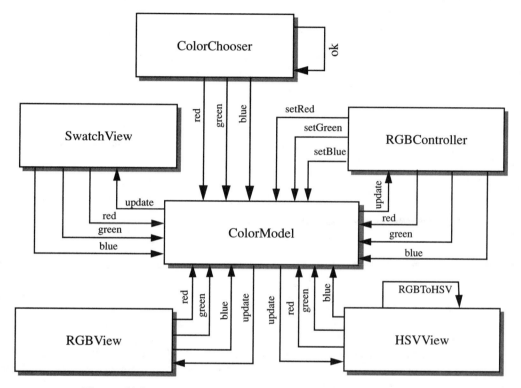

**Figure 11.8**  A message diagram of the ColorChooser component.

## Using the ColorChooser

This section describes a small program that tests the ColorChooser component. This program displays a single Motif XmPushButton widget that displays the ColorChooser dialog when the user clicks on it. The program registers a callback with the ColorChooser that simply prints the values selected using the ColorChooser.

The program defines a ColorTestWindow class that creates a button that allows the user to post the ColorChooser dialog.

```
1    /////////////////////////////////////////////////////////////
2    // ColorTestWindow.h: Test the ColorChooser dialog
3    /////////////////////////////////////////////////////////////
4    #include "MainWindow.h"
5
6    class ColorChooser;
7
```

```
8    class ColorTestWindow : public MainWindow {
9
10     private:
11
12       Widget _button;    // Button used to display ColorChooser
13
14       // Called when user selects a color
15
16       static void colorSelectedCallback ( int, int, int, void * );
17
18       // Called to post the ColorChooser dialog
19
20       static void pickColorCallback ( Widget, XtPointer, XtPointer );
21
22     protected:
23
24       virtual Widget createWorkArea ( Widget );
25       ColorChooser *_colorChooser;
26
27     public:
28
29       // Inline, empty constructor
30
31       ColorTestWindow ( char *name ) : MainWindow ( name ) { }
32   };
```

The ColorTestWindow class is similar to the test classes used to display dialogs in Chapter 7. The function createWorkArea() just creates an XmPushButton widget and registers a callback to be called when the user clicks on the button.

```
1    //////////////////////////////////////////////////////////////
2    // ColorTestWindow.C: Test the ColorChooser dialog
3    //////////////////////////////////////////////////////////////
4    #include <stdio.h>
5    #include "ColorTestWindow.h"
6    #include "ColorChooser.h"
7    #include <Xm/PushB.h>
8
9    Widget ColorTestWindow::createWorkArea ( Widget parent )
10   {
11       // Create a button to post the color dialog
12
13       _button = XtCreateWidget ( "push_to_test",
14                                  xmPushButtonWidgetClass,
15                                  parent,
16                                  NULL, 0 );
17
```

```
18        // Register a callback to post the dialog
19
20        XtAddCallback ( _button,
21                        XmNactivateCallback,
22                        &ColorTestWindow::pickColorCallback,
23                        ( XtPointer ) this );
24
25        // Create a ColorChooser object
26
27        _colorChooser = new ColorChooser ( parent, "colorChooser" );
28
29        return ( _button );
30  }
```

The pickColorCallback() function retrieves the ColorTestWindow object pointer and calls the ColorChooser's pickColor() member function to post the dialog. The function colorSelectedCallback() is registered as a callback function to be called when the user makes a selection. This function does not require any client data, and does not care if the user cancels the dialog, so the final arguments to pickColor() are NULL.

```
31  void ColorTestWindow::pickColorCallback ( Widget,
32                                            XtPointer clientData,
33                                            XtPointer )
34  {
35      ColorTestWindow *obj          = ( ColorTestWindow * ) clientData;
36      ColorChooser    *colorChooser = obj->_colorChooser;
37
38      colorChooser->pickColor ( &ColorTestWindow::colorSelectedCallback,
39                                NULL,
40                                NULL );
41  }
```

The colorSelectedCallback() function is called when the user clicks on the OK button on the ColorChooser dialog. It simply prints the red, green, and blue components of the chosen color.

```
42  void ColorTestWindow::colorSelectedCallback ( int red,
43                                                int green,
44                                                int blue,
45                                                void * )
46  {
47      printf ( "Color Chosen: \n\
48               red   = %d, \n\
49               green = %d,\n\
50               blue  = %d\n",
51               red, green, blue );
52  }
```

The file ColorTestApp.C completes the test program. This file creates an Application object and a ColorTestWindow object.

```
1   ///////////////////////////////////////////////////////////
2   // ColorTestApp.C: Test the ColorChooser dialog
3   ///////////////////////////////////////////////////////////
4   #include "Application.h"
5   #include "ColorTestWindow.h"
6   Application myApp ( "ColorChooserTest" );
7   MainWindow *window = new ColorTestWindow ( "ColorTest" );
```

Before building this program, the classes that implement the ColorChooser should be added to the MotifApp library. The program can then be built using the command:

```
CC -o colorTest ColorTestApp.C ColorTestWindow.C \
      libMotifApp -lXm -lXt -lX11
```

## 11.3 Summary

This chapter explored an architecture based on three different objects, a Model, a View, and a Controller. The Model maintains some abstract data and informs all associated View objects when any aspect of that data changes. A View presents the data represented by a Model. A Controller object allows the user to manipulate the data represented by the Model and to control the way Views present information. Each Model object can support many Controllers and many Views.

The Model-View-Controller (MVC) architecture is particularly useful for applications that need to maintain consistency between different visual representations of data. The ColorChooser component developed in this chapter is one example how a MVC programming model can be applied. In this component, the model is an RGB color. The ColorChooser demonstrates three different view classes, and other views can be added easily.

The MVC architecture demonstrated in this chapter varies in several ways from the original MVC implementation supported by Smalltalk. The model lends itself to many variations, and the key ideas of this architecture can be applied to many situations. In particular, it is often useful to separate presentation aspects of a system from the underlying semantic information. Broadcasting change notifications to collections of dependent objects has applications in any situation that requires synchronization between loosely-coupled objects.

The next chapter presents a more sophisticated example program based on the MotifApp framework. This program demonstrates many of the features of MotifApp, including the Color-Chooser dialog.

C h a p t e r   1 2
# A MotifApp Application

This chapter examines a complete application that exercises more of the MotifApp framework than the small test examples shown earlier. The program is named "bounce" because it allows users to control a simple animation that consists of a set of bouncing balls. The application is designed to be flexible; the appearance and behavior of the animated figures displayed by the program can be altered by defining new classes and making some minor modifications.

Section 12.1 provides an overview of the application, and shows how it takes advantage of the MotifApp framework. Sections 12.2 through 12.7 discuss the application-specific classes used in bounce. Section 12.8 shows how to build and run the application.

## 12.1  An Overview of Bounce

The bounce program is an interactive program that demonstrates a simple animation while exercising many features of the MotifApp framework. Bounce borrows part of its user model from a video player. There is a "screen" on which the animation takes place, and a control panel that allows the user to start, and stop the animation. The user can also control the speed of the animation, and step through the animation one frame at a time.

Unlike video players, bounce allows the user to add and remove elements of the animation interactively. In this respect, bounce borrows some ideas from a play or movie. The area in which the animation occurs is referred to as a "stage", and graphical items that appear on the stage are known as "actors." The user can add actors to the stage by choosing from the available types of actors listed in a pulldown menu. The last actor to be added can be removed by "undoing" the previous command.

In this example, the only available actors are different colors of "bouncing balls," filled circles that bounce off the sides of the stage. However, bounce can support arbitrary actor objects, and radically different animations could be created by defining new actor classes.

Figure 12.1 shows the layout of the bounce program. The stage occupies most of the window, below the menubar. Below the stage is the control area, which provides three buttons that start, stop, and step through the animation. A slider in the lower right allows the user to change the speed of the animation, from one frame per second to thirty frames per second. The menubar along the top of the bounce window contains two pulldown menu panes. The first pane provides an Undo command and a Quit command. The second pane lists the available actors that can be added to the animation.

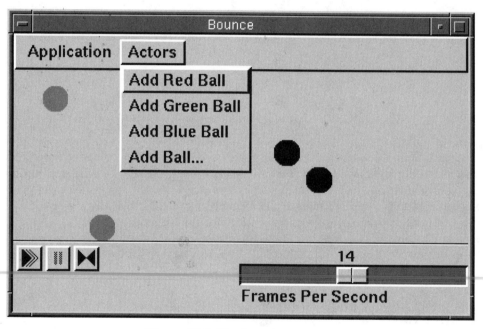

**Figure 12.1**  The bounce program.

Each main area in the bounce window corresponds to a class derived from UIComponent. The stage area in the middle part of the bounce window is implemented as a Stage class. This class not only provides a drawing area, but provides additional support for the Actor classes that display themselves on the Stage. The controls in the window's bottom left are implemented as a Control-Panel class. A general-purpose Clock class provides a control that determines the speed of the animation displayed by the Stage.

The main window layout, including the menubar, is handled by the BounceWindow class, a subclass of MotifApp's MenuWindow class. All commands in the application, including the start, stop, and step commands, are based on classes derived from the Cmd class. This allows the Undo menu item to apply to all operations the user can perform within the program, except changing the clock speed.

Figure 12.2 shows a class inheritance diagram of the bounce program, including those MotifApp classes used directly or indirectly. Only those classes shown in bold must be implemented for the bounce program. MotifApp provides the remaining classes. Of course, bounce does not use every MotifApp class, and this diagram does not show unused MotifApp classes.

The Clock class in Figure 12.2 is not shown in bold, even though it is implemented in this chapter. Although this class is created in response to the bounce program's need for a clock, the Clock class is designed to be reusable and can be added to the MotifApp framework. BounceClock is a subclass of Clock that is specific to the bounce program.

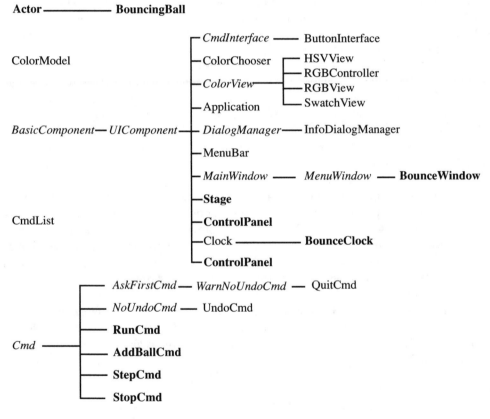

**Figure 12.2** The bounce class hierarchy.

An additional indication of the relative contributions of the bounce program and the supporting framework is the amount of code in each part. Counting all general classes described in earlier chapters, the MotifApp framework consists of just over 2000 uncommented lines of code. Bounce adds just under 700 lines of uncommented code to produce the complete application. The code written specifically for bounce accounts for only twenty-five percent of the total.

The following sections discuss each individual class in the bounce program. Section 12.8 puts all the pieces together and discusses how to build and run the complete application.

# 12.2  The Stage Class

The Stage class provides an area in which individual animated graphical items can be displayed. The simplest implementation of the Stage class would just be an XmDrawingArea widget, into which the application could draw, as needed. This would place the burden of displaying each frame, refreshing the screen when Expose events occur, and so on, on some other part of the program. For example, each Actor placed on the Stage could handle refreshing itself as needed, and could also be responsible for the graphical techniques necessary to produce smooth animation.

However, it requires only a little more effort to create a more powerful class that provides better support for the Actor objects displayed in the stage area. The Stage class described here makes it easy for Actor objects to produce animations by providing *double-buffering*. Double-buffering is a technique that uses two drawing canvases. At any given time, one of these canvases is visible, while the other remains hidden. All objects that will appear in the *next* frame of the animation must be drawn in the hidden canvas. When the entire scene has been rendered, the entire canvas is displayed at once. The previously visible canvas is hidden, erased, and made available for drawing the next frame. The result is a very smooth animation.

In the Stage class, these drawing canvases are implemented as pixmaps.[1] A pixmap can be drawn into the same as a window, but it does not appear on the screen. However, the contents of a pixmap can be copied to a window. The Stage class provides two pixmaps that switch between serving as a back (hidden) buffer and a front (visible) buffer. Actors display themselves in the back buffer. The buffers are then switched. The new front buffer is copied to the Stage window to display the new frame. Whenever the Stage window needs to be redrawn, the current front buffer can be used to restore the contents of the window. Meanwhile, all Actor objects draw themselves in the back buffer to render the next frame. Because each pixmap buffer is erased and completely redrawn with each frame, Actor objects never need to erase themselves, nor do they need to rely on XOR drawing techniques to produce a smooth animation. Each Actor can simply draw itself at the appropriate position for each frame.

The Stage class is derived from UIComponent and is declared as follows:

```
1  ///////////////////////////////////////////////
2  // Stage.h
3  ///////////////////////////////////////////////
4  #ifndef STAGE_H
5  #define STAGE_H
6  #include "UIComponent.h"
```

---

1  There is an X extension that supports multi-buffering. On some machines, this extension may provide hardware support for the technique described here. Although not used in this book, the Stage class could also be implemented using the multi-buffering extension instead of pixmaps.

```
7
8   class Actor;
9
10  class Stage : public UIComponent {
11
12   private:
13
14       static void resizeCallback ( Widget, XtPointer, XtPointer );
15       static void redisplayCallback ( Widget, XtPointer, XtPointer );
16
17   protected:
18
19       GC           _gc;              // Used to clear and copy pixmaps
20       Dimension    _width, _height;  // Current window/buffer size
21       Pixmap       _front, _back;    // Buffers (Always draw to _back)
22
23       virtual void resize();
24       virtual void redisplay();
25       virtual void swapBuffers();
26
27       int     _nActors;    // Number of Actors on the Stage
28       Actor ** _cast;      // List of Actor objects on the Stage
29
30   public:
31
32       Stage ( Widget, char * );
33       ~Stage ();
34
35       virtual void nextFrame();    // Move all actors to the next frame
36
37       void addActor ( Actor * );
38       void removeActor ( Actor * );
39
40       virtual const char *const className() { return ( "Stage" ); }
41  };
42  #endif
```

The Stage class's public protocol consists of a constructor, a destructor, and two methods for adding and removing Actor objects from the Stage. The Stage class also supports a public method that moves the animation to the next frame. The private and protected protocol includes a list of Actor objects, and various member functions and data members that support double buffering.

The Stage constructor initializes all data members and creates an XmDrawingArea widget that serves as the visible Stage window. The constructor installs callbacks to handle widget destruction, resizing and exposure events, and then creates a graphics context to be used in manipulating the pixmaps. Before returning, the constructor calls the resize() member function, which creates pixmaps based on the current size of the class's base widget.

```
1   ///////////////////////////////////////////////////////////
2   // Stage.C
3   ///////////////////////////////////////////////////////////
4   #include "Application.h"
5   #include "Stage.h"
6   #include "Actor.h"
7   #include <Xm/DrawingA.h>
8
9   Stage::Stage ( Widget parent, char *name ) : UIComponent( name )
10  {
11      XGCValues  gcv;
12
13      // Initialize all data members
14
15      _front   = NULL;
16      _back    = NULL;
17      _nActors = 0;
18      _cast    = NULL;
19
20      // Create the visible drawing canvas, and set
21      // up the destruction handler
22
23      _w =  XtCreateWidget ( _name,
24                             xmDrawingAreaWidgetClass,
25                             parent,
26                             NULL, 0 );
27
28      installDestroyHandler();
29
30      // Add callbacks to handle resizing and exposures
31
32      XtAddCallback ( _w, XmNresizeCallback,
33                          &Stage::resizeCallback,
34                      ( XtPointer ) this );
35      XtAddCallback ( _w, XmNexposeCallback,
36                          &Stage::redisplayCallback,
37                      ( XtPointer ) this );
38
39      // A graphics context is needed for copying the pixmap buffers and
40      // erasing the back pixmap
41      // Use the background color of
42      // the base widget for the fill color.
43
44      XtVaGetValues ( _w,
45                      XmNbackground, &gcv.foreground,
46                      NULL );
47
48      _gc = XtGetGC ( _w, GCForeground, &gcv );
49
```

```
50        // Call resize to create the first pixmaps
51
52        resize();
53    }
```

The Stage destructor simply frees the pixmaps and graphics contexts created by this class.

```
54    Stage::~Stage()
55    {
56        // Free the pixmaps and GC, if they still exist
57
58        if ( _front )
59            XFreePixmap ( XtDisplay ( _w ), _front );
60
61        if ( _back )
62            XFreePixmap ( XtDisplay ( _w ), _back );
63
64        if ( _w && _gc )
65            XtReleaseGC ( _w, _gc );
66    }
```

The `resizeCallback()` function is a static member function that just calls the virtual `resize()` member function when the base widget's size changes.

```
67    void Stage::resizeCallback ( Widget,
68                                 XtPointer clientData,
69                                 XtPointer )
70    {
71        Stage *obj = ( Stage * ) clientData;
72        obj->resize();
73    }
```

The `resize()` member function creates the pixmaps used to implement double-buffering. Whenever the Stage window changes size, the old pixmap buffers must be destroyed and replaced by two new pixmaps, whose sizes match the size of the drawing area widget.

Although many Xlib functions work with either windows or pixmaps, pixmaps have no inherent background color. Therefore, neither XClearWindow(), nor XClearArea() can be used to erase a pixmap. Pixmaps must be cleared by calling XFillRectangle() to fill the pixmap with the desired color. Because the pixmaps used in this example are copied to the Stage class's base widget, the pixmap is filled with the base widget's background color.

```
74    void Stage::resize()
75    {
76        // Get the current size of the drawing area
77
78        XtVaGetValues ( _w, XmNwidth,  &_width,
79                            XmNheight, &_height,
```

```
 80                        NULL );
 81
 82       // Pixmaps can't be resized, so just destroy the old ones
 83
 84       if ( _front )
 85           XFreePixmap ( XtDisplay ( _w ), _front );
 86
 87       if ( _back )
 88           XFreePixmap ( XtDisplay ( _w ), _back );
 89
 90       // Create new pixmaps to match the new size of the window
 91
 92       _back = XCreatePixmap ( XtDisplay ( _w ),
 93                               DefaultRootWindow ( XtDisplay ( _w ) ),
 94                               _width, _height,
 95                               DefaultDepthOfScreen ( XtScreen ( _w ) ) );
 96
 97       _front = XCreatePixmap ( XtDisplay ( _w ),
 98                               DefaultRootWindow ( XtDisplay ( _w ) ),
 99                               _width, _height,
100                               DefaultDepthOfScreen ( XtScreen ( _w ) ) );
101
102       // Erase both pixmaps
103
104       XFillRectangle ( XtDisplay ( _w ), _back,
105                        _gc, 0, 0, _width, _height );
106       XFillRectangle ( XtDisplay ( _w ), _front,
107                        _gc, 0, 0, _width, _height );
108   }
```

The Stage class supports animation by displaying the next frame on demand. The `nextFrame()` member function calls `swapBuffers()` to display the frame currently drawn in the `_back` buffer. Then, it sends a `nextFrame()` message to each registered Actor object. The Actor class's `nextFrame()` method expects a Drawable (a Window or pixmap), and the current size of the stage. Notice that the `Stage::nextFrame()` member function passes the `_back` pixmap as the drawable. The Actor objects drawn during any given frame will not be visible until the next frame.

```
109   void  Stage::nextFrame()
110   {
111       // For each new frame, simply swap buffers and have each
112       // Actor object draw its next frame in the back buffer
113
114       swapBuffers();
115
116       for ( int i = 0; i < _nActors; i++)
117           _cast[i]->nextFrame ( _back, _width, _height );
118   }
```

The swapBuffers() member function is very simple. If the Stage object's base widget is not realized, the function does nothing. If the widget has been realized, this function swaps pointers to the pixmap buffers and copies the previously hidden pixmap into the drawing area. The new back buffer is erased by filling it with the drawing area widget's background color, thus making it ready for the next frame.

```
119  void Stage::swapBuffers()
120  {
121      // Switch the front and back buffers
122
123      if ( XtIsRealized ( _w ) )
124      {
125          Pixmap tmp;
126
127          // Do the swap
128
129          tmp   = _front;
130          _front = _back;
131          _back  = tmp;
132
133          // Copy the new front buffer to the drawing area
134
135          XCopyArea ( XtDisplay ( _w ), _front, XtWindow ( _w ),
136                      _gc, 0, 0, _width, _height, 0, 0 );
137
138          // Erase the new back buffer to get ready for the next scene
139
140          XFillRectangle ( XtDisplay ( _w ), _back,
141                           _gc, 0, 0, _width, _height );
142      }
143  }
```

The double-buffering technique used by the Stage class allows bounce to handle Expose events easily. When the Stage window needs to be redrawn, the redisplayCallback() function is called. This function calls the virtual function redisplay(), which restores the window's contents by recopying the contents of the current _front buffer to the XmDrawingArea widget's window.

```
144  void Stage::redisplayCallback ( Widget,
145                                  XtPointer clientData,
146                                  XtPointer )
147  {
148      Stage *obj = ( Stage * ) clientData;
149      obj->redisplay();
150  }
```

```
151  void Stage::redisplay ( )
152  {
153      // Copy the contents of the front pixmap
154      // to restore the window
155
156      XCopyArea ( theApplication->display(), _front,
157                  XtWindow ( _w ), _gc, 0, 0,
158                  _width, _height, 0, 0 );
159  }
```

The final two member functions supported by the Stage class allow Actor objects to be added and removed from the Stage. The addActor() member function simply expands an array of object pointers and adds a new object to the list. The remove Actor() function performs the opposite operation, creating a new, shorter list that excludes the specified Actor object.

```
160  void Stage::addActor ( Actor *newActor )
161  {
162      int i;
163
164      Actor **newList;
165
166      // Allocate a new list large enough to hold
167      // one more object
168
169      newList = new Actor*[_nActors + 1];
170
171      // Copy the old list to the new
172
173      for ( i = 0; i < _nActors; i++ )
174          newList[i] = _cast[i];
175
176      // Add the new object to the end of the list
177
178      newList[_nActors] = newActor;
179
180      // Delete the old list and make _cast
181      // point to the new list
182
183      delete _cast;
184      _cast = newList;
185
186
187      _nActors++;
188  }


189  void Stage::removeActor ( Actor *oldActor )
190  {
191      int     i, j;
```

```
192        Boolean found = FALSE;
193        Actor **newList;
194
195        // Remove the given Actor from the list
196
197        for ( i = 0; i < _nActors; i++ )
198            if ( _cast[i] == oldActor )
199            {
200                found = TRUE;
201                for ( j = i; j < _nActors-1; j++ )
202                    _cast[j] = _cast[j+1];
203                break;
204            }
205
206        if ( !found )
207            return;
208
209        _nActors--;
210
211        // Allocate a new, smaller list
212
213        newList = new Actor*[_nActors];
214
215        for ( i = 0; i < _nActors; i++ )
216            newList[i] = _cast[i];
217
218        delete _cast;
219        _cast = newList;
220    }
```

# 12.3  Driving the Animation

The animation displayed by bounce requires the `Stage::nextFrame()` member function to be called repeatedly, at a fairly rapid rate. Although thirty frames per second is a common speed that produces a smooth animation, users may also want to control the speed of the animation. The bounce program provides a slider control that allows the user to change the rate of the animation from about one frame per second, to the full thirty frames per second required for a smooth animation.

The bounce animation is driven by a variable-speed clock that sends a `nextFrame()` message to the Stage class at the rate determined by the user. The BounceClock class, which sends this message to the Stage class, is derived from an abstract Clock class. The Clock class produces "ticks" at regular intervals and supports the user interface for controlling the speed of the clock. The Clock class is a general-purpose class that can be added to the MotifApp library. The Clock class is similar to the Timer class discussed in Chapters 2 and 3, but adds support for variable speeds and a user interface.

# The Clock Class

The Clock class is an abstract class that calls a pure virtual member function implemented by a derived class at a rate determined by the user. The Clock class is derived from UIComponent, and provides a slider that allows the user to change the clock rate within a fixed range. The minimum and maximum rates supported by a Clock object can be specified as arguments to the Clock constructor. In addition to its interactive user interface, the Clock class also supports a programmatic interface that allows the clock to be started and stopped.

The clock can also be forced to issue a single pulse programmatically. This is useful because it allows applications to control each tick of the clock, if needed. For example, the bounce program uses this feature to allow the user to step though an animation frame by frame. Rather than bypassing the clock to step the Stage through individual frames, bounce always allows the Clock to control the animation. However, the control panel allows the user to control the Clock manually, if desired.

The Clock class is designed to be useful in many situations and is independent of any specific application. Connections to other classes must be made by creating a derived class that defines a pure virtual function, tick(). The Clock class handles the mechanisms that allow the user to control the clock rate, produce clock ticks at regular intervals, and so on. Derived classes must simply define the tick() member function to interface with other objects.

Most of the members supported by the Clock class are for internal use only and are declared to be private. The public interface consists of the constructor and destructor, plus methods for starting, stopping, and single-stepping the Clock. The subclass protocol consists of a single pure virtual member function that must be defined by derived classes.

The Clock class is declared as follows:

```
1    /////////////////////////////////////////////////////
2    // Clock.h
3    /////////////////////////////////////////////////////
4    #ifndef CLOCK_H
5    #define CLOCK_H
6    #include "UIComponent.h"
7
8    class Clock : public UIComponent {
9
10     private:
11
12        int        _delta;       // The time between ticks
13        XtIntervalId _id;        // Xt Timeout identifier
14
15        virtual void timeout();  // Called every delta milliseconds
16        virtual void speedChanged ( int ); // Called if the user moves
17                                           // the speed control
18        //  Xt Callbacks
19
20        static void timeoutCallback ( XtPointer, XtIntervalId * );
21        static void speedChangedCallback ( Widget, XtPointer, XtPointer );
22
23     protected:
```

```
24
25      virtual void tick() = 0;  // Hook for derived classes
26
27   public:
28
29      Clock ( Widget, char *,
30              int,            // Minimum speed, in frames per second
31              int );          // Maximum speed, in frames per second
32      ~Clock ();
33
34      void stop();    // Stop the clock
35      void pulse();   // Make the clock tick once
36      void start();   // Start or restart the clock
37
38      virtual const char *const className() { return ( "Clock" ); }
39   };
40   #endif
```

The Clock constructor initializes various data members and creates an XmScale widget that allows the user to control the clock rate. After checking for a valid lower bound on the time range, the constructor calculates an initial speed that lies midway between the given minimum and maximum clock rates.

The Clock class uses XtAppAddTimeOut() to generate each clock pulse. This function requires an argument that specifies the time between clock pulses, in milliseconds. This number is computed on line 27, and stored in the _delta member, because the timeout function must be re-installed each time it is called.

The Clock constructor is written as follows:

```
1    /////////////////////////////////////////////////////////
2    // Clock.C
3    /////////////////////////////////////////////////////////
4    #include "Clock.h"
5    #include <Xm/Xm.h>
6    #include <Xm/Scale.h>
7
8    Clock::Clock ( Widget parent, char *name,
9                   int minFPS, int maxFPS ) : UIComponent ( name )
10   {
11       int middle;
12
13       _id      = NULL;    // We have no timeout yet
14
15       // Check for a valid minimum speed
16
17       if ( minFPS < 1 )
18           minFPS = 1;
19
20       // Start out in the middle of the designated range
```

```
21
22        middle = ( ( maxFPS - minFPS ) / 2 );
23
24        // Compute the time delta in milliseconds
25        // that corresponds to the given frames per second
26
27        _delta = 1000 / middle;     // 1 / FPS * 1000 milliseconds/second
28
29        _w = XtVaCreateWidget ( _name, xmScaleWidgetClass, parent,
30                                   XmNminimum,      minFPS,
31                                   XmNmaximum,      maxFPS,
32                                   XmNvalue,        middle,
33                                   XmNshowValue,    TRUE,
34                                   NULL );
35
36        installDestroyHandler();
37
38        // Set up a callback to handle changes in the clock rate
39
40        XtAddCallback ( _w,
41                          XmNvalueChangedCallback,
42                          &Clock::speedChangedCallback,
43                          ( XtPointer ) this );
44    }
```

The Clock destructor checks for a pending timeout function, removing it if necessary.

```
45   Clock::~Clock()
46   {
47        if ( _id )
48           XtRemoveTimeOut ( _id );
49   }
```

The start() member function must be called programmatically to start the Clock. This function simply adds the timeoutCallbackFunction() as a timeout callback. Notice that XtAppAddTimeOut() requires an XtAppContext structure as its first argument. The Application class supports a member function that can be used throughout MotifApp when an XtAppContext is needed. However, the Clock class supports a widget from which this structure can readily be retrieved, using the Xt function XtWidgetToApplicationContext(). There is no reason to create unnecessary dependencies, and using this function allows the Clock class to be independent of the rest of the MotifApp framework.

```
50   void Clock::start()
51   {
52        // Start the clock by installing a timeout
53
54        _id  = XtAppAddTimeOut ( XtWidgetToApplicationContext ( _w ),
55                                   _delta,
```

```
56                              &Clock::timeoutCallback,
57                              ( XtPointer ) this );
58  }
```

Xt calls the `timeoutCallback()` function when `_delta` milliseconds have expired. Like most callbacks, this function just retrieves the object pointer and calls a corresponding member function, `timeout()`.

```
59  void Clock::timeoutCallback ( XtPointer clientData, XtIntervalId * )
60  {
61      Clock *obj = ( Clock * ) clientData;
62      obj->timeout();
63  }
```

The `timeout()` member function calls the `tick()` member function, which must be implemented by a derived class. Then, `tick()` re-installs the `tickCallback()` function to be called again in `_delta` milliseconds.

```
64  void Clock::timeout()
65  {
66      tick();    // pure virtual function
67
68      _id = XtAppAddTimeOut ( XtWidgetToApplicationContext ( _w ),
69                              _delta,
70                              &Clock::timeoutCallback,
71                              ( XtPointer ) this );
72  }
```

The `stop()` member function removes the timeout, if one is currently active. The Clock class uses the `_id` member to indicate whether the clock is currently running. Therefore, after removing the timeout, `stop()` sets the `_id` member to NULL.

```
73  void Clock::stop()
74  {
75      if ( _id )
76          XtRemoveTimeOut ( _id );
77
78      _id = NULL;
79  }
```

The `pulse()` member function simply calls the `tick()` member function provided by derived classes. Calling `pulse()` does not involve a timeout, but simply triggers a "tick" immediately. This function can be called whether the Clock is currently running or not. It has no effect on the regularly scheduled clock tick.

```
80   void Clock::pulse()
81   {
82       tick();
83   }
```

The speedChangedCallback() function is called whenever the user changes the value of the Clock's XmScale widget. This function retrieves the object pointer for the Clock object and calls the object's speedChanged() member function with the current value of the XmScale widget.

```
84   void Clock::speedChangedCallback ( Widget,
85                                      XtPointer clientData,
86                                      XtPointer callData )
87   {
88       XmScaleCallbackStruct *cb = ( XmScaleCallbackStruct * ) callData;
89       Clock * obj = ( Clock * ) clientData;
90
91       obj->speedChanged ( cb->value );
92   }
```

The speedChanged() member function computes a new value for _delta, based on the new clock rate. If the clock is running, as indicated by a non-NULL _id member, speed-Changed() removes the current timeout, and adds a new timeout callback with the new value.

```
93   void Clock::speedChanged ( int value )
94   {
95       // Compute the new interval between calls
96
97       _delta = 1000 / value;
98
99       if ( _id )
100      {
101
102          // Remove the old timeout, and set a new one using the
103          // new interval (Note that there may be a glitch before
104          // the first call, depending on how much of the old
105          // time has already elapsed)
106
107          XtRemoveTimeOut ( _id );
108          _id = XtAppAddTimeOut( XtWidgetToApplicationContext ( _w ),
109                                 _delta,
110                                 &Clock::timeoutCallback,
111                                 ( XtPointer ) this );
112      }
113  }
```

Figure 12.3 shows the completed Clock user interface component, as used in bounce.

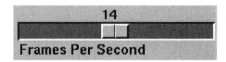

**Figure 12.3** The Clock user interface component

## The BounceClock Class

Now we can look at a class derived from Clock that drives the bounce program's Stage object. The BounceClock class just defines the pure virtual `tick()` member function and sends a `nextFrame()` message to the Stage object with each clock pulse.

The BounceClock class is declared as follows:

```
1    ///////////////////////////////////////////////////////////////
2    // BounceClock.h
3    ///////////////////////////////////////////////////////////////
4    #ifndef BOUNCECLOCK_H
5    #define BOUNCECLOCK_H
6    #include "Clock.h"
7
8    class Stage;
9
10   class BounceClock : public Clock {
11
12     private:
13
14       Stage *_stage;     // The Stage controlled by this clock
15
16     protected:
17
18       virtual void tick();  // Called by base class
19
20     public:
21
22       BounceClock ( Widget, char *, Stage *stage );
23
24       virtual const char *const className() { return ( "BounceClock" ); }
25   };
26   #endif
```

Like all classes derived from UIComponent, the BounceClock constructor requires two basic arguments: a widget to be used as the parent of the user interface component, and a name. In addition, the BounceClock constructor requires a pointer to the Stage object it is to control. The constructor passes the parent widget and the name on to the Clock constructor, along with minimum and maximum clock rates. The constructor stores a pointer to the Stage object for later use.

```
1     ////////////////////////////////////////////////////////////////
2     // BounceClock.C: The clock that controls the animation in bounce
3     ////////////////////////////////////////////////////////////////
4     #include "BounceClock.h"
5     #include "Stage.h"
6
7     BounceClock::BounceClock ( Widget parent, char *name, Stage *stage ) :
8                                         Clock ( parent, name, 1, 30 )
9     {
10        _stage = stage;
11    }
```

The `tick()` member function is called by the Clock base class with each pulse of the clock. This function simply calls the `nextFrame()` member function for the Stage object controlled by this clock.

```
12    void BounceClock::tick()
13    {
14        _stage->nextFrame();
15    }
```

Figure 12.4 shows a message diagram that charts the interactions between the Stage, Clock, and BounceClock classes.

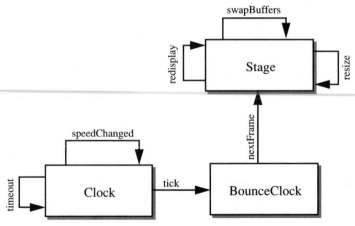

**Figure 12.4** Message diagram of the Stage and Clock classes.

# 12.4 The Control Panel

Bounce uses the command architecture introduced in Chapter 8 to implement the commands that start, stop, and step the animation. This section examines these classes, which are the RunCmd, the StopCmd, and StepCmd. These classes are all similar, and simply provide an interface between the Clock member functions and a visible user interface component. Using the command architecture also allows bounce to take advantage of the undo facility provided by the Cmd and related classes.

## The RunCmd Class

The RunCmd class is derived from Cmd and supports both doit() and undoit() member functions. The RunCmd class maintains a pointer to a Clock object. Executing the RunCmd calls this Clock object's start() member function, and undoing the command calls the Clock's stop() member function.

The RunCmd class is declared as follows:

```
1   ////////////////////////////////////////////////////////////
2   // RunCmd.h
3   ////////////////////////////////////////////////////////////
4   #ifndef RUNCMD_H
5   #define RUNCMD_H
6   #include "Cmd.h"
7
8   class    Clock;
9
10  class RunCmd : public Cmd {
11
12    protected:
13
14      Clock   *_clock;        // Clock controlled by this Cmd
15
16      virtual void doit();    // Start clock
17      virtual void undoit();  // Stop clock
18
19    public:
20
21      RunCmd ( char *, int, Clock * );
22
23  };
24  #endif
```

The RunCmd constructor requires a pointer to a Clock object, which is stored for later use. The doit() member function calls the start() member function for this Clock object, while the undoit() member function calls stop() for the same Clock object. Notice that the RunCmd's undoit() member function is based on the assumption that the clock is in a stopped state before the RunCmd's execute() function is called. This is a reasonable assumption, because the Clock object has only two states: stopped, or running. In more complex cases, a Cmd object like RunCmd might need to query the object it controls to determine its previous state to support undo.

```
1    ///////////////////////////////////////////////////////////
2    // RunCmd.C
3    ///////////////////////////////////////////////////////////
4    #include "RunCmd.h"
5    #include "Clock.h"
6
7    RunCmd::RunCmd ( char *name, int active, Clock *clock ) :
8                                                Cmd ( name, active )
9    {
10       _clock = clock;     // Store the Clock for later use
11   }

12   void RunCmd::doit()
13   {
14      _clock->start();    // Start the animation
15   }

16   void RunCmd::undoit()
17   {
18      _clock->stop();     // Stop the clock, and the animation
19   }
```

## The StopCmd Class

The StopCmd class is very similar to the RunCmd class. StopCmd is derived from Cmd and supports both doit() and undoit() member functions. The StopCmd class is the opposite of the RunCmd class. It calls the Clock object's stop() member function when the command is executed, and calls the Clock's start() member function when the command is undone.

The StopCmd class is declared as follows:

```
1    ///////////////////////////////////////////////////////////
2    // StopCmd.h
3    ///////////////////////////////////////////////////////////
4    #ifndef STOPCMD_H
5    #define STOPCMD_H
6    #include "Cmd.h"
7
8    class Clock;
9
10   class StopCmd : public Cmd {
11
12     protected:
```

```
13
14      Clock *_clock;
15
16      virtual void doit();
17      virtual void undoit();
18
19    public:
20
21      StopCmd ( char *,  int , Clock * );
22  };
23  #endif
```

The StopCmd constructor stores a pointer to a Clock object. The doit() member function stops the associated Clock object, while undoit() restarts the clock.

```
1   ///////////////////////////////////////////////////////
2   // StopCmd.C
3   ///////////////////////////////////////////////////////
4   #include "StopCmd.h"
5   #include "Clock.h"
6
7   StopCmd::StopCmd ( char *name, int active, Clock *clock ) :
8                                              Cmd ( name, active )
9   {
10      _clock = clock;
11  }

12  void StopCmd::doit()
13  {
14      _clock->stop();     // Stop the animation
15  }

16  void StopCmd::undoit()
17  {
18      _clock->start();    // Restart the animation
19  }
```

## The StepCmd Class

The StepCmd class does not support an undoit() member function and is therefore derived from the NoUndoCmd class. Neither the Clock class nor the Stage class support moving backwards, so there is no way to undo a clock pulse. Like the other commands, the StepCmd class maintains a pointer to a Clock object. The StepCmd::doit() member function calls the associated Clock object's pulse() member function when the command is executed.

```
1   /////////////////////////////////////////////////////////
2   // StepCmd.h
3   /////////////////////////////////////////////////////////
4   #ifndef STEPCMD_H
5   #define STEPCMD_H
6   #include "NoUndoCmd.h"
7
8   class Clock;
9
10  class StepCmd : public NoUndoCmd {
11
12    protected:
13
14      Clock *_clock;
15      virtual void doit();
16
17    public:
18
19      StepCmd ( char *, int, Clock * );
20  };
21  #endif
```

```
1   /////////////////////////////////////////////////////////
2   // StepCmd.C
3   /////////////////////////////////////////////////////////
4   #include "StepCmd.h"
5   #include "Clock.h"
6
7   StepCmd::StepCmd ( char   *name,
8                      int     active,
9                      Clock *clock ) : NoUndoCmd ( name, active )
10  {
11      _clock = clock;
12  }
```

```
13  void StepCmd::doit()
14  {
15      _clock->pulse();    // Cause the clock to issue a single tick
16  }
```

## The ControlPanel Class

The ControlPanel class implements the row of buttons in the lower left of the bounce window, as shown in Figure 12.1. The ControlPanel class instantiates each of the command classes described in the previous section and also creates a ButtonInterface object for each command object. The widgets supported by the ButtonInterface objects are managed by an XmRowColumn widget. Chapter 9 demonstrated how the Cmd and CmdInterface classes could be used to create menu items, but these classes can also be used in many different situations. Here, they simply create a row of buttons that can be used to issue commands.

The ControlPanel class is derived from UIComponent and supports only a constructor. The class is declared in the file ControlPanel.h as follows:

```
1    /////////////////////////////////////////////////////////
2    // ControlPanel.h:
3    /////////////////////////////////////////////////////////
4    #ifndef CONTROLPANEL_H
5    #define CONTROLPANEL_H
6    #include "UIComponent.h"
7
8    class Clock;
9
10   class ControlPanel : public UIComponent {
11
12      protected:
13
14      public:
15
16        ControlPanel ( Widget, char *, Clock *clock );
17
18        virtual const char *const className() { return ( "ControlPanel" ); }
19   };
20   #endif
```

The ControlPanel controls the BounceClock object, which in turn drives the Stage object. The ControlPanel constructor requires a pointer to the Clock object to be controlled, as well as the usual parent widget and name string. The constructor creates an XmRowColumn widget to hold a row of button widgets, and then creates an instance of each command class described in the previous section. The Clock object, given as an argument to the ControlPanel constructor, is passed to each of these command objects.

The bounce program enables and disables commands in the ControlPanel depending on what actions are available to the user at any given time. The RunCmd and StepCmd objects are initially active, and the StopCmd object is inactive, because the Clock is stopped when the program begins. The ControlPanel constructor also specifies various dependencies between the commands, to allow the Cmd architecture to activate and deactivate these commands automatically.

Finally, the ControlPanel constructor creates a ButtonInterface object for each Cmd object. The ControlPanel's base widget, an XmRowColumn widget, arranges these buttons in a single row.

```
1    /////////////////////////////////////////////////////////
2    // ControlPanel.C
3    /////////////////////////////////////////////////////////
4    #include "ControlPanel.h"
5    #include "ButtonInterface.h"
6    #include "Clock.h"
7    #include "RunCmd.h"
```

```
8   #include "StopCmd.h"
9   #include "StepCmd.h"
10  #include <Xm/RowColumn.h>
11
12  ControlPanel::ControlPanel ( Widget parent,
13                               char   *name,
14                               Clock *clock ) : UIComponent ( name )
15  {
16      CmdInterface *runBtn, *stopBtn, *stepBtn;
17      Cmd          *runCmd, *stopCmd, *stepCmd;
18
19      // Manage all command buttons in a single horizontal row
20
21      _w = XtVaCreateManagedWidget ( _name, xmRowColumnWidgetClass,
22                                     parent,
23                                     XmNnumColumns, 1,
24                                     XmNorientation, XmHORIZONTAL,
25                                     NULL );
26      installDestroyHandler();
27
28      // Instantiate one object for each command
29      // The clock will initially be stopped, so activate the
30      // step and run commands, but deactivate the stop command
31
32      runCmd  = new RunCmd  ( "Run",  TRUE,  clock );
33      stopCmd = new StopCmd ( "Stop", FALSE, clock );
34      stepCmd = new StepCmd ( "Step", TRUE,  clock );
35
36      // Set up dependencies between the various commands
37      // A running clock can be stopped, but not stepped
38      // A stopped clock can be run, or stepped (It doesn't
39      //  make sense to stop a stopped clock, or to run a
40      // running  clock, so have these commands deactivate
41      // themselves automatically)
42
43      runCmd->addToActivationList ( stopCmd );
44      runCmd->addToDeactivationList ( stepCmd );
45      runCmd->addToDeactivationList ( runCmd );
46
47      stopCmd->addToActivationList ( runCmd );
48      stopCmd->addToActivationList ( stepCmd );
49      stopCmd->addToDeactivationList ( stopCmd );
50
51      stepCmd->addToActivationList ( runCmd );
52      stepCmd->addToDeactivationList ( stopCmd );
53
54      // Finally, create the user interface (buttons) for
55      // each of the commands
56
```

```
57      runBtn   = new ButtonInterface ( _w, runCmd );
58      stopBtn  = new ButtonInterface ( _w, stopCmd );
59      stepBtn  = new ButtonInterface ( _w, stepCmd );
60
61      runBtn->manage();
62      stopBtn->manage();
63      stepBtn->manage();
64   }
```

Figure 12.5 uses a message diagram to show the connections between the objects contained in the ControlPanel and the Clock classes.

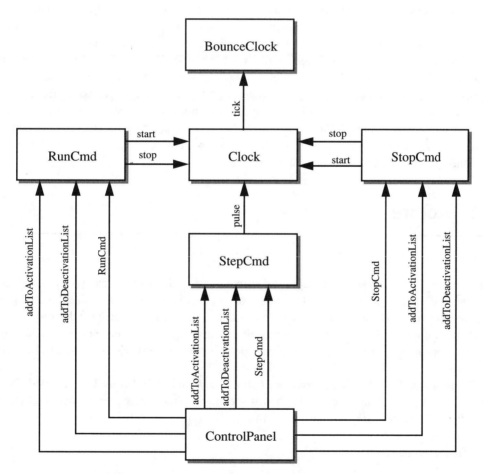

**Figure 12.5** Message diagram of the control panel.

It is interesting to consider whether the ControlPanel class should be re-designed to handle a more general case. For example, the MenuBar class described in Chapter 9 completely hides the process of creating ButtonInterface objects for each command, and also creates the manager widgets that hold these button widgets. It might be useful to create a generic Panel class that does essentially the same thing. This class could take a CmdList and create a panel of controls automatically. While such a class would be easy to write, this approach seems to offer few advantages.

The ControlPanel class, as implemented here, is nearly as simple as possible. Even with a more general Panel class, some part of the program would still need to instantiate Cmd objects, set up any dependencies between them, and create a CmdList. In the current example, using a more general class would replace the three lines of code that create the ButtonInterface objects with five lines of code needed to instantiate a CmdList, add each Cmd to the list, and create the generic Panel object.

While "lines of code" is far from the only consideration, the benefits of a general-purpose Panel class do not seem to be overwhelming, at least for the bounce program. Still, there could be advantages to implementing assorted command and control panels based around the Cmd and CmdInterface architectures. Groups of related applications often have similar needs that can be addressed by such a Panel class. For example, related application may have similar customizable parameters. A PreferencePanel class that supports a common interface for setting user preferences could be very useful in such situations. A general PreferencePanel would be useful in this case because it is possible to support application-specific features that go beyond the capabilities of a generic widget set like Motif. A PreferencePanel class could support an architecture for applications that need to provide user-settable preferences, and enforce both behavioral and visual consistency across the applications that use the component.

# 12.5  Actors

This section introduces classes that represent graphical items that can be displayed in the stage area as elements of an animation. The Actor class is an abstract base class that defines a basic protocol for all objects that can be added to a Stage. In addition to defining a protocol for derived classes, the Actor class automatically registers and unregisters all instances with a Stage object, as needed. The protected portion of the Actor class maintains a pointer to the Stage object in which an Actor object is displayed.

The BouncingBall class is derived from Actor. The BouncingBall class draws a filled circle that moves across the Stage in a randomly-chosen speed and direction. When a BouncingBall object encounters a Stage boundary, it bounces off in a new direction.

## The Actor Class

The Actor class declares a pure virtual member function, `nextFrame()`, that must be implemented by all derived classes. The Stage object calls this member function to request each Actor object to draw itself in the next frame. The Stage passes a Drawable in which the Actor should render itself.

Some Actor objects may find it useful to know the size of the Stage, and therefore `nextFrame()` also takes width and height arguments.

The Actor class is declared as follows:

```
1    /////////////////////////////////////////////////////////////////
2    // Actor.h: Abstract base class for all "actor" objects
3    /////////////////////////////////////////////////////////////////
4    #ifndef ACTOR_H
5    #define ACTOR_H
6    #include <Xm/Xm.h>
7
8    class Stage;
9
10   class Actor {
11
12     protected:
13
14       Stage *_stage;     // The Stage on which this object appears
15
16     public:
17
18       Actor ( Stage * );
19       virtual ~Actor();
20
21       // Must be implemented by derived classes
22
23       virtual void nextFrame ( Drawable, Dimension, Dimension ) = 0;
24   };
25   #endif
```

The Actor constructor saves a pointer to the given Stage object and registers the Actor object with the Stage object. Derived classes may be able to use the `_stage` member, but it is meant primarily for the Actor destructor. The destructor must remove the deleted object from the list of Actors maintained by the Stage, to prevent the Stage object from referencing a pointer to a freed object.

```
1    /////////////////////////////////////////////////////////////////
2    // Actor.C: Abstract base class for all "actor" objects
3    /////////////////////////////////////////////////////////////////
4    #include "Actor.h"
5    #include "Stage.h"
6
7    Actor::Actor( Stage *stage )
8    {
9        _stage = stage;
10       _stage->addActor ( this );   // Add this object to the Stage
11   }
```

```
12   Actor::~Actor()
13   {
14       _stage->removeActor ( this );   // Remove this object from the Stage
15   }
```

## The BouncingBall Class

The bounce program only supports one type of Actor, a "bouncing ball." The BouncingBall class is derived from the Actor class, and defines the behavior of a graphical object that can appear in the bounce stage area. The BouncingBall class displays a small colored circle that moves across the stage at a random velocity. When a BouncingBall object encounters the boundary of the Stage, it changes direction, simulating a ball that bounces off a wall.

The BouncingBall class allows a named color to be specified as an argument to the constructor. If no color is specified, the BouncingBall class uses the ColorChooser class described in Chapter 11 to let the user pick a color interactively.

The BouncingBall class is declared as follows:

```
1    ///////////////////////////////////////////////////////
2    // BouncingBall.h
3    ///////////////////////////////////////////////////////
4    #ifndef BOUNCINGBALL_H
5    #define BOUNCINGBALL_H
6    #include "Actor.h"
7    #include "Xm/Xm.h"
8
9    class Stage;
10
11   class BouncingBall : public Actor {
12
13     protected:
14
15       GC          _gc;        // GC needed to draw the object
16       XPoint      _delta;     // The velocity in terms of dx,dy
17       XRectangle _bounds;     // The bounding box of the ball
18
19       // Called from the ColorChooser when the user has picked a color
20
21       static void colorSelectedCallback ( int    red,
22                                           int    green,
23                                           int    blue,
24                                           void *clientData );
25
26       // Called from the ColorChooser if no color has been selected
27
28       static void canceledCallback ( void * );
29
30       virtual void colorSelected ( int red, int green, int blue );
31
```

```
32    public:
33
34        BouncingBall ( Stage *, char *);
35
36        void nextFrame ( Drawable, Dimension, Dimension );   // Draw one frame
37    };
38    #endif
```

The BouncingBall constructor initializes the size, color, and initial velocity of each ball. The size of each object is determined by a hard-coded parameter, defined here as twenty-five pixels. The initial velocity is based on the value returned by drand48(). This function returns a floating point number between 0.0 and 1.0. The initial velocity of each BouncingBall is computed by multiplying this random number by the size of the object.

The _bounds structure stores the current position of the object between frames. This information is used to detect collisions between an object and the sides of the stage area and to compute the object's position in each frame. Each ball is initially placed in the upper left corner of the stage.

Finally, if the constructor's second argument specifies a named color, BouncingBall tries to allocate a color from the default colormap. If the color allocation fails, the ball defaults to black, which should be available on all X displays. Once a color has been allocated, the constructor creates a graphics context to be used when drawing this object. Color allocation is a complex topic and outside the scope of this book. If necessary, see [Scheifler90] for detailed information about the X color model and the functions used in this example.

If no color is specified, the BouncingBall constructor posts the ColorChooser dialog described in Chapter 11 to allow the user to choose a color. Because the ColorChooser uses a callback model, the ball must not create a graphics context or render itself until the user has chosen a color. Setting the _gc member to NULL provides a way to check whether the object can be drawn while waiting for the user to select a color.

```
1     /////////////////////////////////////////////////////////
2     // BouncingBall.C
3     /////////////////////////////////////////////////////////
4     #include "Application.h"
5     #include "Stage.h"
6     #include "BouncingBall.h"
7     #include "ColorChooser.h"
8     #include "InfoDialogManager.h"
9     #include "libc.h"
10
11    #define SIZE 25
12
13    BouncingBall::BouncingBall ( Stage * stage,
14                                 char *colorName ) : Actor ( stage )
15    {
16        // Get an initial velocity at random
17
18        _delta.x = ( int ) ( SIZE * drand48() );
19        _delta.y = ( int ) ( SIZE * drand48() );
```

```
20
21        // Initialize the current location and bounding box of the object
22
23        _bounds.width = _bounds.height = SIZE;
24        _bounds.x     = _bounds.width  + 1;
25        _bounds.y     = _bounds.height + 1;
26
27        _gc = NULL;
28
29        // If a color name has been specified, try to allocate a color
30        // Otherwise, use the ColorChooser to let the user pick a color
31
32        if ( colorName )
33        {
34            XGCValues  gcv;
35            Display   *dpy = theApplication->display();
36            int        scr = DefaultScreen ( dpy );
37            Colormap   cmap = DefaultColormap ( dpy, scr );
38            XColor     color, ignore;
39
40            // If color allocation fails, use the default black pixel
41
42            if ( XAllocNamedColor ( dpy,
43                                    cmap, colorName,
44                                    &color, &ignore ) )
45                gcv.foreground = color.pixel;
46            else
47                gcv.foreground = BlackPixel ( dpy, scr );
48
49            // Create a graphics context used to draw this object
50
51            _gc = XtGetGC ( _stage->baseWidget(),
52                            GCForeground,
53                            &gcv );
54        }
55        else
56        {
57            ColorChooser *colorChooser =
58                        new ColorChooser ( theApplication->baseWidget(),
59                                           "colorChooser" );
60
61            colorChooser->pickColor ( &BouncingBall::colorSelectedCallback,
62                                      &BouncingBall::canceledCallback,
63                                      ( void * ) this );
64        }
65    }
```

The nextFrame() member function draws the ball in a new position each time it is called.
The function begins by checking for a valid _gc member. If _gc is NULL, nextFrame() simply

returns. Otherwise, `nextFrame()` updates the current position of the ball and checks this object's bounds to determine if the ball has hit the side of the Stage area. If so, the velocity is recomputed to make the ball appear to bounce off the side of the Stage. In any case, the ball is drawn in its new position. Recall that the drawable passed to all Actor objects is a pixmap, which is currently the Stage object's "back" buffer. Therefore, the ball drawn by this method does not appear until the next frame.

```
66  void BouncingBall::nextFrame ( Drawable  d,
67                                 Dimension width,
68                                 Dimension height )
69  {
70      if ( !_gc)    // Return if no color has been chosen yet
71          return;
72
73      // Update the current position
74
75      _bounds.x += _delta.x;
76      _bounds.y += _delta.y;
77
78      // If we have hit the right wall, reposition and
79      // reverse the x component of the  velocity
80
81      if ( _bounds.x + _bounds.width >= width )
82      {
83          _bounds.x = width - _bounds.width;
84          _delta.x  = -_delta.x;
85      }
86      else if ( _bounds.x <= 0 )  // Check for hitting the left wall
87      {
88          _bounds.x = 0;
89          _delta.x  = -_delta.x;
90      }
91
92      // If we have hit the floor, reposition and
93      // reverse the y component of the velocity
94
95      if ( _bounds.y + _bounds.height >= height )
96      {
97          _bounds.y = height - _bounds.height;
98          _delta.y  = -_delta.y;
99      }
100     else if ( _bounds.y <= 0 )  // Check for bouncing off the top
101     {
102         _bounds.y = 0;
103         _delta.y  = -_delta.y;
104     }
105
106     // Draw the object at the new location
```

```
107
108         XFillArc ( theApplication->display(), d, _gc,
109                    _bounds.x,       _bounds.y,
110                    _bounds.width,  _bounds.height,
111                    0, 360 * 64 );
112   }
```

The remaining BouncingBall methods work with the ColorChooser to allow the user to choose an object's color interactively. The ColorChooser calls colorSelectedCallback() when the user has chosen a color. This function passes the red, green, and blue components of the chosen color to colorSelected() for further processing.

```
113  void BouncingBall::colorSelectedCallback ( int    red,
114                                             int    green,
115                                             int    blue,
116                                             void *clientData )
117  {
118      BouncingBall *obj = ( BouncingBall * ) clientData;
119
120      obj->colorSelected ( red, green, blue );
121  }
```

The colorSelected() member function tries to allocate a color based on the red, green, and blue color components provided by the ColorChooser. This function fills in the members of an XColor structure, scaling the 0-255 range of values provided by the ColorChooser to the 0-65535 range expected by X. Then colorSelected() calls XAllocColor() to allocate the color and determine a pixel value that can be used to create a graphics context. If the color allocation fails, the system's default black pixel is used instead. Once a valid pixel is available, the _gc member can be initialized by calling XtGetGC(). Notice that the base widget of the Stage object is used for the call to XtGetGC(). Also, the BouncingBall class takes advantage of the global theApplication object to retrieve a display to be passed to the various Xlib functions.

```
122  void BouncingBall::colorSelected ( int red, int green, int blue )
123  {
124      XGCValues  gcv;
125      Display   *dpy  = theApplication->display();
126      int        scr  = DefaultScreen ( dpy );
127      Colormap   cmap = DefaultColormap ( dpy, scr );
128      XColor     color;
129
130      color.red   = red   * 256;
131      color.green = green * 256;
132      color.blue  = blue  * 256 ;
133
134      if ( XAllocColor ( dpy,
135                         cmap, &color ) )
136          gcv.foreground = color.pixel;
```

```
137      else
138          gcv.foreground = BlackPixel ( dpy, scr );
139
140      _gc = XtGetGC ( _stage->baseWidget(),
141                       GCForeground,
142                       &gcv );
143  }
```

The `canceledCallback()` function can be called by the ColorChooser component if the user fails to select a color. This function uses MotifApp's InfoDialogManager object to post a warning message and then calls `colorSelected()` with the color components for the color "Black."

```
144  void BouncingBall::canceledCallback ( void *clientData )
145  {
146      BouncingBall *obj = ( BouncingBall * ) clientData;
147
148      theInfoDialogManager->post ( "Using Black as the default color" );
149      obj->colorSelected ( 0, 0, 0 );
150  }
```

Figure 12.6 shows the connections between the BouncingBall class and other closely related classes.

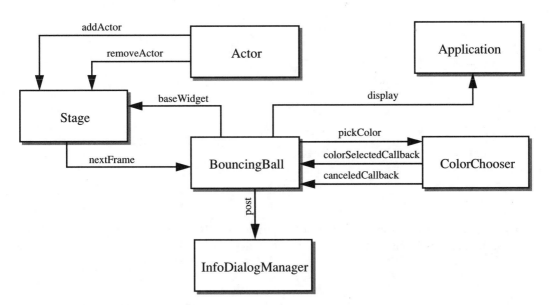

**Figure 12.6** A message diagram of BouncingBall and its related classes.

## 12.6  The AddBallCmd Class

The bounce program allows the user to add new Actor objects by choosing a command on a pulldown menu. This requires one more command class, an AddBallCmd class. The AddBallCmd class creates a BouncingBall object when it is executed. The AddBallCmd is derived from Cmd and supports an `undoit()` member function, which just deletes the BouncingBall object created in the `doit()` member function.

The AddBallCmd class is declared as follows:

```
1    //////////////////////////////////////////////////////
2    // AddBallCmd.h
3    //////////////////////////////////////////////////////
4    #ifndef ADDBALLCMD_H
5    #define ADDBALLCMD_H
6    #include "Cmd.h"
7
8    class Stage;
9    class Actor;
10
11   class AddBallCmd : public Cmd {
12
13     protected:
14
15       Stage    * _stage;
16       Actor    * _ball;
17       char     * _color;
18
19       virtual void doit();
20       virtual void undoit();
21
22     public:
23
24       AddBallCmd ( char *, int active,
25                    Stage*, char *color = ( char * ) 0 );
26   };
27   #endif
```

The AddBallCmd constructor requires both a pointer to a Stage object and the name of a color to create a BouncingBall object.

```
1    //////////////////////////////////////////////////////
2    // AddBallCmd.C
3    //////////////////////////////////////////////////////
4    #include "AddBallCmd.h"
5    #include "BouncingBall.h"
```

```
6
7    AddBallCmd::AddBallCmd ( char   *name,
8                            int    active,
9                            Stage *stage,
10                           char  *color ) : Cmd ( name, active )
11   {
12       _stage = stage;
13       _color = color;
14       _ball  = NULL;
15   }
```

The doit() function instantiates a BouncingBall object, which immediately adds itself to the Stage. Notice that AddBallCmd saves a pointer to this object to allow the undoit() member function to delete the object to remove it from the Stage, if needed.

```
16   void AddBallCmd::doit()
17   {
18       _ball = new BouncingBall ( _stage, _color );
19   }
```

The undoit() member function deletes the ball created by this object, and sets the object pointer to NULL as insurance against future references. The Actor destructor removes the object from the Stage.

```
20   void AddBallCmd::undoit()
21   {
22       delete _ball;
23       _ball = NULL;
24   }
```

## 12.7  The BounceWindow Class

Previous sections in this chapter have discussed all the key elements of the bounce program. All that remains is to create the top-level window that contains and connects these elements. The Bounce-Window class is a subclass of MenuWindow. The MenuWindow class automatically creates the menubar used by bounce. The BounceWindow class arranges the Stage, ControlPanel, and Bounce-Clock components in the window's work area. The BounceWindow class maintains pointers to these three major elements of the application in the private portion of the class. The protected portion supports the pure virtual functions, createWorkArea() and createMenuPanes(), which must be implemented by classes derived from MenuWindow. The public protocol consists of the constructor and destructor.

The BounceWindow class is declared as follows:

```
1   /////////////////////////////////////////////////////////
2   // BounceWindow.h:
3   /////////////////////////////////////////////////////////
4   #ifndef BOUNCEWINDOW_H
5   #define BOUNCEWINDOW_H
6   #include "MenuWindow.h"
7
8   class Clock;
9   class Stage;
10  class ControlPanel;
11
12  class BounceWindow : public MenuWindow {
13
14   private:
15
16      Clock       * _clock;
17      Stage       * _stage;
18      ControlPanel * _controlPanel;
19
20   protected:
21
22      virtual Widget createWorkArea ( Widget );
23      virtual void   createMenuPanes();
24
25   public:
26
27      BounceWindow ( char * );
28      ~BounceWindow();
29  };
30  #endif
```

The BounceWindow constructor initializes all data members to NULL, after calling the MenuWindow constructor.

```
1   /////////////////////////////////////////////////
2   // BounceWindow.C
3   /////////////////////////////////////////////////
4   #include "Application.h"
5   #include "BounceWindow.h"
6   #include "Stage.h"
7   #include "ControlPanel.h"
8   #include "BounceClock.h"
9   #include "QuitCmd.h"
10  #include "UndoCmd.h"
11  #include "CmdList.h"
12  #include "AddBallCmd.h"
13  #include "MenuBar.h"
14  #include <Xm/Form.h>
15  #include <Xm/Separator.h>
```

```
16  BounceWindow::BounceWindow ( char *name ) : MenuWindow ( name )
17  {
18      _clock        = NULL;
19      _stage        = NULL;
20      _controlPanel = NULL;
21  }
```

The BounceWindow destructor deletes the objects created in the `createWorkArea()` member function. The widgets created by BounceWindow are destroyed automatically when the UIComponent destructor destroys the window's shell.

```
22  BounceWindow::~BounceWindow ()
23  {
24      delete _clock;
25      delete _stage;
26      delete _controlPanel;
27  }
```

The `createWorkArea()` member function handles the creation of the other components of the bounce window and sets up the layout shown in Figure 12.1. This function must return a single widget that is installed as the work area widget for the XmMainWindow created by the MainWindow class. The BounceWindow creates an XmForm widget that serves as the work area widget, and arranges all other components of the interface as children within that form.

```
28  Widget BounceWindow::createWorkArea ( Widget parent )
29  {
30      // The BounceWindow work area is implemented as a
31      // form widget that contains the other components
32      // of the bounce interface
33
34      Widget form =  XtCreateWidget ( "workArea",
35                                      xmFormWidgetClass,
36                                      parent,
37                                      NULL, 0 );
38
39      // Create each major component of the bounce window
40
41      _stage        = new Stage ( form, "stage" );
42      _clock        = new BounceClock ( form, "clock", _stage );
43      _controlPanel = new ControlPanel ( form, "control", _clock );
44
45      // Set up the attachments to achieve the layout shown in Figure 12.1
46
47      XtVaSetValues ( _controlPanel->baseWidget(),
48                      XmNtopWidget,        _clock->baseWidget(),
49                      XmNtopAttachment,    XmATTACH_OPPOSITE_WIDGET,
50                      XmNleftAttachment,   XmATTACH_FORM,
51                      XmNrightPosition,    50,
```

```
52                              XmNrightAttachment,  XmATTACH_POSITION,
53                              XmNbottomAttachment, XmATTACH_NONE,
54                              NULL );
55
56      XtVaSetValues ( _clock->baseWidget(),
57                              XmNtopAttachment,    XmATTACH_NONE,
58                              XmNleftPosition,     50,
59                              XmNleftAttachment,   XmATTACH_POSITION,
60                              XmNrightAttachment,  XmATTACH_FORM,
61                              XmNbottomAttachment, XmATTACH_FORM,
62                              NULL );
63
64      Widget sep =
65        XtVaCreateManagedWidget ( "sep",
66                                  xmSeparatorWidgetClass,
67                                  form,
68                                  XmNleftAttachment,   XmATTACH_FORM,
69                                  XmNrightAttachment,  XmATTACH_FORM,
70                                  XmNtopAttachment,    XmATTACH_NONE,
71                                  XmNbottomWidget,     _clock->baseWidget(),
72                                  XmNbottomAttachment, XmATTACH_WIDGET,
73                                  NULL );
74
75      XtVaSetValues ( _stage->baseWidget(),
76                          XmNtopAttachment,    XmATTACH_FORM,
77                          XmNleftAttachment,   XmATTACH_FORM,
78                          XmNrightAttachment,  XmATTACH_FORM,
79                          XmNbottomWidget,     sep,
80                          XmNbottomAttachment, XmATTACH_WIDGET,
81                          NULL );
82
83      // Manage all child widgets and return the form
84
85      _controlPanel->manage();
86      _stage->manage();
87      _clock->manage();
88
89      return ( form );
90  }
```

The MenuWindow class calls createMenuPanes() to add items to the menubar. The BounceWindow class adds two menu panes to the menubar. The first contains the object theUndoCmd, described in Chapter 8, and the "user friendly" QuitCmd described in Chapter 9. This menu pane is labeled as the "Application" pane. The second pane allows the user to add new Actors to the Stage. In this example, createMenuPanes() creates four instances of the AddBallCmd class. The first three are pre-selected to use the colors red, green, and blue, while the fourth allows users to choose a color interactively. Each of these commands is added to a CmdList and placed in a second menu pane, labeled "Actors."

```
91  void BounceWindow::createMenuPanes ()
92  {
93
94      // Create the main application menu, with just a quit and undo cmd
95
96      CmdList *cmdList  = new CmdList();
97      Cmd     *quit     = new QuitCmd ( "Quit", TRUE );
98
99      cmdList->add ( theUndoCmd );
100     cmdList->add ( quit );
101     _menuBar->addCommands ( cmdList, "Application" );
102
103     // Create a menu for adding actors to the screen
104
105     CmdList *actorList = new CmdList();
106
107     Cmd *addRed   = new AddBallCmd ( "Add Red Ball",   TRUE,
108                                      _stage, "Red" );
109     Cmd *addGreen = new AddBallCmd ( "Add Green Ball", TRUE,
110                                      _stage, "Green" );
111     Cmd *addBlue  = new AddBallCmd ( "Add Blue Ball",  TRUE,
112                                      _stage, "Blue" );
113     Cmd *addAny   = new AddBallCmd ( "Add Ball...",    TRUE,
114                                      _stage );
115
116     actorList->add ( addRed );
117     actorList->add ( addGreen );
118     actorList->add ( addBlue );
119     actorList->add ( addAny );
120
121     _menuBar->addCommands ( actorList, "Actors" );
122  }
```

Figure 12.7 shows the interactions between the BounceWindow class and other closely associated classes.

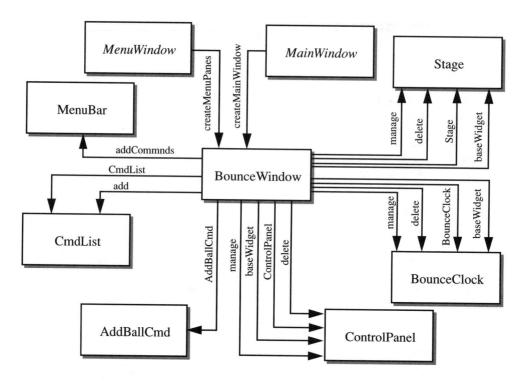

**Figure 12.7**  Message diagram of BounceWindow and associated classes.

## 12.8  Building and Running Bounce

Now we can build and run the bounce program. First, we must create the "main body" of the program. Like all MotifApp programs, the body of the program is extremely simple. The file BounceApp.C instantiates an Application object followed by a BounceWindow object.

```
1  //////////////////////////////////////////////
2  // "Main" program
3  //////////////////////////////////////////////
4  #include "Application.h"
5  #include "BounceWindow.h"
6
7  Application *bounceApp = new Application ( "Bounce" );
8  MainWindow *window = new BounceWindow ( "Bounce" );
```

The bounce program can be built by compiling all the classes described in this chapter and linking them with the MotifApp library. The Clock class should be added directly to the MotifApp library first. The following commands can be used to build bounce:

```
CC -c Actor.C BounceApp.C BounceWindow.C \
     BounceClock.C BouncingBall.C ControlPanel.C \
     Stage.C StepCmd.C StopCmd.C RunCmd.C AddBallCmd.C

CC -o bounce  Actor.o BounceApp.o BounceWindow.o \
              BounceClock.o BouncingBall.o ControlPanel.o \
              Stage.o StepCmd.o StopCmd.o RunCmd.o AddBallCmd.o \
              libMotifApp.a -lXm -lXt -lX11
```

The program can now be tested by typing "bounce" in a terminal window. To start the animation, the clock can be started by clicking on the Run button, and "actors" can be added by choosing an entry from the "Actors" menu pane. The Undo command on the Application pane allows the user to undo the most recent command, whether the command was to add a new actor to the stage area, or to stop or start the animation. Changes to the speed of the animation cannot be undone.

Another interesting experiment is to modify the file BounceApp.C to create multiple Bounce-Window objects. Just like the "Hello World" example in Chapter 6, this is very easy to do.

```
1  ///////////////////////////////////////////////////////////
2  // "Main" program for multiple animation windows
3  ///////////////////////////////////////////////////////////
4  #include "Application.h"
5  #include "BounceWindow.h"
6
7  Application *bounceApp = new Application  ( "Bounce" );
8  MainWindow *window     = new BounceWindow ( "Bounce" );
9  MainWindow *window2    = new BounceWindow ( "Bounce 2" );
```

Because the BounceWindow class encapsulates every object involved in an animation, it is easy to create multiple, semi-independent animation windows. Each window can be started or stopped independently, and the speed of each animation can be controlled separately.

The appearance of most applications can be improved by providing some default resource settings. For example, the following application resource file produces the bounce window shown Figure 12.1:

```
1  !!!!!!!!!!!!!!!!!!!!!!!!!!!!!!!!!!!!!!!!!!!!!!!!!!!!!!!!!!!!!
2  ! Appdefaults file for bounce program
3  !!!!!!!!!!!!!!!!!!!!!!!!!!!!!!!!!!!!!!!!!!!!!!!!!!!!!!!!!!!!!
4  Bounce*clock*titleString:            Frames Per Second
5  Bounce*fontList:  -*-helvetica-bold-r-normal--14-*-*-*-*-*-iso8859-1
6  Bounce*quit*labelString:             Quit
7  Bounce*XmScale*orientation:          horizontal
8  Bounce*colorChooser_popup*title:     Color Chooser
```

```
9   Bounce*stage*width:                    400
10  Bounce*stage*height:                   250
```

In Figure 12.1, the ControlPanel buttons are shown as icons. This can be done very easily, by creating a bitmap image using the bitmap program available on most X systems. Once these bitmaps have been saved to a file, they can be displayed by setting resources that name these files as the XmNlabelPixmap resource for the ControlPanel buttons. For example:

```
11  Bounce*Run*labelType:                  pixmap
12  Bounce*Run*labelPixmap:                run
13  Bounce*Run*labelInsensitivePixmap:     runI
14
15  Bounce*Stop*labelType:                 pixmap
16  Bounce*Stop*labelPixmap:               stop
17  Bounce*Stop*labelInsensitivePixmap:    stopI
18
19  Bounce*Step*labelType:                 pixmap
20  Bounce*Step*labelPixmap:               step
21  Bounce*Step*labelInsensitivePixmap:    stepI
```

Figure 12.8 shows the widget tree formed by the bounce program. The grey areas show some of the component boundaries. The largest area shows the widgets controlled by the BounceWindow class, which includes the menubar and the entries in the menu. The ControlPanel, Stage, and BounceClock classes encapsulate subparts of the overall widget tree.

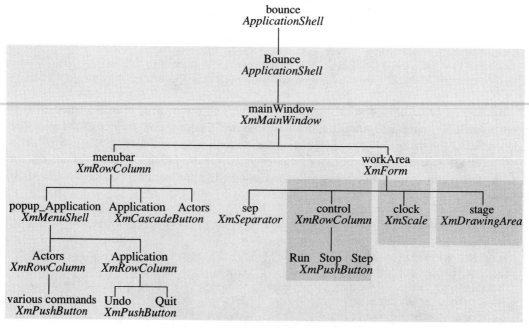

**Figure 12.8** The bounce widget tree.

# 12.9 Summary

The bounce program provides an example of a typical application based on the MotifApp framework. The power of the application framework approach is that it captures a portion of the structure common to a set of applications so that each application requires the programmer to implement only the unique parts of each application. The MotifApp framework is a very simple framework that tries to support a broad set of applications. The "Hello World" program in Chapter 6, the wordCount program in Chapter 10, and the bounce program in this chapter are all very different applications. Yet, MotifApp is able to provide significant support for all three. However, because MotifApp imposes few limits on the types of applications it can support, it cannot provide as much support as a framework that has a more restricted domain. As the range of applications a framework must support narrows, the amount of support the framework can provide increases dramatically.

For example, imagine a framework that supports programs that display animations, like bounce. Such a framework could start with many of the elements present in both MotifApp and the bounce program. However, this framework could provide a more powerful way for the programmer to control various aspects of the animation. For example, one might start by replacing the simple clock-driven approach with a mechanism that allows more flexibility. Perhaps some type of Score class that allows applications to describe each step of the animation in arbitrary units of time could be designed.

Similarly, many animations require different phases. A framework for animation programs might also support a Scene class that somehow determines what Actors appear at any given time. An animation framework could also provide better support for Actors. For example, we could consider separating an Actor's visual presentation from its behavior. Perhaps each Actor object could be associated with a Script object that determines its behavior in any Scene. If the framework were extended sufficiently, it could reach a point where no programming is required, in the traditional sense, to create an application. An animator could simply draw animated figures and write scripts to control their movements. (There are, of course, several commercial systems based on similar ideas.)

As a framework supports more and more specific features, it becomes less useful for applications outside the domain for which it was designed. The animation framework described above would probably not provide the right kind of support for a word processor. However, it would be possible to design frameworks to support word-processing, graphical editors, spreadsheets, and many other types of applications.

Regardless of the domain, it is always useful to identify features and characteristics common to a set of programs and provide as much support as possible in a library. The application framework approach is useful because it can capture the structural characteristics common to a group of applications, in addition to supplying user interface components, utility routines, and so on.

Using an appropriate application framework can reduce the time spent designing, developing, and maintaining most applications. A good framework can also promote consistency across a set of applications. A framework can provide structural consistency, which helps the programmers working on a system, as well as visual and behavioral consistency, which benefits the eventual user of any application.

# Bibliography

| | |
|---|---|
| Asente90 | Asente, Paul, and Ralph Swick, *The X Window System Toolkit*, DEC Press, 1990. |
| Beck89 | Beck, Kent, and Ward Cunningham, "A Laboratory for Teaching Object-Oriented Thinking," *OOPSLA '89 Conference Proceedings*, 1989. |
| Berlage91 | Berlage, Thomas, *OSF/Motif: Concepts and Programming*, Addison-Wesley, 1991. |
| Booch89 | Booch, Grady, "What Is and Isn't Object-Oriented Design," *American Programmer*, Vol 2., Nos 7 and 8, Summer, 1989. |
| Booch91 | Booch, Grady, *Object-Oriented Design with Applications*, Benjamin Cummings, 1991. |
| Budd91 | Budd, Timothy, *An Introduction to Object-Oriented Programming*, Addison-Wesley, 1991. |
| Coad90 | Coad, Peter and Edward Yourdon, *Object-Oriented Analysis*, Prentice Hall, 1990. |
| Cox86 | Cox, Brad, *Object-Oriented Programming*: *An Evolutionary Approach*, Addison-Wesley, 1986. |
| Foley82 | Foley, J.D., and A. Van Dam, *Fundamentals of Computer Graphics*, Addison-Wesley, 1982. |
| Gorlen90 | Gorlen, Keith, Sanford M. Orlow, and Perry S. Plexico, *Data Abstraction and Object Oriented Programming in C++*, John Wiley and Sons, 1990. |

424

| Johnson88 | Johnson, R., and B. Foote, "Designing Reusable Classes," *Journal of Object-Oriented Programming*, Vol. 1 (2), June/July, 1988. |
|---|---|
| Jones89 | Jones, Oliver, *Introduction to the X Window System*, Prentice Hall, 1989. |
| Kobara91 | Kobara, Shiz, *Visual Design with OSF/Motif*, Addison-Wesley, 1991. |
| Linton89 | Linton, Mark A., John M. Vlissides, and Paul R. Calder, "Composing User Interfaces with InterViews," *IEEE Computer*, Vol. 22, No. 2, February, 1989. |
| Lippman89 | Lippman, S., *C++ Primer*, Addison-Wesley, 1989. |
| Meyer88 | Meyer, Bertrand, *Object-Oriented Software Construction,* Prentice Hall, 1988. |
| OSF90 | *OSF/Motif Programmer's Guide, OSF/Motif Programmer's Reference, OSF/Motif Style Guide*, Prentice Hall, 1990. |
| Schlaer88 | Schlaer, Sally, and Stephen Mellor, *Object-Oriented Systems Analysis: Modeling the World in Data*, Yourdon Press, 1988. |
| Shapiro90 | Shapiro, Jonathan, *A C++ Toolkit*, Prentice Hall, 1990. |
| Sklar91 | Sklar, David F., "Modality and synchronicity and in Xt dialogs", *The X Journal*, Vol 1., No. 2, November/December, 1991 |
| Stroustrup91 | Stroustrup, Bjarne, *The C++ Programming Language*, Second Edition, Addison-Wesley, 1991. |
| Stroustrup90 | Stroustrup, Bjarne, *The Annotated C++ Reference Manual*, Addison-Wesley, 1990. |
| Swick91 | Swick, Ralph, and Mark Ackerman, "To Subclass or Not to Subclass," *Proceedings of the 5th Annual X Technical Conference*, 1991. |
| Rosenthal88 | Rosenthal, David S., "A Simple X.11 Client Program, or, How Hard Can It Really Be to Write 'Hello, World'?," *Proceedings of the Winter, 1988 USENIX Conference*, 1988. |
| Scheifler90 | Scheifler, Robert W. and James Gettys, *X Window System*, Second Edition, DEC Press, 1990. |
| Vlissides89 | Vlissides, John, and Mark Linton, *Unidraw: A Framework for Building Domain-specific Graphical Editors*, 4th Annual X Technical Conference: Technical Papers, 1989. |
| Wilson90 | Wilson, David, Larry Rosenstein, and Dan Shafer, *C++ Programming with MacApp*, Addison-Wesley, 1990. |
| Wirfs90 | Wirfs-Brock, R., B. Wilkerson, and L. Wiener, *Designing Object-Oriented Software*, Prentice Hall, 1990. |
| Young90 | Young, Douglas A., *The X Window System: Programming and Applications with Xt,* OSF/Motif Edition, Prentice Hall, 1990. |

# Index

# X

# Getting Source Code

The sources for the examples described in this book are available free of charge to anyone with network access, or they may be purchased from Prentice Hall. The following sections provide instructions for obtaining the sources.

## Downloading Sources over a Network

If you have access to the Internet, the examples in this book may be downloaded from export.lcs.mit.edu using the "ftp" command. Since anyone is free to distribute these examples, you may also find the sources at other ftp or UUCP sites. On export, the source code can be found in the contrib directory, in a compressed tar file named young.c++.tar.Z. Assuming you have access to export, you can download the software with the following command sequence. (Type "ftp" or "anonymous" at the login prompt, and your name or system name as a password.)

```
% ftp export.lcs.mit.edu
ftp > cd contrib
ftp > binary
ftp > get young.c++.tar.Z
ftp > quit
```

Once you have retrieved the compressed tar file, you can unpack the sources with the commands:

```
% uncompress young.c++.tar.Z
% tar xvf young.c++.tar
```

These commands will create a directory named C++Motif which contains subdirectories for each chapter in this book, as well as several other files and directories. Be sure to read the README file in the C++Motif directory for additional information about the software, instructions on how to build the examples, and so on.

## Purchasing the Software from Prentice Hall

For those without network access, Prentice Hall can provide copies of the software for a small fee. The software is available on a floppy disk readable from a PC or a Macintosh. To read the disk, you will need a 3 1/2' disk drive capable of reading a 3 1/2" double-sided, double-density 720KB floppy disk formatted for an IBM PC or compatible (MS-DOS or PC-DOS 3.2 or higher), or a Macintosh.

The examples are intended to be built on a UNIX system, and should be copied from your PC or Macintosh to a UNIX system. As distributed by Prentice Hall, the software is packed into a single file, known as a "shell archive." The examples are in an ASCII file named "examples.shar". The diskette also contains a second text file, named "examples.readme", which contains up-to-date information about unpacking and installing the software. Please read this file first, for further instructions.

To unpack the software, copy examples.shar from your PC to a UNIX system. Then type the following command in a terminal window on the UNIX machine:

```
% sh examples.shar
```

This command creates the C++Motif directory as described in the previous section. Check the README file in the C++Motif directory for up-to-date information and instructions for building the software.

To order, please make a copy of the form below, fill in all necessary information, and mail to:

PRENTICE HALL
Book Distribution Center
Route 59 at Brook Hill Drive
West Nyack, New York 10995

Please send the item checked below. The publisher will pay all shipping and handling charges.

_____ Macintosh (78599-8) _____ IBM (78598-0)

Sample software to accompany *Object-Oriented Programming with C++ and OSF/Motif.*

_____ $12.95 Payment Enclosed

Name _____

Title _____

Name of Firm _____

Address _____

_____

_____

_____

I prefer to charge to my __ VISA __ Mastercard

Card Number _____

Expiration Date _____

Signature _____